YHWH'S DIVINE IMAGES

ANCIENT NEAR EAST MONOGRAPHS

Jeffrey Stackert
Juan Manuel Tebes

Editorial Board:
Pablo R. Andiñach
Jeffrey L. Cooley
Roxana Flammini
Tova Ganzel
Lauren Monroe
Emanuel Pfoh
Stephen C. Russell
Andrea Seri
Bruce Wells

Number 29

YHWH'S DIVINE IMAGES

A Cognitive Approach

by
Daniel O. McClellan

SBL PRESS

Atlanta

Copyright © 2022 by Daniel O. McClellan

All rights reserved. No part of this work may be reproduced or transmitted in any form or by any means, electronic or mechanical, including photocopying and recording, or by means of any information storage or retrieval system, except as may be expressly permitted by the 1976 Copyright Act or in writing from the publisher. Requests for permission should be addressed in writing to the Rights and Permissions Office, SBL Press, 825 Houston Mill Road, Atlanta, GA 30329 USA.

Library of Congress Control Number: 2022944998

Contents

List of Illustrations vii
Preface ix
Acknowledgements xv
Abbreviations xvii

Introduction 1

1. What Is Deity? 21

2. Encountering Divine Agency 51

3. Deity in the Hebrew Bible 75

4. YHWH in the Hebrew Bible 109

5. YHWH's Divine Agents: The Ark of the Covenant and the *Kābôd* 133

6. YHWH's Divine Agents: The Messenger and the *Šem* 157

7. YHWH's Divine Agents: Texts 175

Conclusion 195

Appendix: Divine Agency and Early Christology 201
Bibliography 207
Ancient Sources Index 249
Modern Authors Index 261
Subject Index 271

List of Illustrations

1.1. The Katumuwa Stele	33
1.2. The Khirbet el-Qôm Inscription	40
2.1. The eighth-century BCE *debir* of the temple at Arad	59
2.2. Stelai and offering tables from Hazor's Area A	62
2.3. A shrine model discovered at Khirbet Qeiyafa	66
2.4. Two shrine models discovered at Khirbet Qeiyafa	66
2.5. A bronze calf and clay shrine model discovered at Ashkelon	67
2.6. The Taanach Cult Stand	68
2.7. Pithos A from Kuntillet 'Ajrud	71
3.1. Illustration of "radius" profiled against a circle	77
3.2. Illustration of "aunt" profiled against the kinship system	78
4.1. Bronze and gold foil deity figurines	113
5.1. A reconstruction of a closed shrine model from Megiddo	137
5.2. Tiglath-Pileser III wall relief depicting a shrine model	138
5.3. Sennacherib wall relief depicting cultic objects	139
7.1. A fifth- or sixth-century amulet discovered at Arbel	178
7.2. The Ketef Hinnom Silver Scrolls	180
7.3. The Mesha Stele	186

Preface

My primary target audience with this book is scholars and students—formal and informal—of the Bible and of religion more broadly, as well as cognitive scientists of religion and cognitive linguists. As someone trained in biblical studies but adopting methodologies from the cognitive sciences, I don't believe I'll ever fully shake the sense of imposter syndrome from presuming to have something to say about fields in which I am not a specialist. However, I have been reassured by many kind and generous scholars from across these fields that that's just the nature of interdisciplinary research. I have tried to widen the scope of accessibility of this book to include interested laypeople, whom I hope can also find some value in it. I anticipate some readers will approach this book from a devotional perspective, while others will approach it from a perspective adjacent to a devotional one, and still others in the absence of any such perspective. Though I write as a faithful Latter-day Saint, this book is strictly academic, and I have made a concerted effort to recognize and mitigate the potential influence of any devotional lenses that may color my methodologies and my readings. There is certainly no conscious attempt on my part to promote any particular theological perspective in this book, though I do offer some critiques of the influence on the scholarship of certain theological sensitivities (including from my own tradition). Having said that, I suspect there are ways the book will horrify my coreligionists as well as others who are suspicious that I'm just trying to import Mormonism wholesale into the Bible. If such criticisms come in from all sides, I'll consider that a win.

One of the goals of this book is to begin to disrupt some of the scholarly conventions that are common to the study of the Hebrew Bible. As a subtle and yet influential means of structuring power and values, terminology is precisely one of those conventions. As a result, this book will be somewhat idiosyncratic in the terms it employs, and I'd like to take the opportunity here to explain myself. I begin with perhaps the least idiosyncratic terminological choice: I render the proper name of Israel's patron deity as YHWH, with the consonants of the Tetragrammaton in all caps (normally a standard when transcribing unvocalized names from ancient Southwest Asia). When vocalizing the name, a reader may obviously substitute Yahweh, Adonai, HaShem, the Lord, Jehovah, or whatever their preference. A bit *more* idiosyncratically, however, I use the term "deity" instead of the gendered terms *god* and *goddess*. I also use gender-neutral pronouns in reference to deity, except where I am quoting secondary literature or other translations of primary sources, or where I am translating texts that are marked for gender. Though it is not unilateral, YHWH's performance of maleness is in many places central to the rhetorical goals of the biblical authors, and so I will preserve the gendered language of ancient authors (cf. Clines 2021b but also Levinson 2022). Elsewhere, however, if the gender of an individual, divine or human, cannot be clearly demonstrated, I use gender-neutral pronouns. I will do my best to mitigate the ambiguity that can arise from the collision in the same context of singular *they* and distinct plural subjects and pronouns.

Because of the interdisciplinary nature of this book, I am importing some technical terminology from other disciplines that may not be familiar to readers. I have tried to reduce the jargon as much as possible, but there are a number of terms that I have maintained for the sake of economy and specificity. Some of these need explanations. A word I use in the very first sentence of the introduction is *conceptualize*, which is a verb that refers to the production in our minds of concepts, images, or ideas about something (as opposed to words). These concepts and ideas are frequently conventionalized and shared by speakers of a given language within a given society in order to make communication more efficient, and this dynamic frequently influences the way people think and talk about things. I'll discuss some examples of how this works in more detail in the introduction. There are two other verbs that I will use in the introduction that might cause confusion. The first is *index*. When I use it as a verb, I am referring to the way an object can cue a viewer to some other entity and also store information about that entity. For instance, the great poet (Taylor Swift) once wrote of a former lover who kept a scarf in his drawer because it reminded him of her. The scarf serves to cue the person's mind to their former lover and to aspects of their presence that the scarf may signify. In that sense, the scarf "indexes" the former lover. Similarly, a cultic object that is intended to represent a specific deity cues the viewer's mind to that deity and can store information about them, such as their name or deeds, qualities, or relationships or events associated with them.

The last verb that requires some explanation is *presence*. In this book, to presence an agent is to reify their presence, or cause their presence to be manifested, according to someone's perception. There is overlap between the notions of indexing and presencing, but the latter refers more directly to the generation of the perception of the presence of someone or something. I will discuss this cognitive mechanism in more detail in the first chapter, but as a simple example, that great poet mentioned that the former lover kept her scarf because it smelled like her. Smell is strongly linked to memory, and the former lover likely smelled the scarf on occasion in order to generate that perception of presence, however fleeting. In that sense, he is "presencing" the former lover.

I also try in this book to avoid a number of rather colonizing terms that have become common in biblical scholarship. For instance, *ancient Near East* privileges a Western perspective, and even *Western* is itself a rather problematic dichotomy. Instead of the former, I use *ancient Southwest Asia*, and instead of the latter, I use *Eurocentric*. I use neither of these terms to refer to anything approximating a discrete and clearly delineable semantic category. As my discussion of prototype theory in the introduction will make clear, conceptual categories do not commonly form and are not commonly learned or used in reference to clear and consistent boundaries. Such boundaries are not inherent to most conceptual categories but form rather arbitrarily when a need for them arises, and these and the other conceptual categories I employ throughout this book are no different. I understand the terms ancient Southwest Asia and Eurocentric to focus on the exemplars of the categories and to extend outward to an ambiguous periphery where boundaries can be quite fuzzy, fluid, and debatable. In other words, the terms I use should not imply the assertion of any clear boundaries unless I indicate otherwise.

This is also true of my use of the rather loaded word *mind*. I use it to refer not just to the biological brain and associated structures, but to the collection of networks that facilitate thinking, moving, knowing, and our different senses. These are physical processes carried out through material channels, and in this sense the mind is not necessarily limited to the brain or even to the body. I thus adopt an "embodied mind" paradigm, which "insists that the mind is irreducible to the workings of any single organ or system" (Pitts-Taylor 2016, 44).[1] I will also frequently use it etically (that is, from an analytical perspective that is outside looking in) in reference to other groups' conventionalized understandings of the various internal loci of cognition and emotion, which tend to accrete around the head, the chest, or even the abdomen. In other words, I will use the word mind to refer to a society's reasoning about cognition and emotion, even if they explicitly identify those processes with, say, the heart (cf. Berendt and Tanita 2011).

Israel and Judah are also somewhat problematic designations. The data suggest Israel was the earlier of the two states, and that Israel and Judah existed separately (but with some manner of relationship) until the destruction of Israel in the late-eighth-century BCE. As Jerusalem and Judah grew in significance, their institutions seem to have appropriated Israel's literature and history. By the Neo-Babylonian period (626–539 BCE), Judah was really the most salient

---

[1] Note that I use *embodied* not to refer to some process of incarnation, but to the fundamentally material nature of cognition and its constituent processes (Lakoff and Johnson 1999, Wilson 2002).

identity that was left. To simplify things a bit, when I refer in general to the societies that occupied the regions prior to the Neo-Babylonian period, I will refer to *Iron Age Israel and Judah*. While this roughly covers the period between 1200 BCE and 586 BCE, I am primarily focused on the first millennium BCE, which covers the Iron Age II period. When speaking more specifically about the northern or southern kingdoms, I will refer to either Israel or Judah, and exclusively the latter from the exile on (unless I am referring to the Hebrew Bible's own use of "Israel" as a shared identity).

A final and perhaps unexpected lexical omission from this book is the term *religion*. Any attempt to reconstruct ancient ideologies and worldviews must engage with the imposition of modern conceptual frameworks to schematize the data, and religion is a framework employed by virtually all scholars to structure data regarding deities and their care and feeding. This significantly impacts the results of their reconstructions.[2] Every reference to religious *texts*, religious *beliefs*, religious *practices*, and to any other religious domains of experience evokes an entire suite of conceptual structures and content that will differ from reader to reader, but may not be warranted in any configuration, and may be significantly distorting. Far beyond simply shaping our discourse about these issues and the conclusions we reach, when these frameworks cease to be provisional heuristics that are consistently critiqued and compared to others, they can become cemented into our conceptual architecture, and they can govern how we are able to *think* and *communicate* about them. At that point, they become "stultifying conventions" (Saler 2000, 74–75) that might not only evade detection but might effectively marshal academic consensus and other power structures against their uprooting.[3] Religion can be one such stultifying convention.

These conventions cannot be overcome through the continued application of the same theoretical models that have for so long fostered and nurtured them. Rather, what is required is the imposition of outside methodologies, and the most robust of those methodologies have demonstrated the socially constructed nature of the category of religion.[4] If religion is to be gainfully studied going forward, it must be as a modern social construct that is discursively reified (that is, brought about or created through discourse), and not as a transhistorical and transcultural

---

[2] For examples of how the framework of religion influences our structuring of the data, see Nongbri 2008, 2013.

[3] Scholarship that benefits from this prophylaxis is overwhelmingly produced by elite, white, straight, Eurocentric males, which privileges a small set of perspectives that tend to be more closely tied to the power structures that have given shape to the contemporary conceptualization of religion.

[4] See Nongbri 2013 for one of the more accessible examples. For recent comments on the construction of this category in concert with the construction of the concept of politics, see Fitzgerald 2015.

constant.⁵ In light of this, the category of religion, irrespective of the specific framework or definitional approach, is not helpful as a heuristic or organizing principle for the study of the Hebrew Bible, which has no word for "religion" (Barton and Boyarin, 2016). There is no religion in the Hebrew Bible in anything approximating an analytically useful sense.⁶ The central principles of that framework are incommensurate with the priorities and ideological foci of individuals living in first millennium BCE Southwest Asia. The division of their world into sociocultural domains, of which religion is simply one, sits at odds with the worldviews of non-Eurocentric and non-contemporary people and societies.

Unless otherwise noted, all the translations in this book are my own. I quote the Hebrew Bible (in transliteration) from the *Biblia Hebraica Stuttgartensia* (*BHS*) edition of the Hebrew Bible. I also draw occasional quotations from the Rahlfs and Hanhart (2006) edition of the Septuagint, and from the NA^{28} edition of the Christian scriptures.

---

⁵ Kocku von Stuckrad (2013, 17) provides the following discursive definition of religion: "*RELIGION is the societal organization of knowledge about religion*" (see also Neubert 2016, Hjelm 2020). This highlights the fact that the one and only feature shared among all those phenomena that are labeled religion—and only those phenomena that are labeled religion—is precisely that they are labeled religion. As a result, any analytically useful reduction to necessary and sufficient features—in other words, any *definition*—must isolate that one feature alone. Religion is whatever a given social group decides is religion.
⁶ A concern may be raised with my willingness to use mind emically (that is, from an insider's perspective) while refusing to use religion in the same way. There are two reasons for this inconsistency. First, linguistic and conceptual proximates to the notion of the mind as the seat of cognition are frequently used in the societies I am interrogating, so the concept is not an entirely novel retrojection. The same is not true of religion. Second, I am concerned for the distortion that the application of the framework of religion has wrought within contemporary Hebrew Bible scholarship. I feel a convenient means of challenging that distortion is by demonstrating that the avoidance of the term poses no real threat to the integrity or clarity of the scholarship.

Acknowledgements

First and foremost, I must acknowledge the support of my sweetheart, Aleen. Across multiple states and even countries, she has been a constant source of encouragement, support, and refuge. This book would not have been possible without her. Nor would this book have been at all possible without Francesca Stavrakopoulou's encouragement, support, and especially her kindness while I was her doctoral student with the University of Exeter. That program was also made possible by the generous funding of Brigham Young University's Religious Education Dissertation Grant Program. In connection with that funding (and extending back to my undergraduate education), I especially appreciate Dana Pike's mentorship and support.

I was also very privileged to have my research featured—thanks to Eva Mroczek's generosity and concern for early-career scholars—on the first "New PhD Showcase" of the Bible and Religions of the Ancient Near East Collective (BRANE). For that showcase, a summary of my research was circulated to registered participants beforehand, and during a live online event in October 2020, prepared responses were offered by Debra Scoggins Ballentine, Mark McEntire, Brian Rainey, and Jen Singletary. Other participants were also invited to share feedback during a Q&A portion. I am incredibly grateful for their participation and for the opportunity to have my research engaged so thoughtfully and generously in that venue. Feedback from all four presenters and other commenters has made its way into this book. (I beg forgiveness for not remembering all the individuals who offered helpful comments.) I am also grateful for the opportunity to spend some additional time after the meeting continuing the conversation with Eva, Seth Sanders, and Mark Smith. Several friends and colleagues have also read all or part of some version of this book and offered helpful encouragement, guidance, and critiques, including István Czachesz, Davina Grojnowski, Jenny Labenz, Emma Loosley, Tyson Putthoff, Brandon Shumway, Mark Thomas, Ryan Thomas, and Nicolas Wyatt. The no doubt many infelicities that remain and about which I will no doubt hear are, of course, entirely my own responsibility.

Acknowledgements

First and foremost, I must acknowledge the support of my sweetheart, Aleen. Across multiple states and even countries, she has been a constant source of encouragement, support, and refuge. This book would not have been possible without her. Nor would this book have been at all possible without Francesca Stavrakopoulou's encouragement, support, and especially her kindness while I was her doctoral student with the University of Exeter. That program was also made possible by the generous funding of Brigham Young University's Religious Education Dissertation Grant Program. In connection with that funding (and extending back to my undergraduate education), I especially appreciate Dana Pike's mentorship and support.

I was also very privileged to have my research featured—thanks to Eva Mroczek's generosity and concern for early-career scholars—on the first "New PhD Showcase" of the Bible and Religions of the Ancient Near East Collective (BRANE). For that showcase, a summary of my research was circulated to registered participants beforehand, and during a live online event in October 2020, prepared responses were offered by Debra Scoggins Ballentine, Mark McEntire, Brian Rainey, and Jen Singletary. Other participants were also invited to share feedback during a Q&A portion. I am incredibly grateful for their participation and for the opportunity to have my research engaged so thoughtfully and generously in that venue. Feedback from all four presenters and other commenters has made its way into this book. (I beg forgiveness for not remembering all the individuals who offered helpful comments.) I am also grateful for the opportunity to spend some additional time after the meeting continuing the conversation with Eva, Seth Sanders, and Mark Smith. Several friends and colleagues have also read all or part of some version of this book and offered helpful encouragement, guidance, and critiques, including István Czachesz, Davina Grojnowski, Jenny Labenz, Emma Loosley, Tyson Putthoff, Brandon Shumway, Mark Thomas, Ryan Thomas, and Nicolas Wyatt. The no doubt many infelicities that remain and about which I will no doubt hear are, of course, entirely my own responsibility.

Abbreviations

GENERAL

BCE	before the Common Era
CE	Common Era
CREDs	credibility enhancing displays
CSR	cognitive science of religion
D	Deuteronomic source
DH	Documentary Hypothesis
DN	divine name
Dtr	Deuteronomistic Source
E	Elohist source
ET	English translation
GN	geographic name
J	Yahwist source
KJV	King James Version
LXX	Septuagint
MT	Masoretic text
Non-P	Non-Priestly (and non-Deuteronomistic) source
NRSV	New Revised Standard Version
P	Priestly source
PN	personal name
PT	Pyramid Texts
SP	Samaritan Pentateuch

REFERENCE WORKS

AA	*American Anthropologist*
AB	*Anchor Bible*
ABD	Freedman, David Noel, ed. *The Anchor Yale Bible Dictionary*. New Haven, CT: Yale University Press, 1992.
AE	*American Ethnologist*
AJSLL	*American Journal of Semitic Languages and Literature*

ANET	Pritchard, James B., ed. *Ancient Near Eastern Texts Relating to the Old Testament*. 3rd ed. Princeton: Princeton University Press, 1969.
APJA	*Asia Pacific Journal of Anthropology*
ARAM	*ARAM Periodical*
ARN	*Annual Review of Neuroscience*
ARP	*Archiv für Religionspsychologie*
BA	*The Biblical Archaeologist*
BAR	*Biblical Archaeology Review*
BASOR	*Bulletin of the American Schools of Oriental Research*
BBR	*Bulletin for Biblical Research*
BBS	*Behavioral and Brain Sciences*
BHS	Elliger, Karl, and Wilhelm Rudolph, eds. *Biblia Hebraica Stuttgartensia*. Stuttgart: Deutsche Bibelgesellschaft, 1983.
BibInt	*Biblical Interpretation*
BiolRev	*Biological Review*
BL	*Biology Letters*
BRev	*Bible Review*
BRPBI	*Brill Research Perspectives in Biblical Interpretation*
BT	*The Bible Translator*
CAD	Roth, Martha T., ed. *The Assyrian Dictionary of the Oriental Institute of the University of Chicago*. 26 vols. Chicago: The Oriental Institute of the University of Chicago, 1956–2010.
CBQ	*Catholic Biblical Quarterly*
CD	*Cognitive Development*
ChildDev	*Child Development*
ClassAnt	*Classical Antiquity*
CogPsych	*Cognitive Psychology*
CogSci	*Cognitive Science*
COS	Hallo, William W., ed. *The Context of Scripture*. 3 vols. Leiden: Brill, 1997–2002.
CRR	*Critical Research on Religion*
DAACH	*Digital Applications in Archaeology and Cultural Heritage*
DDD	Van der Toorn, Karel, Bob Becking, and Pieter W. van der Horst, eds. *The Dictionary of Deities and Demons in the Hebrew Bible*. 2nd ed. Leiden: Brill, 1999.
DevPsych	*Developmental Psychology*
DevSci	*Developmental Science*
DSD	*Dead Sea Discoveries*
EHB	*Evolution and Human Behavior*
EHS	*Evolutionary Human Sciences*
EHLL	Khan, Geoffrey, ed. *Encyclopedia of Hebrew Language and Linguistics*. Leiden: Brill, 2013.
EJJS	*European Journal of Jewish Studies*

EncJud	Skolnik, Fred, and Michael Berenbaum, eds. *Encyclopedia Judaica*. 2nd ed. 22 vols. Detroit: Macmillan Reference, 2007.
EP	*Evolutionary Psychology*
ESIC	*Evolutionary Studies in Imaginative Culture*
ETR	*Études théologiques et religieuses*
FHN	*Frontiers in Human Neuroscience*
FiP	*Frontiers in Psychology*
G&H	*Gender and History*
HALOT	Koehler, Ludwig, Walter Baumgartner, and Johann J. Stamm. *The Hebrew and Aramaic Lexicon of the Old Testament*. Translated and edited under the supervision of Mervyn E. J. Richardson. 4 vols. Leiden: Brill, 1994–1999.
HBT	*Horizons in Biblical Theology*
HeBAI	*Hebrew Bible and Ancient Israel*
HJET	*Hau: Journal of Ethnographic Theory*
HN	*Human Nature*
HTR	*Harvard Theological Review*
HUCA	*Hebrew Union College Annual*
ICS	*Intercultural Communication Studies*
IEJ	*Israel Exploration Journal*
IJPsychRel	*International Journal for the Psychology of Religion*
JAB	*Journal for the Aramaic Bible*
JAEI	*Journal of Ancient Egyptian Interconnections*
JAJ	*Journal of Ancient Judaism*
JANER	*Journal of Ancient Near Eastern Religions*
JAOS	*Journal of the American Oriental Society*
JARCE	*Journal of the American Research Center in Egypt*
JBL	*Journal of Biblical Literature*
JCC	*Journal of Cognition and Culture*
JEA	*Journal of Egyptian Archaeology*
JEPG	*Journal of Experimental Psychology: General*
JESP	*Journal of Experimental Social Psychology*
JHS	*Journal of Hebrew Scriptures*
JISMOR	*Journal of the Interdisciplinary Study of Monotheistic Religions*
JJS	*Journal of Jewish Studies*
JN	*Journal of Neuroscience*
JNES	*Journal of Near Eastern Studies*
JPSP	*Journal of Personality and Social Psychology*
JRAI	*Journal of the Royal Anthropological Institute*
JRS	*Journal of Ritual Studies*
JSNT	*Journal for the Study of the New Testament*
JSOT	*Journal for the Study of the Old Testament*
JSQ	*Jewish Studies Quarterly*
JTS	*Journal of Theological Studies*

KAI	Donner, Herbert, and Wolfgang Röllig, eds. *Kanaanäische und aramäische Inschriften*. 5th ed. Weisbaden: Harrassowitz Verlag, 2002.
KTU	Dietrich, Manfried, Oswald Loretz, and Joaquín Sanmartín, eds. *Die keilalphabetischen Texte aus Ugarit*. Münster: Ugarit-Verlag, 2013.
LangCog	Language and Cognition
MR	Material Religion
MTSR	Method and Theory in the Study of Religion
Muséon	Le Muséon: Revue d'Études Orientales
NA28	Aland, Barbara, Kurt Aland, Johannes Karavidopoulos, Carlo M. Martini, and Bruce M. Metzger, eds. *Novum Testamentum Graece*. 28th rev. ed. Based on the work of Eberhard Nestle and Erwin Nestle. Stuttgart: Deutsche Bibelgesellschaft, 2012.
NBR	Neuroscience and Biobehavioral Reviews
NEA	Near Eastern Archaeology
NLM	Neurobiology of Learning and Memory
NTT	Nederlands Theologisch Tijdschrift
PBR	Progress in Brain Research
PEQ	Palestine Exploration Quarterly
PNAS	Proceedings of the National Academy of Sciences
PPS	Perspectives on Psychological Science
PS	Psychological Science
PSPB	Personality and Social Psychology Bulletin
PsychBullRev	Psychonomic Bulletin & Review
PsychRev	Psychological Review
RAAO	Revue d'Assyriologie et d'archéologie orientale
RB	Revue biblique
RBB	Religion, Brain and Behavior
RC	Religion Compass
RE	Review and Expositor
RelS	Religious Studies
SAK	Studien zur Altägyptischen Kultur
SBA-IAS	Strata: Bulletin of the Anglo-Israel Archaeological Society
SJOT	Scandinavian Journal of the Old Testament
SJT	Scottish Journal of Theology
SPPC	Social and Personality Psychology Compass
SRC	Science, Religion and Culture
TA	Tel Aviv
TynBul	Tyndale Bulletin
TCS	TRENDS in Cognitive Sciences
TDOT	Botterweck, G. Johannes, and Helmer Ringgren, eds. *Theological Dictionary of the Old Testament*. Translated by John T. Willis et al. 8 vols. Grand Rapids, MI: Eerdmans, 1974–2006.

T&R	*Thinking and Reasoning*
UF	*Ugarit-Forschungen*
VEE	*Verbum et Ecclesia*
VT	*Vetus Testamentum*
WO	*Die Welt des Orients*
ZAW	*Zeitschrift für die alttestamentliche Wissenschaft*
ZDMG	*Zeitschrift der Deutschen Morgenländischen Gesellschaft*

Introduction

This book is about the ways deity and divine agency are conceptualized. It focuses on the deities, divine images, and representatives in the Hebrew Bible, and will ultimately focus on the way that text itself became a channel for hosting divine agency. The book is also about categories and how we develop and use them. This includes categories like "deity" and "divine agent," but also the conceptual categories scholars use to evaluate and to talk about them, and more specifically, the dichotomies that scholars often use to draw clear lines around those categories. It simplifies our task when we can draw hard and fast lines to distinguish deity from humanity, monotheism from polytheism, the religious from the secular, and cultic images from the deities they index.[1] However, the continued use of these dichotomies does not so much serve the interests of inquiry as it does the interests of the theological and academic structuring of power and values.[2] There is a saying attributed to George E. P. Box that all models are wrong, but some are useful. Many of these dichotomous models on which scholars have been relying have remained useful all these years for reasons that are often problematic. Now, certainly the model I will develop and apply will also be wrong in many ways, but this book is mostly an argument for its usefulness in helping to break some of

---

[1] Brett Maiden's (2020) *Cognitive Science and Ancient Israelite Religion* is an application of the cognitive science of religion to ancient Israelite and Judahite ideologies that includes a chapter on "rethinking" the popular/official religion dichotomy, but the volume still treats "religion" and "ontology" as central categories. Maiden's fifth chapter addresses many of the same questions as this volume, but is quite distinct in methodology and in scope. For other discussions of deity in the Hebrew Bible within a cognitive framework, see Singletary 2021; Stowers 2021.

[2] Note Brittany Wilson's (2021, 6) comments regarding Christianity's accommodation of Platonism: "Within this worldview, we find a range of related dichotomies that have their roots in Platonic thought and that often bubble to the surface in discussions of biblical embodiment (divine or otherwise). Such dichotomies include (but are not limited to): reality/representation, being/becoming, divine/human, immaterial/material, invisible/visible, form/matter, Creator/creation, soul/body." For more thorough discussions of some of these dichotomies and their entanglement with power, see Stroumsa 2010, 2021.

the stultifying molds in which the study of deity in the Hebrew Bible has been confined.

The main question I address in this book is related to the last dichotomy listed above: how is it that cultic images and certain divine representatives can appear to be simultaneously identified *with*, as well as distinguished *from*, the deities they index? As an example, Num 10:35–36 states that as the ark of the covenant set out each day, Moses would declare, "Advance, O YHWH! Your enemies shall scatter!" As it returned each day, he would declare, "Bring back, O YHWH, the ten thousand thousands of Israel!" In 2 Sam 7:2, David laments that he dwells in a house, while "the ark of the Deity dwells within curtains." Four verses later, YHWH responds through the prophet Nathan, stating, "From the day I brought the children of Israel up out of Egypt until this very day, I have not dwelled in a house, but have traveled around dwelling in a tent." These passages indicate the deity's own presence and actions were directly entangled with those of the ark.

Some cultic objects are identified with the deity, but in ways that are not authorized. Exodus 32:8, for instance, has YHWH explain that the Israelites referred to the molten calf as, "your deities, O Israel, who brought you up from the land of Egypt!" The text condemns worship of the calf, but the identification of the deity with a material object requires no explanation in the text, and is consistent with the treatment mentioned above of YHWH's relationship to the ark. Similarly, there are several narratives in the Hebrew Bible in which the messenger of YHWH is identified as a messenger in one verse, but then identified as YHWH in another. For example, Exod 3:2 explains that a "messenger of YHWH" appeared to Moses, but in verse 6 this messenger declares, "I am the Deity of your father, the Deity of Abraham, the Deity of Isaac, and the Deity of Jacob." This is different from other appearances of the messenger, such as Exod 23:20, where YHWH explicitly describes it as a separate entity: "Look, I am sending a messenger before you, to protect you along the way."

This ostensible paradox is more implicit and ambiguous in the Hebrew Bible than it is in texts from regions like Mesopotamia, where the evidence is far more widespread and explicit and extends to texts that prescribe lengthy ritual processes by which the deity was "installed" within a wide variety of often elaborate cultic objects. Largely because of the abundance of material remains in Mesopotamia bearing on this question, it has been most thoroughly addressed by scholars working within the field of Assyriology.[3] Patterns emerging from that field reveal significant progress regarding the conceptual foundations of the relationship of the deity to its cultic images, yet substantial methodological obstacles remain. As a result of the material and ostensibly artistic channels in which these phenomena

---

[3] For engagements with this phenomenon in other fields of study, see Bird 2014 (early Christianity); Mylonopoulos 2010; Platt 2011 (ancient Greece and Rome); Davis 1997 (modern India); Bynum 2015 (Roman Catholicism); Whitehead 2013 (England).

have been preserved, those images have long been interrogated as representative art, which has failed to adequately resolve the issue (cf. Morgan 2018). Scholars increasingly acknowledge that the cultic image was thought to have been divinized and to have somehow materially "presenced" the deity itself, or manifested its presence, while still maintaining some degree of autonomy (Bahrani 2003; Herring 2013; Sonik 2015; Schaper 2019).

In 1987, Thorkild Jacobsen (1987, 18) proposed a philosophical foundation for this problem:

> The contradiction of *is* and *is not* in the matter of the cult statue is so flagrant and cuts so deep that there must seem to be little hope of resolving it unless one goes to the most basic levels of understanding and attempts to gain clarity about the very fundamentals of ancient thought, about what exactly 'being' and 'nonbeing' meant to the ancients. We must consider, if only briefly, the ontology of the ancients, their ideas of what constituted 'being' and 'reality.'[4]

Jacobsen's observation that this ostensible paradox arises because of the disparity between our modern conceptualizations of ourselves and the world around us and those of first millennium BCE Southwest Asia touches on the root of the problem;[5] but despite his methodological sensitivity, Jacobsen still frames the issue in terms of "ontology" and "being," imposing modern philosophical frameworks where there is no indication they belong.[6] Neither "ontology" nor "being" in today's philosophical sense are anywhere discussed in the literature from ancient Southwest Asia related to the nature and function of divine images. It is not an ancient conceptual category; it is a thoroughly modern one, but twenty-first century scholarship continues to uncritically employ it. A notable exception that seems to me to be the most fruitful engagement with this issue from within Assyriology comes from Beate Pongratz-Leisten's phenomenal essay, "Divine Agency and Astralization of the Gods in Ancient Mesopotamia" (2011).[7] Her approach, which has inspired my own in many ways, incorporates frameworks from the cognitive sciences to build on the theoretical model for distributed agency developed by Alfred Gell in his posthumously published *Art and Agency* (1998).

---

[4] A. Leo Oppenheim (1977, 182) has written that it "is open to serious doubt whether we will ever be able to cross the gap caused by the differences in 'dimensions.'" This book will demonstrate that there are significant strides that can be made toward crossing that gap.
[5] By *conceptualize* and *conceptualization* I refer to the formation or interpretation of concepts using imagery and mental spaces that do not isometrically represent reality, but utilize idealized cognitive models or generalized mental representations. This will be discussed in more detail below.
[6] Jacobsen goes on to describe ancient Mesopotamians as *"monists"* (Jacobsen 1987, 19).
[7] Another notable exception is Stowers 2021.

Most of the Hebrew Bible scholarship that treats this problem is grounded in Assyriological research and similarly incorporates the frameworks of "hypostasis" (Lewis 2020, 338–92; cf. Allen 2015) and of Rudolph Otto's (1952) concepts of the numinous (Schaper 2019, 180–81), of *mysterium* (Smith, 2001, 94–95), of the tension of the *fascinans* and the *tremendum* (Sommer 2009, 97), and the notion of the deity as "the wholly other." The most influential engagement within Hebrew Bible scholarship has been Benjamin Sommer's *The Bodies of God and the World of Ancient Israel* (2009), which formulates a conceptual model for thinking through this phenomenon that Sommer calls the "Fluidity Model."[8] According to this model, there are two types of "fluidity" characterizing divine selfhood in ancient Southwest Asia. The first is *fragmentation*, or the ability of divine selfhood to fragment and simultaneously occupy multiple different bodies. The second is *overlap*, or the ability of divine selves to overlap, inhabit each other, or converge (Sommer 2009, 13–19).[9] The fluidity metaphor is intended to help us grasp the concept of the divine self being manifested in a variety of "bodies" that occupy different points in space at different or the same points in time. This fluidity makes them utterly unique, according to Sommer, who states, "For the peoples of the ancient Near East, the gods were made of a different sort of stuff, not only physically, but also ontologically." They were "radically unlike human beings in ways that may seem baffling to people in the contemporary Western world" (Sommer 2009, 12).

Sommer has brilliantly extrapolated this framework of divine personhood from a careful interrogation of ancient Southwest Asian literature, but he happens to closely approximate a widespread anthropological framework for personhood that views the self as fundamentally relational, and frequently partible and/or permeable. Sommer briefly and perhaps incidentally engages some of the features of the framework, but rejects its relevance to his fluidity model (Sommer 2009, 195 n. 145):

> Other cases outside Greece might suggest that human bodies can be seen as somewhat similar to what I describe in Mesopotamian divine bodies, but none

---

[8] Other thorough analyses are Schaper 2019; Lewis 2020, 333–426; Putthoff 2020, 118–55; cf. Wagner 2019. Two papers published in the course of finalizing this book that deploy the cognitive sciences within a discussion of deity in the Hebrew Bible are Singletary 2021 and Stowers 2021.

[9] These two types of fluidity are a bit too dichotomous in Sommer's framework, however, and the term *bodies* reflects too modern a notion of selfhood. The sharp lines Sommers draws seem largely to be responsible for his conclusion (2009, 124) that the Priestly and Deuteronomic strata "completely rejected this conception," and "insisted that God has only one body and one self." As we will see in chapter 5, these authors and editors were engaged more in a nuanced renegotiation than in a rejection.

overturns the basic contrast I outline. A person who believes in transmigration of the soul would argue that a human being does have more than one body, but not at any one moment in time. In some cultures we find a belief in possession or out-of-body experiences (especially mystic unity with a divinity), albeit as exceptional experiences noteworthy precisely because the human goes beyond the bounds of the normal human body. In any event, the ancient Near Eastern cultures under discussion here do not evince such beliefs, so that they posit the fundamental contrast between human and divine bodies.

As the next chapter will demonstrate, ancient Southwest Asian societies show clear evidence of such beliefs, as do modern societies, including those within which the scientific and philosophical frameworks of the Renaissance and Enlightenment are normative. Those beliefs are socioculturally mediated variations on the intuitive partibility of the body and of certain loci of agency. Even in contemporary English-speaking cultures we speak of people in terms of relationality, as well as "being a part of us," "taking a part of us with them," "being there in spirit," having their hearts in conflict with their brains, and in many other ways that reflect the underlying cognitive predispositions to relationality and the associated concepts of partibility and permeability, including—particularly in cases of deceased persons—inhabiting material media. The ability of ancient Southwest Asian deities to be present simultaneously in multiple different bodies is a difference of degrees, not of kind, that primarily emerges from widespread social demands for immediacy and presence, and from the conceptual flexibility of agents whose bodies are not otherwise available for scrutiny.

Assyriological and Hebrew Bible scholarship recognizes that these societies understood deities to in some way be able to inhabit material media and reify their presence through that media while the primary locus of their presence was understood to be located elsewhere. The scholarship also recognizes that this understanding seems to obtain in many different societies across time and space, suggesting there is some kind of underlying compulsion towards that conceptualization of deity and divine agency. A significant obstacle in this scholarship, however, is the tendency to rely for explanation on the many different emic rationalizations of those practices that emerge situationally (that is, they emerge in response to specific circumstances and situations) within the different societies in which they are found. This results in a tangled mess of accounts of deity and in the many different theoretical models that have been posited to explain the complexities of the sacred, the numinous, the hypostatic, and even of religion more broadly. This book offers a unifying theoretical framework that can account for that intuitive compulsion, can accommodate the diversity of explanations, and can also demonstrate the relationship of that intuitive compulsion to other phenomena associated with deity in the Hebrew Bible that are rarely recognized as such.

THE APPROACH OF THIS BOOK

The primary data pool from which I draw is the Hebrew Bible and other material remains from first millennium BCE Israel and Judah. Some preliminary remarks are warranted regarding my approach to those data. It is not my intention to forward any new theoretical models related to source criticism or the dating of the biblical texts, and so I will adopt existing models that I consider broadly representative of the state of the field. While early West Semitic poetry has an obscure *terminus post quem* (that is, earliest possible date of origin) the preponderance of evidence indicates that narrative prose developed in the regions around the highlands of Israel and Judah no earlier than the mid-ninth century BCE, which suggests that texts employing narrative prose to describe events preceding that period were committed to writing no earlier than the mid-ninth century.[10] That is not to say they cannot reflect historical events from earlier periods, only that their textualization would have followed a period of oral/material transmission during which there would have been a higher likelihood of change (despite some degree of constraint imposed by different sociomaterial dynamics).[11] Additionally, the commitment of earlier traditions to writing would have been refracted through the lenses of the sociocultural contexts and concerns of the later authors and editors.[12] What this means for this book is that I will consider historical narratives describing periods preceding the Mesha Stele and the rise of an Israelite monarchy to have been committed to text in a later period, and therefore to have in some way reflected the rhetorical goals of the latter authors and editors. The growth of the Omride kingdom in the ninth century would have provided ample administrative support for the development of royal histories—and scholars have long pointed to indications of northern origins for

---

[10] The Mesha Stele is the earliest example of narrative prose writing in the regions of and around early Israel and Judah (Sanders, 2010, 113–14). The reference on the Mesha Stele to Omri's oppression of Moab prior to Mesha suggests that Omri's kingdom had administrative structures at least as developed as Moab's, and therefore may have been capable itself of producing narrative prose around the same time period, though nothing survives.

[11] By *sociomaterial* I refer to the fundamentally material objects and channels through and with which society and sociality are created and maintained. By *oral/material* I refer not only to orally transmitted stories, but also to the association of mnemohistory with material media, such as cultic objects, buildings, geography, and even ruins. For discussions of mnemohistory, materiality, and the Hebrew Bible, see Pioske 2018; Wilson 2018; cf. Miller 2021, 189–92.

[12] See Pioske 2018, 80: "as older memories aggregate within a stream of oral tradition, they often, by necessity, adapt and cohere to 'new social and symbolic structures' within a community so that this remembered past retains its meaning and significance for those listening to a past they never experienced themselves."

several traditions (Rendsburg 1990; Finkelstein 2013, 141–51; Stahl 2021, 63–74)—but with the destruction of the Israelite kingdom in 722 BCE, and the subsequent maturation of the Judahite kingdom under Assyrian hegemony, any such literature was appropriated by whatever scribal structures were in place among officials in Jerusalem.[13]

The traditions of early Israel thus come down to us through the scribal filters of various cult centers and the Judahite royal court (Schniedewind 2004; Carr 2005; van der Toorn 2007). Some of the earliest of these likely include the charter myths of the patriarchal and exodus narratives (Finkelstein and Römer 2014, 321–22; Schmid 2018, 491–92), traditions associated with the conquest narratives (Römer 2007, 81–90), portions of the book of Judges known as the "Book of Saviors" (Römer 2007, 90–91; Knauf 2010, 140–49; Finkelstein 2017, 431–49), some prophetic literature,[14] and traditions regarding the rise of Saul (Edelman 1991; Wright 2014, 35–50). Judah produced its own literature between the eighth and seventh centuries BCE, which likely included early editions of prophetic texts and its own regnal histories (Aster 2017). An additional editorial filter for many of these texts is that of the so-called "Deuteronomic school," which refers to authors and editors who were responsible for the composition, compilation, and/or redaction of Deuteronomy (D) and the Deuteronomistic literature (Dtr), which runs from Deuteronomy through 2 Kings (Weinfeld 1972; Person 2012; Edelman 2014). The main outcome of this campaign is the book of Deuteronomy, the earliest edition of which I date to the late Neo-Assyrian period of the seventh century BCE.[15] Reconstructions propose this first edition began with Deut 6:4–5, included portions of Deut 12–13 and 21–25 as its core, and concluded with the curses of chapter 28 (Römer 2007, 78–81).

The Deuteronomistic school during the Neo-Assyrian period also produced portions of what would become the books of Joshua, Judges, Samuel, and Kings. While all these books drew in part from earlier literary traditions, and were also later edited within Neo-Babylonian (626–539 BCE) and Achaemenid (539–330 BCE) phases of Deuteronomistic production, their compilation was likely initiated by royal scribes working in Jerusalem under the reign of Josiah. Several prophetic books were composed or expanded upon between the late seventh century and the Neo-Babylonian period, including Jeremiah, Ezekiel, Deutero-Isaiah, Habakkuk, and others (Albertz 2003; Middlemas 2007; Becking and Human 2009).

---

[13] Note Pioske's observation that "when reading stories about the early Iron Age period we find that it is events and figures associated with the central hill country, from Shechem in the north to Hebron in the south, that are most often within the purview of the biblical writers. When we move outside of these bounds the picture presented becomes somewhat more murky" (Pioske 2018, 216).
[14] Portions of Hosea, for instance (Emmerson 1984; Blum 2009, 291–321).
[15] The reconstruction I adopt here is based on Römer 2007, 45–106.

Another widely acknowledged source for the biblical literature is the Priestly source, or P (Guillaume 2009; Schectman and Baden 2009; Baden 2012, 169–213). This source is characterized by a transcendent view of deity and by concern for genealogy, authority, purity, and ritual law.[16] Understood to begin with the creation account of Gen 1:1–2:4a, the earliest version of P is also thought to include a genealogy of Adam and of Shem, a flood account, the table of nations, portions of the books of Genesis and Exodus, Leviticus (including another source comprising Lev 17–26 known as the Holiness Code, or H), and portions of the book of Numbers (and perhaps Joshua). An original P corpus likely circulated independently,[17] perhaps during the sixth or early fifth century BCE,[18] but at some point, it was brought together with D and other narrative strands to produce the macronarrative of the Pentateuch.

Perhaps the most controversial aspect of the development of biblical literature I will address is the question of the Yahwist (J) and Elohist (E) sources. According to the classical formulation of the Documentary Hypothesis (DH), J and E were two of the earliest documentary sources for the Pentateuch, and many theoretical models attribute the initial combination of the patriarchal and exodus narratives to J (Römer 2006, 24–25). They have been unstable sources in some ways, however, and questions regarding their relationship to each other and to the broader Pentateuchal macronarrative have occupied the attention of source critics for some time.[19] Many—particularly German—scholars have recently forwarded the theory that the two corpora operated as independent traditions of Israelite origins until initially joined by P (Gertz, Schmid, and Witte 2002; Dozeman and Schmid 2006; Schmid 2010, 2012a). This would confine J to the early patriarchal narratives and render it less of a discrete documentary source and more of a collection of Yahwistic fragments. I think the arguments in favor of this view are strong, and so in this book I adopt the convention of referring to D, P, and either pre- or post-P sources.

I understand the rest of the biblical literature to have been composed between the Neo-Babylonian and Greco-Roman periods, with Daniel being the last, written around 164 BCE.[20] Some of these texts preserve traditions from earlier time

---

[16] The concern for the temple cult is understood by many to have been introduced in a later phase of P. In this view, P "provided the chronological and narrative thread of the compilation of the Torah" (Knauf and Guillaume 2016, 183).

[17] For an English translation of one proposed original P document, see Guillaume 2009, 13–30. A somewhat related attempt to delineate P is Propp 1996, 458–78.

[18] For a preexilic context for P, see Milgrom 1999; Faust 2019; cf. Meyer 2010, 1–6.

[19] Recent concerns about J are usually traced to Rendtorff 1976, 1977; cf. Römer 2006.

[20] Although the traditions still circulated separately, continued to be edited, and were characterized by a great deal of textual fluidity, as demonstrated, for instance, by the variability between MT, the Dead Sea Scrolls, and the Septuagint (Tov 2012, 174–90).

periods, and I will address them as the discussion warrants, but for the most part, I understand them to primarily reflect the social and ideological circumstances of the periods in which they were completed. Because these later texts will not be particularly germane to my discussion, I will address any questions of dating or sources, again, as the discussion warrants.

One main motivation for the ongoing revision, expansion, rearrangement, and reinterpretation of the texts of the Hebrew Bible in these periods is particularly relevant to this discussion, and that is the exigencies (that is, needs or demands) of social memory. The redaction of old material, the composition of new material, and the reconfiguring and reinterpreting of both socially narrativizes the circumstances and experiences of the group. This contributes to the making of meaning by renegotiating the past in light of the present and emplotting the group within the broader historical macronarrative, which reinforces identity and orients members towards desired values and goals. As Jan Assmann (2010, 14) has put it, "Memory enables us to orient ourselves in time and to form out of the stuff of time a 'diachronic identity.' Political myths are about forming a collective or political identity, and they achieve this by giving time the form of a narrative structure and charging this structure with values, emotions, and ideals." Controlling that narrative emplotment also facilitates boundary maintenance and the structuring of values and power. Conceptualizations of deity and divine agency are deeply entangled with those dynamics of power, values, and identity. The same is also frequently true of the contemporary study of deity and divine agency, which brings us to the cognitive sciences.

In order to disrupt the categories and conventions I believe have prevented researchers from more productively engaging with the problem of deities and their agents in the Hebrew Bible, and to address the frequent methodological myopia of a purely historical-critical approach, my approach in this book will be informed by insights from cognitive linguistics and the cognitive science of religion.[21] The material remains of ancient Israel and Judah that bear on the question of deities and divine agency are material products of mental representations within socio-historical contexts. Historians have long worked under the unstated assumption that "understanding arises simply by situating mental products in their context" (Martin 2013, 16), but the cognitive sciences have made clear that environmental input alone is not sufficient to determine mental output—the mind is not a blank slate (*tabula rasa*). The shared cognitive features of humanity's evolutionary history contribute, along with top-down environmental affordances, influences,

---

[21] While the cognitive science of religion is only beginning to be applied to the study of the Hebrew Bible (e.g., Maiden 2020), Ellen van Wolde (2003, 2005, 2007, 2009a, 2009b, 2013) has been productively applying the insights of cognitive linguistics for years. For the use of prototype theory to interrogate deity in relation to divine kingship in Mesopotamia, see Selz 2008.

and constraints, to the production, direction, and structuring of those outputs. Both configurations are critical to a more precise understanding of those outputs. Because our reconstruction of the ancient world unavoidably requires theoretical leaps over the gaps between lived experiences and material remains (and particularly texts), a more careful and robust methodological bridging of that gap is critical to advancing the field.[22]

Before describing my approach in more detail, a couple of caveats must be noted. The cognitive sciences are based on research with living informants, and this book begins from the assumption that the findings of experimentation today are more or less transferable to ancient minds. No available empirical data verify or falsify this assumption as of yet, but several considerations lend strong support to it. For instance, the main cognitive features that will be identified as central to the development of my thesis are understood to be products of evolutionary adaptations from very early in, and even prior to, the rise of modern humans. The conditions that give rise to many of those features have not changed since then: humans still give live birth to infants whose growth requires extensive support over several years from human persons who physically and personally interact with them within a broader social group. Additionally, many of the widespread mental outputs identified by scholars today as culturally mediated products of the relevant shared cognitive features are abundant in the material remains of first millennium BCE Southwest Asia, at least provisionally suggesting the presence and influence of those shared cognitive features. As Luther H. Martin has observed, "Given the scale of evolutionary time and change, it is reasonable to conclude that our cognitive capacities, like our behavioral biases, have remained significantly unaltered since the emergence of modern humans by the late Pleistocene Era, some 60,000 to 50,000 years ago" (Martin 2013, 16; cf. Wynn and Coolidge 2009).

A related complication is the disproportionate use of experiment participants from societies that are "WEIRD," or "Western, Educated, Industrialized, Rich, and Democratic" (Henrich, Heine, and Norenzayan 2010). College students in and from Eurocentric societies have long provided the vast majority of the data used to construct psychological theories and models, based on the untested assumption that their perspectives are universal. The experiences of people in these societies can differ wildly from those of societies from the other ends of those continua, which includes the societies of ancient Southwest Asia. While our underlying cognitive architecture is often consistent, mental outputs differ when cognition gets shone through the various cognitive filters those experiences afford us. While this has problematized much older data, subsequent cognitive research has more consistently incorporated informants from societies that do not fall exclusively under

---

[22] For a cognitive perspective on text as a technology that facilitated the formation of Jewish culture, see Levy 2012.

that rubric, and I have tried to construct my theoretical framework on that more recent research.

For this book, one of the most important insights I draw from the cognitive sciences is the influence of automatic and unconscious cognitive processes on our conscious and reflective cognition. In simpler terms, our subconscious thought precedes our conscious thought and can and does influence and even conflict with it. Within the cognitive science of religion, this insight is most commonly manifested in the concept of "dual-process cognition," which is usually and unfortunately represented as a dichotomy that divides "intuitive cognition" (quick, automatic, linked to the mind's "default settings") apart from "reflective cognition" (slow, conscious, open to contextual influence; Evans and Stanovich 2013; De Neys 2014; Morgan 2014; White 2021, 39–41). Many scholars have identified a variety of cognitive processes underlying our cognition that can straddle both sides of this proposed dichotomy (Glöckner and Witteman 2010; Mugg 2016; Grayot 2020). My interest in this model is focused on the capacity for cognition to operate unconsciously, which has been demonstrated by an array of experimental data, as has the potential for such unconscious cognition to influence and to conflict with more reflective cognition (Kelemen, Rottman, and Seston 2013; Järnefelt, Canfield, and Kelemen 2015; Järnefelt et al., 2019). In cases of such conflict in a person's cognition, they may apply reflective reasoning to the justification, explanation, or elaboration of the intuitive response (I refer to this as "rationalizing"), or they may employ reflective reasoning to revise or override it (I refer to this as "decoupling").

This cognitive conflict again raises a rather significant impediment to the study of deity that was briefly discussed above, namely the widespread scholarly prioritization of reflective and emic explanations in reconstructing the fundamentals of thought regarding deity from the available texts.[23] The overwhelming majority of emic explanations of deity—past and present—represent reflective reasoning about deity. Such reasoning, however, tends to be influenced by identity politics and power structures, and it is less likely to be relevant to the origins of the deity concepts. One result of the centering of this reflective reasoning is an insistence on treating the conceptualization of and engagement with deities and divine images as something unique, transcendent, and/or ineffable.[24] This may

---

[23] This prioritization obviously extends beyond just accounts of deity concepts. Theological explanations for ritual also tend to represent rather ad hoc rationalizations that serve the structuring of power and often have little to do with the historical and cognitive underpinnings of ritual acts (cf. Whitehouse 2021, 40–46). As Claire White (2021, 40) notes, "belief is often a poor predictor of behavior."

[24] Note Sommer's suggestion that "an interpreter should first of all at least consider the possibility that we can understand a religious text as manifesting religious intuitions that are essentially timeless" (Sommer 2009, 97). The next chapter will demonstrate that these

obscure our attempt to identify influences underlying their transmission, change, and elaboration (Boyer 2012).

Until reflective explanations become salient (usually because of strong social institutions), deity concepts tend to develop and circulate on the "folk" level, and to be more closely tethered to intuitive reasoning. Additionally, reflective explanations are often situationally emergent and contingent on power structures. Those explanations may become authoritative and govern subsequent accounts, or they may be altered or abandoned because of changing circumstances, but deity concepts cannot escape the gravitational pull of intuitive reasoning.[25] To use the most salient *reflective* explanations to account for the production, elaboration, or transmission of the concept is to put the cart firmly before the horse. Unfortunately, that has been the trend in many scholarly accounts of deity and divine agency.[26] The cognitive science of religion, on the other hand, gives significant weight to the *intuitive* explanation. This is thought to hit closer to the cognitive roots of cross-cultural patterns of thought and behavior, and this makes for a more solid foundation for explanation than does privileging the far more socially and historically contingent reflective structuring of knowledge. I am by no means suggesting that these cognitive roots are the only relevant sources of explanation, that they should always take unilateral priority over those more socially contingent modes of knowledge, or that the latter do not merit study in their own right. I am suggesting those roots have been neglected for far too long, and that they can facilitate a great deal of progress.

One of the outcomes of the priority of our intuitive cognition is that our minds mediate our perception of the world around us, and this extends to our senses (it's what makes most optical illusions work), but even to how we *think* about ourselves and the world around us (cf. Ramachandran 2011). This leads to an important insight: our perception and experience of the world is the result not just of the passive processing of stimuli, but also a projection of experience. Our minds

---

intuitions are actually the same intuitions responsible for our conceptualizations of ourselves and the rest of the world around us. The assumption that there are intuitions unique to religion is a distorting framework.

[25] Justin Barrett and Frank Keil (1996, cf. Barrett 1999), for instance, have shown that when reasoning about the activity of deity, people most commonly default to a thoroughly anthropomorphic conceptualization, which is more intuitive. When primed regarding the particular theological orthodoxies they endorsed, the appeals to anthropomorphism were reduced.

[26] It seems to me this is particularly common in the study of early christology. This scholarship frequently gives priority of place to rationalizations attributed to the authors of the biblical texts, which serves the interests and power structures of scholars operating within the perception of a shared tradition. This seems to me to be a brand of what is referred to in the study of religion as "protectionism." For an excellent discussion of this phenomenon, see Young 2019.

take a fraction of a second to process stimuli, but there are sometimes circumstances in which that gap can be the difference between life and death. As a result, our minds have evolved to cover that gap by using available clues to project expectations onto our perceptions (Bubic, von Cramon, and Schubotz 2010). This evolutionary adaptation can be exploited for entertainment purposes:

A
BIRD
IN THE
THE BUSH

If you read "A BIRD IN THE BUSH," your mind skipped the second occurrence of "THE" on the fourth line. Not everyone will be tripped up by this illustration, but expectations can trip us up enough that it's one of the main reasons it's good to have others proofread our writing.

A theoretical model known as "predictive coding" describes the human brain as "a statistical organ that constantly tests its own hypotheses about the world through an ongoing process of error minimization" (Anderson 2019, 71).[27] Predictive coding suggests the mind's experiences in the past inform expectations (or predictions) regarding the sensory input most likely to come from its environment.[28] These expectations inform those projections that cover gaps in processing time and in the reliability of sensory input. When that reliability is low, such as in darkness, expectations drawn from prior experience can dominate perception (and imagination), while the sensory input will usually dominate when it is more reliable and precise.[29] The mind's model of its own body and its environment, seen and unseen, and expectations going forward, are revised and corrected in accordance with the input received. This feature of our cognition will have particular significance in the next chapter's discussion of our sensitivity to the presence of agents in the world around us.

---

[27] On this model, see further Hohwy, 2013; Clark et al., 2013; van Elk and Aleman 2017; Van Eyghen 2018; Anderson et al. 2019.

[28] See Uffe Schjødt's description (2019, 364): "Predictive coding elegantly explains how the brain uses Bayesian inference to minimize the energy spent on perception and cognition. Mental representations consist of top-down models based on prior experience which are constantly compared with bottom-up information from the senses. If prediction errors are detected, the brain corrects and updates its models in order to minimize prediction error in the future."

[29] This theory's prioritization of domain-general cognitive processes instead of domain-specific (or "modular") processes offers a helpful corrective to the salience of modularity within CSR. Cognitive linguistics developed out of opposition to the modular theories of generative grammar (Lakoff 1987a, 582–85).

While these insights help us better understand the cognitive processes involved in the production, elaboration, and transmission of deity concepts, it's not as simple as drawing a straight line from those cognitive processes to the biblical texts as we have them today. In addition to the fact that the Hebrew Bible represents the repeatedly edited and decontextualized writings of a tiny minority of members of elite scribal classes, they are overwhelmingly instruments of propaganda intended to further the authors' and editors' own rhetorical goals. As a result, they reflect carefully curated perspectives with a broad spectrum of proximities to actual lived experiences today. To more carefully bridge the gap between cognition and text, and to help navigate the complexities of biblical rhetoric, this book also incorporates insights from cognitive linguistics.

The foundational principle of cognitive linguistics is that language is not an autonomous faculty that operates independently of our cognition, but is one of many integrated functions *of* that cognition. In other words, language is not an independent tool we just pick up and manipulate. It originates in and is governed by our experiences within our cognitive ecologies—it is an outgrowth of our individual experiences with cognition.[30] Perhaps the most important insight that results from this principle is that linguistic meaning is contingent on our cumulative embodied experiences. We construct meaning from language because we have experience with usage in contexts, not because words, phrases, or sentences have inherent or autonomous semantic value. They do not. Words and texts have no inherent meaning. Meaning is generated in, and is confined to, the mind of the hearer, reader, or viewer, and based on the interpretive lenses their cumulative embodied experiences afford.

Among many other things, this insight helps us to better understand how what we consider theologically problematic biblical texts could be preserved by theologically sensitive editors and redactors. A text composed to communicate a perspective that later circumstances rendered theologically problematic need not necessarily be revised or excised in order to resolve the problem, since it carries no meaning independent of the hearers, readers, or viewers. As the shared texts of Judahite societies arrogated more and more authority, their alteration became an increasingly sensitive issue. All that was usually required to resolve theologically thorny issues, however, was for the consumers to bring interpretive frameworks to the text that facilitated an alternative reading. In many instances, powerful social institutions can propagate and enforce such alternative readings without making any changes to the texts at all, either by slightly revising entirely distinct texts, or by composing entirely new texts. As one example from the Christian scriptures, Jas 2:24 seems to represent a direct challenge to Rom 3:28. The author

---

[30] William Croft and D. Alan Cruse (2004, 3–4) explain, "categories and structures in semantics, syntax, morphology and phonology are built up from our cognition of specific utterances on specific occasions of use."

of Romans states, "for we determine that a person is justified by faith without the works of the law" (*logizometha gar dikaiousthai pistei anthrōpon xōris ergōn nomou*), while the author of James asserts, "you see that a person is justified by works and not by faith alone" (*horate hoti ex ergōn dikaioutai anthrōpos kai ouk ek pisteōs monon*). James 2:21–22 also directly challenges the example of Abraham evoked by Paul in Rom 4:2–3. While Martin Luther dismissed James as an "epistle of straw" (*strohene Epistel*) in the introduction to his 1522 translation of the Bible, subsequent Protestant readers have largely reconciled the two texts not by altering them, but by imposing a new interpretive lens that flips the relationship of faith and works and rereads works as the fruits or the manifestation of faith. According to this reading, the author of James and the author of Romans are actually in perfect agreement, and the second chapter of James is just explaining that one's justification is still achieved by faith alone and only *manifested to others* through works. Readers of the biblical texts are not as confined as we frequently assume to the readings that we find most likely. In chapter 5 I will suggest that a passage in Exodus was composed precisely to provide an alternative interpretive lens for other problematic passages that scholars still have not managed to resolve to widespread satisfaction.

In addition to being confined to the minds of hearers, readers, and viewers, cognitive linguistics suggests that meaning is conceptual, or based on concepts, which can be described as "a person's idea of what something in the world is like" (Dirven and Verspoor 2004, 13). Concepts are not coextensive with linguistic expressions; they are the semantic structures conventionally indexed by those expressions. To facilitate the more efficient and consistent construal of conceptual content, our minds create and deploy basic metaphorical frameworks called "image schemas" (Hampe 2005; Mandler and Cánovas 2014). These are "abstract, preconceptual structures that emerge from our recurrent experiences of the world" (Kövecses 2020, 9). They serve to give structure to more developed or abstract concepts. A very basic example is the UP-DOWN schema, which is used to map abstract concepts against a vertical spatial relationship.[31] This schema may derive intuitively from the upright stance and gait of healthy and abled humans. It appears to be nearly universal, and a vast array of abstractions is intuitively mapped against it to produce what are called conceptual metaphors (Kövecses 2020; Nyord 2009, 6–23).[32]

The following are common English-language examples based on the UP-DOWN schema:[33]

---

[31] I follow the convention here of putting the names of image schemas and conceptual metaphors in small caps.
[32] Sometimes the terms *image schema* and *conceptual metaphor* are conflated (cf. Lakoff 1987b, 219–22).
[33] The examples here are drawn primarily from Saeed 2003, 347.

good is up; bad is down
 "Things are looking *up*"
 "Well, this is an all-time *low*"

happy is up; sad is down
 "My spirits are *up*"
 "He's feeling *down*"

virtue is up; depravity is down
 "She has *high* standards"
 "I wouldn't *stoop* that *low*"

control is up; subjugation is down
 "She's in a *superior* role"
 "They are *under* my control"

Another very basic image schema that research suggests develops intuitively in preverbal infant cognition is the CONTAINER schema (Mandler 1992; Tilford 2017, 17–23), which leads to the widespread conceptual metaphor THE BODY IS A CONTAINER. According to this metaphor, the skin functions as a boundary to keep everything inside on the inside, and everything outside on the outside. As we will see in the next chapter, this conceptual metaphor leads intuitively to the perception that the self is contained inside the body (and most commonly located in the area of the head, the chest, or the abdomen). With this understanding of the relationship of conceptual metaphors to cognition, we can more confidently reconstruct some of the intuitions, assumptions, and foundations of thought that were likely held by ancient writers about the person, about the world, and about the former's place within the latter. This will be particularly relevant to the discussion of personhood in the first chapter.

Prototype theory is another important framework that will inform this book's engagement with conceptual categories (Rosch 1973, 1975; Lakoff 1987a; Taylor 2003; Geeraerts 2006). According to this theory, the human mind does not intuitively learn or use categories according to the classical Aristotelian approach of a binary set of necessary and sufficient features (the foundational approach of most dictionaries).[34] That is a distorting framework. Experimental data indicate that conceptual categories are not strictly binary, but can be internally graded—that is, there are "better" and "worse" members of a category—and tend to lack

---

[34] John Taylor provides a summary of the Aristotelian method of categorization, and he identifies four basic assumptions inherent to it: (1) "Categories are defined in terms of a conjunction of necessary and sufficient features," (2) "Features are binary," (3) "Categories have clear boundaries," and (4) "All members of a category have equal status" (Taylor 2003, 21–22).

natural boundaries. Attention is focused inward on the center of the category and on its prototypical members, not outward on its boundaries or on the total membership. As a result, categories do not develop and are not learned through the delineation of the boundaries, but through experiences with the prototypical members of a category.[35] For instance, you can almost certainly distinguish furniture from non-furniture, but can you define "furniture"?[36] Can you list the widely accepted necessary and sufficient features? We understand a category because we have experience with items identified as members of it, not because we memorize lists of features that delineate the category.[37] Boundaries tend to arise rather arbitrarily as a need arises for them, meaning those boundaries are often fuzzy, arbitrary, and/or debatable, and are often the products of attempts to structure values and power.[38] Rather than learning and using categories based on necessary and sufficient features, prototype theory suggests that categories are learned and used based on the perception of some manner of similarity to a prototype. These prototypes are not usually individual members of a category, but cognitive exemplars or idealized conceptualizations that arise from experiences with the category.[39] While this theory will inform my engagement with all the conceptual categories discussed throughout this book (and is why I do not define any terms), it will be a particular focus of my discussion in chapter 3 regarding the conceptualization of deity in the Hebrew Bible. Among other things, prototype

---

[35] The "is a hotdog a sandwich" debate shows how prioritizing necessary and sufficient features can result in (mostly) humorous distortions of the ways categories are used.

[36] Cf. Wittgenstein 1958, §1.68: "How is the concept of a game bounded? What still counts as a game and what no longer does? Can you give the boundary? No. You can draw one; for none has so far been drawn. (But that never troubled you before when you used the word 'game.')."

[37] Ask someone on the street in San Antonio to describe a "boot" in as much detail as possible and they'll almost certainly describe a cowboy boot. Ask someone on the street in Liverpool, UK, and they'll almost certainly describe an army boot, if not the trunk of a car. The different experiences with the category "boot" between these two societies will produce different conceptualizations.

[38] For example, there is a lot at stake in debates about what does or does not constitute a deity, a religion, or even a woman, which is one of several reasons the definitions are so contested. For an example of sociological research on what's at stake in how the concept of "racism" is defined, see Unzueta and Lowery 2008.

[39] Describing developments in the field of prototype theory, Patrizia Violi (2000, 107) states, "It became clear that it was not possible, at least for semantic applications, to think of the prototype as the concrete instance of the most prototypical member of any given category, and consequently as a real individual. Instead, it was necessary to turn it into a mental construal: an abstract entity made up of prototypical properties. In this way the prototype, being the result of a mental construction, frees itself from any concrete evidence, and as such may well never be actualized in reality as any real instance."

theory allows us to acknowledge and engage with overlap and integration at the intersection of distinct conceptual categories, rather than insist on the strict and clear binaries that are prominent primarily because of academic convenience rather than analytical value.

OUTLINE OF THIS BOOK

My first chapter constructs a theoretical model for the nature and origins of deity concepts. Rather than begin with contemporary models of deity, however, it begins with a theoretical model for the origins of deity concepts drawn from the cognitive science of religion. I will then argue that deity concepts originated in elaborations on the intuitive conceptualization of human persons, including deceased kin.[40] The most important function of deities within this framework relate to the facilitation of social cohesion through full access to strategic information, through social monitoring, and through the provision, via ritual, of opportunities for costly signaling and credibility enhancing displays. Cultic media will be shown to be critical not only to the materialization and transmission of deity concepts, but also to the presencing of deities and their agency.

The second chapter treats the material encounter of deity and divine in ancient Southwest Asia, applying the theoretical framework developed in chapter 1 to the material remains of Egypt, Mesopotamia, and Anatolia, and finally ancient Israel and Judah. This will demonstrate the heuristic value of that framework and set the stage for the discussion in subsequent chapters of YHWH's presencing media. Chapters 3 and 4 will address deity in the Hebrew Bible, employing insights from cognitive linguistics to bridge the gap between the material and phenomenological aspects of deity and divine agency and their representation in the biblical texts. Chapter 3 will explore the contours and boundaries of the semantic field of the generic concept of deity. Chapter 4 will then interrogate YHWH's profile as an instantiation of that generic concept. Depriviliging YHWH's conceptualizations by examining them through the frameworks of generic deity will reveal their roots in that generic framework, and also show that the more distinctive aspects of YHWH's divine profile do not represent conceptual revolutions, but incremental elaborations on generic features and functions.

In the fifth chapter I interrogate YHWH's own divine agents, focusing on the ark of the covenant and the *kābôd* (traditionally translated "glory"). By tracing the developmental trajectory of these agents, this interrogation will demonstrate that there was no revolutionary paradigm shift that resulted in the abandonment of Israelite or Judahite presencing media. Rather, the nature of those media was

---

[40] My discussion will focus on the cognitive science of religion. A related discussion from archaeological and anthropological perspectives, with several points of contact, is found in Wunn and Grojnowski 2016.

incrementally revised to serve the changing perspectives, circumstances, and needs of the elite. The chapter begins with the ark of the covenant, which is the closest thing in the Hebrew Bible to an authorized Yahwistic cultic image. The chapter will argue that it paralleled, in form and function, shrine models that housed and mobilized small divine images. The chapter then moves on to the *kābôd*, or "glory" of YHWH, which in its earliest iterations represented the very body of YHWH, but later became compartmentalized as a partible divine agent that both presenced the deity and also obscured its nature.

Chapter 6 turns its attention to the enigmatic messenger of YHWH, who in several biblical narratives is alternatively distinguished *from* YHWH and also identified *as* YHWH. This phenomenon closely parallels the similar identification elsewhere in ancient Southwest Asia of divine images as simultaneously the deity and *not* the deity. The chapter will identify three main approaches to accounting for this conflation of identities, concluding that the theory of the interpolation of the word *messenger* in these narratives best accounts for the data. The theoretical framework developed earlier in the book regarding the intuitive communicability of loci of agency will account for the survival of these seemingly paradoxical narratives. Exodus 23:20–21 appeals to that framework when it attributes divine prerogatives to the messenger of YHWH in virtue of the messenger's possession of one of the main loci of YHWH's agency: the divine name. The remainder of the chapter will explore the use of the *šem*, or "name," elsewhere in the Hebrew Bible to presence the deity, and particularly in the Jerusalem temple.

In chapter 7, I will examine the further textualization of YHWH's presencing media. I will argue that the de facto centralization of cultic worship following the invasion of Sennacherib and the later loss of the Jerusalem temple left a void in the sociomaterial presencing of YHWH that was quickly filled with inscriptions, amulets, and the texts of the Torah. Amulets like the Ketef Hinnom inscriptions demonstrate the private apotropaic (that is, for warding off evil) use of texts as presencing media. Meanwhile, in narratives from the authoritative literature, versions of the Torah were written upon more traditional cultic media like stelai (that is, standing stones, e.g., Deut 27:1–10). In this way, texts that not only bore the divine name, but also the first-person speech of the deity, merged with and activated the older presencing media. In later periods, these texts were rhetorically democratized as authoritative literature. They would also prescribe the installation of amulets containing portions of some Torah texts on the posts of their doorways (similar to the placement of stelai at city gates), as well as their wearing as emblems on the forehead. In this way, the Torah replaced icons and divine images, not by way of rejection, but assimilation.

The conclusion will summarize the most important findings of the book, including the nature of deity concepts as elaborations on the intuitive conceptualization of partible and permeable persons, the divine/human continuum, and the relationship of presencing media to communicable divine agency in the Hebrew Bible. I will also highlight the productivity and robustness of the theoretical frameworks developed in the book and discuss their applicability to other aspects of the study of the Hebrew Bible, as well as the study of deity beyond the Hebrew Bible. A brief appendix following the conclusion will also discuss the relevance of the messenger of YHWH and the divine name to early perspectives on Jesus's relationship to the God of Israel.

1.
What Is a Deity?

A question that is central to my thesis is one that Vitor Hurowitz once scribbled into the margins of an early draft of Mark Smith's (1990, 6–8) book *The Early History of God*: "What is an *ilu* [deity]?"[1] This chapter will set the stage for answering that question, but instead of proposing a provisional definition, or plowing ahead as if we already all agree regarding what constituted a deity in ancient Southwest Asia,[2] this chapter will aim for a more methodologically sound and heuristically robust theoretical framework for the origins and functions of deity concepts. This will inform the next three chapters' interrogations of ancient Israel's and Judah's presencing media and authoritative literature. Rather than begin this interrogation with textual data, I begin with what cognitive scientists of religion have suggested is the conceptual taproot of deity: agency. Those scholars have done a lot of the heavy lifting already with their development of the so-called supernatural agency hypothesis, and the first section of this chapter will outline the most promising features of that hypothesis.[3] The bulk of the chapter will then be dedicated to interrogating personhood and its relationship to agency. The focus will ultimately be trained on deceased persons and the blurred lines that separate deceased persons from deities, and particularly in ancient Southwest Asia and the Hebrew Bible. The final section will address theories regarding the relationship of socially concerned deities to large and complex societies.

---

[1] A wonderful contribution to this discussion within Assyriology is Porter 2009.

[2] Note Stanley Stowers's (2021, 387) comments regarding the subtext that tends to govern the scholarly responses to this question: "This subtext includes the doctrine that the late Hebrew Bible and Judaism eventually became monotheistic. A narrative about evolution from cruder conceptions of God to (a higher and more spiritual) monotheism frames the discussions either explicitly or implicitly."

[3] Many scholars recognize the problems with the loaded term supernatural, and many have shifted to preference for the framework of counterintuitiveness. I think there is value to this framework, but it seems to me there is still too much that remains to be worked out for me to incorporate it into my own theoretical model here. For discussion, see Purzycki and Willard 2016.

My thesis in this chapter is fourfold. First, the conceptual spark of deity concepts is humanity's hypersensitivity to the presence of *unseen agency* in the world around us. Because this agency, as with our thoughts and intentions, is not visible, it may potentially be anywhere. Second, deity concepts initially develop as elaborations on intuitive reasoning about the agency of the partible and permeable person, particularly after death. Third, the transmission and perpetuation of large-scale socially concerned deities like YHWH rely on their performance of functions that increase social cohesion, such as providing access to "strategic information,"[4] monitoring behavior, facilitating costly signaling, and punishing violators of social mores. Fourth, these functions are facilitated through powerful social institutions and through the use of material media to *presence*—that is, reify or bring about the presence of—the unseen agency, which may, depending on the relevant reflective reasoning, transform the unseen agency into an agent that may be seen, socially engaged, and even handled. While my thesis builds on a number of well-established features of human cognition, some of the discussion will also address prominent but preliminary theories about evolution and universal experiences of infancy that are thought to contribute to the emergence and development of those features.

AGENCY

While there continues to be debate about many of the details of the supernatural agency hypothesis, it builds on the convergence of four insights about agency from cognitive and evolutionary psychology that explain the production of deity concepts on an individual level and their propagation on a social level. According to the first of these insights, human evolution has made us hypersensitive to the presence of mental agents in the world around us. This is thought to derive at the most basic level from genes most consistently being passed on by early primates who most rapidly reasoned that the rustling in the bushes or the shadows darting around in the night were agents that might be focused on them. There was a low cost for false positives—maybe you get made fun of—compared to the high cost of false negatives—death—so evolution embedded that hypersensitivity deep in our intuitive reasoning, giving our minds a hair trigger for the presence of mental agents in the world around us (Guthrie 1993; Barrett 2000, 31; Maij, van Shie, and van Elk 2019).

The second insight is the teleological orientation of our intuitive reasoning, or our tendency to attribute purpose and intention to circumstances, events, or entities for which we lack an adequate explanation. In other words, we tend to

---

[4] This is a technical term within CSR that generally refers to any information that can aid in human decision-making, and particularly related to social interactions. See Boyer 2001, 150–55; Purzycki et al. 2012; Purzycki 2013.

1. What Is a Deity?

assume things we don't understand have happened for a reason. This reasoning has been observed very early in infancy, and it is thought to arise as a result of children accumulating embodied experiences and beginning to recognize that other persons are "like me." This leads to the cognitive mapping of the bodies of others onto an infant's own via the mirror neuron system, resulting in the imitation of others' actions (Rizzolatti and Craighero 2004; Kaysers, Thious, and Gazzola 2013; Wightman 2015, 17–23). Infants also map the relationship between their own bodily actions and mental experiences back onto the actions of others and begin to develop the ability to attribute intention to those actions (Meltzoff 2011; Kim and Song 2015). Within the first year of life, infants begin to attribute goals to unfamiliar and inanimate objects, and to infer unseen and unknown causes and agents based on the perception of intentionality in a variety of environmental cues and conditions (Luo and Baillargeon 2005; Moriguchi and Shinohara 2012; Muentener and Schulz 2014). This teleological outlook stays with us throughout adulthood (Kelemen and Rosset 2009; Kelemen, Rottman, and Seston 2013; Järnefelt, Canfield, and Kelemen 2015), and when we combine it with our hypersensitivity to the presence of agents, we are embedded in a world potentially teeming with intentional agents that we do not see, but that may be responsible for any number of unexplained circumstances, entities, or events.

Predictive coding is a feature of cognition that may stimulate the mental representation of novel agents.[5] Inferring the nature of hidden or unknown causes in our environment most often involves projecting known patterns and values. These inferences are likely to include known agents where the available stimuli are symptomatic, according to our experiences, of their presence. Our minds are open to the possibility of encountering previously unknown agents, however, so our existing expectations can be revised in terms of scale, intensity, distance, and other properties based on variations in the stimuli. To illustrate, Tommaso Bertolotti and Lorenzo Magnani (2010, 253) suggest the following thought process could underlie the intuitive response to a person seeing some rocks falling:

1. An animal climbing on a cliff causes some gravel and rocks to move and fall when it treads over them.
2. *Hence, falling rocks are likely to be symptomatic of an animal stepping up hill.*
3. I notice rocks falling down.
4. *Therefore, I must be in presence of an animal stepping uphill.*

A similar physical event, but with a significant shift in magnitude, may be interpreted according to this experience, but with a similar shift in magnitude.

---

[5] Some scholarship has argued that overreliance on content biases and not context has distorted the findings of the cognitive science of religion (Gervais and Henrich 2010).

Without a strong reflective framework for experimentation or investigation, we will intuitively reach into our experiential repertoire for the closest conceptual match. If we witness boulders careening down a mountainside, but we are unfamiliar with the responsible phenomena, we may revise existing agent concepts (e.g., "an animal climbing") to produce novel agent concepts, such as an enormous or enormously powerful animal climbing on a cliff (Bertolotti and Magnani 2010, 254). Similar inferences drawn from the many and varied experiences of early humans within their cognitive ecologies likely contributed to the initial production of a variety of novel agents.

The third insight is what I refer to as body-agency partibility. As a result of the Eurocentric reification of the mind as the locus of cognition, this is generally referred to as "mind/body dualism" in the cognitive sciences, but this is an imprecise and infelicitous term that is too often equated with Cartesian duality.[6] In short, the sensitivity of our minds to mental agents in the world around us does not necessarily posit a body. This again is thought to be a byproduct of the universal experiences of human infancy. Around the end of the first year of life, infants begin to intuitively perceive that thoughts and motivations are different from *things*, that people have different mental attitudes, and that those mental attitudes can be hidden and can differ from bodily states and behaviors (Kinzler and Spelke 2007; Boyer and Barrett 2016). The result is the perception that psychological agents are "in here," while physical objects—including the body—are "out there" (Wellman 2014, 266). These intuitions remain into and throughout adulthood (Forstmann and Burgmer 2015) and interact with sociocultural frameworks and influences to result in the production and propagation of a variety of entities associated with cognition (e.g., "mind"), emotion (e.g., "heart"), animacy (e.g., "spirit," "life force"), and selfhood (e.g., "soul," "Ego").[7] As children begin to be able to engage in contemplation and imagination about the nature of these loci of agency—unobservable as they are—they also contemplate and imagine their constraints, and particularly the degree to which they are and are not confined to the body, and most importantly, their continued existence after death (Bering and Bjorklund 2004; Astuti and Harris 2008).

The fourth insight is humanity's "symbolic faculty," or our ability to symbolically structure knowledge about ourselves and the world around us. This faculty is widely thought to have begun developing before the isolation of *Homo sapiens sapiens* (modern humans), and it has been observed in some non-human animals, but its development in modern humans was accelerated well beyond other animals by the development of human language (Gamble 2007, 87–110;

---

[6] The Cartesian echoes of this terminology are frequently lamented and often distort discussion of these findings (Hodge 2008).

[7] Cohen and Barrett 2011, 114–17; Johnson 1990; Roazzi, Nyhof, and Johnson 2013; Weisman, Dweck, and Markman 2017.

Tattersall 2009). That innovation allowed us to communicate in increasingly complex ways about ourselves, about our mental states, and about the world around us. It also allowed us to share, and thus to propagate and elaborate on, concepts of alternative realities (circumstances, states, and entities that are not immediately available or observable), which exponentially increased the complexity and sophistication of our capacity for imagination (Dor 2015).

We take this capacity for granted today, but the ability to symbolically structure and then socially transmit mental representations of complex circumstances, agents, roles, structures, and norms that are not based on immediately available data is a uniquely human evolutionary adaptation that burst a cognitive dam. This technology made it possible to reason and to pass on knowledge about alternative realities such as "yesterday," "tomorrow," who "we" are, and "the way things should be" (Van Leeuwen 2016; Wood and Shaver 2018, 9–10). This fundamentally altered the constitution of human sociality, and among many other things, it made it possible to reason together about all the agents in the world around us that we do not see, including their intentions, their faculties, and whatever sociality might obtain among them. In virtually all societies across time and space, this resulted in the development of concepts of unseen agents with biographies, faculties, personalities, relationships, and even institutions.[8] Because the agents that are most familiar and important to us are other human persons, they are the most available and accessible templates for elaboration, and thus the most common. Concepts of unseen agency, more often than not, build on salient features of personhood.

On the individual level, these concepts of unseen agency are usually fleeting, since they are tethered to the individual's own situationally emergent intuitions. To spread and preserve them across time and space requires their social transmission through more reflective reasoning and discussion. Human language was one important catalyst for this, but the material representation of such concepts was another. Materially representing concepts of unseen agency anchors them in media that can more efficiently and reliably "store" and transmit certain features. This frees up cognitive real estate that might otherwise be required to maintain or transmit those features so that it can be dedicated to further elaboration and development.[9] (How many phone numbers have you memorized in the last five years?) This material mode of transmission is particularly important for more counterintuitive agent concepts like theriomorphic (that is, having animal form) or hybrid agents, which require more cognitive effort to process (cf. Mithen 1998).

---

[8] According to the most common theories, these features become culturally adaptive as they are deployed in the maintenance of social cohesion. See Atran 2012; Purzycki, Haque, and Sosis 2014. For critiques of this approach, see Pyysiäinen 2014, Vlerick 2020.
[9] This "ratcheting effect" is frequently referred to as "cumulative culture." See Dean et al. 2014; Haidle 2019.

PERSONHOOD

PERSONHOOD IN TODAY'S SOCIETIES

This brings us to intuitive conceptualizations of personhood, which derive in large part from our symbolic structuring of the relationship of the loci of agency to the body. I was born and raised in, and I live and work (most of the time) in, societies in North America that descend intellectually from the scientific and philosophical frameworks of the Renaissance, Reformation, and Enlightenment. As a result, personhood in my cognition and discourse is heavily influenced by structures descended from classical Greek and Christian literature and praxis (Elkaisy-Friemuth and Dillon 2009; King 2012; Long 2015). When discussing personhood *reflectively*, people in such societies will generally stress "a persistent personal identity ... over relational identities" (Fowler 2004, 7), and will often prioritize ontological dimensions like the biological or the cognitive. However, in everyday discourse, more *intuitive* conceptualizations move within a variety of dimensions of personhood that are more relational and more closely linked with the conceptualizations of personhood that we can reconstruct from the material remains of ancient Southwest Asia.

For example, I have lived my whole life associating my brain with my intellect, my heart with my desires, and my gut with fear and anxiety. These associations are not just an arbitrary metaphor—they obtain reliably across time and space. Cognitive linguistic research examining the most socially common loci of faculties of feeling, thinking, and knowing in languages from around the world found that results consistently fell into one of three different models: abdominocentric, cardiocentric, or dual cephalocentric/cardiocentric (Sharifian et al. 2008; Yu 2009; Slingerland and Chudek 2011). In Eurocentric societies, the autonomy of these regions and their compartmentalized faculties are commonly reflected through references to conflict between the emotional heart and the analytical head. The fact that these independent parts can reify the presence of the person as a whole in certain circumstances is reflected in stories like Frankenstein's monster (and its many variations), or stories of the loved ones of deceased organ donors feeling reunited with the deceased by meeting with the recipients of the organs (almost always the heart). The easy ability to feel or even recognize another's heartbeat provides a sensory reinforcement of the identification of the organ as a primary locus of agency, and thus presence.

As an example, when twenty-year-old organ donor Abbey Connor died, her heart was given to twenty-one-year-old Loumonth Jack Jr. When Abbey's father, Bill, met Loumonth, he listened to his heartbeat with a stethoscope and later commented, "Abbey is alive inside of him—it's her heart having him stand up straight. I was happy for him and his family, and at the same time, I got to reunite with my daughter" (Earl 2015). Herein lies an issue with Sommer's fluidity model, which is concerned primarily with the ability of deities to "exist simultaneously in several *bodies*" (Sommer 2009, 12, emphasis added). Loumonth's body was not identified as Abbey's body, but the constituent element of her personhood that had been implanted in him reified Abbey's *presence* for her father, even if not her *body*. Sommer (2009, 2) defines body as "*something located in a particular place at a particular time, whatever its shape or substance*" (emphasis in original), and the goal of this definition seems to me to be to extend the category over cultic objects made of wood and stone.[10] Without endorsing a definition, I believe most English speakers associate the body with an agent's primary visible locus of self, *whatever that may constitute*. At the same time, however, the cognitive research indicates presence can be reified through partible aspects of personhood that are not necessarily identified as an individual's body.[11] I think Sommer's choice to use this term may have contributed in part to his drawing of such clear and firm lines of distinction between the fluidity model and its rejection by the P and D strata.[12]

Notions about loci of agency departing the body, entering other bodies, and existing autonomously are also widespread and have been the subject of a great deal of cognitive and anthropological research (Pyysiäinen 2009, 57–94). In societies where the biological dimension of personhood is less important than other relational dimensions, the person in reflective reasoning is constituted more by material and social relationships, is less restrained by the container of the body, and is less socially diminished in death. A classic example of such societies is that of Melanesia, as discussed by Marilyn Strathern in her important work, *The Gender of the Gift* (1988).[13] As with all societies, Melanesian societies hold both dividual and individual conceptualizations of the person in tension, with priority emerging situationally (Hemer 2013, 92–93). Practices and beliefs related to the body are quite variable, but in broad terms, the body is conceptualized as the observable embodiment of the relationships with the food, the people, and the

---

[10] Others have criticized Sommer's definition as too broad (Knafl 2014, 72; Smith 2016, 13–14; Wilson 2021, 14–18), but they also appeal to definitions to draw lines of demarcation.
[11] One may argue that the heart is a part of a deceased person's body, but if their heart reifies their presence as a vehicle of agency after transplantation into another person's body, the partibility and permeability of the self is overlapping with Sommer's fragmentation framework. If the rest of the deceased person's body also still reifies their presence—for instance, if one still visits their grave in order to be in their presence—then their presence can at least be perceived to be reified simultaneously in different "bodies."
[12] This will be discussed in more detail in chapter 5.
[13] Melanesian persons, she states, "are as dividually as they are individually conceived. They contain a generalized sociality within. Indeed, persons are frequently constructed as the plural and composite site of the relationships that produce them" (Strathern 1988, 13; cf. Mosko 2010).

spirits responsible for its development and state, with illness reflecting deficiency somewhere among those relationships (Knauft 1999, 26–28).

Gift exchange is a formative aspect of these societies, and it can serve as a means of remedying those deficiencies. The gifts that are exchanged can themselves take on gender, agency, and a biography according to the social relations they produce. They are not commodities that one possesses, but partible aspects of one's personhood they employ in the creation and maintenance of relationships and power structures that constitute identity.[14] In marriage, for example, each partner brings their parents' two bloodlines together for a total of four distinct lines, with no redundancies allowed in the union. In the case of redundancies, the exchange of pigs and other goods facilitates the return of the secondary bloodlines to the clans of their origin, detaching each partner from the bloodline. At death, this process of "deconception" is repeated at a mortuary feast, but now with permanent effect, dissolving the individual identity of the deceased into the clan identity (Mosko 1992, 703–4).[15] Endocannibalism (mortuary cannibalism) takes place in some Melanesian societies, which facilitates the further distribution of the person's partible substances to their kin (Conklin 1995, 77). This postmortem dissolution of the individual into a corporate ancestral identity is a widespread feature of societies where relational personhood, and particularly kinship, is more salient.[16] The person in these societies is much more thoroughly integrated into, and constituted by, the broader material environment.[17]

As a result of sociocultural elaborations on intuitions about agency and the continuation of some unseen locus of agency after death (Bering 2002; Pereira, Faísca, and Sá-Saraiva 2012), concepts of disembodied spirits (Richert and Harris 2008), spirit possession (Cohen and Barrett 2008), out-of-body experiences (Craffert 2015), and reincarnation (White 2015, 2016) have long been salient in Eurocentric as well as many other societies around the world.[18] These are

---

[14] This may sound unusual to an individual from a more Eurocentric society, but when we think about the people we know, their personalities, as far as we conceptualize them, are commonly entangled with the material—their clothing, their hairstyle, their jewelry, their home, their car, their workspace.

[15] In the nineteenth century, when Melanesian men died, their dissolution took with them so much of their wives' partible personhood that the latter were compelled by custom to beg to be strangled so they could follow close behind. Custom did not compel men to do the same (Lindstrom 2013, 263–64).

[16] A period of individual burial followed by a secondary commingled burial is understood by many anthropologists to reflect this concept of dissolution into a generic ancestral group after the memory of the individual as an individual had faded (Cradic 2017; cf. Duncan and Schwarz 2014).

[17] For related findings from other societies, see Busby 1997; Lambek and Strathern 1998; Carsten 2004; Hess 2009; Appuhamilage 2017.

[18] As in Afro-Brazilian cults in South America (Cohen 2013), the Pacific islands (Mageo

reflective ways to employ unseen agency—conceptually flexible precisely because it cannot be observed—to account for otherwise unknown phenomena associated with illness, behavioral changes, disability, and the many different ways we perceive agency to inhabit and influence the world around us. Across societies and across time, some patterns are discernible that demonstrate the anchoring of these phenomena in humanity's intuitive reasoning. The number, nature, and function of these entities is, of course, largely a product of social factors and counterintuitive properties that still require much further study (Boyer 2003; Chudek et al. 2018).

A particularly relevant phenomenon related to these unseen loci of agency is the conceptualization of deceased loved ones. It takes time for the loss of a loved one to be incorporated into the mind's mediation of our experience of the world, and the smells, sights, and objects that were associated with the presence of loved ones can continue to trigger our minds to the sense of their presence.[19] Photographs and objects created by or strongly associated with the loved one can be particularly powerful presencing media, and are frequently employed intentionally for that purpose (Hallam and Hockey 2001, 129–54; Christensen and Sandvik 2014; Kjærsgaard and Venbrux 2016). This is not mere memory, but the mind projecting the sensation of presence that it produced when that individual was present. Even in thoroughly secularized societies, people regularly speak with the dead, and the gravestone in particular can play a central role in facilitating these discussions. In this view, it can be "animated as the body of a person in that it is washed, cared for, gazed at, dressed with flowers, offered drinks, and surrounded by household and garden ornaments" (Hallam and Hockey 2001, 151; cf. Christensen and Sandvik 2014). It can even be addressed in the second person as the deceased person. The widespread use of gravestones to index or house the unseen agency of deceased loved ones, and particularly kin, is a byproduct of our intuitive reasoning about the loci of agency of deceased persons.[20]

PERSONHOOD IN FIRST MILLENNIUM BCE SOUTHWEST ASIA

These patterns were also common in the conceptualization of the person from first millennium BCE Southwest Asia, and as in today's societies, the partibility and independence of the unobservable loci of agency are most clearly represented in

---

and Howard 1996), Niger (Rasmussen 1995), Laos (Holt 2009, 15–75), the Northern Philippines (Mikkelsen 2016), and many others.

[19] This sense that the dead are present has been demonstrated to be present even among those who explicitly reject the reality of ghosts and spirits. See Bering, McLeod, and Shackelford 2005; Bering 2006; Barrett 2011, 104; Walter 2017, 20–22.

[20] To my knowledge, gravestones as indices for the agency of the deceased has not been extensively studied by cognitive scientists There is some discussion in the context of conceptual blend theory in Fauconnier and Turner 2002, 204–10.

death (though the accident of preservation also skews our evidence towards mortuary remains). Because there were fewer philosophical and scientific frameworks within the reflective discourse to temper intuitive reasoning, these entities in the ancient world were more elaborate and variable. The CONTAINER schema was salient in places like Egypt and Mesopotamia, evinced not only by the frequent use of prepositions that demonstrate the body's interiority and exteriority, but also by the concern for the integrity of the body and the skin's protection of the vulnerable interior from malevolent spirits and other potentially contaminating entities that existed outside the body.[21]

In Egypt, the most popular iconography and texts from the Third Intermediate period describe several *kheperu*, or "manifestations," as central to personhood.[22] Among these are the *akh*, the spirit of the deceased that could aid the living (Hays 2015, 76), the *ib* ("heart"), which was the locus of intelligence and morality that testified for or against the person in the afterlife,[23] and the *rn*, or "name," which represented the reputation of the person, was materially manifested in the cartouche (that is, a hieroglyphic name or title enclosed within an oval), and took on a life of its own, particularly in the afterlife.[24] There was also the *ka*, an animating force or "twin" that could exist on in a deceased person's statue once their corpse had disintegrated (Gordon 1996; Assmann 2005, 96–102), and the *ba*,[25] which was the most dynamic element of personhood that survived the body.[26] During life, the *ba* was largely dormant. At death it was endowed with divine abilities and could travel freely during the day but had to return to the corpse by night.[27] This mobility was expressed in the iconographic representation of the *ba* as a saddle-billed stork or a bird with a human head (Janak 2011; Steiner 2015, 56).

---

[21] In Egypt, women were particularly susceptible and were expected to perform purifying rituals following events like menstruation. See Gahlin 2007, 337–38; Frandsen 2007. See also Zgoll 2012.

[22] Taylor 2001, 16; Meskell and Joyce 2003, 18–21, 67–70; Assmann 2012; Hays 2015, 76–77; Putthoff 2020, 17–38.

[23] The heart exercised a degree of autonomy that was sometimes a source of anxiety for the person (Assmann 1998, 385).

[24] Meskell and Joyce 2003, 69–70; Leprohon 2013, 5–7; Allen 2014, 101; Quirke 2015, 55–56.

[25] Taylor 2001, 20–23; Meskell 2002, 59–60; Assmann 2005, 90–96; Janak 2011; Gardiner 1957, 173; Žabkar 1968.

[26] The *ba* was a flexible concept that referred in earlier periods to the manifestation of a deity, later to a king's endowment with divine powers in the afterlife, and by the time of the New Kingdom, to any (properly buried) deceased person's unseen locus of agency. See Žabkar 1968, 11–15, 51–89.

[27] Janak 2011, 144–45; Keel 1997, 64–65. On the anxiety regarding the potential for the *ba*'s return to the body to be disrupted, see Steiner 2015, 128–62; Hays 2015, 51–53.

At least three loci for agency or animacy are identified in the material remains of ancient Mesopotamia, including the *eṭemmu* ("body spirit" or "ghost"; Abusch 1999; Steinert 2012, 299–347, 365–84; MacDougal 2014, 110–12), the *napištu* ("animating force"; Steinert 2012, 271–93), and the *zaqīqu* ("breath," wind," or "spirit"; Steinert 2012, 347–84). These overlapped in nature and in function (similar to contemporary concepts of mind, soul, and spirit), but the *eṭemmu* was central to the selfhood of the deceased and appears in a variety of contexts and ways.[28] It frequently represented the spirit of a deceased person that could leave the underworld and invade the bodies of the living, usually through the ear (Black and Green 1992, 88–89; Stol 1999; Verderame 2017). This ghost/spirit was also associated with ideologies related to mortuary practices, and as with the Egyptian *ba*, the Akkadian *eṭemmu* could remain tethered postmortem to the corpse's bones (Asher-Greve 1997, 447), suggesting the *eṭemmu* functioned more like a "body-soul" than a "free-soul" (which seems to align more with the *zaqīqu*).[29] Much like the *ka*, the *eṭemmu*, which was often marked with the divine determinative DINGIR (Abusch 1999, 309; Hays 2015, 45), could be petitioned for help and had access to strategic information (Hays 2015, 43).

Some elite practices suggest the relationship of these loci of agency to the deceased individual did not necessarily require a *biological* body. Julia Asher-Greve (1997, 452) asserts that "The self is located in the inseparable unity of body and spirit," but goes on to note that the self,

> can replicate itself in other manifestations such as statues or monuments which are more than symbolic proxies but less than distinct duplicates. The spirit, not a replica but a unique entity, can apparently inhabit several objects simultaneously. In a sort of reciprocal interaction the deity bestows life not only on the human individual but also on all its subsequent images (such as statues or monuments) and these in turn can independently and eternally converse or negotiate with the deity.[30]

---

[28] The Mesopotamian anthropogonies all included clay as a fundamental element of the creation of humanity, but the Akkadian tradition includes the spit from the igigi and the flesh and blood of the slaughtered deity, Wê-ila. From that blood is drawn the *ṭēmu*, or "intelligence," and from the flesh is drawn the *eṭemmu*, the "ghost/spirit" (see Asher-Greve 1997, 447–52; Abusch 1998; Bauks 2016, 186–89; Putthoff 2020, 62–66).

[29] On the *zaqīqu* as a "free-soul" that may have been conceptualized as a bird, see Hays 2015, 44; Steiner 2015, 56–57.

[30] Cf. Scurlock 2002, 1–6. Asher-Greve (1997, 453) notes that while the *eṭemmu* can thus inhabit other "bodies" in life and in death, reifying the "body and spirit" pairing, it is never associated with intelligence or "mind." For this reason, she asserts the "mind/body dichotomy was absent" from early Mesopotamia. Steinert (2012, 337–40) points out that there are texts which discuss thought and emotion among the dead, but more directly related to the heart (*karšu* and *libbu*).

Such objects helped facilitate the *kispu* ritual, or the "post-funerary ritual meal that called forth the deceased from the netherworld to eat and drink with the living" (MacDougal 2014, 149). This rite, according to Nicolas Wyatt, "involved three features, a communal meal, *šuma zakāru*—'remembering the name,' and *mē naqû*—'pouring the water.' The dead were represented by statues called en-en-ku-ku—'lords who are sleeping'" (Wyatt 2012, 261).[31]

This notion of a separable locus of a person's agency or presence inhabiting material objects after death was by no means confined to Mesopotamia or to the ancient world. Indeed, as mentioned above, people today commonly treat gravestones intuitively as presencing the deceased. From ancient Southwest Asia, however, one of the most striking examples of the same phenomenon comes from an inscribed basalt mortuary stele known as the Katumuwa Stele (fig. 1.1), discovered in situ in the Syro-Hittite town of Zinçirli and dated to the eighth century BCE (Struble and Herrmann 2009; Herrmann and Schloen 2014; Steiner 2015, 128–31). The Katumuwa Stele depicts a figure seated before a table, holding a cup and a pinecone. The table has a duck, a vessel, and a stack of pita-like bread. The negative space is expertly filled with an inscription that prescribes meal offerings for Katumuwa's *nbš* ("self" or "life"),[32] which "(will be) in this stele" (*bnṣb.zn*).[33] Scholars suggest the small room in which the stele was set up constituted a "mortuary chapel" (Struble and Herrmann 2009; Steiner 2015, 148–50), which would have provided a space for the provision of food for the deceased's designated locus of agency, which, as in Egypt and Mesopotamia, was understood to be able to inhabit material objects.

The Katumuwa Stele and its mortuary chapel represent one of the most pristine examples of a setting for funerary/mortuary food offerings, a significant feature of the sociocultural matrix of ancient Southwest Asia (Maher and Lev-Tov 2001; Lewis 2014; Draycott and Stamatopoulou 2016). This practice, associated with primary burial/memorialization and repeated at intervals, provisioned the dead with needed sustenance and perpetuated their afterlife through

---

[31] MacDougal (2014, 183) points out that figurines or statues may have been linked with a chair during the ritual as the "locus for the soul during the rituals. It is possible that images were employed to house the transitory spirit of the family deceased, just as a magic figurine for an unsettled *eṭemmu* was made to receive *kispum*."

[32] On the relationship of *nbš* to Hebrew *nepeš*, see Steiner 2015, 137–39.

[33] The term used here to refer to the stele, *nṣb*, is cognate with the Hebrew *maṣṣēbâ*, which derives from the root *nṣb*, "to stand, set up." Multiple Aramaic funerary stelai from the mid-first millennium BCE are known that bear inscriptions identifying themselves as the *nepeš* of their owners, although the term is usually translated "tomb" in these contexts. See, for instance, Beyer and Livingstone 1987, 288–90. The transcription and translation are from Pardee 2009, 53–54.

1. What Is a Deity?

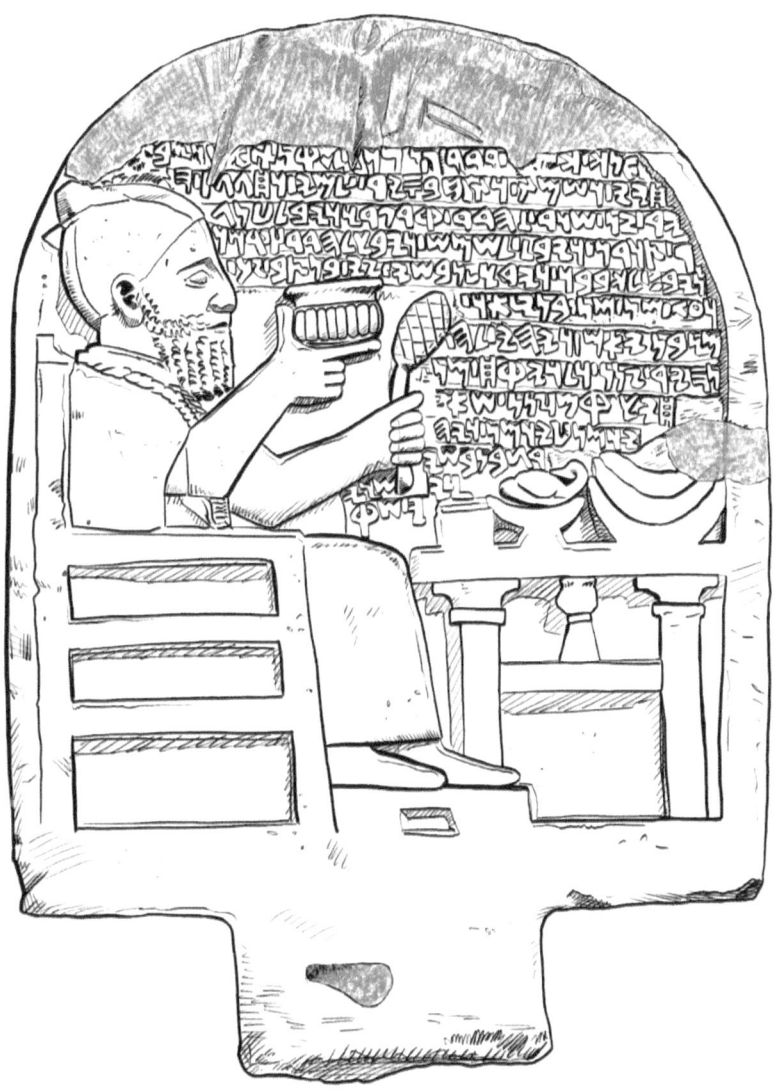

Figure 1.1. The Katumuwa Stele. See Struble and Herrmann 2009. Drawing by the author.

their ritual memorialization. Where the remains were inaccessible or buried at a distance, stelai or other ritual objects could host the deceased's locus of agency and facilitate the necessary interactions.[34] Katumuwa's patron, Panamuwa, for instance, had the following inscribed on a statue of Hadad that was discovered at a cultic installation in Sam'al (*KAI* 214.17): "May the *nbš* of Panamuwa eat with you, and may the *nbš* of Panamuwa drink with you" (*COS* 2.36:156–58; Niehr 2014). Matthew Suriano states, "The establishment of Panamuwa's *mqm* for his name and soul right beside (and along with) Hadad's stele insured that his defunct-soul would be fed so long as the storm god received food and drink offerings" (Suriano 2014, 403). This is related to the concern manifested in the Egyptian and Mesopotamian rituals for the provision of food and the invocation of the name, which facilitated the continued memory, and therefore existence, of the deceased's loci of agency.[35] The dependence on kin and on others for provisioning that would ensure a lengthy and successful afterlife punctuates the fundamentally relational as well as material nature of personhood within these societies.

PERSONHOOD IN FIRST MILLENNIUM BCE ISRAEL AND JUDAH

The bulk of the materials that bear on the question of the conceptualization of the person in first millennium BCE Israel and Judah comes from the Hebrew Bible and from mortuary remains. Both demonstrate continuity with the partibility and permeability of the person that is represented more explicitly in other Southwest Asian material remains. Consistently throughout the biblical texts, the most important constituent elements of the person were the *bāśār*, "flesh," the *lēb*, "heart,"[36] the *rûaḥ*, "breath" or "spirit," and the *nepeš*, "soul."[37] The consistent treatment of these elements as central to personhood across biblical and other texts suggests that centrality obtained beyond the texts as well, with different social and material dimensions no doubt influencing the situationally emergent structuring of the person. The *lēb* was the most dynamic locus of agency, representing vitality, affection, cognition, and will (Fabry 1995; Schroer and

---

[34] In later periods in ancient Egypt, bust portraits kept in residences may have served to facilitate the dead's participation in family feasting at any time. See Borg 1997.

[35] For a discussion on the relationship of funerary/mortuary drinking bowls to materiality and memory, see Feldman 2014, 119–37. On the innovations in the relationships of the dead to the living, see Sanders 2012.

[36] The *lēb* in many contexts is not to be identified with the organ of the heart so much as with the region of the body, which can sometimes be as general as the torso.

[37] While "soul" is admittedly a loaded term, I use it here as shorthand for the concept of a person's primary locus of animacy that continues to exist after death. I certainly do not mean to assert conceptual contiguity with the modern concept of the soul. Cf. Bauks 2016, 181–84; Newsom 2020.

Staubli 2001, 42–44).³⁸ Proverbs 4:23 states that life springs from the *lēb*, while food strengthens and restores the *lēb* in Gen 18:5 and Judg 19:5, 8, 22. From this sense of vitality develops an emotional dimension, and particularly intense emotions like excitement, fear, and grief (cf. Pss 4:8; 13:3; 34:19).³⁹ A cognitive dimension is also salient. Deuteronomy 29:3, for instance, refers to YHWH's provision of a *lēb lāda'at*, "heart to know."⁴⁰

Because it was unobservable and interior, the *lēb* was also *āmōq*, "deep" (Ps 64:7), and *'ên ḥēqer*, "unsearchable" (Prov 25:3). This relationship to the inner person facilitated the identification of the heart as a primary locus of the self (Pss 22:15; 27:3; Gen 18:5; Exod 19:4). After Saul's anointing as king at the hands of Samuel, YHWH gives him *lēb 'aḥēr*, "another heart" (1 Sam 10:9), which likely serves a function similar to the promise in verse 6 that YHWH's *rûaḥ* would *ṣālḥâ 'al*, "force entry into,"⁴¹ Saul, turning him into *'îš 'aḥēr*, "another person" (Hausmann 2003). This story also illustrates the permeability of the person, as well as the communicable nature of the *rûaḥ* in the biblical conceptualizations (Newsom 2020).⁴² This episode additionally reflects the activation of THE BODY IS A CONTAINER, which is elsewhere demonstrated in the frequent references to the *nepeš* and the *rûaḥ* as located inside the person.⁴³

Scholars have long been opposed to understanding the *nepeš* or the *rûaḥ* as elements of personhood that could depart from the body in the Hebrew Bible, but Richard Steiner's (2015) monograph on the *nepeš*, *Disembodied Souls*, has adduced strong evidence that the conceptualization of these elements as they appear in the Hebrew Bible was much more closely related to those of the broader Southwest Asian societies than has been previously recognized (Steiner 2015, 43–92; Feder 2019). In addition to showing the *nepeš* could function as a "dream

---

³⁸ For a consideration of the symbolic function of *lēb* in rabbinic Judaism, see Kiperwasser 2013. On the relationship and overlap between the *lēb* and the *kābēd*, "liver," see Smith 1998; Tilford 2017, 8–9.

³⁹ Prov 14:30 reflects this relationship: "a calm heart enlivens flesh." The author of Ps 38:9 groans because of the *nahămat lēbî*, "tumult of my heart," while in Ps 22:15, the author's *lēb* is like wax, and "is melted within my breast."

⁴⁰ In 1 Kgs 3:9, Solomon requests from YHWH a *lēb šōmē'a*, "hearing heart," in order to govern the people.

⁴¹ HALOT, s.v. צלח.

⁴² Because of space, I do not discuss YHWH's *rûaḥ* as a divine agent in this book but for a discussion of the *rûaḥ* as a vehicle for divine presence, see MacDonald 2013.

⁴³ Isa 26:9, for instance, refers to *rûḥî bəqirbî*, "my *rûaḥ* inside me." 1 Kgs 17:22 narrates a child's revivification at the hands of Elijah, explaining that his *nepeš* returned *'al-qirbô*, "inside him." See Fabry 2004, 375 for more examples of passages showing the *rûaḥ* was consistently conceptualized as internally located.

soul" that departed from the body during sleep,⁴⁴ Steiner shows the *nepeš* could be conceptualized as capable of flight. The representations of the Egyptian *ba* and the Mesopotamian *zaqīqu* as birds provide important comparative context (Steiner 2015, 55–58), but the biblical texts themselves also make use of THE SOUL IS A BIRD as a conceptual metaphor:⁴⁵ "how can you say to my *nepeš*, 'Flee to the mountains like a bird?'" (Ps 11:1); "Our *nepeš* has escaped like a bird from the snare of the fowlers" (Ps 124:7). Isaiah 8:19 also describes the spirits of the dead chirping and cooing like birds.⁴⁶ Much like the Egyptian *ba*, the Hebrew *nepeš* could also be addressed by its owner in the vocative, suggesting a degree of independence. This is most common in the Psalms (Pss 103:1, 2, 22; 104:1, 35), with one of the most explicit examples in Ps 42:12: "Why are you dissolving, O my *nepeš*, and why are you restless within me?"

Steiner also argues for a separate component of the *nepeš*, namely the *nepeš habbāśār* ("*nepeš* of the flesh"), which was physically located in the blood (Lev 17:11). This concept is similar to that of the "body soul," or the animating element that is native to the body and remains with it until decomposition.⁴⁷ This, according to Steiner, is to be distinguished from the animating *rûaḥ* which departed the body at death.⁴⁸ The *nepeš*, the *nepeš habbāśār*, and the *rûaḥ* appear to have survived the death of the body.⁴⁹ Later texts that elaborate on these concepts suggest the *rûaḥ* returned to the deity (Eccl 12:7), the *nepeš habbāśār* remained with the body, while the *nepeš* continued on as the deceased's primary locus of agency and self.⁵⁰ Steiner has marshaled considerable support for recognizing a

---

⁴⁴ Steiner (2015, 23–42) argues that the sense of the two unique nouns in the enigmatic Ezek 13:18 (*kəsātôt* and *mispāḥôt*) is not to be found in Akkadian, but in Mishnaic Hebrew, where they refer to pillowcases and pillow filling. The passage is not about women hunting lives with wristbands and headbands but using pillowcases and pillow filling to capture and ransom *napāšôt* that had departed from the body during sleep.

⁴⁵ Steiner attributes the two references to Lys 1959, 161.

⁴⁶ The two verbal roots are *ṣpp* and *hgh*, which appear in Isa 38:14 associated with birds: "Like a swallow or a swift, so I chirped (*'ăṣapṣēp*), I cooed (*'ehgeh*) like a dove."

⁴⁷ JoAnn Scurlock (2002, 3) describes the Mesopotamian *eṭemmu* as a body-soul, which may find support in the reference with in the Atrahasis to the *eṭemmu* originally being drawn from the flesh and the blood of the deceased deity (Atr. 1.2.215, 217). Cf. Abusch 1998, 372. For a review of the different typologies of the soul within a cognitive context, see Pyysiäinen 2009, 58–68.

⁴⁸ Steiner (2015, 84–85) also finds this concept of a distinct *pneuma* and *psychē* within the writings of Philo of Alexandria (Her. 55) as well as Josephus (Ant. 1.1.2.34).

⁴⁹ Yitzhaq Feder (2019, 417) argues that extra-biblical evidence "corroborates the view, suggested by numerous biblical texts, that the *nepeš* refers to the soul of the deceased which resides in the grave after death."

⁵⁰ Job 19:26 may invoke the latter concept when it states, "After my skin is thus shredded, without my flesh I will see God." Feder (2019, 421) states, "it seems reasonable to infer

significant degree of autonomy and partibility in biblical representations of the *nepeš* and the *rûaḥ* that have long been obscured by otherwise well-meaning attempts to steer clear of the gravitational pull of Cartesian dualism. Those representations show much closer relationships to the concepts of the person found in the other Southwest Asian societies discussed above than more conservative commentators have been willing to acknowledge.

This can be further established through an interrogation of the ancient Israelite and Judahite conceptualizations of, and interactions with, the dead. The bench tombs common to the highlands of Israel and Judah by the eighth century BCE facilitated multiple close burials and included a repository for secondary burials when additional space was required.[51] Commentators are in wide agreement that such tombs supported the integrity and continuity of the household and its territory.[52] Archaeologists have even noted that the bench tomb and the four-room house share similarities in design and in their multigenerational use (Suriano 2018, 93–95). This may be related to the preferred outcome of being "gathered" (*'sp*) following death, but that outcome depended in large part upon the living (Cook 2007, 672–78; Teinz 2012; Feder 2019, 411–17). The most important task for the living was the continued remembrance of the deceased's name, which could be facilitated by stelai that materialized the name and that were the responsibility of the deceased's offspring to erect and attend. According to 2 Sam 18:18, David's son Absalom was left without a son of his own to guarantee the perpetuation of his memory, so he commissioned a stele himself:[53] "In his lifetime, Absalom took and set up for himself a stele (*maṣṣebet*) that is in the Valley of the King, because he said, 'I have no son to cause my name to be remembered.' And he called the stele (*maṣṣebet*) by his own name, so it is called the Monument of Absalom (*yad 'abšālōm*) to this day."[54]

---

that the spirit's power to animate the body was considered to gradually leave the body at the time of decomposition. According to this understanding, some of the *nepeš* was assumed to disseminate from the corpse immediately following bodily death, constituting the difference between the animating spirit activating the living person and the inactive shadow existence of the resting spirit in the grave."

[51] Bloch-Smith 1992b, 215–16. Regarding secondary burials, see Meyers 1970; Cradic 2017; Suriano 2018, 45–53.

[52] "The protective ties of extended family and kin-group are literally cut into the rock of ancient Israel's family tombs, built to symbolize the protective huddle of kinfolk that one hoped to join in the Hereafter" (Cook 2009, 113; Schmitt 2012, 471–73; Stavrakopoulou 2010).

[53] 2 Sam 14:27, of course, mentions three sons born to Absalom.

[54] Note "monument" renders the Hebrew *yād*, "hand," perhaps suggestive of some kind of conduit for agency or power (cf. 2 Sam 8:3; 1 Chr 18:3). In Isa 56:4–5, YHWH promises the following to the eunuchs who observe sabbath requirements: "I will give, in my house and within my walls, a monument (yad) and a name better than sons and daughters; I will

The name here seems to function as a locus of presence, not just a facilitator of simple memorialization (cf. Radner 2005; Westenholz 2012). This practice is strikingly similar to those attested at Egypt, Mesopotamia, and Samʾal, but we have precious little data to cast light on the specific conceptualizations of the stele's reflective functions.[55] Intuitively speaking, however, there can be no doubt that for many there was an element of the deceased's presencing associated with such memorials (as is the case even today). An authoritative line of division is unlikely to have been maintained between memorialization and the more intuitive presencing without leaving any trace in the normalizing literature.[56] Absent regulation and other powerful reflective frameworks to decouple it, the trend will be in the direction of the more intuitive conceptualization.

The notion that the dead live on in some manner, but require support from the living, is further manifested in the provisioning of the deceased with "items of personal adornment, lamps, cosmetic containers, cooking pots, bowls, and jugs with food" (Schmitt 2012b, 457; cf. Suriano 2018, 51–53, 154–76).[57] There is a great deal of overlap between burial assemblages and those of domestic settings, suggesting some continuity between the needs of the living and those of the dead.[58] Lamps, for instance, are frequently left in burials, perhaps to provide light in the dark underworld.[59] Vessels with small amounts of animal bones have been found in many burials that likely reflect food offerings for the dead, very much in line with—if not as elaborate and explicit as—the funerary and mortuary feeding of the dead in the societies discussed above (Bloch-Smith 1992a, 122–26; Schmitt 2012, 457–59).[60] Textual data can be brought to bear on this question, although the Hebrew Bible is notoriously reticent regarding such practices (Friedman and Overton 1999; Lewis 2002). What little is in the texts is largely proscriptive or

---

give them an everlasting name that shall not be cut off." Cf. van der Toorn 1996, 208.

[55] Stavrakopoulou (2010, 15) notes, "The extent to which standing stones are seen to manifest, deify, or merely symbolize or represent the dead is uncertain—and likely dependent on the (changing) context-specific particularities of the stones themselves, including, perhaps, the perspective of the viewer before whom the stone is exhibited."

[56] See Kerry Sonia's (2020, 127) comment: "death-related practices do not always rely on a well-articulated or widely accepted rationale for those practices."

[57] On burial goods more generally, see Bloch-Smith 1992a, 61–108; Schmitt 2012b, 438–49.

[58] "Based solely on archaeological evidence, it is not possible to reconstruct death cult rituals in tombs; identical finds in both tombs and houses and public buildings preclude identifying distinctive mortuary practices" (Bloch-Smith 2009, 126).

[59] See, for instance, Ps 88:6; 143:3; Lam 3:6. As Suriano (2018, 47–48 and n. 27) notes, many lamps were found placed next to the head of the deceased, sometimes lacking any indication of soot, indicating they were never lighted and were likely intended for the use of the dead. Suriano describes their function as "symbolic."

[60] Wayne Pitard (2002, 150) has been skeptical about many of the data that have been adduced for such practices.

polemical, but several references are made to feeding the dead in ways that presuppose its ubiquity, if not its normativity.⁶¹ Deuteronomy 26:14, for instance, calls upon those offering their tithes to declare the following regarding tithed food: "I have not eaten from it while in mourning, and I have not removed any of it while unclean, and I have not given any of it to the dead." This text appears to address both commemorative meals as well as meal offerings to the dead, without appearing to prohibit either, in or of themselves. Rather, the sense appears to be that food offered to the dead is to be kept separate from food offered to YHWH.⁶²

The dead also appear to have been in need of protection, primarily through provision with apotropaic and prophylactic beads and amulets, which have been found in numerous burials (Bloch-Smith 1992a, 81–86; Schmidt 2016, 124–28).⁶³ The most well-known are the two tightly rolled silver scrolls discovered in 1979 in the repository of a bench tomb in Ketef Hinnom (Barkay 1992; Suriano 2018, 123–26). The scrolls, which were designed to be threaded on a necklace and worn for protection, had inscribed upon them a version of the "Priestly Blessing" from Num 6:24–26 that praises YHWH's power to deliver from evil.⁶⁴ An inscription that can be read as a similar prayer for protection was etched in the rock of a multi-chambered tomb from Khirbet el-Qôm (fig. 1.2):⁶⁵

1. *'ryhw . h'šr . ktbh*	Uriyahu the notable has written it
2. *brk̲ . 'ryhw . lyhwh*	Blessed be Uriyahu to YHWH,
3. *wmṣryh . l'šrth . hwš'lh.*	Now from his enemies, to Asherah, deliver him

---

⁶¹ Tryggve N. D. Mettinger (1995, 192) notes that cultic practices among the societies surrounding and preceding early Israel and Judah involved ritual slaughter of a sacrifice followed by a meal shared among the worshippers. "It is this communal meal and its ritual accoutrements, rather than the feeding of the gods known from Mesopotamian cult, that are central to the meaning of West Semitic sacrifices."

⁶² Kerry Sonia (2020, 51) notes, "this passage is concerned primarily with avoiding contamination of the tithe." Schmitt (2012b, 459) notes that Isa 65:3–5, while being quite late, may refer to an actual practice in its polemicizing of those who spend the night in tombs and eat the flesh of swine, since pig bones have been found in two Iron Age IIC graves in Lachish. The apocryphal book of Tobit tells the reader, "Place your bread on the grave of the righteous, but give none to sinners" (Tobit 4:17 [NRSV]).

⁶³ Egyptian influence is particularly salient. Scarabs, *wedjat*-eye, Pataeke, and Bes amulets are the most common (cf. Albertz 2008, 101). For the most thorough analysis, see Herrmann 1994–2006.

⁶⁴ This is the earliest known attestation of any text from the Hebrew Bible (Berlejung 2008; Schmidt 2016, 123–44; Smoak 2016, 12–42).

⁶⁵ See Zevit 1984; Hadley 1987; Margalit 1989; Dobbs-Allsopp et al 2005, 408–14; Schmidt 2016, 139–40. On the material context of the inscription, see Mandell and Smoak 2017.

4. (hand)	l'nyhw	(hand)	to Oniyahu
5.	wl'šrth…		and to Asherah…
6.	wl'šrth[…		and to Asherah[…

A downward oriented hand was carved under the third line, which could be interpreted to identify the inscription as Uriyahu's *yād*, "monument," as a reference to the underworld (Schmidt 2016, 140; Schroer 1983; Suriano 2018, 117), or it may represent YHWH's own hand, reaching down to save (Parker 2006, 89).

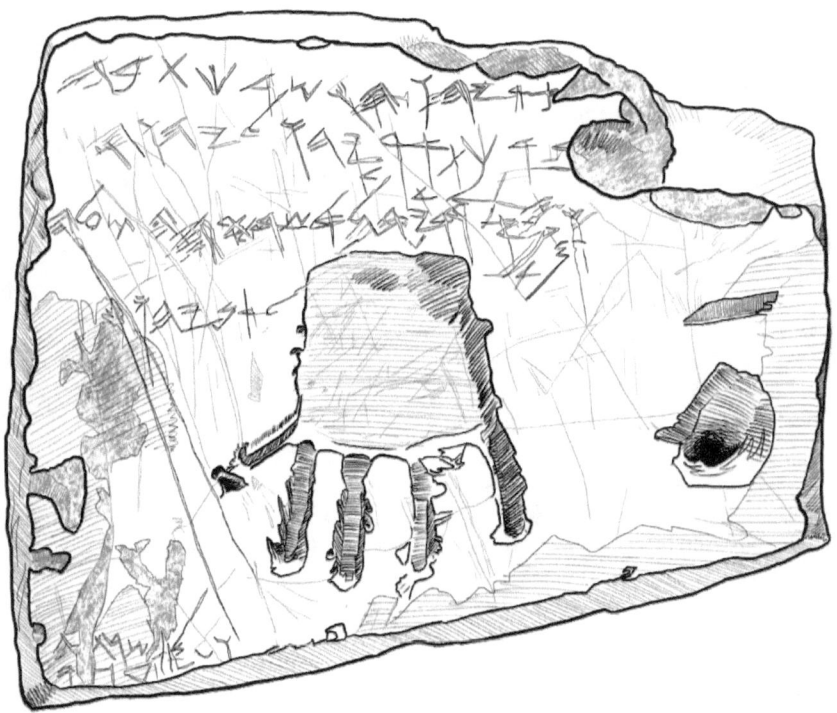

Figure 1.2. The Khirbet el-Qôm Inscription. Drawing by the author.

The worry expressed in these texts may be for robbers or desecrators of graves, but if the biblical literature reflects salient beliefs about the underworld, the other inhabitants of that underworld may also have been in view for some.[66]

---

[66] The Royal Steward Inscription from the Silwan Necropolis (Silw 1) expresses this concern: "This is the [sepulcher of PN-]iah, the royal steward. There is neither silver nor gold [he]re, / [but] only [his bones] and his concubine's bon[es] w[ith] him. Cursed be the one who / opens this (sepulcher)" (Suriano 2018, 103–5). Feder (2019, 422) argues, "the

The biblical texts refer to the *mētîm* ("dead"⁶⁷), *'ôb* (traditionally "medium," but perhaps "ancestor, image"⁶⁸), *yiddʿōnîm* ("knowing ones"⁶⁹), *'iṭṭîm* (meaning unknown, but likely cognate with Akkadian *eṭemmu*, "body spirit/ghost"⁷⁰), and *rəpā'îm* ("benefactors" or "noble ones"?).⁷¹ While there was likely a broad spectrum of conceptualizations of these entities, where they came from, and any threat or benefit they posed to the dead, they appear only in reference to their relationship to the living (Hays 2015, 183–84), and most frequently in the rhetorical denigration or marginalization of their power over or within the world of the living (Bloch-Smith 1992a, 121–22). This oft-repeated refrain suggests representative portions of ancient Israelite and Judahite societies believed or feared they exercised precisely such power.⁷² If the etymological roots of *yiddʿōnîm* are any indication, for instance, the dead, and particularly one's deceased kin, may have been thought to have special access to strategic information.⁷³

This perception of special access raises a critical point that will provide a segue into the next section's discussion. The nature, function, and treatment of the dead overlaps in significant ways with that of deity. The Hebrew Bible's repeated—though not unilateral—denunciations of the powers of the dead to influence the living suggests that the perception they had such power was salient enough to demand direct engagement. The clearest example of the power of the dead to heal is likely the story of the corpse thrown into Elisha's tomb being revivified upon contact with his bones (2 Kgs 13:20–21). While this reflects the perception of the capacity of Elisha's bones to retain divine agency and its healing power, the story denies Elisha any agency, and merely suggests YHWH's own agency (or some generic divine agency) remained residually in the prophet's bones.

---

existence of apotropaic objects and amulets in Judean burial contexts from the preexilic period and later reveals a concern that can only vaguely be inferred from biblical texts, namely the fear of the threat posed to the spirit of the dead by disturbances and looting."

⁶⁷ Isa 26:14; Ezek 24:17; Ps 106:28.

⁶⁸ Lev 19:31; Deut 18:11; 1 Sam 28:3, 7–9; 2 Kgs 23:24; Isa 19:3; 29:4. The "ancestor, image" gloss comes from the etymological connection with Egyptian *ȝbwt* made in Hays and LeMon 2009; cf. Hays 2015, 171–73.

⁶⁹ It always appears in conjunction with *'ôb* (Lev 19:31; Deut 18:11; 1 Sam 28:3, 9; 2 Kgs 23:24; Isa 8:19; 19:3).

⁷⁰ Isa 19:3 is the only occurrence.

⁷¹ Isa 14:9; 26:14; Ps 88:11; Prov 9:18. On the most likely etymology of *rəpā'îm*, see Galbraith 2019, 215–17.

⁷² Leviticus repeatedly prohibits consulting the dead (Lev 19:31; 20:6, 27). Isa 18:11–12 condemns anyone who "consults [*š'l*] an *'ôb*," or "inquires [*drš*] of the *mētîm*." Eccl 9:5 asserts that the dead know nothing.

⁷³ Kerry Sonia (2020, 67 and n. 5) refers to "privileged information," which she describes as "information that the living attain only through divine assistance, such as knowledge of the future."

Regarding the deceased's access to strategic information, the Hebrew Bible has more to say.[74] An intermediary for the dead is described in Deut 18:11 as a consulter of an *'ôb* and a *yiddʿōnî*, as well as a *dōrēš 'el-hammētîm*, "seeker of the dead." Isaiah 8:19 says "there is no dawn" for those who say, "Inquire of the *'ōbôt* and the *yiddʿōnîm* who chirp and mutter! Should a people not inquire of their gods—the dead on behalf of the living?" (cf. Sonia 2020, 71–79). The most well-known example of this practice is that of Saul's visit to a necromancer (Hebrew: *baʿălat-'ôb*, "Lady of *'ôb*") at En-dor in 1 Sam 28:3–25 (Hamori 2015, 105–30; Sonia 2020, 71–79).[75] In the narrative, Saul is unable to get a response from YHWH regarding what to do about the armies of the Philistines,[76] so in disguise he visits a necromancer—a profession he had banned—asking her to bring up the deceased prophet, Samuel.[77] She does, and the sight of the deceased prophet somehow tips her off to Saul's identity. When Saul asks what she sees, the necromancer explains, "I see deities [*'ĕlōhîm*] rising up from the underworld."[78] Saul states why he has come, and Samuel explains that on the following day, YHWH would deliver Saul into the hands of the Philistines, and he and his sons would be joining Samuel. The story thus appropriates a practice the authors viewed as marginalized or inappropriate in order to convey a prophecy concerning Saul's death, rhetorically illustrating YHWH's ultimate sovereignty over the dead and their access to prophetic knowledge (cf. Boyer 2001, 152; Purzycki et al. 2012).

Note that in Isa 8:19 and 1 Sam 28:13, the word *'ĕlōhîm* is used in reference to the dead (albeit polemically in the former instance). Such terminological overlap is also found in personal names, where theophoric elements are frequently exchanged with kinship terms. Among Hebrew names, for instance, Rainer Albertz (2012, 340) identifies "five divinized designations of kinship, including *'āb* 'father,' *'āḥ* 'brother,' *'am* 'uncle,' *ḥam* 'father-in-law,' and probably also

---

[74] "The exception to the apparent weakness of the dead in the Hebrew Bible is necromancy; the idea that the dead are a source of divinatory knowledge is richly attested" (Hays 2015, 168). Kerry Sonia (2020, 13) notes, "the terminology used for biblical necromancy suggests that the dead are, in fact, divine. That biblical writers use the term *'ĕlōhîm* for the dead in some biblical texts describing necromancy suggests that (in these texts, at least) the dead belong to the same conceptual category as other divine beings."

[75] On prophecy and women more broadly, see the essays in Claassens and Fischer 2021.

[76] It is not insignificant that 1 Sam 28:6 mentions Saul's failed use of *'ûrîm*, "Urim," to divine YHWH's will. These were divinatory objects that overlapped in nature and function with other prohibited methods of divination, but because they were means YHWH had prescribed for priestly divination (Num 27:21), they were considered appropriate.

[77] "And he said, 'Divine for me an *'ôb*, and bring up for me the one I tell you'" (1 Sam 28:8).

[78] On the interpretive problems, see Wright 2009, 256 and n. 78; Schmidt 2016, 187–90. Whether singular or plural, Samuel is identified as an *'ĕlōhîm*.

'ēm 'mother.'"[79] These kinship terms constitute 43.5 percent of all theophoric elements in Hebrew names, while Yahwistic theophoric elements only make up 24.4 percent. Karel van der Toorn (1996, 230) highlights even more explicit examples: "The divine nature of the ancestor is made explicit in the name Ammiel: 'My Ancestor is god' (עמיאל, cf. אליעם, Eliam, 'My god, the Ancestor'). A similar significance is to be attributed to the name Ammishaddai (עמישדי), which proclaims the ancestor to be one of the Šadday gods, chthonic deities that were credited with powers of protection."

There is also significant overlap in the care and feeding of deceased kin and of YHWH.[80] Offerings to YHWH are most commonly framed within the biblical literature as signaling commitment to YHWH's commands, but there can be little doubt that requirements to provide food of various kinds on a daily basis stem not only from the perception that there is some reciprocal benefit for the one making the offering, but that the recipient is in some sense in need of it.[81] The most likely source of this perception for deities is the identical perception of the dead attested in the various offerings mentioned above. Even the structures that housed deities and the deceased, or the loci of their agency, shared features of form and function. For instance, the use of lamps in burial contexts aligns with the use of the lampstand within the temple (Exod 27:20).[82] Some kind of chair or throne is also often represented in the depictions of both (see the Katumuwa Stele discussed above). Altars are so parallel in form and function to offering tables that archaeologists often disagree about their identification.[83] Isaiah 56:4–5 mentions

---

[79] He notes, "Names containing these units amount to 13.1% of all theophoric names and 12.1% of all instances." Albertz (2012, 351) has proposed that these terms reflected "early designations of personal gods," rather than an ancestral cult, as van der Toorn concludes, but acknowledges that van der Toorn's position, "is now widely accepted." He notes the close overlap in the roles of family deities and divinized ancestors, suggesting, "all divinized kinship terms may be considered semantically equivalent to designations of family gods."

[80] Sonia (2020, 14) notes, "the different modes of offering and maintenance that constitute the cult of deities are strikingly similar to those constitutive of the cult of dead kin" (cf. Sanders 2015, 82–83 n. 62).

[81] "Care for the dead (e.g., provision of offerings, protection, commemoration) is strikingly similar to the care of a deity in a temple cult, and the underlying logic of such cult assumes reciprocity between the one who sacrifices and the divine recipient" (Sonia 2020, 17).

[82] Lamps are known from cultic settings in the second and first millennia BCE from around ancient Southwest Asia. See Meyers 2003. See also Hachlili 2001, 11–16: "candelabra were used for illumination in cultic settings, as indicated by their location at the time of discovery, be it in a temple, tomb, or palace."

[83] The same artifacts at Arad were identified by Elizabeth Bloch-Smith (2015, 101) as "incense altars or offering tables," by Ze'ev Herzog (2010, 174) as incense altars, and by Menahem Haran (1993, 237–47) as offering tables. See also Douglas 1999, 241: "a very

an eternal name within YHWH's temple, which reflects the hope mentioned in 2 Sam 18:18 that one's name be remembered after their death. This resonates with the Jerusalem temple's function as a place for YHWH's name (*šēm*).[84]

In these settings, both deities and the dead could also be represented and presenced by the same cultic objects.[85] Absalom's *yad* (also called a *maṣṣebet*) and the stele set up by Jacob at Rachel's tomb (Gen 35:20) demonstrate the association of stelai with the deceased in early biblical narratives. Isaiah 56:4–5 even provides a postexilic suggestion that such monuments might be located within the temple:[86] "For thus says YHWH: / To the eunuchs who keep my sabbaths, / and choose those things that please me, and take hold of my covenant— / I will give, in my house and within my walls, / a *yād* and a name better than sons and daughters. / I will give them an eternal name that will not be cut off."[87]

Stelai are also directly associated with deities in biblical narratives as well as in other material remains (Bloch-Smith 2006, 2007). While many authors polemicized the cultic use of stelai, they are favorably or neutrally associated with El and/or YHWH in the Jacob cycle (Gen 28:22; 35:14–15), by Isaiah (Isa 19:19–20), and perhaps even Hosea (Hos 3:4; Stavrakopoulou 2010, 15–17; Bloch-Smith 2015, 106–10; LaRocca-Pitts 2001). The Judahite temple excavated at Arad boasted at least one stele in its inner sanctuary that almost certainly represented YHWH (Aharoni 1968; Herzog 2002; Köckert 2010, 378), and some 450 stelai have been identified by archaeologists around the Negev. Elizabeth Bloch-Smith (2015, 111) has commented:

> Given the dead's divine status, marked by the designation elohim and the receipt of tithes, standing stones erected for the dead also localized (lesser) divinities (Deut 26:12–14; 1 Sam 28:13). Recognizing a divine association for

---

strong analogy between table and altar stares us in the face." Cf. Zevit 2001, 276, 295–98.

[84] Stavrakopoulou 2010, 129: "in its very claim to perpetuate life in spite of death, the temple exhibits a function akin to that performed by the tomb: both represent and materialize the ongoing perpetuation of existence in the face of death—and the illustrations given in this discussion of a reciprocal appropriation of imagery and ideology between temple and tomb display this shared role. Both temple and tomb mark the interconnectedness of life and death, rather than their separateness."

[85] Rüdiger Schmitt (2012, 433) argues that the dead were not considered divine, but see Sonia 2020, 12–14.

[86] Schmitt (2009) suggests such stelai served exclusively as landmarks or materials memorials. He has elsewhere argued against the existence of any ancestor cults (Schmitt 2008, 9–10).

[87] Note, again, that "name" here seems to function in connection with the *yād* as a locus of agency. To have an everlasting name that shall not be cut off would have been to have perpetual existence through the presencing function of the name.

all stones, either through a deity or the divinized dead, contrasts with earlier categorizations of massebot that restricted divinity to solely those stones explicitly identified with a god.

To summarize and conclude this section: the societies of first millennium BCE Southwest Asia absolutely evinced body-agency partibility, which was not exceptional, but widespread and intuitive. While there was a great deal of variability in the situationally emergent conceptualization of the person within and between these different societies, the intuitive reasoning described above is revealed by a number of shared frameworks. The person was a partible assemblage of different socially and materially determined loci of agency, animacy, emotion, cognition, and selfhood (Pongratz-Leisten 2011). These loci were generally confined to the body in life, but in death—now as an unseen agent—they enjoyed differing degrees of independence from the body and could even inhabit and be presenced by cultic objects and other material media. This is true even in societies around the world today, including those in which strong reflective frameworks widely and actively suppress those intuitions. The overlap with the conceptualization of deity has already been noted, but the following section will further unpack the nature and origins of concepts of deity.

DEITY

This section addresses the question of how we get from concepts of unseen agency to concepts of enormously powerful deities who reign over national pantheons. Above I addressed the centrality of human language and material media to the initial propagation of concepts of unseen agency. Here I focus more attention on the role of social institutions in the "cultural evolution" of deity concepts. The concept of cultural evolution has some important differences from biological evolution.[88] In the latter, genetic mutation is random, while cultural change may be accidental, incidental, or intentional (cf. Scanlon et al. 2019). Cultural adaptations, additionally, may have nothing to do with adaptive fitness (an entity's ability to survive within a given ecology). Cultural innovation is not always the product of extensive testing and trial and error. Instead, the survival of a particular tool, process, or practice may be the result of authority, tradition, economic value, identity politics, or other influences that may insulate it from competition and incentivize its adoption, proliferation, and/or perpetuation. The dynamics are thus very different, and a coevolutionary approach is certainly more complex, but it is necessary to account for the development of concepts of unseen agency beyond the purview of individual cognition.

---

[88] This section draws in part from Shennan 2004, 21–25. See also Mesoudi 2011.

While material media like statues, stelai, or plaques expand the communicability and the perseverance of concepts of unseen agency, there are limits, as those concepts will not resonate equally with all members of a social group. To increase their relevance and circulation within larger social groups, the concepts must "transcend the dimension of the singular observer and break our intuitive pre-assumptions" (Bertolotti and Magnani 2010, 253). That is, transmission must also take place on a level that is not under the control of individual perspectives and impulses; social pressures are needed to incentivize individuals to support and share a concept that may not resonate with them intuitively (cf. Stagnaro and Rand 2021). Kinship is frequently the most fundamental and powerful framework for prosociality (cf. Crespi 2021), but as populations grew and diversified beyond the boundaries of kinship, anonymity increased, and people were more and more likely to interact with and need to rely on people they did not know (Tuzin 2001; de Waal 2008; Richerson et al. 2016). At this point, additional frameworks were needed for mitigating competition and increasing cooperation and social cohesion.[89]

Scholars have identified a rough typology of unseen agency that runs from concepts of spirits, ghosts, and other types of agents that are less concerned about human affairs and less likely to intervene in them, all the way to spirits, ghosts, and other types of agents that are very concerned about human affairs and very likely to intervene in them. They have also observed that the types of deities closer to the former end of the spectrum are predominant within smaller subsistence-based societies that often lack in technologies and access to resources, while those concentrated on the latter end of the spectrum tend to predominate within moderately complex large-scale societies that tend to be more rich in technologies and access to resources.[90] Significantly, however, after societies grow beyond a certain point in complexity and size, the prominence of those deities begins to drop off slightly (Kay et al. 2010).

Synthesizing these data, Ara Norenzayan and several other scholars contend across multiple publications that deities concerned with the "morality" of the societies with which they have relationships—so-called moralizing deities—

---

[89] Technological advances are one example of a partial solution. As an example, commerce in smaller communities was governed by public agreements witnessed by individuals who knew both parties, whereas the development of writing could facilitate the documentation of more private transactions between more or less anonymous people. See Aufrecht 1997, 123–24; Sanders 2010, 114–20; Routledge 1997. For a reconstruction of this process based on urbanization and rapidly expanding economic institutions, see Collard 2013.

[90] This is not to say ghosts and spirits are not a common part of large and complex urban societies, only that they tend not to be the predominant agents on the broader social level (Roes and Raymond 2003; Sanderson and Roberts 2008, 454–56; Norenzayan 2013, 126–30).

either provided or developed prosocial mechanisms that made significant contributions to maintaining social cohesion within growing societies, allowing them to become increasingly large and complex (Slingerland, Henrich, and Norenzayan 2010; Norenzayan et al. 2016). According to this theoretical model, as these agents gained salience and influence within societies, they became more reliably linked with morality. Moralizing deities with greater access to strategic information and greater abilities to covertly monitor and to punish developed the most fitness within such cognitive ecologies. Regarding the mechanism for the origins of these deities, Norenzayan et al. (2016, 46) state, "They arise from modifications of preexisting beliefs and practices that over historical time become targets of cultural evolutionary selection pressures." Rather than catalyzed by biological evolution (like our sensitivity to agency), the social salience of deity concepts is a product of their capacity to perform prosocial functions—to increase social cohesion and cooperation, allowing the society to continue to grow in size and complexity. The primary insight I want to draw from this model is that large-scale deity concepts, such as those found in the Hebrew Bible, tend to become or to remain salient because of their performance of prosocial functions such as offering access to strategic information, monitoring behavior, and punishing behavior that threatens social cohesion. This increases their adaptive fitness from the perspective of cultural evolution. Production of a deity concept based on individual sensitivity to agency, teleological reasoning, etc., is one thing, but the perseverance of that concept across a large and complex society for century after century is another entirely. "Optimal" deity concepts will satisfy both ends of this spectrum (cf. McNamara et al. 2021).

Another clue regarding the transition from unseen agency concept to socially-concerned deity is the observation that the emergence of these deities appears to follow *after* a society's rituals become more frequent and standardized. From the perspective of Harvey Whitehouse's (1992) "modes of religiosity" framework,[91] low-frequency, high-arousal "imagistic" ritual tends to give way with increased social size and complexity to high-frequency, low-arousal "doctrinal" ritual, which affords greater oversight and closer control through that growth (Whitehouse and Hodder 2010; Tsoraki 2018; Whitehouse 2021, 53–126). This is because the performance of higher-frequency ritual tends toward greater standardization and less tolerance for deviation, increasing the function of the rituals as costly signaling or as credibility enhancing displays, or CREDs (Henrich 2009; Liberman, Kinzler, and Woodward 2018). This reinforces group identity and aids in boundary maintenance, while also transmitting and embedding ideologies associated with that identity and its boundaries.[92] The cognitive,

---

[91] See also McCauley and Lawson 2002.
[92] Harvey Whitehouse and Ian Hodder (2010, 123) explain, "High-frequency ritual performances allow complex networks of ideas to be transmitted and stored in memory as

emotional, and physical costs associated with such rituals could also vary depending on competition and pressures. During times of war, for instance, they may become both highly costly and highly valued as demonstrations of group membership (Sosis, Kress, and Boster 2007). There is an important balance to strike with the deployment of "doctrinal" ritual over and against "imagistic," however. The subordination of high-arousal and low-frequency ritual to more routinized ritual can increase oversight, but it can also increase boredom and reduce motivation, which can result in campaigns to expand "imagistic" practices or can even result in revolt. Both ritual modes thus tend to occur in states of flux within individual social groups as the interests of the individual participants compete with the interests of the institutions (Whitehouse and Hodder 2010, 123–25).

So, an increase in "doctrinal" ritual can increase the salience of socially concerned deities, but there is more. As growing anonymity in larger and larger societies made the monitoring of "doctrinal" ritual performance more difficult for the institutions, socially concerned deities could become even more critical to the society's survival.[93] Agents thought to be able to covertly monitor everyone's actions may exploit the tendency for people who believe they are being watched to engage in more prosocial behavior (Bateson, Nettle, and Roberts 2006; Bateson et al. 2013).[94] This is particularly true if those agents are also thought to be willing and able to punish (Bourrat, Atkinson, and Dunbar 2011; Atkinson and Bourrat 2011; Johnson 2016). Growing urbanism would increase population density and interactions with material media, which would include media related to deity, contributing to a heightened sense of divine monitoring, particularly if sociocultural institutions were in place to enforce mores and even administer public punishment on behalf of the socially concerned deity (Hodder 2006, 195; Shults and Wildman 2018, 39). An increased capacity to monitor would also likely increase the perceived access to strategic information. These features could contribute to the mitigation of the occurrence of freeriding and other violations of

---

relatively schematized encyclopedic knowledge, leading to the standardization of teachings in collective memory. Unauthorized deviations from the standard canon thus become easy to identify."

[93] The monitoring of ritual performance by socially concerned deities in smaller societies likely developed in the interest of "stimulating and rationalizing (i.e. explaining costly behaviours with appeals to unverifiable agents) religious ritual" (Purzycki, Haque, and Sosis 2014, 81).

[94] It should be noted, however, that prosocial behavior and normative behavior are not the same thing. Because lying and cheating could have prosocial functions within a society, even if they do not align with normative behavior, cues of being watched tend not to mitigate that behavior (Oda, Kato, and Hiraishi 2015; Cai et al. 2015; Pfattheicher, Schindler, and Nockur 2018).

norms, as well as to the reinforcement of the deities' monitoring and punitive features (cf. Pyysiäinen 2014, 638–39; Norenzayan 2013, 13–14).

I would suggest that deceased kin would make particularly fit candidates for such deity concepts, given the high salience of their existing social relationships with the living and the higher likelihood of the perception of their concern for the social well-being of the living (Barrett 2011, 103–04; cf. Pyysiäinen 2009, 68). As societies stratified and elite groups emerged, elevating their own deceased kin over the broader social group would initially grant them unique access to and control of cultic authorities. In this way, the framework of kinship would be maintained for elite groups while others would engage with a high deity that may or may not have been perceived as kin.

While prosocial behaviors in complex anonymous societies are not exclusively facilitated by the conceptualization of deities as socially concerned agents (Nichols et al. 2020), a strong correlation has been shown between socially concerned deities and prosocial behavior. This prosociality, however, is predominantly parochial, or "in-group" in orientation.[95] That is, the sociocultural mores and ritual practices established, promoted, and enforced by deities tend to benefit those within the boundaries of a given social group while increasing antisocial behavior towards out-groups. One review of studies found conflicting evidence for religious prosociality, but when the authors distinguished between "religious" principles (which they understood as relating to the broader "package" of practices and beliefs conventionally associated with a given community's deities) and "supernatural" principles (understood as relating specifically to deity), the picture became clearer. They found that "religious" principles were associated with in-group-specific prosociality (i.e., protection of in-group values, antisocial behavior toward outgroup members), while the latter was associated with outgroup prosociality. They concluded that belief in an omniscient, omnipresent, and benevolent deity may promote inclusion of all peoples within the boundaries of the social group over which the deity is thought to preside (Preston, Ritter, and Hernandez 2010; Preston and Ritter 2013). Such deity profiles are quite complex philosophical elaborations, however, and though they are common today, they still manage to facilitate all kinds of identity politics. The story is much more nuanced for first millennium BCE Southwest Asia.

---

[95] Some of the criticism leveled at the theoretical model of Ara Norenzayan et al. is based precisely on the observation that the prosociality facilitated by "Big Gods" tends to be oriented exclusively in-group (Galen 2016; Hobson and Inzlicht 2016; McKay and Whitehouse 2016).

CONCLUSION

What this chapter has argued is that concepts of deity originate in intuitions about unseen agency in the world around us. These agents could be discussed within social groups, represented in material media, utilized by social institutions, deployed to explain unknown phenomena, and assigned features, biographies, and character traits. At some point along the way, social institutions would begin to link ritual acts with interactions with these agents. The ability of such agents to covertly monitor others, to provide special access to strategic information, and to punish would have provided the institutions with leverage over a host of prosocial forces. The increased use of material media to presence the deities, and ritual to curate the relationship of individuals to such agents, would have also increased the perception that those agents were present and monitoring behavior. This would increase discourse within the society regarding those agents, further embedding them in the prior expectations of individuals, causing them to more frequently appeal to them as explanations for unknown and unexplained events. It's probably at this point that these agents could be called "deities" according to the most representative use of the term in English today, but there is no analytically useful way to draw to a firm line of distinction between what is and what is not a deity in an ancient society. If it is important to have a boundary, we must hope to identify those drawn by the society itself, though even those boundaries will usually be fuzzy and debated, as entangled as they will so often be with the situational structuring of values and power by people and institutions, particularly within large and complex societies.

Because deities are not unique categories that occur in nature, there is no acid into which we can dip a text to see if deity is present. They are constructed and curated by individual cognition, by cultural evolution, and by social institutions, which means the most direct answer to the question posed by the title of this chapter is rather simple, if a bit disappointing: a deity is whatever a group says is a deity. In the next chapter I will apply the theoretical framework developed above to the material remains of first millennium BCE Israel and Judah in order to see what insights that framework can generate regarding the use of material media to presence divine agency. Following that, the third and fourth chapters will apply the resulting framework first to the generic concept of deity in the Hebrew Bible, and then to the representation of YHWH in the Hebrew Bible. This will demonstrate YHWH's foundation upon the fundamental frameworks of generic deity and its material presencing.

2.
Encountering Divine Agency

Now that a theoretical framework is in place for the origin and function of deity concepts, as well as the intuitive reasoning that facilitates their presencing through material media, we can apply that framework to an interrogation of the material media employed in ancient Southwest Asia to presence divine agency. This will reveal some of the reflective logic and reasoning undergirding the presencing media employed by the relevant societies. This chapter will briefly consider the larger empires of Mesopotamia, Egypt, and Anatolia, where the use of that media was much more widespread, elaborate, and explicit, and then move on the material remains of Israel and Judah. This interrogation will help me to begin to fill in my reconstruction of ancient Israel and Judah's concept of deity and its use of material media to presence it. It will also provide important context for the discussions in subsequent chapters regarding the relationship of YHWH's divine profile and presencing media to the broader concept of generic deity and to the broader repertoire of practices associated with presencing divine agency. These chapters will demonstrate that the Hebrew Bible's representations of YHWH and their material presencing do not represent revolutionary departures from widespread conventions regarding the representation and presencing of deity, but rather incremental elaborations on both.[1]

ENCOUNTERING DIVINE AGENCY IN ANCIENT SOUTHWEST ASIA

The basic logic of presencing media is that an unseen agent whose presence is desired for one reason or another can be presenced through appropriate material media. A deity without a means of being in some sense materially *present* is of little value or utility in a society that does not have the institutions available to impose the kinds of philosophical notions of omnipresence, omniscience, and omnipotence that are widely considered "theologically correct" in many societies today. While the seeds of those institutions were germinating in the

---

[1] On the embedded nature of Israel's history, sociomaterial conventions, and relationships with deity in the broader West Semitic world, see Smith 2002.

central Mediterranean in the first half of the first millennium BCE, they were not nearly so salient in the societies of and around Israel and Judah during that time period.

Indications that both deceased kin and deity were presenced via cultic objects is evident in the use of stelai in burials and cultic installations that correspond with the rise of pastoralism in the Neolithic Negev (Avner and Horwitz 2017; Avner 2018). These stelai appear to have initially marked the location of burials, as they are widely found collocated with burials, but this indexing seems to have given way to presencing functions, as indicated by later intentional configurations of stelai set up at great distances from burials and associated with rituals such as mortuary feasts. An analysis of sites from the fifth to third millennia BCE identified two different arrangements of stelai that the authors concluded represented two different groups (Arav et al. 2016).[2] Larger stones arranged in standardized numbers and groupings were thought to represent deities, while smaller stones arranged individually and arbitrarily were thought to represent ancestors.[3] In some mortuary locations, as well, stelai set up near the perimeter of tombs were understood to represent protective deities, while the stelai in the interior were understood to presence deceased kin.[4]

As noted by most scholars who address the function of stelai, they could serve multiple different functions, and often simultaneously, depending on the associated institutions and the experiences and perspectives of the person encountering them (e.g., Graesser 1972, 37). Central to all the different functions that have been identified is their use to cue the viewer's attention to their intentional upright orientation and whatever function the viewer may associate with that intention, which could obviously be quite subjective and fluid. The appropriation of older material media for new purposes illustrates a central feature of sociomaterial ecologies: as the identities and the meanings associated with objects and behaviors fade from communal memory or lose salience because of

---

[2] The authors noted that while ancient and modern societies around the world treated stelai as representing ancestors, the desert stelai of the Negev have always been treated as representative of deities. The authors refer to *KTU* 1.17.i.26–27, which describes establishing a stele for ancestors. (cf. Avner 2002, 65–92).

[3] Arav et al. 2016, 20: "It is most likely that in sites of this group there is a combination of stones for deities and stones for ancestors. In ancient records and anthropological studies ancestors are perceived as sitting and dining in communion with the gods."

[4] Avner and Horwitz 2017, 36: "In tombs, two types of *maṣṣeboth* were set. Those incorporated in the tomb's perimeter, mostly on the eastern side and facing east, are explained as representing the deities that guard the tombs and the deceased. *Maṣṣeboth* set within tombs are usually narrow, set separately and face north; these are interpreted as representing the ancestors."

circumstances, the objects as well as the behaviors often remain to be repurposed for use in new circumstances and in the service of new exigencies and ideologies.

For reflective elaborations on the use of material media to presence the divine pantheons of ancient Southwest Asia, the clearest examples come from the large and powerful empires of Mesopotamia and Egypt, where multiple texts preserve descriptions of special rituals referred to as the *mīs pî*, "washing of the mouth," and the *pīt pî* (or *wpt-r*), "opening of the mouth," that transformed human-made divine images into heaven-born deities (Boden 1998; Berlejung 1998; Walker and Dick 1999, 2001; McDowell 2015). While there are many references to these rituals across the Akkadian corpora, the prescriptive ritual texts themselves are limited to a few surviving Akkadian fragments that all date to the first millennium BCE. The number and order of the incantations and the ceremonies differ between the surviving fragments, but the core of the process was the ceremonial washing of the mouth, which purified the image for contact with the deity, and the ceremonial opening of the mouth,[5] which actually enabled the image to breathe, smell, eat, and drink (Walter and Dick 1999, 151). Both the secondary references to the ritual and the ritual texts themselves use language related to gestation, birth, and manufacturing as part of a two-day ritual process that transitioned the deity into the cultic image.[6]

According to the version of the ritual from Babylon, on the first day, the image is set within an orchard while a tamarisk trough representing the divine womb (the *buginnu*) was filled with water (representing Ea's semen), gold, silver, oil, carnelian, lapis lazuli, and tamarisk.[7] After a series of "mouth washings," the image and the *buginnu* were left to "gestate" overnight. The mouth, ears, heart, and mind were understood to be operative to some degree at this point, but on the second day, the *buginnu* was placed on a birthstone before a panel of artisan deities who were petitioned to enable the image to eat, hear, and breath.[8]

---

[5] The opening of the mouth could also be performed for images representing living kings and other persons (Walker and Dick 2001, 13).

[6] Hurowitz (2003, 150–53) and McDowell (2015, 69–80) agree with Boden (1998, 101–5) against Berlejung (1998, 137–41) and, to some degree, Walker and Dick (1999, 21), that birth provides an overarching conceptual framework for the rituals, although manufacturing terminology also features prominently.

[7] A separate "holy-water basin of mouth-washing" was filled with "an assortment of precious metal, gems, oils, wood, salt, syrup, and ghee" (McDowell 2015, 55). McDowell (2015, 74–80) criticizes Berlejung's (1998, 137–41) rejection of the birthing framework on the grounds that she conflates this basin with the *buginnu*.

[8] See McDowell 2015, 72: "Its creation is attributed, ultimately, not to human craftsmen but to a group of creator-gods who, through a collaborative effort, form the divine embryo which then gestates overnight while divine powers are transferred to the materials collected in the tamarisk 'womb.' On the following day, the god is 'born' on the brick of *Bēlet-ilī* and its mouth is washed a final time, allowing for its initial life-giving breath. With its

According to the text, after reciting an incantation that includes, "Go, do not tarry," the performer "makes (him) enter the form."[9] The Ninevite Ritual Text has the artisan whisper in the ear of "that god," [*itti ilāni*] *aḫḫēka manâta*, "You are counted among your brother gods" (Walker and Dick 2001, 94–95). When the rituals associated with the liminal phase were complete, the image was installed in its temple and given its first meal. At this point, according to Pongratz-Leisten (2011, 149), "the divine statue was perceived as a self-propelled agent." Rather than treat such an agent as "secondary," however, we may more accurately think of it simply as an extension of the deity's self, with more detailed reflective accounts of the relationship of the agent to the deity contingent upon rhetorical context and exigencies.

Two aspects of these rituals that should be highlighted are the materials used and the role of the artisan. Only certain materials were considered to have qualities that were appropriate for creating the image or that could facilitate the process of enlivenment (Hurowitz 2006; Benzel 2015). Even in their raw state, for instance, pure gold and silver do not oxidize, but maintain their color and shine. This quality could very easily become associated with the enduring brilliance of deity, and thus be conceptualized either as coming from divine realms or as a more pure or suitable habitation or conduit for divine presence. This may account for the inclusion of gold and silver in the *buginnu*, and the use of gold and silver plating over cultic images. While the core of the image was composed of wood instead of precious metals, specific types of wood were still preferred. The tamarisk, called *eṣemti ilī*, "bone of the gods," was probably most prominent (Hurowitz 2003, 5–6).[10] If so, the use of a tamarisk *buginnu* and the inclusion of tamarisk in the mixture placed within it may have been intended to materially link the cultic image with the womb in which the precious materials gestated overnight.

While these materials could be considered divine in origin or especially suited to transmitting or housing divinity, whether inherently or otherwise, certain acts were required to commission them for divine inhabitation. The washing and opening of the mouth ceremonies transitioned the image from an earthly creation to a self-created divine entity, and in these larger empires, some concomitant ritual

---

sensory organs activated and functioning, the image is clothed, installed in its temple, and fed its first meal."

[9] As Walker and Dick note, this may indicate the deity is compelled to inhabit the image (cf. Winter 1992, 23), but the Sumerogram GIŠ.ḪUR.ME could also be read as the Akkadian *gišhuru*, which would be "magic circle," reflecting the notion of the "magic circles of the gods" (Walker and Dick 2001, 81–82, n. 81).

[10] McDowell (2015, 75) summarizes, "The tamarisk from which the *buginnu* was made ... may have been understood both as a component of the divine statue's formation, perhaps its skeletal system, and as a cleansing and purifying agent, possibly for the womb and the gestating divine embryo."

was usually included to signal the dissociation of the image from its natural/human origins.[11] This would have amplified the perception of the image as inhabitable by divine agency and was accomplished through the symbolic amputation of the artisan's hands and declarations such as *anāku lā ēpu[šu ...]*, "(I swear) I did not make (the statue)" (Walker and Dick 2001, 94–95). An additional reason for this dissociation may have been to rhetorically undercut the criticism of attributing deity to the products of human industry—a criticism well-known from the Hebrew Bible (Dick 1999, 16–45; Smith 2004b).

A similar "opening the mouth" ritual is attested in texts from across the history of Egypt. Its full name was "Performing the Opening of the Mouth in the Workshop for the Statue of PN," but it could also be referred to as the "Opening of the Mouth and the Eyes," or just "Opening of the Mouth" (*wpt-r* or *wn-r*) (McDowell 2015, 85–109). As with the *pīt pî*, the *wpt-r* ceremony was a ritual of animation that could be used to cultically enliven a variety of inanimate objects (which included the mummies of certain deceased persons, demonstrating the similar conceptual and cultic overlap of the deceased and the divine in Egypt).[12] Similar to the rituals in Mesopotamia, the instruments and terminology of the *wpt-r* reflect its conceptual undergirding by the frameworks of both birth and manufacturing.[13] The materials used were also critical to the success of the endeavor—gold and silver again figure prominently, as well as lapis lazuli and other precious stones—but the role of the human artisan was not repudiated in Egypt.[14]

---

[11] Note the following comments from Pongratz-Leisten and Sonik (2015, 8): "The Greek term *archeiropoieta* ... identifies miraculous portraits or representations that were 'not made by any [human] hand,' encompassing in the Christian tradition such images as the Mandylion (Image of Edessa). The *archeiropoieta* are not limited to this context, however; ancient Greek sources include various accounts of divine images that had miraculously *appeared*, having fallen perhaps from the heavens or yielded by the seas, and that were understood as products of the divine rather than human agency."

[12] McDowell (2015, 87) notes that the majority of references to the ritual in ancient Egyptian literature are funerary in nature. "The earliest mortuary attestation comes from the tomb of Metjen, a prominent Old Kingdom official from Fourth Dynasty (ca. 2600 B.C.E.). The ritual is also mentioned in the earliest edition of the Pyramid Texts (PT), the PT of Unas (ca. 2375–2345 B.C.E.) from the Fifth Dynasty and in the PT from the Sixth Dynasty."

[13] For instance, funerary texts describe two blades being used to open the mouth of the mummy, which may reflect the use of two fingers to clear mucus from the mouth of newborns, enabling it to breath. Additionally, the enlivened entity is immediately breastfed. See McDowell 2015, 104–9, following Roth 1992.

[14] For a comparison of the Mesopotamian and Egyptian rituals, see McDowell 2015, 109–15.

There is also a relevant Hittite text from the late fifteenth or early fourteenth century BCE that prescribed an eight- or nine-day regimen for commissioning a satellite cult installation for the "Deity of the Night" (in the case of this text, the female deity Pirinkir) (Miller 2004; Beckman 2010). The deity itself was to be made from gold, decked out in accoutrements of a variety of precious stones. The process for installing the deity is long and complex, but on the fifth day, before leaving the old temple behind, the text in section 22 prescribes the following utterance: "Honoured deity! Preserve your being, but divide your divinity! Come to that new house, too, and take yourself the honoured place!"[15] As with the Akkadian rituals described above, once the statue is installed in the cult place, sacrifices are made to facilitate the deity's first meal. Gary Beckman points out that communal meals are the most frequent rituals described in the Hittite temple texts (Beckman 2010, 88). He also highlights "the frequent attribution of the construction to deities rather than the actual human builders" (2010, 89).

These rituals represent the most explicit reflective practices associated with the intuitive conceptualizations of divine agency as communicable, and of certain inanimate objects and substances as animable by that agency.[16] The variations in details, including the degree of independence of the image, the number of manifestations, the associations between the deities and the locations, and the types of materials used are all products of diverse reflective considerations taking place within different economies and sociomaterial ecologies. If the question of whether or not the image was a "full" or "partial" manifestation of the deity emerged at all, it would have done so situationally and would have been addressed within the relevant rhetorical contexts. There is no need to impose a systematic ontology on the discussion.

What is consistent across all these practices and societies is the intuitive perception of the partibility of divine agency and its communicability through material media. These intuitions need not be explicitly manifested in praxis or in reflective rationalizations of that praxis in order for them to be influential, of course. Related rituals and concepts of enlivened statues from other societies

---

[15] The translation is from Miller 2004, 290. Beckman (2010, 83) renders, "O esteemed deity, guard your person, but divide your divinity!" For a specific discussion of the verb "divide," see Beal 2002. For a broader discussion of the Hittite conceptualization of the divine, see Taggar-Cohen 2013.

[16] Herbert Niehr (1997, 78) notes related features of some Phoenician and Aramaic inscriptions: "After a Phoenician temple had been built or restored, the divine statue had to be erected in the sanctuary. This is referred to with the phrase 'I/we caused the deity to dwell in it' (*yšb yiphil*). In a Punic inscription, a god's entrance into a sanctuary is indicated by the verb *bw'* without mentioning the statue, but by stating the divine name only. Several Phoenician and Aramaic inscriptions mention votive statues or stelae placed in front of the divine statues in the temples."

around the world and down to the present time demonstrate the trans-cultural and trans-historical intuitiveness of this approach to divine agency. These concepts do not stand in contrast or contradiction to intuitive notions of human personhood and agency, but rather represent more flexible and dynamic elaborations on both (contra Sommer 2009, 195, n. 145). Their general intuitiveness and broad consistency across ancient Southwest Asia, along with significant overlap in rituals and traditions associated with deity, support the preliminary application of the same conceptual frameworks to the interrogation of the way deities were encountered in Iron Age Israel and Judah.

ENCOUNTERING DIVINE AGENCY IN IRON AGE ISRAEL AND JUDAH

We have no direct attestation of prescriptions for rituals associated with enlivening presencing media in the material remains of first millennium BCE Israel and Judah (Hundley 2013, 352–54),[17] but there is a rich tradition in the region of materially presencing deity that reaches back into Neolithic periods and drew in the Bronze and Iron Ages from the same conventions and intuitive concepts of deity in circulation in the surrounding societies.[18] The clearest example of this is the building and maintenance of temples in Iron Age Israel and Judah, which was closely patterned after the temples of surrounding societies, and was first and foremost a means of facilitating the deity's presence and nearness (Levine 1974, 2011; Hundley 2013). The points of contact do not end there, however.

According to Othmar Keel and Christoph Uehlinger (1998, 96), the material representation of deity in the highlands of Israel and Judah in the Late Bronze Age reflected heavy Egyptian influence, particularly in the prevalence of enthroned male Egyptian deities, and especially those who represented political domination and war. Bull imagery was particularly prominent, but while in earlier periods it could represent either fecundity or ferocity, by the Iron Age, it almost exclusively reflected the latter. The role of the female deity was diminished in Egypt, but highland artisans appear to have carried on a simplified version of a popular "naked goddess" motif through the production of much more inexpensive terracotta plaques (Keel and Uehlinger 1998, 108). The effacement of Egyptian influence meant the similar withdrawal of wealth and markets it facilitated, so locally produced plaques, statuettes, stelai, and cult stands became less expertly and less expensively produced. By Iron Age I, the fertility aspects of the divine

---

[17] According to Herbert Niehr (1997, 78), this is also a feature of Phoenician and Aramean societies. He states, "This is due to the epigraphic character of the Phoenician and Aramaic inscriptions; they are neither literary nor ritual texts."

[18] Ben-Ami 2006, 132: "Standing stones were an integral (and dominant) part of early Israelite cult places."

were depicted primarily through symbols and "substitute entities" like a tree, a scorpion, or a suckling mother animal (Keel and Uehlinger 1998, 128). This does not represent a significant or intentional departure from trends taking place elsewhere in ancient Southwest Asia.

Finds from Iron I–IIA that likely depict deity include stelai, metal statuary (with a caveat), objects in stone, terracotta cult stands, shrine models, shrine plaques, anthropomorphic terracotta vessels and figurines, worship scenes depicted on seals, and depictions of deity in or on clay (Uehlinger 1997; cf. Lewis 2020, 287–426).[19] Metal statuary depicting male deities does not appear to have been produced—or at least not widely—from the tenth century BCE on, which is sometimes taken as a sign of programmatic aniconism, but is more likely a shift in preference governed by the markets and available resources. Tryggve N. D. Mettinger (1995) convincingly argues that Israel and Judah were initially carrying on a "*de facto* aniconism" that was well known from the broader West Semitic social milieu (cf. Ornan 2005). This aniconism was not "the result of theological reflection. Instead, it must be seen as an inherited convention of religious expression which only later formed the basis for theological reflection" (Mettinger 1995, 195). Theological explanations often represent ad hoc rationalizations of practices that endure for a variety of more ordinary intuitive or reflective reasons. The more widespread use during this period of symbols and substitute entities suggests that the notion was no longer particularly salient—if it ever was—that the cultic image need approximate the appearance of the deity itself. The priority was presencing the deity, not looking like it (cf. Ornan 2004).

While some of the media mentioned above may have had primarily commemoratory or dedicatory functions, according to the institutions responsible for them, many would have been widely understood to presence or transmit divine or otherwise unseen agency, particularly if erected in a public setting and assigned a specific sociomaterial role in the functioning of the society. These media no doubt indexed a spectrum of unseen agency running the gamut from deceased kin to socially concerned deities. The archaeological bias towards the state and its elites has weighted our data overwhelmingly in favor of the few deities who predominated on a national or dynastic level, of course, so this interrogation cannot comment on the full range of that agency. Naturally, there will be more variability in the presencing media utilized privately by individuals and family units, as they generally do not answer to same broader prosocial forces.

Stelai represent the strongest candidates for presencing media from Iron Age Israel and Judah. The most explicit use of stelai in worship from Iron Age Judah no doubt comes from the broadroom temple that occupied Strata X and IX in the Judahite fortress of Arad (Herzog 2002; Bloch-Smith 2015; fig. 2.1). The temple

---

[19] The Kuntillet 'Ajrud inscriptions and the Taanach cult stand contain the most explicit depictions of deity on clay. See Thomas 2016, but see also Gilmour 2009.

2. *Encountering Divine Agency* 59

is widely understood as dedicated primarily or exclusively to YHWH—meaning the stele found in the last phase of the *debir* would have indexed YHWH—

Figure 2.1. A reconstruction of the eighth-century BCE *debir* (cultic niche) of the temple at Arad (the original artifacts are on display in the Israel Museum in Jerusalem). Drawing by the author.

but other material remains can be correlated to broader trends regarding the presencing of other deities. YHWH was not alone at Arad. For instance, fragments from multiple Judean Pillar Figurines (see below) were discovered near the sacrificial altar and in an adjoining storage room (Kletter 1996, 211–12; Bloch-Smith 2015, 102; Darby 2014, 254–58).

Several considerations support interpreting stelai as saliently presencing the agents they indexed.[20] The word *maṣṣēbâ*, meaning "stood up," or "erected," reflects the upright orientation of the stones, which makes the stones stand out within the environment and cues the viewer to intention and agency.[21] Beyond that orientation, the Ugaritic and Akkadian words for "stele"—*skn* and *si-ik-ka-num*—may derive from a verbal root meaning "to inhabit" (Fleming 1992, 75–79; Durand 1998, 24–29; Sommer 2009, 29; Scheyhing 2018, 95, 98). This terminology resonates with Jacob's designation in Gen 28:22 of a stele he set up and anointed with oil as the *bêt ĕlōhîm*, "house of deity." Anointing with oil (see also Gen 35:14–15) may represent a commissioning of sorts, as has been proposed for some Akkadian rituals (Fleming 2000, 86–87), although it is less elaborate than the complex rituals described above, and perhaps intentionally so.[22] The shortened form, *bêt-ēl*, would later become a designation for "stele" that would be adapted in Greek as *baitylos*, "betyl." By the seventh-century BCE, Assyrian sources identify a West Semitic deity named Bethel who also appears in later

---

[20] Iron Age stelai have been found in cult installations and other contexts in Arad, Tel-Dan, Hazor, Bethsaida, Lachish, Tirzah, Tel-Reḥov, Beth-Shemesh, Tel Qiri, Timna, Shechem, Khirbet Qeiyafa, and in other locations (Mettinger 1995, 149–68; Bloch-Smith 2015, 100; Zukerman 2012, 41–43; Garfinkel, Ganor, and Hasel 2018, 131–34; Garfinkel 2018, 55–70; Herring 2013, 53–63).

[21] Carl Graesser (1972, 34) suggests this orientation "served as a marker, jogging the memory. It would arrest the attention of the onlooker because it stood in a position it would not take naturally from gravity alone; only purposeful human. Activity could accomplish such 'setting up.'" While Graesser suggests memorial, legal, and commemorative functions, he insists it is "important to note that a single stone was not limited to a single function but often carried out several at one and the same time" (37).

[22] We already know certain idiosyncrasies were adopted as identity markers to distinguish Israel and Judah from the societies surrounding them, and this certainly may have been an additional way to distinguish themselves in their relationship to their deity/ies. The abandonment of the use of *'eben* in reference to their deity may be another example. Sommer rhetorically asks, "Is it possible that, in these passages, anointing transforms the stele and thus functions in a manner comparable to the *mīs pî* ritual in Mesopotamia?" (Sommer 2009, 49). As Sommer notes in a footnote (207, n. 67), several midrashim insist the oil that anointed these stelai came down directly from heaven, which is reminiscent of the insistence at the end of the Mesopotamian ritual that the stele was not made by human hands. Anointing with oil is prescribed by Lev 8 to consecrate the various appurtenances of the temple.

Aramaic and Greek texts (Sommer 2009, 28–29). In his first century CE text, *Phoenician History* (preserved in Eusebius's *Preparation for the Gospel*), Philo of Byblos describes the betyls as *lithoi empsychoi*, "enlivened stones."[23] The terminology that was in usage suggests the concept of the divine animation of stelai enjoyed wide circulation around ancient Southwest Asia.

Stone may also have been perceived as one of the more suitable materials for hosting the agency of the deceased/divine in light of its durability. Genesis 49:24 refers to a deity (likely El) as the *'eben yiśrā'ēl*, "Stone of Israel," but this very early text seems to preserve a frozen epithet that is nowhere else used to refer to the deity of Israel. The term *'eben* is commonly used to refer to the material out of which stelai were constructed (Gen 28:18; 31:45; 35:14), but it is also frequently used in polemics against divine images (Lev 26:1; Deut 4:28; 28:36, 64; 29:17). The association of deity with the term *'eben* may have been abandoned by later authors and editors, who clearly prefer the term *ṣûr*, "rock" (Deut 32:4, 15, 18; 1 Sam 2:2; 22:3; Isa 17:10; 26:4) in reference to the deity. As *'eben* likely did originally, the term *ṣûr* seems to refer to the deity's eternal nature and ability to provide protection and refuge. The occasional denial of *ṣûr* ("rock") status to other deities suggests that status may even have been considered prototypical of deity (Deut 32:37; 2 Sam 22:32; Isa 44:8).

Unworked stone may also have boasted the additional feature of a more natural state (perhaps the state in which a deity was thought to have left it), rather than one forced on the stone by human industry. Flat stones placed horizontally before stelai to function as offering tables suggest rituals similar to those performed for the deceased were likely performed for the deities indexed by the stelai (Garfinkel, Ganor, and Hasel 2018, 131–32).[24] For instance, two open air sanctuaries at Hazor dating to the eleventh century BCE prominently featured stelai and included cultic assemblages. The elevated arrangement of stelai at Area A was surrounded by offering tables (Ben-Ami 2006, 123–27; see fig. 2.2). A recently excavated Iron IIA Judahite temple from Tel Moẓa features a room near the entrance with five stelai at the base of a bench (Kisilevitz 2015, 51). Several clay figurines were also discovered among cultic vessels, including horses showing the remains of riders, as well as two hand-modeled anthropomorphic heads.[25] At Khirbet Qeiyafa, three tenth-century-BCE cult rooms featuring stelai

---

[23] Philo of Byblos, *Phoenician History* 810.28 (see Baumgarten 1981, 16, 202–3).

[24] According to Mettinger (1995, 191–92), stelai functioned primarily to facilitate sacrifices and shared communal meals. Note the communal meal mentioned in Exod 24:10–11 after the elders of Israel "saw the God of Israel" (*yir'û 'ēt 'ĕlōhê yiśrā'ēl*). Mark Smith (2008, 58–61) elaborates on the importance of the communal meal to covenant ritual.

[25] The context does not yet make clear the intended referents of the figurines, but excavations are ongoing. Yosef Garfinkel (2020) suggested in a *Biblical Archaeology*

Figure 2.2. An arrangement of stelai and offering tables discovered in Hazor's Area A. Source: Ben-Ami 2006, 124 (fig. 2). Drawing by the author.

were discovered. Room J in Building D and Room G in Building C3 each featured large stelai with stone offering tables at their bases and benches adjacent to them (Garfinkel, Ganor, and Hasel 2018, 134–46). The former appears to have been a public cult installation, while the latter was found among a row of houses, and was likely private. Similar private installations dating to the end of the second

---

Review article that these heads in connection with the horses depicted YHWH, but the head of the Tel Moẓa excavation responded with others in a subsequent article (Kisilevitz et al. 2020, 41) pointing out that anthropomorphic clay figurines were also frequently used as votive offerings or as "charms used in rituals." Zevit (2001, 274) explains: "Those figurines which represented deities evoked their presence, while those which may have been votives representing the donor were prayers in clay." Even the latter function, however, involved the intuitive notion that some manner of agency was channeled in one direction or another through the material media.

millennium BCE have been found at Lachish and Tel Qiri.[26] A ninth-century-BCE open air sanctuary is known from Tel Reḥov that featured a raised platform with two stelai, an offering table, a pottery altar, and a large number of animal bones (Mazar 2015, 27–28). The offering of food and the ritual sharing of meals before these stelai suggest the presence and participation of the indexed agents.[27]

Another potential means of presencing generic divine agency that has long eluded scholarly consensus is the use of free-standing clay figurines known today as Judean Pillar Figurines, or JPFs (Kletter 1996; Byrne 2004; Darby 2014).[28] These objects were long assumed to represent the deity Asherah and to facilitate fertility and successful childbirth, but the lack of any representation of the genitals complicates the assumption. Erin Darby's recent reanalysis of the archaeological contexts and the comparative data suggests they exercised somewhat generic apotropaic and healing functions, and show no signs of identification with specific deities.[29] They may also have functioned for some to facilitate access to divine agency for those excluded from participating in—or who otherwise lacked access to—temple ritual.[30] With their form likely developing from the earlier naked

---

[26] See Ben-Tor and Portugali 1987, 82–90 (the authors note the abundance of animal bones, and particularly right forelimbs, which they suggest indicates their use in cultic activity [89–90]); Zukerman 2012; Garfinkel, Ganor, and Hasel 2018, 144–45, and nn. 9–11 (I exclude Megiddo room 2081 [see Bloch-Smith 2007, 33–35]). Some refer to these installations as "cult corners" (Zevit 2001, 123; Hitchcock 2011).

[27] 1 Sam 9:12–13, in which Saul seeks help in the recovery of lost donkeys, provide a biblical perspective on this context. He asks if the seer is around, and the locals respond, "He is. Look, just ahead of you. Hurry up. He's come to the town today because there's a sacrifice for the people today at the shrine [bāmâ]. As soon as you enter the town, find him before he goes up to the shrine to eat. See, the people won't eat until he arrives, since he's the one who blesses the sacrifice. After that, those who are invited can eat. Now head on up. Now's the time to find him."

[28] As the name suggests, these figurines were most prominent in Judah, and were particularly prolific from the eighth through the sixth centuries BCE. There have been around 1,000 JPFs discovered in the region. They were small (13–16 cm) free-standing figurines that depicted a female with hands holding or supporting the breasts and a pillar base extending from below the breasts. The figurines had heads made of two types: a hand-made type that was executed by pinching the clay to roughly form a nose and eye sockets, and a molded type connected to the body by a clay tang. Some are also depicted holding a disc or a child.

[29] Francesca Stavrakopoulou (2016, 356–57) suggests they were tied in domestic contexts to lactation rituals and signaled the transformation of the personhood of the mother/feeder and the child.

[30] Darby (2014, 390) appeals to Hector Avalos's (1995) analysis of healing ritual, favorably summarizing: "The sick may have originally travelled to shrines where rites took place. At some point, perhaps as early as the Iron IIB, the sick were excluded from temple space; and healing rituals must have taken place in the home."

female deity plaques,[31] female deity appliqués from shrine models and cult stands, and Phoenician and Israelite pillar-based figurines, their function appears to have been influenced by "magico-medical, apotropaic, and exorcistic figurine rituals" to which Judahites were exposed by their Assyrian vassalage (Darby 2014, 393).[32]

Darby's analysis includes some intriguing overlap with the discussion so far of communicable agency. She argues that clay seems to have been perceived as an effective conduit for purity/holiness as well as impurity.[33] For example, rituals in Lev 14 and Num 5 prescribe the use of earthen vessels to facilitate the transmission of impurities to/away from individuals in need of cursing/healing. Prescriptions from Lev 11 show that an earthen vessel coming in contact with unclean animals renders unclean any food or water it touches, and therefore must be shattered. The idea here seems to be that the clay vessel was charged with or stored impurity which could only be dispelled through the shattering of the vessel.[34] This could easily extend to removing other contaminates thought to operate on the level of communicable agency. As with stone, fired clay did not naturally deteriorate, and that permanence may have subtly influenced its suitability as a host for divine agency. Its fragility, however, allowed for the deliberate breaking of clay objects to take on significance of its own. Not only could it dispel impurity, but execration rituals meant to curse a specific target could involve the deliberate breaking of clay. The ability to conduct/transmit purity and impurity could have served a wide array of domestic functions related to exorcism, apotropaism, as well as execration, which would account for their presence in domestic contexts.[35] Whatever the precise nature of the agency they

---

[31] Two figurines discovered at Tel Reḥov may represent a transitional phase between the plaques and the JPFs. According to Amihai Mazar (2015, 39), they "comprise a strange combination of a mold-made plaque figurine and a standing 'pillar figuring;' each has a broad base, enabling it to stand on its own."

[32] Darby goes on to discuss the possible role of the figurines in developing national identity or resisting Assyrian hegemony.

[33] Another way of understanding the function of fired clay was that whatever quality it had absorbed could be transmitted, but could not be removed. Thus, pottery that becomes impure must be destroyed, as it could never be purified (Faust 2019, 186–90). Faust notes that many Iron Age four-room homes that have been excavated contained rooms devoid of pottery, which he interprets as an indication people needed a location free from pottery for the process of purification. (His paper argues for a preexilic context for the composition of the majority of P.)

[34] Darby 2014, 277–83. Ritual and contamination have been important frameworks within the cognitive science of religion. See, for instance, McCauley 2011, 177–82.

[35] Darby (2014, 394) concludes, "it is tantalizing to hypothesize that the preference for pillar figurines might relate to their ability to stand guard unaided in open and liminal areas, such as windows and doorway, much as pillar-based females do on the Yavneh fenestrated stands. Additionally, free-standing figurines could be configured in any number of ways,

were thought to transmit, they represent another example of material media with a socially constructed capacity for the transmission of some manner of perhaps generic agency.

The shrine model was a more likely means of presencing deity in ancient Southwest Asia. Such shrines were ubiquitous in ancient Southwest Asia and the Mediterranean.[36] The only examples that have been preserved have primarily been made of clay or sometimes stone, and the models generally fall into one of three different broad types (Katz 2016): (1) closed models, which were usually rectilinear or cylindrical, closely resembling buildings or sometimes pots, jars, or pithoi; (2) *naos* models, which tended to have an opening in the front that usually included a closing door, as well as concentric recesses to suggest compartmental depth (see figs. 2.3 and 2.4); and (3) open models, which tended to be taller and to be used as offering tables or altars of some kind. Across the three types, shrine models could perform a number of different functions. In early periods, and especially in Egypt, they seem to have been intended for the deceased. Many contain soot that suggest incense and other substances were burned in or upon them. Katz (2016, 126) suggests closed cylindrical models were likely intended as containers for food intended for priests or for deities. Some interpret the shrines as containers for offerings, or even as votive offerings themselves.

A distinct presencing function is suggested by a number of *naos* models that have space inside for the placement of miniature cultic media. A Middle Bronze IIB clay shrine model discovered in Ashkelon likely housed a bronze calf figurine covered in silver plating that was discovered in the same context (fig. 2.5). Temples were not as scarce in Iron Age Israel and Judah as previously thought (Nakhai 2015, 90–101; Finkelstein 2020), but the discovery of shrine models in cultic and other contexts suggests there was a desire to localize or perhaps mobilize the access to the divine that temples were thought to facilitate. The miniaturization and localization specifically of temple space is most likely for those shrines that had large openings flanked by pillars, by lions, or by sphynxes, represented roof beams, held doors at one time, concentrically represented progression through temple spaces, and included space for the placement of a

---

including being stationed around the body of a sick individual…. Finally, the base of a pillar figurine might be wielded by hand during a ritual." On a personal note, one night in 2017 while I was contemplating the apotropaic function of pillar figurines, my then-five-year-old daughter came to me and announced that she had arranged her dolls in a perimeter around her bed to protect her from monsters while she slept. Surely the intuitions undergirding these ancient practices live on.

[36] Shrine models have been discovered in many locations in and around Israel and Judah, including Tel Dan, Tel Rekhesh, Tel Reḥov, Tirzah, Megiddo, Jerusalem, Khirbet Qeiyafa, and elsewhere. See Zevit 2001, 328–43; Mazar and Panitz-Cohen 2008; Garfinkel and Mumcuoglu 2015; Mazar 2015, 36–38; Garfinkel, Ganor, and Hasel 2018, 146–55.

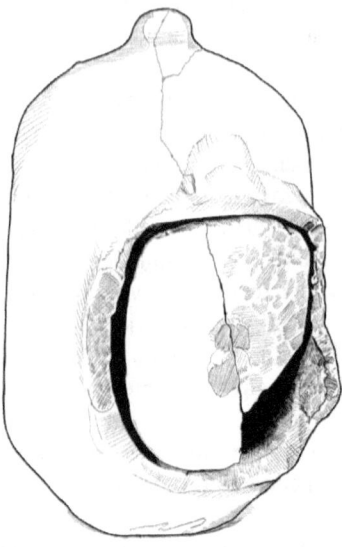

Figure 2.3. A shrine model discovered at Khirbet Qeiyafa that includes a mostly preserved door. Source: Zilberg 2018. Drawing by the author.

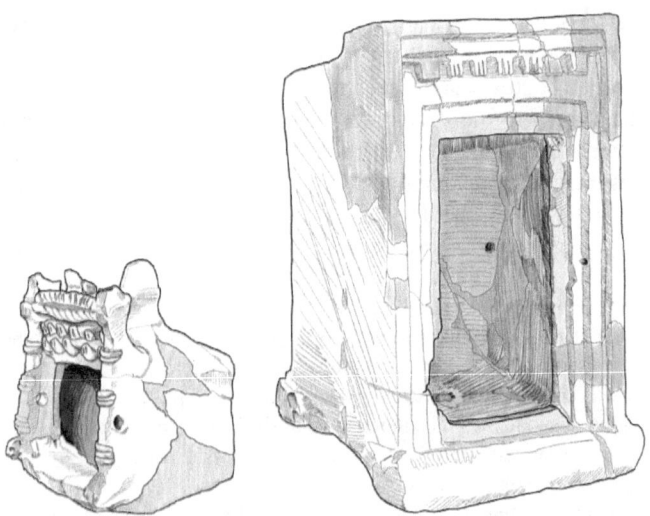

Figure 2.4. Two shrine models discovered at Khirbet Qeiyafa. Source: Garfinkel and Mumcuoglu 2018. Drawing by the author.

figurine or some representation of a deity, whether anthropomorphic or otherwise, iconic or otherwise. The temple space may have been a means of more fully facilitating access to divine agency, it may have allowed the image to be carried in processions throughout the community, or it may have "democratized" access to temple worship.[37] The use of clay and stone correlates with the perception, already discussed, that both substances were efficient and/or effective means of channeling unseen agency.

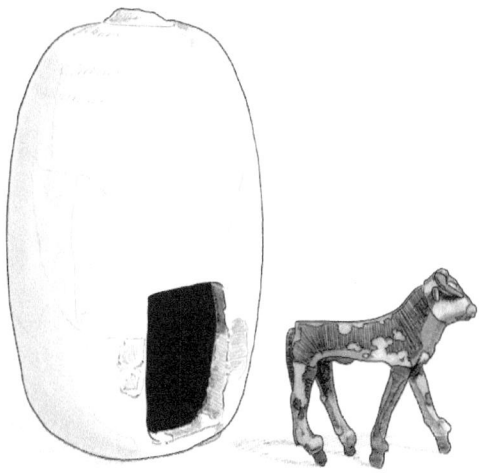

Figure 2.5. A bronze calf and clay shrine model discovered in Ashkelon. The calf measures about 4.5 inches long and 4.25 inches high. Drawing by the author.

The Taanach cult stand (fig. 2.6), dated to the tenth century BCE, may represent a hybrid of two or more of the shrine model types (Hestrin 1987; Beck 1994; Keel and Uehlinger 1998, 154–60; Hadley 2000, 169–79; Doak 2015, 129–32). The terracotta stand features four vertically arranged sections that, beginning from the bottom, depict (1) a nude female with outstretched arms touching the ears of lions on each side of her (the depictions of the flanking animals continue along the sides of the stand); (2) sphynx figures on each side of an empty space; (3) a stylized tree with feeding goats flanked by lions; and (4) a horse below a sun disk, flanked by outward facing volutes (spirals).[38] Above the top register is a row

---

[37] Garfinkel, Ganor, and Hasel (2018, 155) suggest the ark of the covenant may have functioned as a shrine model.

[38] There has been some debate about these representations, and particularly regarding the animal in the upper section. Early interpreters understood it as a bull, perhaps as a result of

of clay circles likely representing roof beams. The four sections may vertically arrange the rooms of the shrine, rather than depict concentric entryways ("recessed doorframes") surrounding the image in the inner sanctuary, as in other shrine models (Garfinkel and Mumcuoglu 2013). If this is the case, the empty

Figure 2.6. The Taanach Cult Stand. Note the lions flanking the female figure in the first register, the sphynx figures flanking what may be the entry, and the representation of roof beams at the top. Drawing by the author.

---

the interpretation of the stand as Yahwistic in orientation. On the protective role of the naked female and her attendant animals on cult stands, see Darby 2014, 330–38.

space between the sphinx figures may represent the entrance to the shrine (rather than aniconically signaling YHWH's presence between "the cherubim" [*hakkərubîm*]). According to this understanding, the lions and the female figure on the bottom section would be guarding the entrance.

Brian R. Doak (2015, 129) contends that several observations support interpreting the stand as entirely devoted to a female deity. First, the clearest indications of the stand's referent are the bottom and third friezes, which depict a female deity anthropomorphically and as a tree. The other two friezes have the empty space—perhaps representing the entryway—and the horse underneath the sun disc. The horse was used in ancient Southwest Asia predominantly to represent Anat and Astarte, as noted by Keel and Uehlinger (1998, 160).[39] They also note that Early Iron Age terracotta figures predominantly represent female agents (160).[40] The multiple manifestations of the deity on the shrine may have been intended to increase the accessibility or potency of her agency. Many shrine models were likely too elaborate for widespread private use, but local cult installations carrying them could increase access to the agency of the (primarily female) deities they indexed for those living nearby. More basic models could have been utilized privately or by smaller social groups (Ziffer 2020).

In connection with female deities, we must consider that most vilified of cultic objects from the Hebrew Bible, the *'ašerah* (Sommer 2009, 44–49; Thomas 2017). The Hebrew term occurs forty times in the Hebrew Bible, sometimes in reference to the deity (1 Kgs 18:19), and sometimes in reference to a cultic object (2 Kgs 13:6; 17:10, 16). Keel and Uehlinger (1998, 229) have argued that worship of Asherah was waning by the Iron Age, which has led many scholars to prefer understanding most uses of *'ašerah* from Iron Age Israel and Judah to refer to the cultic object.[41] The use of the roots *'md* and *nṣb* (both roughly meaning "to stand")

---

[39] "It is much more likely that the striding horse is to be interpreted, in light of the Late Bronze and early Iron Age iconographic tradition … as an attribute animal of Anat-Astarte" (160). See also p. 141: "We encounter the *war horse* in the Late Bronze Age as an attribute animal upon which the warrior goddess Anat stands.… The horse appears as the animal on which the goddess rides on Iron Age IIA seal amulets.… But consistent with the tendency to avoid using anthropomorphic images, the attribute animal replaces the goddess altogether." On the relationship of Astarte and Asherah, see Anthonioz 2014.

[40] Darby (2014, 333) also notes that "almost every cult stand combines female figurines with zoomorphic images." The fifty-seven clay figurines and zoomorphic vessels discovered at Tel Reḥov lend further support to this observation. Almost half of the figures were anthropomorphic, and almost all of those were female. Ten of the twenty-nine zoomorphic figurines and vessels depicted equids (Mazar 2015, 38–39).

[41] Putthoff 2020, 126–28. Shmuel Aḥituv, Esther Eshel, and Ze'ev Meshel (2012, 131) note "Asherah's name had even vanished in Phoenicia in the 1st millennium BCE. It is not mentioned in the whole corpus of Phoenician inscriptions, not even as a theophoric element in personal names."

in connection with the installation of the cultic object suggests it was something erected (similar to JPFs and stelai), and the use of the roots *krt* ("to cut") and *śrp* ("to burn") in connection with their destruction (2 Kgs 18:4; 23:4) suggests the *'ašerah* was made of wood. A number of Israelite and Phoenician seals depicting sacred trees—in isolation or flanked by hybrid or other creatures, as in the Taanach cult stand and the illustration on Pithos A from Kuntillet 'Ajrud (Beck 2012, 143–56)—have been marshalled as evidence the *'ašerah* was a special tree or wooden pole of some kind (Keel and Uehlinger 1998, 233–46; cf. Hestrin 1987; Lewis 2020, 236–43).

Judahite inscriptions dating to the eighth century BCE from Khirbet el-Qôm and Kuntillet 'Ajrud bless others by, and attribute blessings to, YHWH and *l'šrth*, "to Asherah" (Finkelstein and Piasetzky 2008; Carmi and Segal 2012). In line 3 from the Khirbet el-Qôm inscription, Uriyahu writes, "Now from his enemies, to Asherah, deliver him" (*wmṣryh . l'šrth . hwš'lh*). Asherah is mentioned in multiple inscriptions from Kuntillet 'Ajrud (Aḥituv, Eshel, and Meshel 2012, 87–100, 105–7):

Kuntillet 'Ajrud, Inscription 4.1.1

1. *y]'rk. ymm. wyśb 'w*[...] *ytnw.l*[*y*]*hwh*[...] *tymn. wl'šrth*[
2.]. *hyṭb. yhwh. hty*[*mn. .*]*y. hyṭb. ym*[*m*

1. he will] lengthen their days and they will be filled [...] they will give to [Y]HWH[ ]of Teman and to Asherah[
2.] do good, YHWH of Te[man ...]make [their] days good

Kuntillet 'Ajrud, Inscription 3.9

1...] *lyhwh . htmn wl'šrth.* [...]   to YHWH of Teman and to Asherah

Kuntillet 'Ajrud, Inscription 3.6

5. *brktk. ly*
6. *hwh tmn*
7. *wl'šrth. yb*
8. *rk wyšmrk*

I have blessed you to Y-
HWH of Teman
and to Asherah. May he bl-[42]
ess you and protect you

---

[42] The verb here is singular, which is a datum that is sometimes marshalled in support of the interpretation of *'šrth* as a cultic object, but it may indicate nothing other than YHWH's priority (Lewis 2020, 240–43). Asherah may still be understood as a vehicle for YHWH's agency without being rendered a cultic object (cf. the discussion of the messenger of YHWH in chapter 5).

Kuntillet 'Ajrud, Inscription 3.1

1. *'mr. '[…]°°[…](m)[…]k. 'mr. lyhl(y). wlyw'śh. wl[…] brkt. 'tkm*
2. *lyhwh. šmrn. wl'šrth*

1. '[…]°°[…](M)[…]K said, "Speak to Yahel(i) and to Yô'aśa, and to[…] I have blessed you
2. to YHWH of Shomron and by Asherah

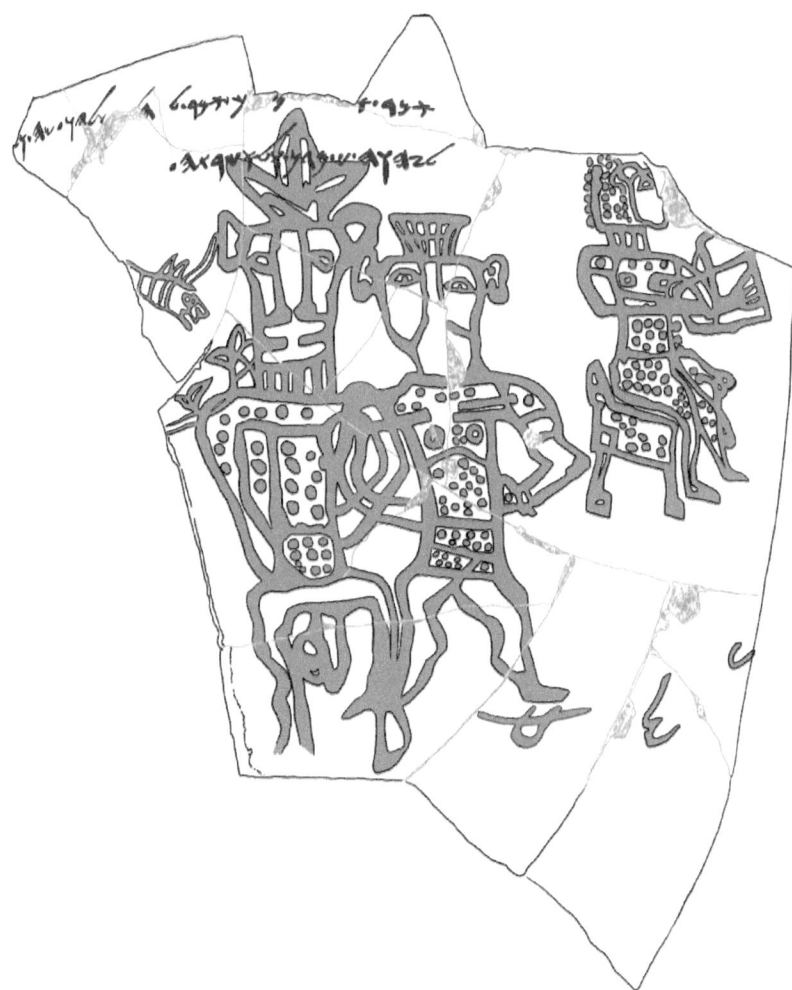

Figure 2.7. Pithos A from Kuntillet 'Ajrud, featuring Inscription 3.1 and drawings. Drawing by the author.

The drawings that appear under the inscription seem to depict male and female figures with overlapping or interlocking arms (with a female playing a stringed instrument off to the side). The features of these figures have been commonly associated with the Egyptian deity Bes, but some scholars have pointed out that the imagery associated with Bes was frequently appropriated by other deities. In Egypt, that imagery was used to represent Aha, Hayet, Soped, Tettetenu, Amon, Horus, Baal, and Reshef (Zevit 2001, 388). Outside of Egypt, Bes iconography seems to have been adapted as a more flexible and generic symbol for deity that commonly served apotropaic functions (Thomas 2016, 146–52).

It has become quite common to see the final *he* of *'šrth* interpreted as the third masculine singular pronominal suffix "his." Because that pronoun cannot appear attached to personal names, the argument goes, the term must be understood to refer to a cultic object (e.g., Emerton 1999; Sommer 2009, 44–49; Aḥituv, Eshel, and Meshel 2012, 130–32; cf. Stein 2019). The interpretation that predominated through the end of the twentieth century CE held that the sacred tree would have lost associations with the inactive female deity and would have been appropriated as a Yahwistic cult symbol. The inscriptions would then represent extra-biblical witnesses to the cultic objects decried in the Hebrew Bible. This would be an attractive example of a cult object channeling divine agency, but the situation is not so cut and dry. As Richard Hess has demonstrated, the epigraphic corpus consistently shows final *he* for the spelling of the deity's name (Hess 1996; Thomas 2017). The Hebrew Bible's spelling without final *he* is absent from the inscriptions, suggesting it may not be as simple as a pronoun.

A more helpful explanation may be that of Josef Tropper (2017), who sought to reconstruct the development of the pronunciation of the Tetragrammaton, YHWH, through Neo-Babylonian and Achaemenid period onomastic data. He notes that the divine name consistently ended in *-a* when it occurred in the final position of a name, but with *-ú* when occurring medially. This final *-a* he ultimately interprets as an absolutive case ending that was indicated in Hebrew with *he* functioning as a *mater lectionis*. This accounts for the biblical YHWH, and when this case ending is applied to *'šrh*, the existing *he* converts to *taw*, resulting in *'šrth*. If Tropper's reconstruction is accurate, all three inscriptions could refer to the female deity, whose worship was retained at least into the eighth century BCE in Judah.

CONCLUSION

This brief interrogation shows that the theoretical framework of communicable divine agency productively situates the material remains of ancient Israel and Judah within the broader conceptual and practical matrix of divine presencing through cultic media. While reflective reasoning regarding the nature and function of this agency was far more elaborate and institutionally supported in the larger and more complex nations surrounding Israel and Judah, that rationalizing was not necessary for the underlying conceptual frameworks to be operative. The sharing of a ritual meal with stelai, and other social interactions with the object, whether they were commissioned with complex rituals, a simple anointing, or perhaps without any ritual at all, would have facilitated the perception of divine presence for the majority of sympathetic participants. While the final section focused on the most explicit manifestations known from the worlds of Iron Age Israel and Judah, any degree of a deity's agency could potentially be facilitated through appropriate media, from a portion of its power or authority all the way up to the primary locus of the deity's own self.

The perception (perhaps rationalization) of clay/terracotta and of stone as particularly effective conduits for divine agency may help explain the ubiquity of divine images crafted from those materials during the early first millennium BCE. The abandonment of metal and other costlier materials and complex processes around the tenth century BCE was likely the result of market forces, which would have increased the salience of clay and stone as media for the production of divine images, as well as the perception of its suitability and effectiveness. The decreased threat of theft could also have contributed to this perception. As with JPFs, the data are limited that indicate the presencing function of shrine models and cult stands, but the presence of the latter in cultic installations, and in connection with figurines, points in the direction of divine presencing, and if shrine models did mobilize the deity for processions, that case is even stronger. This will have more relevance in the discussion of the ark of the covenant in chapter 5, but we now turn to the generic concept of deity in the Hebrew Bible.

3.
Deity in the Hebrew Bible

This chapter will interrogate the generic category of deity as preserved in the texts of the Hebrew Bible and in related inscriptions. This chapter will focus on the conceptual structures of generic deity, and the next chapter will move on to a parallel interrogation of YHWH as an instantiation of that generic concept (cf. Cornell 2020). Some additional methodological care is necessary in this chapter. Synthesizing the presentation of deity across all the texts of the Hebrew Bible will result in a largely artificial profile of deity that would never have been espoused by any single person living in the societies responsible for the relevant texts. The texts also privilege a small number of elite perspectives that are engaging with their community's past and with their own situational exigencies. There is, in addition, an unknown tangle of other diachronic (that is, occurring through time) and synchronic (that is, occurring at one time) influences.[1] Data are not available that allow us to fully unravel that tangle and entirely discount those perspectives, but with the aid of the theoretical framework developed in chapter 1 and some principles from cognitive linguistics, we can more carefully parse the data that are available and make progress bridging the gap between the texts and the lived experiences that contributed to their composition. This will get us a few significant steps closer to understanding ancient Southwest Asian conceptualizations of deity.

In doing that parsing in this chapter, I make two broad assumptions. First, I assume that elite perspectives about the nature and function of deity were not entirely decoupled from more widespread and less elite perspectives. There were important differences, to be sure, but the gravitational pull of intuitive reasoning

---

[1] We also have no living informants to interview, so there will be significant gaps in my ability to reproduce a representative sample of the entire spectrum of lived experiences that would have been brought to bear on the generation of meaning from the texts of the Hebrew Bible. As an example, the texts of the Bible are textual artifacts, which were not the primary media for communicating or thinking about deity anciently. It privileges the modern prioritization of text to ground the interrogation primarily in the written word, and particularly when the relationship to that written word was so distinct for ancient Israelites and Judahites, few of whom could access it directly.

about deity still would have been quite strong, and with an understanding of that intuitive foundation, those perspectives that appear to serve the specific structuring of power of those elite groups can be distinguished from other more representative perspectives. The second assumption is that the perspectives of elite groups will betray the perspectives of less elite groups (with varying degrees of accuracy) to the degree they engage in polemics against them. In other words, if biblical authors and editors polemicize a specific perspective regarding deity, or insist a problematic perspective was widespread among Israelites and Judahites, we can excavate from that rhetoric data regarding more widespread conceptualizations of deity.

A further note of caution, however: any attempt to discern the conceptualization of generic deity in the Hebrew Bible is complicated by the fact that the overwhelming majority of references to deity in the texts are to YHWH, the deity of Israel. While conceptualizations of YHWH in the earliest periods of their worship were more directly influenced by the features of more generic conceptualizations in circulation within other societies, by the time of the rise of the biblical texts, YHWH had developed, through generations of curation in competition with other nations and their deities, a more distinctive profile.[2] In an effort to mitigate the potential for inadvertently reading uniquely Yahwistic features into my reconstruction of the generic concept of deity, my primary data set for this chapter will be those texts from the Hebrew Bible and other inscriptions that refer (or most likely refer) specifically to deities other than YHWH (or to the abstract concept of divinity) (cf. Wardlaw 2008). There obviously remained a significant degree of overlap between conceptualizations of YHWH and those of other deities, and even where Yahwistic conceptualizations diverged into unique roles and features, the prototypical features of deity and divine agency will show themselves to have been remarkably resilient (Hayman 1990, 8; cf. Ben-Dov 2016). YHWH's divine profile did not escape the gravitational pull of prototypical features of generic deity, but rather remained firmly anchored to them.

Prototype theory was introduced briefly in the introduction, and it will continue to inform this chapter's engagement with conceptual categories, but in the next section I will also briefly introduce semantic profiles, bases, and domains, which will be more directly relevant to the conceptual structures that were evoked by the terms for deity. This will go a long way to reducing the influence of contemporary philosophical frameworks and scholarly assumptions in the construal of the data.

---

[2] In *The Early History of God*, Mark Smith (2002) referred to "convergence" and "differentiation," and in *God in Translation* (2008, 18), he refers to "the general shift from translatability to non-translatability." For a related discussion, see Dearman 2020.

SEMANTIC PROFILES, BASES, DOMAINS, AND MATRICES

Linguistic concepts do not function autonomously; they function in relation to other concepts within larger conceptual configurations. According to Ronald Langacker (1987, 183), "The semantic value of an expression … derives from the designation of a specific entity identified and characterized by its position within a larger configuration."[3] For example, one cannot understand the concept of a "radius" unless they understand the concept of a "circle." Figure 3.1 illustrates the relationship of these two terms. The concept "radius" is *profiled* against the conceptual *base* of the concept "circle."[4] Many semantic units have multiple and complicated conceptual bases, and many involve more than one profile. As an example, we may profile the concept of "aunt" against the kinship system illustrated in figure 3.2.[5] The parent/child, spouse, sibling, and male/female concepts are all required on at least the intuitive level for an adequate conceptualization of the prototypical sense.

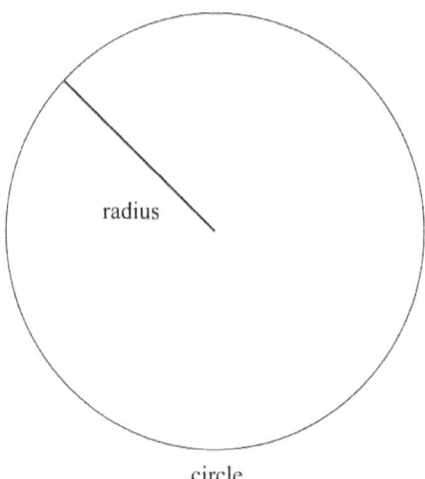

Figure 3.1. Illustration of "radius" being profiled against a circle.

---

[3] John Taylor argues a base is "the conceptual content that is inherently, intrinsically, and obligatorily invoked by the expression" (Taylor 2002, 195).
[4] The profile is not to be confused with an expression's referent (Taylor 2002, 194). The former is a conceptualization that inhabits a mental space, while the latter is an instantiation in the real world of that concept.
[5] This image is adapted from Langacker 2002, 15.

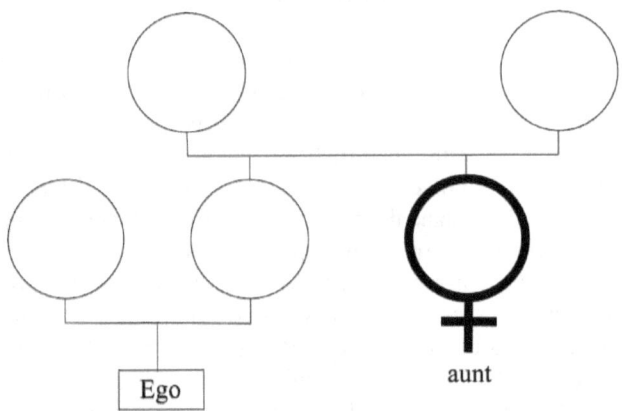

Figure 3.2. Illustration of "aunt" profiled against the kinship system.

A conceptual base is required for a basic understanding of a semantic expression, but there are other aspects of the broader conceptual backdrop against which an expression can be profiled for a fuller conceptualization. That backdrop is what cognitive linguists call a *domain*, and this term suggests a conceptual field within which there can be movement and differentiation. John Taylor (2002, 195) notes, "the distinction between base and domain is not always clear-cut. Essentially, the distinction has to do with how intrinsic the broader conceptualization is to the semantic unit, how immediately relevant it is, and to what extent aspects of the broader conceptualization are specifically elaborated." He provides the example of "thumbnail," which profiles against "thumb" as its base. "Thumb," in turn, profiles against "hand," which itself profiles against "arm," which profiles against "torso," or even "human body." It would be imprecise to say "thumb" profiles against "human body" as its base, though. Rather, human body constitutes the conceptual domain within which multiple profile/base relationships may operate, with or without direct reference to the former.[6]

Just as a domain may contain multiple different profiles and bases, most semantic expressions can be conceptualized against multiple domains, or a conceptual matrix. An example is the concept "mother." George Lakoff (1987a, 74) identifies five different domains that may be activated by the term in reference to a human:[7]

---

[6] For the conceptual domain for HUMAN BODY, see Langacker 1987, 147–54.
[7] He uses the term *model*, but the concept is the same as our term *domain* (cf. Taylor 2003, 87–90).

(1) Birth domain: "the person who gives birth is the *mother*."
(2) Genetic domain: "the female who contributes the genetic material is the *mother*."
(3) Nurturance domain: "the female adult who nurtures and raises a child is the *mother*."
(4) Marital domain: "the wife of the father is the *mother*."
(5) Genealogical domain: "the closest female ancestor is the *mother*."

In order to adequately understand the contextual uses of the term *mother*, we must be aware of these domains and how they may be activated in discourse. In the prototypical matrix associated with the concept mother, these domains all converge, with the birth domain generally prioritized. Any particular instantiation of the concept, however, may profile against any number of these domains. For instance, a *birth mother* might not raise her child or be married to the father, thus only activating domains (1), (2), and (5), with domain (1) prioritized. A *donor mother* does not give birth to her child and may only activate domain (2). A *foster mother* will not have given birth to the child or have contributed genetic material, activating only domains (3) and (4), with the former taking priority. In each case, the context or some qualifier will make it possible for listeners with adequate encyclopedic knowledge to identify the activated domains, hierarchize them, and generate an adequate meaning for the expression. Along with the fact that conceptual categories are not commonly formed with reference to boundaries, this dynamic is a primary contributor to the fuzziness of the boundaries of conceptual categories, including that of deity. A hearer, viewer, or reader who is not aware of these domains will not adequately understand when a less prototypical domain or configuration of domains is activated independently. In the same way, to adequately understand the concept of "deity" as it was deployed in the biblical literature, we must be able to distinguish the main domains that could be activated by the use of the term, as well as to understand the less prototypical configurations of those domains.

Positing a semantic base for the profile "deity" is more complex than that of "radius," but it allows us to set aside the artificial dichotomies inherent in reducing the category to necessary and sufficient features, and it gives us a foundation upon which to begin to more confidently reassemble the conceptual frameworks of deity and divine agency. Such a base is not the *essence* of deity—other concepts can share the same base—it is simply a conceptual foundation apart from which the profile cannot be adequately conceptualized. Once the domains and matrices that constitute the literary manifestations of deity are identified, we can examine their prioritization and hierarchization to better understand what aspects of deity served what rhetorical functions in what contexts. Beginning with prototypical features and then moving to the unique, unexpected, and innovative features allows us to better understand not only the core and contours of the concept, but its fuzzy and contested boundaries. Interrogating the contexts in which authors wrangled with those boundaries further clarifies the areas of contention and, when examined diachronically, the developmental trajectories of the concept. In this way, the universals of the structure and function of language can be used to fill in some of the sociomaterial gaps that have so frequently frustrated scholars and compelled us toward more presentistic assumptions and the imposition of anachronistic philosophical frameworks.

TERMS FOR DEITY IN THE HEBREW BIBLE

The three primary terms used to refer generically to deity across the Hebrew Bible are *'ĕlōhîm*,[8] *'ēl*,[9] and *'ĕlôha*.[10] The most basic form from which these derive is *'ēl*, and Marvin Pope's conclusion from over sixty years ago will be our point of departure regarding its etymology: "the problem is philologically insoluble on the basis of the materials now at our disposal. The word *ilu*, *'ēl* is simply a primitive noun and as such cannot be further analyzed" (Pope 1955, 19).[11] These terms were lexicalized well before the isolation of Hebrew as a discrete language and their textualization in the traditions that would become the Hebrew Bible (cf. Sanders 2010, 103–55).

All three terms are used primarily with an appellative sense, which means they function as common nouns applicable to members of a given class. This can include a generic use (e.g., a mother, a prophet) or a titular sense (e.g., Mother, the Prophet). While YHWH is by far the most common referent of all three terms, and particularly when the titular sense is activated, the continued salience of the generic sense is demonstrated by the regular use of *'ĕlōhîm* in reference to YHWH with pronominal suffices (984 occurrences, or 38 percent of all occurrences).[12] All three terms are also used in roughly synonymous ways in reference to the generic concept of deity (Burnett 2001, 54–57). For instance: *'ĕlōhê nēkar*, "foreign deities" (Deut 31:16; Josh 24:20; Jer 5:19); *'ēl nēkār*, "a foreign deity" (Deut 32:12; Mal 2:11; Ps 81:10); *'ĕlôha nēkār*, "a foreign deity" (Dan 11:39); *'ĕlōhîm 'ăḥērîm*, "other deities" (Exod 20:3; Deut 5:7); *'ēl 'aḥēr*, "another deity" (Exod 34:14); *lō' 'ĕlōhîm*, "not deity" (Hos 8:6); *lō'-'ēl*, "not deity" (Deut 32:21;

---

[8] About 2,600 occurrences (227 not in reference to YHWH, or 8.7 percent).
[9] 237 occurrences (thirty-one not in reference to YHWH, or 13 percent).
[10] Fifty-eight occurrences (eight not in reference to YHWH, or 13.7 percent).
[11] Burnett 2001, 2, n. 4; Wardlaw 2008, 92, n. 4; cf. Ringgren 1974, 273; Zimmermann 1962.
[12] Fifty-seven of those occurrences refer to deities other than YHWH. *'Ēl* occurs twelve times with a pronominal suffix, or in roughly 5 percent of occurrences. Nine occurrences are in the Psalms, and the only use in reference to a deity other than YHWH is in the exilic Isa 44:17 (*'ēlî*). *'Ĕlôha* occurs once with a pronominal suffix in reference to generic deity (*'ĕlôhô*, Hab 1:11).

Isa 31:3).¹³ Note, however, that many of the parallel constructions employing *'ēl* and *'ĕlôha* in ways that suggest interchangeability with *'ĕlōhîm* occur primarily in texts dating to the Babylonian exile and later, which suggests either their semantic harmonization in later periods, or a growing concern for lexical variation in the relevant constructions.¹⁴ In the earlier periods, *'ĕlōhîm* is almost always the noun of choice, and particularly when used with a proper noun.¹⁵ The frequent references to "other deities," "foreign deities," "their deities," and "deity of GN," as well as *'ēl/'ĕlōhê (ha) 'ĕlōhîm*, "deity of deities" (Deut 10:17; Josh 22:22; Ps 84:8; 136:2) demonstrate that YHWH was conceptualized as one member of a generic class that had many other members. I would suggest the most precise construal of this semantic field in English is a spectrum from concrete to abstract: Deity ↔ deity ↔ divinity. Any point along this spectrum may be profiled by a given contextual use of the relevant terms.

Much has been made of the morphologically plural form of *'ĕlōhîm* used with singular referents, including YHWH (Gen 1:1; 1 Kgs 11:33; 18:27).¹⁶ The most common explanation has for some time been the notion of a "plural of majesty," which views the plural as honorific or intensifying. ¹⁷ Three observations complicate that explanation, however: (1) the plural *'ĕlōhîm* appears in pejorative references to individual foreign deities, ¹⁸ (2) *'ēl* and *'ĕlōhîm* are used

---

¹³ Deut 32:17 is an interesting case. It refers to worship of *šēdîm* (*shaddays* or perhaps "demons") as *lō' 'ĕlôha*. This is frequently translated as "not deity," but the appositional clause that immediately follows refer to them as *'ĕlōhîm lō' yədā'ûm*, "deities they did not know." In agreement with Michael Heiser (2008b), I would argue *'ĕlōhê* there is to be understood in the titular sense: "they sacrificed to *shaddays*, not to the Deity."
¹⁴ For example, all three terms occur with the same general sense in Dan 11:36–38.
¹⁵ There are eighteen occurrences of the plural "deities of [PROPER NOUN]," and an additional seven occurrences of the singular "deity of [PROPER NOUN]," and all utilize *'ĕlōhîm*. "Deity of Israel" (*'ĕlōhê yiśrā'ēl*) occurs 196 times, with the highest frequency of occurrence in Ezra (1.68 times per 1,000 words), Jeremiah (1.49 times per 1,000 words), and 2 Chronicles (1.03 times per 1,000 words). There are no occurrences in Leviticus or Deuteronomy.
¹⁶ Sometimes plural verbs occur alongside what appear to be singular referents. Discussing Exod 22:8–9, David Wright (2009, 256, n. 78) calls this an "emphatic formulation," citing in addition, Gen 20:13; 31:53; 35:7; Josh 24:19; 2 Sam 7:23. Multiple other Semitic languages attest to the morphologically plural use of words for "god" with singular referents. Extensive coverage is found in Burnett 2001, 7–53.
¹⁷ Gesenius 1910, 124g; Ember 1905; Waltke and O'Connor 1990, 7.4.3a–f; Joüon and Muraoka 2006, §136d; Byrne 2011, 28; Beckman 2013, 3.145–46.
¹⁸ For example, 1 Kgs 11:33; 2 Kgs 1:2–3, 6, 16. This demonstrably non-honorific usage of the "plural of majesty" is found in other Semitic literature as well. For instance, a "plural of majesty" in the Amarna correspondences is particularly undermined by the occurrence of the morphologically plural IR.MEŠ ("servant") with a singular referent in EA 47:11. It

interchangeably in many places (e.g., Exod 20:3 // 34:14; Deut 32:21 // Hos 8:6; Ezek 28:2 // 9), and (3) no heightened sense of honor or majesty is demonstrable in any occurrence of *'ĕlōhîm*.[19] The difference seems to be one of style, not sense (Burnett 2001, 24).

The most compelling explanation of this phenomenon comes from Joel Burnett (2001, 7–53), who argues that the most common use of *'ĕlōhîm* is as a "concretized abstract plural." That is, the abstract plural *'ĕlōhîm* had the sense of "divinity," but became concretized in reference to actual manifestations of divinity, and over time came to mean "deity."[20] This final sense is synonymous with the primary senses of singular *'ēl* and *'ĕlôha*, but as Burnett notes (2001, 57–60), an abstract nuance was preserved for *'ĕlōhîm* and is evoked in some places. For instance, in 1 Kgs 11:33 the masculine plural *'ĕlōhîm* appears in reference to a single feminine deity. The abstract sense of "deity" is gender neutral, while nonabstract "god" is masculine. While Biblical Hebrew does not explicitly attest to a word for "goddess"—leaving the author little choice—the masculine plural *'lm* in reference to singular feminine deities is also found in Phoenician, which does have a word for "goddess" (*'lt*) (Burnett 2001, 27). This is not definitive proof of the same usage in Hebrew, but it is suggestive, and it demonstrates the same construction in a cognate language that is not accounted for by the plural of majesty.

This theory also makes better sense of the use of *'ĕlōhîm* as the *nomen rectum* in construct phrases. Rather than conjuring up a superlative sense for the term, for instance, we may understand it as the adjectival genitive. Thus *ḥerdat 'ĕlōhîm* (1 Sam 14:15) is not "a very great panic" (NRSV), but "divine panic," or a panic caused by or associated with divine activity (Burnett 2001, 57–59; cf. Joüon and Muraoka 2006, §141*n*). Similarly, *bənê 'ĕlōhîm*, traditionally translated "sons of God" (Gen 6:2, 4; Job 1:6; 2:1; 38:7), is not necessarily a reference to the offspring of the high deity, but perhaps members of the class of deity, and could therefore

---

is not "honorific," or "majestic," it just highlights whatever abstract semantic qualities the word evokes. In other words, it derives directly from the abstract plural (this is Gesenius' explanation of the plural of majesty [1910, §124g]).

[19] The notion of intensification seems to sit at the root of most arguments for the plural of majesty (Waltke and O'Connor 1990, §7.4.3a–b; Wardlaw 2008, 104), with contradictory data dismissed as "exceptions" (Waltke and O'Connor 1990, §7.4.3b n. 16).

[20] In essence, the abstract sense expressed the salient abstract qualities associated with the noun. Concretization took place through the firm and repeated association of those qualities with some entity. Burnett (2001, 22) cites as another example of a concretized abstract plural the word *bətûlîm* (Deut 22:15), meaning "evidences of virginity," rather than the abstract "virginity."

be glossed as "deities."[21] This reading is supported by the grammatically parallel use of *bənôt hā'ādām*, "daughters of the human," or "women," in Gen 6:2. This reading harmonizes with the variant construction *bənê 'ēlîm*, "deities," in Pss 29:1 and 89:7.[22]

The primary sense of *'ĕlōhîm*, *'ēl*, and *'ĕlōha* is thus the appellative sense "deity," with *'ĕlōhîm* carrying an additional abstract sense of "divinity" that could also be used in the adjectival genitive. This does not tell us much about what was understood by the term "deity," though. To begin to fill in this picture, we may add the observation that *'ĕlōhîm* is used not only in reference to the dead, but also to cultic objects (e.g., Gen 31:30; Exod 32:31; Judg 18:24; Isa 44:15).[23] While the use of terms for deity in reference to cultic objects was frequently sarcastic or intentionally put in the mouths of foreign or less pious individuals, there are multiple references to cultic objects as *'ĕlōhîm* without any hint of polemic or irony.[24] We cannot so easily dismiss this usage. The term was also occasionally used in reference to humans with special authority or relationships with deity, as in the vocative references to the king *'ĕlōhîm* in Ps 45:7–8, or in Exod 7:1 (*nətattîkā 'ĕlōhîm ləpar'ōh*, "I have made you a deity to Pharaoh"), Isa 9:5 (*šəmô pele' yô'ēṣ 'ēl gibôr*, "his name will be called Counselor of Wonder, Mighty Deity"), and Exod 4:16 (*wə'attâ tihyeh-lô lē'lōhîm*, "and you will be to him a deity").[25] Lest the *lamed* prefix in the final example be interpreted to be qualifying the divinity attributed to Moses (i.e., "you will be *like* a deity"; Wardlaw 2008, 108), note the *lamed* prefix in YHWH's promise to Israel to be, *ləkā lē'lōhîm*, "to you a deity" (Gen 17:7; Deut 26:17; 29:12).

This suggests deity was fundamentally understood as a relational designation and not an ontological one. To the degree they performed the right functions and roles, the designation "deity" could extend to include the dead, humans, and even cultic objects. The ability to perform certain functions humans cannot normally perform is absolutely an aspect of that designation, but there is no reason that such

---

[21] By analogy with, for example, *bənê hannəbî'îm*, "children of the prophets" or "prophets" (1 Kgs 20:35), or *ben-'ādām*, "child of a human" or "human" (Ezek 8:5).

[22] It should be noted that *bənê 'elyôn*, "children of Elyon," in Ps 82:6 suggests a change in the sense of the offspring of the high deity, possibly under the influence of the broader Semitic tradition of the divine council inhabited by the offspring of El (Mullen Jr. 1980; Handy 1994; Smith 2001, 54–66). This text is quite late, however (see McClellan 2018).

[23] In light of this, the references in Exod 21:2–6 and 22:7–8 to appearing before *ha'ĕlōhîm* may have reference to stelai located at city gates or by the entry to a house. While these references could be sarcastic in the exilic literature, they reflect the disputed boundaries of the concept. The prototype effects of "deity" will be discussed further below.

[24] For instance, Gen 35:2, 4 have Jacob and the narration itself refer to cultic objects as *'ĕlōhê hannēkar*, "foreign deities."

[25] See Lewis 2020, 505–7 for a discussion of these passages that borrows Irene Winter's (2008, 88) notion of kings being "infused by the divine."

abilities must be rooted in a unique ontology, particularly when there is no indication that ontology was a concept with any currency in Iron Age Israel or Judah. Those abilities, when they were attributed to humans, seem to have been rooted, rather, in special relationships to deity or in special dispensations from deity. We do no justice to the literature to impose on the texts our own theologically and philosophically driven prescriptiveness regarding what the word "deity" is allowed to mean. A clearer understanding of how these entities fit into the conceptual category of deity for ancient Israel and Judah demands a careful interrogation of the conceptual structures that constituted and shaped the category, and it is to that interrogation that I now turn.

THE CONCEPTUAL STRUCTURES OF DEITY

In this section I will propose a semantic base for deity and identify the main conceptual domains and profiles that would have been activated in the minds of hearers/readers/viewers when the concept of deity was evoked. Identifying these structures in a sense separates out the different interpretive lenses through which deity was conceptualized, allowing a more careful interrogation of the category and its constituent elements. Because the conceptual structures discussed in this section will be among the most broadly representative of deity, they stretch across the full chronological range of the Hebrew Bible, but I will discuss dating and change where relevant.

The discussion to this point provides a much broader semantic range for the concept of deity than is generally recognized by scholars, but as we saw above with "mother," not every occurrence of the word evoked that entire semantic range. Different semantic fields within it would have had different degrees of salience depending on the region, the time period, and the contexts of the usage. Those contexts signaled to the hearer/reader/viewer which profiles were activated, which semantic domains were to be prioritized, and how they were to be configured. That process must build on a conceptual base, however, and I suggest that base derived from the intuitive frameworks outlined in the first chapter. That chapter argued that the early Israelites and Judahites, including those involved in the composition, editing, and transmission of the biblical texts, conceptualized deity according to the intuitive frameworks that are still operative in the conceptualization of deity today. As a result, I propose UNSEEN AGENCY as the semantic base for deity in the Hebrew Bible.[26]

---

[26] I use small caps to identify bases and domains and scare quotes to identify profiles.

THE CONCEPTUAL DOMAINS AND PROFILES OF DEITY

DEITY. I identify both a domain in reference to the abstract and generic notion of deity, as well as a profile in reference to a concrete instantiation of that notion: a "deity." YHWH was the most common referent for both in the Hebrew Bible, and particularly when terms for deity were used in the titular sense. However, because there were other appellative senses very closely related to the titular sense, there would naturally have been fuzzy usage that could have been understood as referring either to YHWH or to unnamed instantiations. One example is Exod 22:27a: *'ĕlōhîm lō' təqalēl*, which NRSV renders, "You shall not revile God." The KJV, on the other hand, renders, "Thou shalt not revile the gods." Burnett (2001, 60–61) renders, "You shall not revile a deity." While a hearer/reader close to the text's composition and rhetorical context might have an easier time identifying the referent, our expertise and experience is not remotely native enough to be able to arrive at a firm conclusion with the available contextual clues.

This fuzziness would have provided for some flexibility as pantheons were being renegotiated, allowing for earlier references to deities other than YHWH, to humans, or to cultic objects to be accommodated to an increasingly narrowed Yahwistic worldview. All that would have been required for those engaged in renegotiating the pantheon was the conventionalization of a Yahwistic or even a humanistic interpretation of such passages (e.g., Gen 6:2, 4; Exod 22:7–8; Ps 82). This could happen through discourse,[27] through interpolation,[28] or through the production of parallel or allusive traditions that more explicitly identify a reference to deity as YHWH or as something other than a deity.[29] This also allowed authors to curate the boundaries of the category and rhetorically deny that entities commonly referred to as deities actually qualified as deities. The use of substitutions in order to avoid using terms for deity became conventional for many authors, as well (cf. Dick 1999; Smith 2008).

PATRONAGE. Note that roughly half of all the occurrences of terms for deity occur in the construct, mostly marking a genitive relationship with individuals, groups, or territories, as in the following: "deities of the peoples/nations" (*ĕlōhê hā'ammîm/haggôyim*, Deut 6:14; 29:17; 2 Kgs 18:33; Ps 96:5); "foreign deities"

---

[27] This would be difficult to identify, but later traditions of vocalization reflected in *qere* variants or in Septuagint renderings might indicate such discursive re-readings of a passage.

[28] For example, YHWH is entirely absent from Gen 14:19–22 in the earliest Septuagint manuscripts but is added to verse 22 by the time of MT, likely to more directly identify El Elyon as YHWH. The interpolation of the "messenger" (*mal'āk*) is another option that will be discussed in more detail in chapter 6.

[29] Exod 6:3 strikes me as the most explicit example of this.

(*'ĕlōhê* [*han*]*nēkar*, Gen 35:2, 4);[30] "Baal Zebub, the deity of Ekron" (*baʿal zəbûb ĕlōhê ʿeqrôn*, 2 Kgs 1:2, 3, 6, 16); "Let the deity of Abraham and the deity of Nehor judge between us" (*ĕlōhê ʾabrāhām wēʾlōhê nāḥôr yišpəṭû bênênû*, Gen 31:53).[31] Except for certain references to cult objects (e.g., Gen 31:30), the genitive here does not indicate possession, but rather patronage, as demonstrated in Judg 11:24: "Shouldn't you take possession [*tîrāš*] of what your deity Chemosh conquers for you [*yôrîšəkā*]? Likewise, we will take possession [*nîrāš*] of all that our deity YHWH conquers [*hôrîš YHWH*] before us."[32]

This is the PATRONAGE domain, or the notion that deities were sovereign over specific social or geographical divisions, which reflects the fundamental prosocial function of divine agents. This is widespread in ancient Southwest Asian discourse about deity.[33] Parallel references to "your deity" and "our deity" in the Hebrew Bible suggest the underlying patron/client relationship was embedded in the generic understanding of deity.[34] Mark Smith (2008) uses the term "translatability" to refer to this trans-cultural sharing of superordinate conceptualizations of the nature and function of deity.[35] The fact that almost half of occurrences of words for deity are found within constructions that indicate such relationships demonstrates that the PATRONAGE domain is widespread and should be considered one of the prototypical features of deity in the Hebrew Bible. The prototypes of deity were patrons over peoples and lands.

Of course, there was no single conceptualization of patronage. The specific nature of the relationship was construed according to salient social frameworks and a society's mnemohistory. Where deceased kin may have been understood to have purview over a smaller kinship unit (as assumed of premonarchical periods,

---

[30] Note these passages refer to cultic objects. They are not owned by foreign peoples, rather they index deities understood to be patrons of foreign nations.

[31] While the first part of this passage refers to YHWH, the translatability of the ability of the two different deities to judge between Jacob and Laban displays the generic conceptualization of deity underlying the passage. The same is true of Judg 11:24.

[32] Mark Smith (2008, 102–3 and n. 36) suggests that while Judges and Kings are traditionally characterized as "Deuteronomistic," this example and others that demonstrate translatability in discourse about deity "may be reasonably situated largely in the monarchic period."

[33] See *KAI* 14.19; *KAI* 4.4, 7; *KAI* 222 B.5–6; *ANET* 534–35.

[34] Thus, the Israelite king Ahaziah instructs his messengers in 2 Kgs 1 to enquire of Baal Zebub in Ekron regarding injuries he sustained. Elijah's confrontation with the king tacitly acknowledges the parallelism of the two deities' roles, since Elijah rhetorically asks if he realizes there's a deity in Israel (2 Kgs 1:3; cf. Smith 2008, 114–16).

[35] While there is much that was shared, the biblical authors also sometimes used distinct language and frameworks when representing non-Israelites' discourse about the patronage of deities. This was in the service of the (usually polemical) rhetorical purposes of the author. See, for instance, in 1 Kgs 20:23, 28 (Rendsburg 2013, 1.903–4).

for instance), that patronage could be construed according to a specific conceptualization of kin, such as—in patriarchal societies—the patriarchal household (Smith 2001, 54–66). In such situations, the governing profile may be "father," "patriarch," and/or "ancestor." In the patriarchal tradition, reflected primarily in Genesis, a similar relationship was established by covenant with Abraham (Gen 12:1–3; 17:1–14; 22:15–18) and affirmed by the males of later generations through circumcision. These texts reflect a specific framing of social circumstances that served certain rhetorical goals. In the exodus tradition, on the other hand, the covenant was established with the people of Israel through Moses (Exod 20:1–23:19) and affirmed through obedience to the Law of Moses. Conceptualizations of divine patronage were cumulative as they accreted to the growing authoritative textual traditions. Thus, in Exod 3:6, editors integrate the two traditions (or affirm that integration) by identifying YHWH at the opening of the exodus tradition as "the deity of your father [ĕlōhê 'ābîkā], the deity of Abraham, the deity of Isaac, the deity of Jacob" (Dozeman 2006, Schmid 2010).

A larger nation would likely construe patronage according to whatever frameworks for authority were most salient among elites, such as the KINGSHIP domain (Handy 1994). In such cases, the profile "king" obtains. The frequent use of the word "lord, master" ('ădōnāy), in reference to deities (particularly YHWH) and the root 'bd, "to serve," in reference to worship also evokes the SLAVERY domain (Bridge 2013), activating the "master" profile (Exod 4:10; Deut 3:24; 10:12, 20; Josh 5:14). In the case of textual conflation and change, as in the Hebrew Bible, different conceptualizations could be held in tension, achieving salience in different contexts or among different segments of the society. In the Neo-Babylonian and Achaemenid phases of Deuteronomy, for instance, Assyrian treaty language was combined with the Abrahamic covenant, the Covenant Code, and the concept of "devoted love" in the construction of a more complex framework for Israel's patron/client relationship with YHWH. This framework included a "suzerain" profile (Deut 13:6–11; 17:14–20; cf. Judg 2:1–2)[36] and also embedded the husband/wife metaphor, facilitating a more salient "husband" profile (see Isa 54:5; Ezek 6:8–14; Hos 2:1–20).[37]

A related but slightly more specialized domain that occurs in some instances is that of NATIONAL DEITY, which reflected the superordinate notion of a patron deity over each nation or people of the earth and their relationships to each other (Block 2000). This framework is put on clearest display in Deut 4:19 and 32:8–9:

---

[36] A suzerain is most commonly conceptualized as a strong sovereign state that exercises some manner of control over the foreign policy of a weaker internally autonomous state that usually pays tribute and offers military aid.

[37] On "devoted love," see MacDonald 2003, 97–123. For a summary of the influence of the Covenant Code and Assyrian treaty formulae, see Levinson and Stackert 2012.

Deuteronomy 4:19

so that you wouldn't be compelled, when you lift up your eyes to the heavens and see the sun and the moon and the stars—all the host of the heavens—to bow down to them and to serve those whom your deity YHWH distributed (*ḥālaq*) to all the peoples under the whole heavens.

Deuteronomy 32:8–9

When the Highest apportioned (*bəhanḥēl ʿelyôn*) the nations, when he divided the children of Adam, he set up the boundaries of the peoples according to the number of the deities; and YHWH's portion (*ḥēleq*) was his people—Jacob was the allotment of his inheritance (*ḥebel naḥălātô*).

Deuteronomy 4:19 is likely the later of the two texts, and it reinterprets Deut 32:8–9 by putting YHWH in the position of distributing the deities to the nations, rather than Elyon distributing the nations to YHWH and the other deities. The earlier text understands YHWH's purview to be limited to the nation of Israel—a preexilic concept reflected in multiple passages[38]—and it distinguishes the high deity from YHWH, but both reflect divine patronage over each nation (Olyan 2018). Daniel 10:13–21 reflects a second century BCE iteration of this conceptualization of divine patronage. The text refers to "princes" (*śārîm*) of Israel, Persia, and Greece, framing these "princes" as angelic figures who battle on behalf of their client nations.[39]

Such battling evokes the related DIVINE WAR domain and the associated "warrior" profile (Miller 1973; Kang 1989), both of which extend from the earliest to the latest biblical texts.[40] An example of its activation that includes a deity other than YHWH is found in 2 Kgs 3, which describes an Israelite/Judahite/Edomite coalition against Moab. YHWH promised to deliver Moab into the coalition's hands (vv. 18–19), and it is successful until it reaches the king at Kir-hareseth. Before the coalition is able to breach the city wall, the king of Moab offers his son

---

[38] In addition to Deut 32:8–9, see 1 Sam 26:19; 2 Kgs 3:27; 5:15–17.

[39] The chief angel is called Michael, who is an angelic being in the literature contemporary with Daniel (1 En 20; 89.55–90.19; Jub. 10.22–23; Sir 17:17; T. Naph. 8–10; 4Q403 1.i:1–29). On the development of an angelic interpretation of patron deities in the Greco-Roman period, see Hannah 2007; cf. Smith 2008, 201–2.

[40] See Judg 11:24 above, but also 2 Kgs 19:10, 12, in which the Assyrian king Sennacherib's chief eunuch, Rabshakeh, taunts Hezekiah by appealing to the translatability of the notion of the divine warrior patron: "Do not let your deity on whom you rely deceive you by promising that Jerusalem will not be given into the hand of the king of Assyria," and "Have the deities of the nations delivered them, the nations that my predecessors destroyed?" For the case that Rabshakeh was a Judahite, see Levin 2015.

as a burnt offering, catalyzing a *qeṣep gādôl*, "great fury," that causes Israel to withdraw.⁴¹ In light of the consistent use of *qeṣep* in reference to divine fury—apart from its generic use in two Persian period prose couplets—the text is most reasonably interpreted to be indicating (rather reticently) that the sacrifice successfully invoked the intervention of the Moabite patron deity Chemosh, which forced the retreat of the Israelite forces (Burns 1990; Smith 2008, 116–18; Stark 2011, 91–92).

ACCESS TO STRATEGIC INFORMATION. Another transcultural feature of the NATIONAL DEITY domain highlighted in the episode in 2 Kgs 3 relates directly to one of the central prosocial functions of deity. In that episode it is linked to YHWH, but this domain is ubiquitous around ancient Southwest Asia and in the Hebrew Bible in relation to other deities, including cultic objects and the dead. After initial setbacks, the Judahite king Jehoshaphat asks if a prophet is around through whom they might seek YHWH's direction. A servant of the Israelite king Jehoram directs them to Elisha, who reluctantly inquires of YHWH and then promises them total victory. This evokes the ACCESS TO STRATEGIC INFORMATION domain. Humans operate with limited access within this conceptual domain, but because full-access is central to the prosocial functioning of deities, the "full-access strategic agent" profile is prototypical of deity in the Hebrew Bible.

The most explicit example involving a deity other than YHWH is that of Saul's interaction with the deceased Samuel in 1 Sam 28. As with 2 Kgs 3, the concern was to determine strategy related to warfare (cf. 2 Sam 2:1; Jer 21:1–7), but this was not the only reason full-access strategic agents were consulted. They were also sought after for help judging difficult legal cases (Num 5:11–31), for determining succession of leadership (Num 27:18–21; 1 Sam 10:20–22), for resolving illnesses (2 Kgs 1:2), and for numerous other reasons not clearly reflected in the Hebrew Bible. A variety of tools were available to facilitate divination, including the Urim and Thummim (Num 27:21; Deut 33:8–10; 1 Sam 14:41), the ephod (1 Sam 23:9–10; Judg 17:5), lots (Lev 16:7–8), teraphim (Ezek 21:26; Zech 10:2), and other cultic items.⁴² In the broader world of ancient Southwest Asia, the natural world was saturated with clues about strategic information, and accessing that information was primarily a matter of adequate education in the significance of dreams, the configuration of the stars, the shape

---

⁴¹ Some suggest this terminology indicates a peaceful departure, but the verse employs in conjunction with each other the same two verbs used to refer to Sennacherib's retreat in 2 Kgs 19:36 after the messenger of YHWH decimated his troops.

⁴² See, for instance, the story of Micah in Judg 17 and 18. Micah makes an ephod and teraphim and has a hoard of silver made into a pair of divine images by a silversmith. These are used to facilitate access to strategic information, but are later stolen. When Micah tracks down the thieves, he calls after them, accusing them of stealing, "my deities which I made [*ĕlōhay 'ăšer-'āśîtî*]" (Judg 18:24).

of clouds and livers, the flight of birds, and numerous other phenomena (Seow and Ritner 2003; Nissinen 2004; Beerden 2013).[43]

SOCIAL MONITORING AND PUNISHMENT. Patronage and full access to strategic information also would have cued a hearer/reader to the SOCIAL MONITORING domain (one of the fundamental prosocial functions of deity), which would also be construed according to common conceptual frameworks. "Judge" was a common profile associated with deity in the Hebrew Bible, which was activated most clearly when the root špṭ ("to judge") occurred in some way in reference to a deity's activities (e.g., Gen 18:25; Isa 2:4; 11:4; Ezek 7:8). This could represent a range of ideas about judgment and the conventions associated with them that frequently bled into other notions of authority and governance. For instance, špṭ is used in some texts to refer to the activity of kings, prophets, and even high priests (1 Sam 4:18; 7:16–17), suggesting it was associated somewhat generically with authority, as in 1 Sam 8:5: "give us a king to judge us [ləšāpṭēnû] like all the nations." The deity could even be cast as prosecutor or plaintiff, and particularly in the rîb (roughly, "lawsuit") type-scene (Nielsen 1978, de Roche 1983).

Related to social monitoring is punishment, which was most commonly reflected in the judgments against Israel and the nations for their disobedience and iniquity. Because of the Yahwistic orientation of the vast majority of the biblical literature, punishment is generally exercised *on* the deities of the nations, rather than exercised *by* them. A non-Yahwistic example from the cognate literature, however, is found in the Mesha Stele, which asserts in lines 5–6 that the king of Israel was able to oppress Moab because "Chemosh was angry with his land" (y'np ḳmš b'rṣh).[44] The Hebrew Bible reflects the same perspective in several locations where YHWH allows foreign powers to oppress Israel because of their iniquity or cultic infidelity. In fact, 2 Kgs 17:18 insists that the fall of the Northern Kingdom was the work of YHWH: "YHWH was very angry [wayyit'anap YHWH mə'ōd] with Israel and removed them [waysirēm] from his sight." This reflectively employs the SOCIAL MONITORING and PUNISHMENT domains to rationalize another nation's victory over Israel without acknowledging the failure of YHWH

---

[43] Necromancy may have been the most accessible, natural, and ubiquitous form of divination available to Israelites and Judahites. Threats to YHWH's monopoly on the "full-access strategic agent" profile, however, were a concern for later cultic authorities (cf. Deut 18:13). As a result, many of these channels and means for divination were portrayed in later periods as outlawed in monarchic Israel and Judah, with access to this divine agency rhetorically restricted to an authorized school of Yahwistic prophets (Schmitt 2008; Huffmon 2012). Although these prophets still utilized some of the tools mentioned above, unauthorized, foreign, and non-Yahwistic forms of divination were literarily condemned, particularly if involving the deceased (Exod 22:17; Lev 19:26; 20:6, 27; Deut 18:9–14; 1 Sam 28:3–25; cf. Num 23:23; cf. Stökl and Carvalho 2013; Hamori 2015).

[44] For the text of the Mesha inscription, see Jackson and Dearman 1989.

to fulfill their duties as patron deity and as warrior by protecting their people. Later authors would repeatedly and rhetorically invoke this domain of FAILURE TO ACT in attempting to compel the deity to ease the suffering they felt was unmerited.

DIVINE COUNCIL. The NATIONAL DEITY and SOCIAL MONITORING domains could also be activated within the broader domain of the DIVINE COUNCIL, which represented another one of the projections of human institutions onto the divine realm (Fleming 1989; Kee 2007; White 2014). Profiles operative within the DIVINE COUNCIL domain, depending on the context, include "high deity," "patriarchal deity," "second tier deity," and in later periods, "prophet." The "warrior" and "judge" profiles were salient within this domain in the cognate literature, but the latter primarily obtains in the Hebrew Bible, and specifically in reference to YHWH. The other deities of the divine council could be called upon as witnesses within legal proceedings, however, but only oblique references to such traditions appear to have escaped the blade of editors of the Hebrew Bible who were carefully curating the category of divinity (Amos 3:13 may be an example; Bokovoy 2008). One of the overarching functions of the divine council was to oversee cosmic order and social justice (Miller 1987). The manifestations of this conceptual domain in the Hebrew Bible show very close connections with the comparative literature, and particularly that of Ugarit, but resonances with Mesopotamia are also manifested in iterations from the Babylonian and later periods (cf. Lenzi 2008).

INCOMPARABILITY. A conceptual domain frequently asserted for the patron deities of many nations in Southwest Asia was INCOMPARABILITY. This was the rhetorical assertion that a given deity was so authoritative, transcendent, or prototypical (Singletary 2021), that other deities could not compare to them (Labuschagne 1966; Ready 2012). This rhetoric commonly extended to asserting the deity's military dominance or, in the case of deities associated with creative acts, their preexistence before all other deities and the creation of all things (including the other deities). While the Hebrew Bible never asserts the incomparability of deities other than YHWH, it occurs frequently enough in other societies that we are safe identifying it as common to the Southwest Asian concept of deity. For instance, an Akkadian hymn to the moon deity Sin began, "O Lord, chief of the gods, who alone is exalted on earth and in heaven" (Rogers 1912, 141). At Ugarit, Baal was commonly exalted in this manner (*KTU* 1.3.v.32–33): "Our king is Mightiest Baal, our ruler, / with none above him [*'in.d'lnh*]" (Smith 1994, 327). Even more elaborately, "The Great Cairo Hymn of Praise to Amun-Re" described Amun-Re as "Unique One, like whom among the gods?," "Sole One, who made all that exists, One, alone, who made that which is," and "Father of the fathers of all the gods, Who suspended heaven, who laid down the ground. Who made what exists, who created that which is" (*COS* 1.25.i, iii). The rhetoric of incomparability could be directed by the same text or the same authors at multiple different deities, indicating it did not constitute a particularly consistent praise indicative of consistent and systematic divine hierarchies (Labuschagne 1966, 33), though there was a limited number of deities at whom this rhetoric could be directed (Ready 2012, 68).[45]

HOLINESS. Connected with the concept of incomparability was that of holiness, which is treated as a central attribute of deity across ancient Southwest Asia. The fundamental sense seems to be that of a distinctiveness that is a result of, and is marked by, cleanliness, purity, and radiance. For instance, the Akkadian verbs *qadāšu(m)* and *qašādu(m)*—cognate with Hebrew *qdš* ("holy")—refer in the G stem to becoming clean or pure, and in the D stem to cleansing, purifying, or consecrating (Kornfeld 2003). These terms are overwhelmingly used to refer to the non-divine spaces, objects, and people involved in cultic activities and dedicated to serving deities (Clines 2021). Closely linked to these terms are the Akkadian adjectives *ellu* and *ebbu*, which can mean "clean," "pure," "holy," "lustrous," and "sacred."[46] The deities themselves were qualified with different Akkadian terms that reflected the same conceptual suite, but with some additional nuances. The words *pulḫu* and *melammu* referred to the awesome radiance which with deities were adorned (Aster 2012).[47] That radiance engendered terror as a result of the power that it signaled. It could also be transferred to anything a deity endowed with their agency, including kings, temples, and cultic objects (Oppenheim 1943, Emelianov 2010, Aster 2015). Thus humans and their material spaces and media could approach deity through acts of purification that granted them a degree of "holiness," while certain interactions with the divine could then endow certain humans and their material media with the deities' own *pulḫu* and *melammu*, illustrating overlap and integration at the center of the human/divine continuum.

The Ugaritic literature provides a closer analogy to the Hebrew Bible in its use of *qdš* to refer to deities, who frequently carry the epithet "children of *qdš*" (*KTU* 1.2.i.20–21, 38; 1.17.i.3, 8, 10–11, 13, 22; Smith 2001, 93). El is referred to on a few occasions in the Ugaritic literature as *ltpn w qdš*, "sagacious and holy one" (*KTU* 1.16.i.11, 21–22; ii.49; Rahmouni 2008, 207–9). The word was also

---

[45] Jill Middlemas (2014, 93–102) argues that the prophetic literature of the exile consciously combated idolatry by adapting the rhetoric of incomparability in order to assert aniconism and a philosophical monotheism. She states (95), "This is exclusive monotheism through and though: Yahweh is not God among gods, but God transcendent above the formed shapes of what some (erroneously according to the ideology) worship, tend, and regard as divine." The same rhetoric aimed at other nations (Isa 40:17), or put in the mouths of personified cities (Isa 47:8, 10; Zeph 2:15), however, suggests the rhetoric is not quite so philosophically assertive (cf. Moberly 2004, Heiser 2008a, Olyan 2012).

[46] See *CAD* 4, s.vv. "ellu," "ebbu."

[47] *CAD* 12, s.v. "pulḫu"; *CAD* 10.2, s.v. "melammu"; Enuma Elish 1.138, 2.24.

used in different forms to refer to sacred spaces, cultic offerings, and to cultic personnel (van Koppen and van der Toorn 1999). An associated term in Ugaritic is *ṭhr*, which refers to purity and luminosity (del Olmo Lete and Sanmartín 2015, 875). In *KTU* 1.4.v.18–19 Baal's palace is to be constructed of *ṭhrm.'iqn'im*, "purest lapis lazuli" (a stone frequently associated with deity—note the Akkadian parallel *uqnû ebbu*).[48]

This last passage provides a link to Exod 24:10, which describes the deity of Israel as standing on a brickwork of lapis lazuli, "like the very skies in clarity" (*kəʿeṣem haššāmayim lāṭōhar*).[49] The Hebrew *ṭhr* is used in Lev 12:4, 6 to refer to ritual purification, and specifically for a woman who has given birth. Concepts of cleanliness and purity extend throughout the biblical representations of holiness. The brilliance associated with cleanliness, and the antithetical concept of uncleanliness and pollution, appear to constitute the root metaphors for conceptualizing ritual/moral purity and sin (Feder 2014, 2021). Items purified for ritual use were marked for that use, often with *qdš l-*, "holy to" or "consecrated for." This was a way to indicate the consecration of those items specifically and exclusively for use in cultic contexts.[50] A sense of distinctiveness is developed in the Hebrew Bible to refer to YHWH's people as separated and distinct from the rest of humanity.[51] This sense seems to be intended in Lev 20:26: "You will be holy [*qədōšîm*] to me, for I, YHWH, am holy [*qādôš*], and I have separated you [*wāʾabdil ʾetkem*] from the peoples to be mine" (cf. Deut 7:6, 14:2).[52]

In the Hebrew Bible, the other deities of the divine council can be referred to as *qədōšîm*, "holy ones." The designation even appears to be used in later texts somewhat euphemistically to refer obliquely to subordinate deities without explicitly acknowledging their deity, as in Zech 14:5, which asserts, "And

---

[48] For the text and translation, see Smith and Pitard 2009, 529–38, 569.

[49] For *sappîr* as lapis lazuli, see *HALOT*, s.v. "סַפִּיר."

[50] Two burnished plates discovered by the altar at the temple at Arad were inscribed with what appears to be *qk*, which most scholars understand as an abbreviation for *qōdeš lakkōhănîm*, "consecrated for the priests," indicating their designation for exclusive use by the temple's priesthood (cf. Num 6:20; Aharoni 1968, 20). Similar inscriptions are also known from finds at Beer-sheba, Beit Mirsim, Hazor, Tel Miqne, and Masada (Vriezen 2001, 48).

[51] Cult specialists in societies around the world frequently engage in self-denial—often associated with sex or food—in order to achieve or project a sense of commitment, distinction, and proximity to deity that is associated with their station (Singh 2018, Singh and Henrich 2020).

[52] As will be discussed below, the framing of Israel as being chosen by YHWH from among the nations—rather than the earlier framework of inheritance (Deut 32:8–9)—is likely an innovation that developed following YHWH's accession to rule over all the nations of the earth.

YHWH, my deity, will come, all the holy ones (*kol-qədōšîm*) with him."[53] YHWH is clearly represented as greater than all the "holy ones," as in the rhetoric of incomparability used in Ps 89:7–8: "who among the deities is like YHWH, / a deity dreaded among the council of holy ones (*bəsôd-qədōšîm*), / great and awesome above all who surround him?" The designation of the other deities as *qədōšîm* here may include the notion of awe and fear, particularly in light of the rhetorical emphasis of YHWH's inspiration of far greater dread and awe.

The biblical texts also identify a close conceptual relationship between this awe/terror and the radiance of some of those entities understood to be "holy." While that terror in the Akkadian literature stems from what the radiance signaled about divine power, the biblical literature develops the notion that the radiance itself is deadly to humanity. Thus, in the chapter before the episode with Moses' shining face, YHWH explains to Moses, "you cannot see my face, because a human cannot see me and live" (Exod 33:20). The communicability of that radiance may be reflected in the episode of Moses' shining face in Exod 34:29–35 (provided one interprets *qāran* to refer to the shining of Moses' face; cf. Philpot 2013). The fact that the people feared coming near him suggests the terror associated with it was communicable as well.

Holiness, then, was likely a conceptual extension from more "profane" contexts, but was considered prototypical of the generic concept of deity in the Hebrew Bible, even as it was communicable to humanity and to architecture and cultic objects. The Hebrew Bible's use of "holiness" in reference to some sense of separation or consecration may derive from the expectation that humanity somehow participate in the holiness of deity and the observation that humans rarely radiate their own inherent luminosity. The cultic prescriptions associated with Israel's achieving holiness indicate cleanliness and purity were also included in the conceptualization of "holy," and perhaps even constitute a primary means of facilitating it.

IMMORTALITY. Deities were prototypically immortal, or at least a lot less mortal than humans. A clear reflection of the IMMORTALITY domain is found in Ps 82:6–7, where the deity status of the members of the divine council is contrasted with their condemnation to mortality: "I have declared, 'You are deities, / and children of the Highest, each of you.' Nevertheless, like a human you will die [*təmûtûn*], / and as one of the princes, you will fall [*tippōlû*]." These late verses evoke the prototypical understanding of the immortality of deity, even as they make

---

[53] These vague references to "holy ones" may have been reinterpreted in later years as references to humans in light of both the concern for YHWH's exclusivity and the post-exilic emphasis on Israel becoming holy.

effective rhetorical use of its revocation.[54] Other texts reflect the same understanding of deity. In Gen 3:22, for instance, upon acknowledging the humans' possession of "knowledge of good and evil" (perhaps a merism for full access to strategic information), the deity cuts off access to the tree of life so that the humans do not eat from it and live forever.

Because of its vulnerability, human flesh is used in multiple places as a symbol of mortality over and against the longevity and invulnerability of *rûaḥ*. The reference in such passages is not to the contemporary notion of an immaterial body, but to air, wind, or breath—an indestructible, unseen, and animating agentive force. This is particularly salient when contrasted with vulnerable flesh. See, for instance, Job 19:26, where Job insists that even after his flesh has been destroyed, he will see the deity. This further suggests the partibility of the person, and the positing of a locus of selfhood that outlived the body. YHWH asserts when limiting human life to one hundred twenty years in Gen 6:3, *rûḥî bā'ādām lə'ōlām bəšagam hû' bāśār*, "My spirit will not remain with humans forever, since they are flesh." The withdrawal of YHWH's sustaining spirit allows the flesh to decompose as expected.

Similarly, Isa 31:3 asserts: *ûmiṣrayim 'ādām wəlō'-'ēl wəsûsêhem bāśār wəlō'-rûaḥ*, "Now Egyptians are human, and not divine, and their horses are flesh, and not spirit." The idea here seems to be that the Egyptians and their horses—the symbol of their military might—are still vulnerable flesh rather than invulnerable spirit. Despite some attempts to leverage these contrasts to define deity according to contemporary notions of immateriality (Heiser 2015, 33, n. 8), there is no indication any such concept was in circulation at the time, much less a necessary and sufficient feature of deity (cf. Renehan 1980).[55] We are on much safer methodological ground observing that spirit was unseen, could not be destroyed, but could animate and even be destructive itself. Because of its conceptual derivation from the frameworks of unseen agency and deity, which is immortal—or at least considerably more enduring than flesh—there is a perception of comparative invulnerability.[56]

---

[54] The counterintuitive notion of dying gods actually has some purchase in the ancient literature. See, for instance, Machinist 2011. On the notion of "dying and rising gods," see Smith 2001, 110–20.

[55] "The prophet's intent is not to articulate a flesh-spirit dualism, but simply to warn those who would seek support from Egypt. In comparison to the power of the spirit, the flesh is weak and feeble" (MacDonald 2013, 99).

[56] Deceased kin seem to have been understood to perdure as long as their names and memories survived. Transition to full deity status may have been a way of ensuring a much longer postmortal tenure. Assimilation to generic "ancestor" status could be understood as a transitionary phase.

COMMUNICABLE AGENCY AND ANTHROPOMORPHISM. Two final domains of deity that should be briefly addressed are COMMUNICABLE AGENCY and ANTHROPOMORPHISM. Both seem to be presupposed in most evocations of deity concepts in the Hebrew Bible. The main profile associated with this domain would be "divine image." While the Hebrew Bible's rhetoric takes on a markedly polemical tone in Neo-Babylonian- and Achaemenid-period literature, and frequently placed the terminology for the material mediation of deity in the mouths of foreigners and apostate Israelites, some earlier references to cultic objects as deities seem natural and uncontroversial (e.g., Gen 35:4; Exod 20:23; 34:17; Judg 17:5[?]). The natural semantic fuzziness of the terms for deity may have facilitated the reinterpretation of problematic references so they escaped the editorial knife (Smith 2004a, 156–57; Reed 2020, 81). While anthropomorphic descriptions of deities other than YHWH are rare in the Hebrew Bible, when they are referenced, it is generally within the same conceptual frameworks used to describe YHWH's own anthropomorphic activity, as in, for instance, Ps 82.

CONSTRUING THE DOMAINS

With these conceptual domains and their profiles identified, we can interrogate a passage from the Hebrew Bible and begin to reconstruct a rough approximation of a contemporary hearer/reader/viewer's conceptualization of deity and divine agency. A helpful case study that is among the most thorough engagements in the Hebrew Bible with deities other than YHWH is Ps 82 (Parker 1995; Smith 2008, 131–39; Machinist 2011).[57] This text is additionally instructive because of its renegotiation of the role and function of those deities. I quote the psalm in full and follow with a cognitive-semantic interrogation of the conceptualizations of deity it could have evoked.

> 1 The deity [*'ĕlōhîm*] takes his place in the divine council [*baʻădat-'ēl*];
>   in the midst of the deities [*bəqereb 'ĕlōhîm*] he judges.
>
> 2 "How long will you judge iniquitously,
>   and show favoritism to the wicked? *Selah.*
> 3 Render justice for the poor and the orphan,
>   defend the rights of the afflicted and the destitute.
> 4 Rescue the poor and the needy,
>   deliver from the hand of the wicked."

---

[57] I date the psalm to the Neo-Babylonian or Achaemenid period, based primarily on the psalm's thorough integration into the narrative arcs of Pss 74–76 and 79–82, which address the loss of the temple. I argue Ps 82 is the very fulfillment of the petition in Ps 74:22 for the deity to "rise up" and plead their *rîb* (McClellan 2018).

5 They do not know, and they do not understand,
   in darkness they wander—
   all the foundations of the earth are shaken.

6 Even I have declared, "You are deities [*'ĕlōhîm 'attem*],
   and children of the Highest [*ûbnê 'elyôn*], each of you."
7 Nevertheless, like a human, you will die,
   And as one of the princes, you will fall.

8 Rise up, O Deity [*qûmâ 'ĕlōhîm*], judge the earth!
   For you will inherit all the nations [*tinḥal bəkol-haggôyim*]!

The first verse sets the stage by describing the deity taking their position among the deities of the divine council to render judgment.[58] This imagery immediately invokes the DEITY and DIVINE COUNCIL domains, as well as the "YHWH" profile. The use of *špṭ* profiles "judge" against these domains, which itself activates the SOCIAL MONITORING domain associated with it. This is a divine council court scene, and someone has been naughty. Whatever experiences the hearer or reader has with these domains will be the context within which the rest of the psalm will be interpreted. Verse 2 begins with the question *'ad-mātay*, "how long?," which is prototypically associated elsewhere in the Psalms with the complaint, a motif within the lament genre.[59] The divine council type-scene appears to be conflated with a complaint, which may be an innovative way to frame the divine or prophetic lawsuit known as the *rîb*, and aim it at the deities themselves. Seth Sanders has suggested "judicial complaint" as a possible description of this hybrid genre.[60]

The deities of the divine council are addressed with the second person plural verbs that follow, describing unjust judgment, favor toward the wicked, and neglect of the weak, the low, and the orphan. Verses 2–4 read both as charges against the deities and accusations as part of the complaint. SOCIAL MONITORING comes into greater focus at this point, and the failure to uphold the social standards being described by the ruling deity likely begins to activate the PATRON DEITY, NATIONAL DEITY, and FAILURE TO ACT domains in reference to the responsibilities

---

[58] *'ădat-'ēl* is literally, "council of El," but by this period this was likely a frozen form wherein the *nomen rectum* would be understood as the adjectival genitive (thus "divine council"). The Septuagint's *synagōgē theōn*, "council of deities," may suggest a more original *'ădat-'ēlîm*, "council of deities" (Gonzalez 1963, 299; Tate 1990, 329 n. 1.d).

[59] See, for instance, Pss 74:10; 80:5; 90:13. On the complaint, see Broyles 1989. On the lament, see Mandolfo 2014, 114–30. Susan Niditch includes an insightful discussion of the autobiographical dimensions of the lament in Niditch 2015, 55–63. On genre in the psalms more broadly, see Gunkel and Begrich 1998; Nasuti 1999.

[60] Personal communication.

of the other deities of the divine council over their respective national purviews. Interestingly, the same domains are activated by several other psalms from around this time period that are directed at YHWH's own perceived neglect, so there is clear conceptual overlap (translatability) between YHWH and the deities of the divine council.

The references to the *dal* ("weak"), *yātôm* ("orphan"), *'ānî* ("lowly"), *rāš* ("destitute"), and *'ebyôn* ("needy"), evoke conventionalized symbols of social justice and the related notion of cosmic stability, which are most directly associated with the KINGSHIP and DEITY domains (Fensham 1962). Isaiah 1:17 uses *špṭ* in describing YHWH's pleading to their own people for the *yātôm*, as well as for the *ḥāmôṣ* ("oppressed") and the *'almānâ* ("widow"). The victims here and in Ps 82 were "much less real-world social groups than intellectual constructs. That is, the terms refer to the *ideal victim*" (Silver 1995, 182–83). For the societies that produced the Hebrew Bible, social monitoring was rationalized as a matter of cosmic stability. Social injustices were conceptualized as manifestations of the chaos which deities, rulers, and cultic specialists were responsible to mitigate. The reference to the inhabitants of earth wandering in darkness and the foundations of the earth shaking (verse 5) demonstrates the failure of the council to uphold the cosmic order, of which social justice was a weight-bearing pillar.[61] By this point, FAILURE TO ACT comes front and center. The deities are failing to live up to their primary responsibilities as deities.

Verses 6 and 7 represent the sentence passed on the deities. Verse 6 first affirms the divine status of the deities of the council as *'ĕlōhîm* and *bənê 'elyôn*, which places the most common term for deity in the Hebrew Bible parallel to a unique phrase that appears to be a variation on the somewhat more common *bənê 'ĕlōhîm*, "deities" (Gen 6:2, 4; Job 1:6; 2:1; 38:7).[62] *'Elyôn* is particularly prevalent in the Psalms, and here it invokes the "high deity" profile (and perhaps "patriarchal deity") within the DIVINE COUNCIL domain.[63] It is possible, given the likely Neo-Babylonian or Achaemenid context of the psalm, that this verse serves to clear up any misunderstanding about the divinity of the members of the council, but the main function is to set up a contrast for the deities' consignment to mortality in verse 7 (activating the PUNISHMENT and IMMORTALITY domains). This effectively rescinds their responsibilities over the nations and expels them from the divine council, revoking their status as prototypical deities and hurling them into

---

[61] These figures are frequently misunderstood as the deities that are being tried, but the verse fits far better within the complaint genre's feature wherein the complainant describes the lamentable outcomes of the deity's failure to act (McClellan 2018, 843–44).

[62] As Reed (2020, 74 n. 122) notes, *bənê 'elyôn* especially resonates "with early Enochic traditions about angels."

[63] *Elyôn* is not explicitly identified with the ruling deity, but their conflation by this time with YHWH was likely established enough to be understood without contextual nudges.

the periphery of the semantic field. This act again invokes the DIVINE COUNCIL domain, but specifically to renegotiate it. This would have been a significant paradigm shift for someone experiencing this upheaval of the structures of deity for the first time.

In the final verse, the psalmist calls upon the deity to rise up and inherit (*nḥl*) all the nations. The use of *nḥl*, particularly in connection with '*elyôn*, alludes to the description in Deut 32:8–9 of the people/nation of Israel as YHWH's *naḥălâ*, "inheritance" (Forschey 1975; Sanders 1996, 368–69). This would activate PATRONAGE, PATRON DEITY, and NATIONAL DEITY. While the "second-tier deity" profile should also be activated, since YHWH receives that inheritance from '*elyôn* in Deut 32:9, the two were long conflated by the time of Ps 82, and "second-tier deity" had little currency at that time in connection with YHWH. Whether or not it was activated vis-à-vis the other deities is a question of how far back into the past the authors were reaching for this motif. It is likely there were some for whom the notion of second-tier deities would have been activated, even if others had long consigned them to a conceptual grab-bag of angels, demons, or some other diminutive category. The suggestion that YHWH will now directly rule over all nations also fronts the "high deity" profile (cf. Ps 83:19). The psalm thus combines the divine council type-scene with the complaint genre to rhetorically bring about the deposition of the deities of the nations and YHWH's usurpation of their purviews, entirely restructuring the divine council.

Because Ps 82 consolidates so many different domains and profiles of deity, it will be instructive to hierarchize its domains and profiles. The unseen agency base is presupposed, as are the domains of DEITY and PATRONAGE, and likely KINGSHIP. SOCIAL MONITORING and PATRON DEITY are somewhat salient in the psalm, but DIVINE COUNCIL and FAILURE TO ACT are front and center. The "deity" and "YHWH" profiles were surely activated by the psalm, but as part of the Elohistic Psalter, '*ĕlōhîm* was given preference at some point during the editorial process (cf. Zenger and Lohfink 1998; Joffe 2001; Burnett 2006). '*Ĕlōhîm* feels to us a bit redundant in verse 1, which has compelled some scholars to posit that it replaces an original YHWH (e.g., Morgenstern 1939). Whether the psalm was composed by those giving preference to '*ĕlōhîm* or at some earlier point is unclear from the available data (the redundancy is not determinative), but YHWH would have been presumed to be the active deity.[64] "Judge" also appears to be activated within the juridical context, as well as "high deity" (as part of the divine council framework, but not particularly salient in the psalm). "Second tier deity" is activated in reference to the deities being condemned.

Psalm 82 evokes a number of profiles and domains associated with deity, and largely in order to reconfigure them in response to the crisis of exile and the loss

---

[64] The titular use of '*ĕlōhîm* was likely close enough to lexicalization in reference to YHWH in this period that it could function (a bit idiosyncratically) as a substitution for it.

of the temple. Those subsequent consumers of the biblical literature to whom this text was known and was influential would have approached that literature with a new configuration of interpretive lenses with which to construe data regarding deity. Among other things, the text effectively extends YHWH's PATRONAGE, PATRON DEITY, and NATIONAL DEITY domains over the whole earth, universalizing Israel's deity and subordinating other deities to them. The deities of the nations were no longer peers with whom to compete, but marginalized subordinates. Once this specific configuration became firmly enough embedded in the perspectives of the societies for whom these texts were authoritative, references to other deities—as long as they were not worshipped—would not be as threatening to YHWH's sovereignty and exclusive relationship with Israel. This is likely the conceptual backdrop that facilitated the literary exploration in the Greco-Roman period of the heavens and its hierarchy.[65]

THE BOUNDARIES OF DEITY

This and the next subsection will discuss the boundaries and the prototypes of deity, which will provide a segue to the next chapter's discussion of YHWH as an instantiation of generic deity. To introduce the boundaries of deity, I return to the creation of humanity in Gen 2, and particularly to the observation that the human in that chapter was formed (*yṣr*) from the "dust from the earth [*'āpār min-hā'ădāmâ*]" (or clay) and had the breath of life breathed into their nostrils. The conceptual overlap of this creative act and the creation and enlivening of a cultic image has not gone unnoticed by scholars (Herring 2013; McDowell 2015; Putthoff 2020). The humans' partial deification may represent an attempt to rhetorically frame humanity as the deity's divine image—thereby militating against the use of other cultic objects while also imposing an ethical mandate—without attributing full divine status to them. They thus approximate the fuzzy and debatable boundaries of deity (cf. Ps 8:6). Certain members of the human category who were significantly elevated in life encroached upon the threshold of deity enough to have been referred to as deities in the Hebrew Bible. In death, there seems to have been a natural blurring of the boundaries separating humanity from deity, with deceased kin and influential ritual specialists like the deceased Samuel referred to and cared for as deities, although none seem to have penetrated into the center of the category while maintaining association with their human identity. Indeed, Ps 82's revocation of the immortality of the deities of the nations and their consignment to the outskirts of divinity includes an element of humanization.

---

[65] See Reed 2020, 65: "the beginnings of Jewish angelology and demonology in the third and second centuries BCE may be best understood as part of an ongoing engagement with the past, for which writing, lists, and genealogies served as powerful technologies for both preserving and reframing memory."

The deities of other nations were most explicitly cast as peripheral members of the category of deity, and particularly in later periods. For example, the story of the contest between Elijah and the prophets of Baal rhetorically marginalizes Baal by asserting Baal is not *hā'ĕlōhîm*, "*the* deity." Deuteronomy 32:16–17 is more explicit: "They made them jealous with strange ones, with abominations they provoked them. They sacrificed to *šēdîm* [*shaddays* or perhaps "demons"], not Deity [*lō' 'ĕlōha*]—to deities they did not know [*'ĕlōhîm lō' yədā'ûm*], to new ones that showed up recently, that your ancestors did not fear." Here the divinity of the *šēdîm* is acknowledged, but their prototypicality is rejected in their identification as "strange ones" that were not familiar to them and that their ancestors had not worshipped. This same rhetoric takes a slightly more hyperbolic tone in Deut 32:21, where the divinity of those deities is ostensibly denied: "They made me jealous with what is not a deity [*lō'-'ēl*], they provoked me with their vanities. So I will make them jealous with what is not a people [*lō'-'ām*], with a worthless nation I will provoke them."

The parallel descriptions of the other deities and the other nation as "not a deity" and "not a people" point to the rhetorical exaggeration here.[66] The author was not denying their existence as a deity or a people, they were denigrating them as comparatively meaningless, or "vanities," the way a Denver Broncos fan might insist the Las Vegas Raiders are "not a real football team." This kind of rhetoric was frequently deployed to marginalize and demean the deities of other nations and their misguided citizenry (Isa 44:9; Ps 96:5 // 1 Chr 16:26),[67] but it has frequently been construed by scholars as an explicit assertion of philosophical monotheism (Middlemas 2014, 93–102). The rhetoric of incomparability that described YHWH as deity of deities (Deut 10:17; Josh 22:22; Ps 136:2) and asserted them to be greater than all other deities (Exod 18:11; 1 Chr 16:25; Ps 95:3; 96:4; 97:9) permits a less rhetorically obscured picture of the relationship of YHWH to the other deities. The cultic objects associated with the deities of the nations were more "literally" decried as non-divine in later periods, and those who treated them as deities were also mocked (Deut 28:64; Isa 42:17; 43:10; 44:9–20;

---

[66] Similarly, other authors put the rhetoric of exclusivity into the mouth of the personified Babylon and Nineveh (Isa 47:8, 10; Zeph 2:15), who obviously do not consider themselves to be the only cities in existence, but just the only ones that matters to their constituencies (cf. MacDonald 2003, 81–85).

[67] Christopher Hays (2020) has argued that the Hebrew *'ĕlîlîm* seems to have originated in a borrowing from the Neo-Assyrian references to Enlil/Ellil (likely on the part of the author of Isa 10:10), and to have originally functioned sarcastically as a reference to "false deities." Later it would have developed the pejorative adjectival sense of "worthless." The rhetorical point is that the deities of the nations are insignificant or powerless deities.

Ps 115:2–7; cf. Hos 8:4–6).[68] Ultimately, however, the rhetoric is still aimed at social roles and responsibilities, and not at ontology.

The divine messengers of the Hebrew Bible also seem to occupy the periphery of the category (cf. Köckert 2007). While these messengers operate in ways that indicate some kind of divine status, they are not divine patrons over social groups, they do not (yet) appear to deploy their own communicable agency through any material media, and while they are asserted to have access to strategic information, it seems to derive from YHWH. In the Ugaritic literature, divine messengers—referred to as "deities" (*ilm*) in *KTU* 1.3.iii.32 (Handy 1994, 157)—primarily communicated between one deity and another, and they constituted a servile class of deity operating on the lowest tier of the pantheon (Smith 2001, 49–50; Handy 1994, 149–54). But even in the Hebrew Bible they could be referred to as deities, as in the story of the annunciation of Samson's birth to his parents in Judg 13:21–22: "The messenger of YHWH [*mal'ak YHWH*] did not appear again to Manoah and to his wife. Then Manoah realized that it was the messenger of YHWH. So Manoah said to his wife, 'We will surely die, since we have seen deity ['*ĕlōhîm rā'înû*].'" The received form of the text seems to refer to the messenger as a deity, so for communities in which that text circulated, the messenger would likely have been understood as some manner of deity (although chapter 6 will show that the textual situation is not so cut and dry). This is also indicated by the widespread reinterpretation in the Greco-Roman period of passages that explicitly refer to deities as references to messengers (e.g. 1 Enoch's reinterpretation of Gen 6).

Finally, we must mention a collection of divine beings whose occupation of the periphery of the conceptual category of deity is largely a result of their distance from population centers, social groups, and human institutions. These were divine agents without patronage, and they included the chaos monsters of the sea, such as *liwyātān*, "Leviathan" (Isa 27:1; Ps 74:14; 104:26; Job 3:8; 40:25), and the ghosts and demons thought to dwell in ruins and in the wilderness, such as the *ṣiyîm*, "desert-demons(?)," the *'iyîm*, "howlers(?)," the *śĕ'îrîm*, "goat-demons," *lîlît*, "Lilith," and *'ăzā'zēl*, "Azazel."[69] These entities were not described with any appreciable degree of detail in the texts, which not only contributed to their ambiguity, but to their conceptual elasticity, providing convenient conceptual canvasses for later periods. In the short term, they no doubt served the biblical authors' structuring of divine power.[70] Perhaps they were understood zoomorphically or as hybrid entities, but the texts just don't provide

---

[68] Cf. Dick 1999; Smith 2004b; Levtow 2008, 40–85.
[69] Most of these are mentioned only in Isa 13:21–22; 34:14; Jer 50:39, but for Azazel, see Lev 16:8, 10, 26. See Janowski 1999a, 1999b; Hutter 1999; Frey-Anthes 2008; Blair 2009.
[70] On writing and the postexilic development of angelology and demonology, see Reed 2020.

any detail, which may have been a way to intentionally represent the mystery and the chaos of sea, desert, and separation from civilization (cf. Hutter 2007).

As YHWH's exclusive patronage over Israel became more and more critical to the survival and success of Israelite identity, the fuzzy boundaries of the concept of deity began to constrict around YHWH. This was not to say that other deities were no longer considered deities, only that the increased use and salience of the rhetoric of incomparability elevated YHWH to the degree that they alone represented the divine prototype, shoving other deities toward the periphery where they could be denigrated and dismissed. Psalm 82 effects the universalization of YHWH, which not only deposed the deities of the nations and condemned them to mortality, but also arrogated to YHWH direct political rule over the nations, a radical renegotiation of the heavens that had far-reaching implications that have yet to be fully unpacked by scholars.

THE PROTOTYPES OF DEITY

This subsection interrogates prototype effects associated with deity in the Hebrew Bible, beginning with the cognitive exemplars and then moving outward toward the fuzzy boundaries that were discussed above. Rather than attempt to be comprehensive, I will identify two features treated as diagnostic of deity in the biblical texts, and briefly review a few other features considered prototypical but not necessarily diagnostic. As should be clear by now, the intent is not to list necessary and sufficient features of deity, but to better understand the center of the category. Viewing deity as a neatly delineated category may seem a convenient scholarly heuristic, but it does considerable violence to the way the category was used in the biblical texts and in the sociomaterial ecologies that produced those texts. The effect of that violence is exponentially increased by the deployment of this particular conceptual category in attempts to structure power and values.

YHWH was not the prototypical deity because they asserted features that were entirely unique to them. Rather, they were the prototype precisely because they fit a broader template for deity while also asserting a configuration of largely typical features that answered the specific needs and circumstances of the societies over which they functioned as patron.[71] A significant amount of the polemics aimed at other deities that threatened YHWH's relationship with Israel acknowledged—usually only tacitly—the parallel natures and functions of those other deities. To insist that YHWH out-deitied the other deities required appeal to

---

[71] Cf. Fleming 2021, 245: "By considering the great gods of Babylon and Assyria on one hand and the political gods of South Arabia and Moab on the other, I have weighed analogies that do not place primary significance on job descriptions that are imagined to be original to each deity. What makes each god 'great' for the people in question is his (in these cases) identification with the people bound to him."

cognitive exemplars regarding what a deity was supposed to be, and it is that conceptual ideal that is in view in this section (cf. Smith 1990, 51).

As a result, we must engage the profiles of both YHWH and the other deities to tease out those features considered most prototypical of generic deity. I have advanced the proposition that the cognitive exemplars of deity in the Hebrew Bible were built on a foundation of the prosocial functions that facilitated the development, sociomaterial transmission, and perseverance of deity within their respective societies. Patron deities would be socially concerned deities with full access to strategic information who nurtured patron/client relationships with individuals or social groups whose behavior they monitored and whose social frameworks they were thought to enforce and protect. The prototype of this kind of deity according to the authors and editors of the Hebrew Bible was obviously YHWH, but there are multiple other deities mentioned that match the same profile for their respective constituencies, including Baal, Asherah, Chemosh, Milcom, and others. The significant degree of translatability across these various deities indicates the production and curation of their profiles related to conceptual templates shared across a broader sociomaterial matrix (Smith 2008, 37–130).

If a conceptual domain associated with deity is explicitly described in the Hebrew Bible as diagnostic of deity status, it should be considered to have been prototypical according to the reflective reasoning of the texts' authors and editors. Two such features are referenced on multiple occasions in the biblical literature, and both are directly linked to the intuitive roots of the production and social transmission of deity concepts. The first is full access to strategic information, which we find reflected, for instance, in the serpent's statement in Gen 3:5 that the humans would be "as deities, knowing good and evil" (*kē'lōhîm yōdʿê ṭôb wārāʿ*), which I suggest is a merism intended to refer to all knowledge, from the good to the evil.[72] Isaiah 41:23a, which challenges the deities of the nations to prove their divinity, is even more explicit: "Declare what is to come hereafter so we may know that you are deities [*wənēdʿâ kî ĕlōhîm 'attem*]." In 2 Kgs 1:3, the relevance of full access to strategic information to deity status undergirds the rhetorical question, "Is it because there is no deity ['*ên-'ĕlōhîm*] in Israel that you are going to inquire [*lidrōš*] of Baal Zebub, the deity of Ekron?" Beyond these explicit appeals to that access as central to deity, the feature is widely represented in the literature, particularly relating to YHWH. Saul's visit to the necromancer at En-dor, however, demonstrates that even a deceased human could display this prototypical feature (though here subordinated to YHWH). While Isaiah seems to insist full access to strategic information was a necessary and sufficient feature, that is more a rhetorical flourish than an essentialization of deity. The example

---

[72] A *merism* is a way to refer to a whole by referring to opposite or contrasting ends of it. For example, if I said, "She searched high and low," the idea is that she searched everywhere, from high to low and everywhere in between.

with Samuel demonstrates the category's gradience; YHWH was a prototypical example of deity, while the postmortem Samuel occupied the fuzzy boundaries.

The other feature that occurs repeatedly in rhetoric about classification as deity is immortality. Perhaps the most explicit identification of this feature as constitutive of deity is found in Ps 82:6 (see above), but the contrasting of the divinity of YHWH and the humanity of the Egyptians in Isa 31:3 also appeals to that immortality—or at least relative invulnerability—as representative of deity status. (Death could be experienced by deities, but as with some humans, it was not always permanent.) Ezekiel 28:9 similarly contrasts mortality against deity status, rhetorically asking the ruler of Tyre, "Are you really going to say, 'I am a deity' [*'ĕlōhîm 'ānî*] to the ones who are killing you?" The steps taken by the deity in Gen 3:22–24 to ensure that the humans could not eat the fruit of the tree of life and live forever reflect the rhetorical leveraging of immortality as an additional constitutive feature of deity.[73] They were already *kē'lōhîm*, "as deity," in one sense, and had they eaten the fruit and become immortal they would have arrogated the second of the two main features of deity. The deity prevented that, so humanity remained *like* deity, but still lacking a prototypical feature. One of the primary struggles for the deity within the Primeval History appears to be protecting the integrity of the porous boundaries that separated deity and humanity (Garr 2003, 59–61).

Patronage was another prototypical feature of deity, but rather than being aimed at determining if an entity possessed a faculty that was diagnostic of deity, the rhetoric associated with patronage in the Hebrew Bible seems to have been more directly concerned with demonstrating which deity was the true patron over the people, and therefore the rightful object of worship and fidelity. In this context, the term "deity" primarily designated a relational status.[74] The one who had sovereignty over a region or people was authoritative over that region or people—they were *the* deity.[75] We see this rhetoric most clearly in the story of

---

[73] The salience of immortality to the concept of deity is reflected in many non-biblical texts. As just a single example, in the Epic of Gilgamesh, in which the protagonist—already part deity—seeks to achieve immortality, Gilgamesh laments, "When the gods created mankind, / Death for mankind they set aside, / Life in their own hands retaining" (Epic of Gilgamesh 10.3.3–5 [Speiser 1969]).

[74] It is this sense that is frequently used in contemporary rhetoric about prioritizing commitment to certain entities or ideologies. People do not accuse others of making alcohol or nationalism or some other vice their "god" to indicate they think alcohol or nationalism has full access to strategic information or is immortal. Those accusations reflect the perception of dogmatic and unwavering commitment. As a non-pejorative example, a friend in 1998 commented that if Dave Matthews and Jewel had a baby, it would be his new god.

[75] This is not monotheism; it's just a question of whose authority takes priority and who is owed allegiance. Rhetoric associated with this patronage and with incomparability, however, would facilitate the development of concepts of divine exclusivity that would

Elijah's contest with the prophets of Baal. In 1 Kgs 18:23–24, Elijah describes the contest, which was simply a matter of calling upon their respective divine patrons to light the fire of a burnt offering. Elijah states in verse 24, "So you call on the name of your deity, and I will call on the name of YHWH, and it will be that the deity that answers with fire is the deity [*hû' hā'ĕlōhîm*]." Patron deity status here was demonstrated through the performance of an act associated with the shared natures of the two as storm-deities, namely sending down fire (lightning) to light the sacrifice. YHWH's victory should not be understood to indicate that Baal was not thought to exist, but that the nation of Israel was YHWH's unique purview, therefore they were the only storm-deity authorized to exercise their divine power therein and to be worshipped by that region's inhabitants.

Communicable agency was not a rhetorically salient diagnostic for deity, although it was absolutely prototypical of deity. As stated in the previous chapter, a deity without some means of material presencing, mediation, or representation on earth would have been of little value or utility without philosophical frameworks leveraged by powerful social institutions. The references to such media used in the worship of other deities are ubiquitous, but the Hebrew Bible is also littered with references to material media that was used to presence YHWH or to transmit their agency.[76] Many of these references became increasingly pejorative in later periods, however, as YHWH's rhetorical differentiation from and exaltation over the deities of the nations combined with concern for the vulnerabilities of sociomaterial media to incentivize the restriction of those media to the proprietary modes of the priesthood's literate elite. Stelai, *asherahs*, and other cult objects appear to have been common to YHWH's material presencing, if the polemicizing references to their ubiquity and their removal from the Jerusalem temple approximate historical realities (2 Kgs 17:9–12; 18:4; 21:7; 23:6). These media were frequently described as dedicated to the deities of other nations (Judg 6:25–26; 2 Kgs 10:26–27; 23:13), although that may be largely editorial in origin.[77] Worshipping YHWH the way other nations worshipped their deities became explicitly prohibited (e.g., Deut 12:31). The vilification of these media relied on their prototypicality to the conceptualization of deity—in a sense, the prohibition was acknowledging that everyone else did it, but demanding devotees of YHWH resist the urge to do it themselves. This prototypicality is

---

contribute to the innovation of the category of monotheism in the seventeenth-century CE, although even that concept of monotheism was quite distinct from its contemporary iterations (MacDonald 2003, 5–58).

[76] For example, Exod 3:2–4; 32:4; Num 21:4–9; Deut 4:12; 12:5–7; Judg 17:1–5; 18:1–6; 1 Sam 5:2–4; 1 Kgs 12:27–29; Hos 3:4.

[77] Note Rainer Albertz's suggests everything in Hosea's anti-Baal rhetoric, "had been an uncriticized ingredient of the cult of Yahweh for centuries" (Albertz 1994, 173).

further supported by the preservation of certain sanctioned forms of those media for use only by the appropriate authorities.

CONCLUSION

In this chapter, I've imposed frameworks derived from cognitive linguistics and the cognitive science of religion on the texts of the Hebrew Bible in an effort to try to tease out a better understanding of the extent and contours of the category of generic deity. The conceptualization of deity was constructed in the Hebrew Bible, as it is today, on a foundation of embodied engagement with specific sociomaterial ecologies, most of which are common to the human experience. There is no need to posit the influence of widespread sociocultural idiosyncrasies to which we no longer have access in order to reconstruct the guiding frameworks in this period and for these groups. Nor is there a need to appeal to enigmatic concepts of being and non-being, to ineffability, to the putatively proprietary concerns of theology, or to the inadequacies of human language. The main conceptual filters through which the relevant cognitive processes were refracted to produce the kaleidoscope of divine features we find in the texts were the rhetorical interests and needs of historically situated persons with their own repertoires of experiences with preexisting concepts of deity within specific sociomaterial contexts. We do not have access to these experiences or to all the details of their historical and sociomaterial contexts, but there are data available to improve on where we stand today. For scholars to continue to build on our understanding of the conceptual structures of generic deity and divine agency in ancient Israel and Judah, we will need to engage each of those considerations independently as well as in concert with each other. This is precisely the goal of the next chapter vis-à-vis the conceptualization of YHWH as a member of the generic category of deity.

4.
YHWH in the Hebrew Bible

In the previous chapter, I proposed that the semantic base of deity is unseen agency, and I identified several conceptual domains commonly activated in the Hebrew Bible's representations of the generic concept of deity. I also identified a number of additional profiles and discussed the category's negotiable boundaries and some of the associated prototype effects. The focus in that chapter was primarily on the generic concept of deity and on deities other than YHWH, although there was some discussion of the relationship of these conceptual frameworks to YHWH, given how salient the latter was to the concept of deity within the social worlds that produced the biblical texts. In this chapter I revisit those same conceptual domains and profiles, but with a focus on the way they were deployed to represent YHWH.

Before turning to those conceptual structures, however, I'd like to address a significant difference between the representation of YHWH and of generic deity in the Hebrew Bible. The domains and profiles discussed to this point have been focused on the wider social functions of deity, but deity was also significant as a source of individual and private blessing, comfort, and protection. This domain of DEITY is central to the patriarchal narratives and is represented in many places in the Hebrew Bible in reference to YHWH. Apart from the later wisdom and lament literature, which expands the exploration of individualism (Niditch 2015), even that representation as a deity for the people is embedded in narratives or rhetorical arcs that ultimately serve broader social and institutional interests. Because of the nature of the biblical literature, private and individual relationships are largely omitted from discourse regarding deities other than YHWH. Perhaps the closest we come to exceptions are the discussions in Gen 31 of Nahor's family deity and private collection of teraphim, and in Judg 17–18 of Micah's private shrine and priest. Both, however, are commonly subsumed under a Yahwistic rubric.

Genesis 31:53 mentions "the deity of Nahor" (*'ĕlōhê nāḥôr*) parallel to "the deity of Abraham" (*'ĕlōhê 'abrāhām*). This seems to refer to Nahor's otherwise unattested personal or family deity (van der Toorn 1999b). The text refers appositionally to the two deities as the "deities of their father" (*'ĕlōhê 'ăbîhem*), and some translations conflate the two by rendering "the God of their father"

(KJV, NRSV, ESV), but the text does not support this conflation. When Nahor initially confronts Jacob in verse 29, he refers to "the deity of your [plural] father" (*'ĕlōhê 'ăbîkem*). Jacob also refers in verse 42 to the deity of Abraham as "the deity of my father" (*'ĕlōhê 'ābî*) and "the Dread of Isaac" (*paḥad yiṣḥāq*). In other words, the deity of Jacob's father is *not* the deity of Nahor's father. Rachel had also stolen Nahor's teraphim (*tərāpîm*, often translated "household gods"). When Nahor asks about them, he calls them "my deities" (*'ĕlōhāy*), and Jacob seems to defer to that designation, also referring to them in response as "your deities" (*'ĕlōhêkâ*). The narration, however, always uses "teraphim," a term that seems to refer to some manner of personal presencing media, perhaps similar in form to the Judean Pillar Figurine, but indexing deceased kin (van der Toorn 1990; Edelman 2017). While the term is usually used pejoratively, 1 Sam 19:13 suggests even King David evidently kept teraphim handy.

In Judg 17:3, Micah's mother (the name is "Micaiah" in Judg 17:1–4) uses 200 shekels of silver (that Micah had stolen from her and returned) to create a carved divine image (*pesel*) and a cast divine image (*massēkâ*),[1] which were placed in Micah's own shrine—literally, "house of deity" (*bêt 'ĕlōhîm*)—along with his ephod and teraphim (Cox and Ackerman 2012). These are all treated in the canonical context as dedicated to YHWH, and the text contextualizes these actions in verse 6 by clarifying that there was no king in Israel, and that everyone did what was right in their own eyes. When an itinerant Levite happens by, Micah hires him on to replace his own son as his private priest. Later, a band of Danite scouts stops by and requests the priest seek a prophecy regarding their mission. After the favorable response by YHWH (presumably via the presencing media) and the success of their mission, they return to seduce away the priest and abscond with Micah's presencing media. When Micah later catches up with and confronts them, he complains that they stole "my deities that I made!" (*'ĕlōhay 'ăšer-'āśîtî*).

It should be noted that none of the *national* deities of the other nations of ancient Southwest Asia are treated in the Hebrew Bible as functioning on a personal level. The fact that YHWH saliently operates on both a personal and a national level is not distinctive solely because of an editorial hand heavy with nationalistic rhetoric. Karel van der Toorn (1999a), Seth Sanders (2015), and Daniel Fleming (2021) have noted that YHWH seems in the earliest recoverable literary strata to function on the level of kin-based deity, which is not a common heritage for the national deities of ancient Southwest Asia. Instead, personal deities tend to remain personal deities as a result of their kinship-based purview, while national deities tend to be the distant high deities of the pantheon whose

---

[1] I treat these as two objects, but when Micah's trove of presencing media is mentioned in chapter 18, the text only refers to the cast image. Some read *massēkâ* as appositional to *pesel*, explaining what type of presencing media was created (e.g., NRSV's "an idol of cast metal"), but the terms refer to two different processes of manufacture.

profiles are more conducive to facilitating social cohesion beyond the boundaries of kinship. Sanders (2015, 81) suggests Israel's distinctiveness in this regard results from an early king having adopted the most popular personal deity as patron over the nascent nation of Israel.[2] There is thus a brand of distinctiveness to YHWH's conceptualization in the Hebrew Bible, but one that ultimately derives from the shared conceptual structures of deity.

THE CONCEPTUAL STRUCTURES OF YHWH'S DIVINE PROFILE

As a prototypical deity, YHWH was conceptualized according to the same base of unseen agency, but there is some unpacking to do regarding their occasional visibility. Like other agents, YHWH could be seen when their presence was reified through presencing media, but the biblical literature also suggests the deity's own body, independent of presencing media, was repeatedly seen. Esther Hamori (2008), for instance, has highlighted Hebrew Bible narratives in which the deity appears as a "man" (*'îš*) to biblical figures, interacting in ways that suggest a fully visible and anthropomorphic deity (Gen 18:1–15; 32:23–33). She calls this phenomenon the "*'îš* theophany," and describes it as displaying "a radical degree of what might be called 'anthropomorphic realism'—that is, realistic human presentation and action throughout the appearance in human form." Nevada Levi DeLapp (2018) has also interrogated the theophanic type-scene in the Pentateuch, finding a variety of narrative frameworks that facilitated YHWH's appearance to the people of Israel, including *kābôd* theophanies and other mediated appearances (cf. Savran 2005). Rather than representing a programmatic metaphorization of an "abstract entity beyond our comprehension" (Middlemas 2014, 93), these are manifestations of the intuitive salience of anthropomorphism in the conceptualization of imagined and unseen agency.

The deity was clearly thought to be, in rare circumstances, *seen*; but these occurrences remain confined to biblical narrative in which YHWH's appearance served paraenetic rhetorical functions and came to be assigned strict boundaries. Exodus 33:20 asserted that a human could not see the deity's face and survive, but at the same time, multiple figures still managed to encounter YHWH face-to-face (Gen 16:13; 32:31; Exod 33:11; Deut 34:10). In most cases, they express fear, however, or surprise at their survival, which sends the message that YHWH's face may indeed be accessible for extraordinary circumstances and figures, but it was otherwise utterly devastating. (This rhetoric is to be distinguished from the

---

[2] Sanders (2015, 81, n. 59) argues that van der Toorn's (1996) theory that YHWH was the personal deity of Saul elevated to national deity status at Saul's accession to the throne (1) "would require 11th-century data unavailable to us," (2) places "too much stress on a 'great man' theory of history," and (3) does not explain how the state was able to facilitate the popularity of the deity on a personal level (an unlikely direction of influence).

rhetoric of the many psalms that express the joy of and yearning for seeing the deity's face.) The theophanies of the early biblical narratives are reflective elaborations intended to serve specific rhetorical goals, but they do not fundamentally undermine the observation that deity concepts build on the conceptual base of unseen agency. For those consuming the texts and doing the conceptualizing, the deity—apart from their presencing media—remained unseen.

Despite the prescription in Exod 34:23 and Deut 16:16 to see the face of the deity three times a year,[3] there was still a tension inherent in the deity's cultic visibility.[4] The use of non-anthropomorphic imagery could potentially have been rationalized as a prophylactic practice meant to shield the common viewer from the deity's anthropomorphic form (Ornan 2005). It would have served the interests of those in positions of authority over the cult to limit the perception of access to the deity. Indeed, concerns about the degree to which a cultic object facilitated that access may sit at the root of preexilic attempts to reflectively compartmentalize the loci of the deity's self and agency (see the next chapter). Asserting the deadly nature of the deity's face would address this (Exod 33:20), as would confining the deity's location to the heavens (Deut 4:36). Restricting entry to the inner sanctuary to a single individual on a single day was one of many ways biblical authors and cultic authorities protected the privacy of the divine presence, and even for that single individual, there is a text that insists incense was required so that a cloud of smoke obscured the ark from view (Lev 16:13). Narratives suggesting a fundamentally anthropomorphic nature for the deity—a deity that walks, talks, smells, and gets angry (Stavrakopoulou 2021)—also would have contributed to the perception that the cultic object (which did not do those things) afforded only partial access to the divine presence. So, while Israel and

---

[3] The verbal root *rʾh* in these passages is vocalized in MT as the passive niphal stem (i.e., "appear before my face"), but the consonantal text was likely originally understood in the active qal stem (i.e., "see my face"). This is most directly indicated by the allusion to the requirement in Isa 1:12, which has the root in the infinitive construct—*lērāʾôt*—and is vocalized as a niphal in MT, but it lacks the preformative *he* required by the niphal stem (we would expect *ləhērāʾôt*). There is also no preposition in Isaiah to support interpreting it as "appear *before* my face." (The articulations of the commandment in Exodus and Deuteronomy only have the direct object marker *ʾet*.)

[4] Note Ornan's (2005, 173) observations regarding cult images in Mesopotamia: "Most men or women, therefore, rarely saw the anthropomorphic images of their deities in ninth–sixth-century Assyria and Babylonia. In their daily lives, Babylonians and Assyrians were not surrounded by figures of their prominent gods, but instead by clay statuettes of minor deities, by composite apotropaic creatures and by divine symbols engraved on seals. The ancients saw their prominent human-shaped gods on special occasions, such as cultic processions, but as a rule, cult statues in Mesopotamia were kept closed in shrines and temples, into which ordinary people could not have entered."

4. *YHWH in the Hebrew Bible*   113

Judah's cultic objects made the deity in some sense visible, the deity's fitness seems to have remained tethered to the unseen agency conceptual base.

In contrast to the deadly nature of the deity's face and the compartmentalization of the loci of their identity, the narrative anthropomorphism of the Bible was unlikely to have been a conscious and intentional rhetorical campaign. In chapter 1, I discussed ways in which certain reflective elaborations on concepts of unseen agency aided their sociomaterial transmission, relevance, and perseverance. These reflective elaborations included stories about sociomaterial interactions with humanity; after all, narratives assigning personhood and all its trappings to deity would be more intuitive and thus easier to visualize, to remember, and to transmit. Anthropomorphism is included in the package with narrativization. Because cultic representations of deity are necessarily visible—even if access is restricted—they are a rich medium for further reinforcing those anthropomorphic literary features that facilitated transmission. Thus, for instance, metal statuary representing national deities in and around Israel and Judah in the Late Bronze and early Iron Ages gravitated towards two broad styles associated with central "doctrinal" features of the deities: the striding "smiting" type, often associated with Baal, and the seated "enthroned" type, often associated with El (but see Ornan 2011, 272–80, and fig. 4.1 below).

Figure 4.1. Bronze and gold foil deity figurines (fourteenth–thirteenth century BCE) in the "enthroned" and "smiting" poses. Drawing by the author.

As mentioned above, semiotic anchoring in material media and cult make the transmission and elaboration of properties much more efficient, but the proliferation of repetitive "doctrinal mode" ritual can serve the same function, removing some of the pressures from artistic representation where resources are scarce. This may account in part for the decrease in anthropomorphic representation and the increase in symbolic—which is not to say aniconic—representation during the Iron Age in the regions occupied by Israel and Judah. In short, resources and the markets that supported them (and were supported by them) were scarce, but an increase in "doctrinal mode" ritual in concert with the centralization of authority within developing "secondary states" around the tenth century BCE could have stepped in to carry the weight of transmitting, elaborating on, and perpetuating features of the salient divine profiles. This could have reduced the demand for explicitly anthropomorphic statuary and helped proliferate so-called aniconic representations as these societies and their institutions grew in size and complexity in the seventh century.[5]

THE CONCEPTUAL DOMAINS AND PROFILES OF YHWH

DEITY. In the Hebrew Bible, YHWH is the prototypical representative of the conceptual domain of DEITY.[6] Thus, the most common profile for the terms for deity is "YHWH." We see this demonstrated in places like Isa 13:19: "And Babylon, the splendor of kingdoms, / the beauty and pride of the Chaldeans, / will be as when Deity overthrew Sodom and Gomorrah."[7] The informed hearer/reader

---

[5] Middlemas (2014) and Schaper (2019) both make the case that this abstraction was the answer to the anxiety associated with divine imagery. In the next few chapters I will argue that abstractions absolutely played a role, but with two caveats: first, abstractions only served this function to the degree that institutions and texts could maintain and enforce the desired associations; second, material presencing media were not abandoned, they were simply adapted.

[6] An exception may be Gen 33:20: *'ēl 'ĕlōhê yiśrā'ēl*, which may be translated "El, the deity of Israel," or as a verbless clause: "El is the deity of Israel." The former would represent the only El-oriented variation on the formula "YHWH, the deity of Israel" (*YHWH 'ĕlōhê yiśrā'ēl*), which occurs 119 times, but not in Genesis, suggesting its association with Israel's more developed national identity. This analogy also suggests *'el* is functioning as a DN and not the appellative "deity." Wardlaw argues for the appellative use of *'el* in Gen 33:20 on analogy with the arthrous *ha-'ēl 'ĕlōhê 'ābîkā* in Gen 46:3, which he translates "God the God of your father." While Wardlaw acknowledges that a HIGH GOD domain was likely associated with the lexeme *'el* in ancient Israel, he only identifies five passages where it is plausible (Gen 33:20; Deut 7:9, 21; 10:17; 33:26), and ultimately concludes that it is not used as a DN (Wardlaw 2008, 132–34).

[7] Here the profile YHWH refers not to the (putative) real-world instantiation of the concept, but to the individual's conceptualization of it. In other words, it refers to the conceptual package evoked by the lexeme, not to its actual referent.

would be able to discern from the various contexts that *'ĕlōhîm* is being used as a title that profiles YHWH. The most explicit contextual cue in this passage is the reference to the tradition regarding the destruction of Sodom and Gomorrah from Gen 19:24–25, but the broader context of the author's prophecies, as well as other more explicit references to YHWH as *'ĕlōhîm / 'ēl/ 'ĕlôha* would cue the reader to the same titular use, as would the location and situations attending the passage's consumption in antiquity. The title borders on functioning as a name. Similarly, an informed person on the street today in Salt Lake City, Utah, would understand "the Church" to profile The Church of Jesus Christ of Latter-day Saints, while an informed person on the street in Rome would understand it to profile the Roman Catholic Church. A Latter-day Saint in Rome speaking with a local would know to qualify their references to "the Church" if they intended to refer to the one headquartered in Salt Lake City. Similarly, without a contextual cue to mute the YHWH profile, that would be one of the most intuitive and automatic profiles for the concept. This no doubt helped facilitate the renegotiation of some of the ambiguous uses of *'ĕlōhîm* that likely referred to other deities or to cultic objects in early literature (e.g., Exod 22:27).

All this is not to say that YHWH's identification as the prototypical deity did not merit reinforcement at certain times and in certain circumstances. One of the most frequent objects of the biblical authors' scorn was the tendency for the people of Israel and Judah to dedicate attention and resources to deities other than YHWH, and so asserting YHWH's primacy was a frequent rhetorical necessity. One of the most explicit attempts to emphasize YHWH's claim to deity was Elijah's contest with the priests of Baal, which was intended to demonstrate definitively that YHWH was "Deity in Israel [*'ĕlōhîm bəyiśrā'ēl*]" (1 Kgs 18:36). After YHWH sent down fire from the heavens to burn up the sacrifice and the altar, the gathered people fell to their faces to emphatically acknowledge (v. 39), "YHWH is the deity [*YHWH hû' hā-'ĕlōhîm*]! YHWH is the deity [*YHWH hû' hā-'ĕlōhîm*]!"

PATRONAGE AND NATIONAL DEITY. The previous chapter noted that about half of all biblical occurrences of the terms for deity occur in genitive relationships with individuals, groups, or territories. While a number of those occurrences refer to deities other than YHWH, the majority are direct references to YHWH, who was conceptualized within the same conceptual domains of PATRONAGE and NATIONAL DEITY. YHWH's profile as a national deity came off the same conceptual shelf as other national deities. That YHWH was the national deity over Israel/Judah does not require argument, but there is change in this conceptualization that merits attention. The earliest texts reflecting YHWH's purview over Israel and Judah understood it to be restricted to those nations. YHWH's defeat at the hands of Chemosh in 2 Kgs 3:27 is an example that was discussed earlier, but there are others. In 1 Sam 26:19, David accused Saul of chasing him out of the nation of

Israel ("YHWH's inheritance" [*naḥălat YHWH*]), in effect saying, "Go, worship other gods." Similarly, in 2 Kgs 5:17, the Syrian general, Naaman, after being healed of his disease, asks for two mule-loads of earth to facilitate the worship of YHWH in his home country. Finally, an exiled psalmist in Ps 137:4 laments, "How could we sing a song of YHWH on foreign soil [*'al 'admat nēḥār*]?" The concept tacitly underlying all these passages is that deities are prototypically patrons over a nation and do not appropriately function, or are not accessible, outside that purview. While the relationship was fundamentally with the people, since a nation's identity was as saliently linked with territory, so too the conceptualization of that relationship. In this sense, YHWH did not operate any differently from the other deities of ancient Southwest Asia.

The paradigm shift in YHWH's territorialism came with their universalization in the exilic and/or postexilic periods, which was discussed earlier in relation to Ps 82. Expanding the purview of the patron deity beyond national boundaries may have served the immediate rhetorical need of facilitating the perception of access and oversight to the diaspora populations of a splintered nation, but there were other unintended implications related to their conceptualization as patron deity. If all nations were now the purview of the deity of Israel/Judah,[8] all peoples were potentially YHWH's people. On what grounds were Judahites to assert a unique or exclusive relationship with YHWH? One response was to emphasize Israel's "chosen" or "elected" status, realized either through their covenant relationship with the deity (Deuteronomistic writings) and/or through their purity and holiness (Priestly writings).[9] Exodus 19:5–6 seem to recognize the need for such status in light of YHWH's purview over the whole earth, and consolidates the two ideologies: "And now, if you carefully heed my voice and keep my covenant, you will be my treasure from among all peoples. For the whole earth is mine [*lî kol-hā'āreṣ*], but you shall be for me a priestly kingdom, and a holy nation" (cf. Deut 14:2; 26:18; Ps 135:4). There was thus an expansion of the limits of YHWH's patronage alongside a dichotomization of its nature. Judah/Israel remained a privileged social group, even as YHWH appropriated responsibility over all the nations of the earth.

DIVINE WAR. Some of the earliest texts in the Hebrew Bible present the deity of Israel as a warrior. Exodus 15:1–12—the earliest portions of the Song of the Sea—may represent the most archaic of these, describing YHWH's defeat of

---

[8] Of course, by this time, the population was primarily Judahite, and identified itself as such, even if Israelite identity had been appropriated.

[9] The need to rationalize this exclusive relationship became the seedbed for the ideologies that are frequently identified by modern scholars as the necessary and sufficient features of monotheism. Cf. MacDonald 2003, 151–81.

Pharaoh and the armies of Egypt.[10] The text asserts in verse 3 that, "YHWH is a man of war" (*YHWH 'îš milḥāmâ*). The rest of the poem describes the Egyptian army being slung into the sea, having the sea piled up and then cast over them, and having the earth swallow them up. Similar to the Song of Deborah's depiction of Sisera's army being swept away by the river Kishon, the Song of the Sea describes natural phenomena under the control of the deity defeating the enemy, sidestepping the need to describe an individual warrior somehow singlehandedly destroying an entire army—a counterintuitive narrative that would be cognitively costly to produce, remember, and transmit.[11]

The Song of the Sea's description of the deity's manipulation of the sea for destructive purposes may reflect, at least in part, the "storm-deity" profile, which is known from across ancient Southwest Asia.[12] Generally speaking, the storm-deity was responsible for sustaining agriculture (and thus civilization and cosmic order) through the provision of rain and other terrestrial sources of water (as a result there was a natural conceptual overlap with fertility).[13] There was also a violent dimension to such deities, however, and they could devastate peoples and/or their crops and animals through violent storms, lightning, hail, floods, and drought. These were the media for the storm-deity's conceptualization as warrior, although the mythological narrativization of the deity's battles with other deities also involved other more traditional weapons and warrior motifs.[14]

Apart from 2 Kgs 3:27, one of the most conspicuous examples of war between divine combatants in the Hebrew Bible is the so-called *Chaoskampf* motif, which pits YHWH against a divine sea monster of some kind that is generally

---

[10] See Flynn 2014, 47–58. Ronald Hendel (2015) has suggested that the Song of the Sea represents the accretion of poetic tradition to social memories regarding the collapse of Egypt's hegemony over the hill country in the Late Bronze Age.

[11] Although note Isa 63:1–6 describes the deity returning from battle, covered in blood, castigating those who failed to show up in support and boasting of their singlehanded victory. The actual means of the victory are elided, however, and the hearer/reader is left to imagine the scene themselves.

[12] Pantoja 2017, 56–62. See also Green 2003; Schwemer 2008a, 2008b. On YHWH as storm-deity, see Dion 1991; Müller 2008.

[13] In places like the Southwest Asian hill countries, where rainfall was the central lifeblood of agriculture and, thus, civilization, the balance between prosperity and destruction became increasingly delicate as the size and complexity of a society increased. It is no wonder the storm-deity began to predominate in these regions after the development of the secondary states of the tenth century BCE.

[14] For instance, in the Ugaritic stories of Baal's battle with Yamm, the craftsman deity Kothar-wa-Hasis fashions two maces that Baal uses to defeat Yamm (*KTU* 1.2.iv.10–30). Mark Smith and Wayne Pitard (2009, 57) suggest, however, that these weapons represent Baal's lightning.

thought to represent cosmic chaos or disorder.[15] The deity's victory secures and is symbolic of their sovereignty, often expressed as their kingship. Isaiah 27:1 represents a clear example of this motif: "In that day, YHWH will visit punishment, with his hard and great and strong sword, upon Leviathan [*liwyātān*], the wriggling serpent [*nāḥāš bāriḥa*], and upon Leviathan, the writhing serpent [*nāḥāš 'ăqallātôn*]; and he will kill the monster [*hattannîn*] that is in the sea." This account bears striking similarities to a passage from the Ugaritic *KTU* 1.5.i.1–3 that praises Baal for dispatching a creature named Lotan:[16]

k tmḫṣ.ltn.bṯn.brḥ	When you struck Lotan, the wriggling serpent,
tkly.bṯn. 'qltn.	you finished off the writhing serpent,
šlyṭ.d.šb 't.rašm	the powerful one with seven heads.

While the final passage refers to a powerful one with seven heads rather than to a *tannîn*, "monster," that lives in the sea, the epithet *šlyṭ* occurs elsewhere in connection with the Ugaritic *tnn* (*KTU* 1.3.iii.40), which is cognate with the Hebrew *tannîn* and has similar reference to the notion of chaos and disorder (Smith and Pitard 2009, 250–54). There can be little doubt that a tradition directly related to the one underlying *KTU* 1.5.i.1–3 is reflected in Isa 27:1 (Tsumura 2005, 192–95), again demonstrating that the traditions undergirding YHWH's divine profile were drawn from the broader conceptual matrices for deity. Psalm 74:12–14 similarly describes the deity's defeat of *tannînîm* and Leviathan, although in that exilic text the tradition begins to bleed into rhetoric about the deity's creative prowess, particularly in verses 15–17 (Tsumura 2015; cf. Greene 2017). In the Ugaritic literature, divine warfare is tied to rule over the pantheon, and not to creation, although the Babylonian Enuma Elish incorporates both.[17]

The figures prominent in the *Chaoskampf* motif are present in the Priestly account of creation, but those authors seem reticent to describe creation as a product of a battle against antagonistic divine forces, and so while the figures were retained, they were only conceptual husks, stripped of their agency and

---

[15] Recall that the danger and chaos of the sea conceptually contrasts with the order and safety of civilization. On the use of "chaos" in the Hebrew Bible, see Watson 2005.

[16] This translation is my own, but cf. Wyatt 2002, 115; Smith and Pitard 2009, 252. The second and third lines appear almost identically in *KTU* 1.3.iii.41–42 (the verb at the beginning of line 2 is different [*mḫšt*], as well as being in the first person). Lotan is cognate with the Hebrew *liwyātān* (Emerton 1982).

[17] For a brief outline of some different ways the Ugaritic and Akkadian literature treat the rise to divine kingship, see Smith and Pitard 2009, 16–19. David Tsumura (2005) argues that scholars have been too eager to find Enuma Elish in Gen 1. Cf. Day 1985, but against Tsumura, see Cho 2019.

narratives.[18] Enuma Elish's sea monster Tiamat may be reflected in the inert "deep" (*təhôm*) (Gen 1:2), while the great *tannînîm* became the deity's own creation, created to inhabit the waters of the sea (Gen 1:21) (Cho 2019, 76–87). Psalm 104:26 describes the deity having formed (*yṣr*) Leviathan as a plaything. None of these conceptualizations of YHWH or their relationship to the broader divine world was created *ex nihilo* within Judahite or Israelite society; they were negotiated from preexisting conceptual frameworks that were drawn from broader sociocultural contexts.

Returning to the Song of the Sea, we see in this poem an appeal to the deity as warrior in its description of YHWH's harnessing the sea to defeat the Egyptian army, but this does not directly invoke the classical motifs of storms or flooding usually associated with the storm-deity as warrior. Rather, the references to the sea and its manipulation seem to allude obliquely to the mythological story of the storm-deity's battle with, and victory over, the personified sea.[19] In the Ugaritic literature, this deity was El's own son, Yamm (also called Nahar, "River"), and their defeat at the hands of the outsider Baal (referred to as the son of Dagon) secured the latter's kingship over the deities.[20] The Song of the Sea may be recasting that battle, describing YHWH's opponent as a human army and turning the sea into a de-deified weapon, with YHWH's victory still securing sovereignty over all. The echo of the battle between deities is still heard in the rhetoric of incomparability from Exod 15:11, "Who is like you [*mî kāmōkâ*] among the deities [*bā'ēlîm*], YHWH?"

Judges 5:4–5, a portion of the Song of Deborah, more directly draws from the classical imagery of the storm-deity as warrior vis-à-vis humanity: "YHWH, when you went out from Seir, / when you marched from the fields of Edom, / the earth convulsed, / and the heavens poured, / indeed, the clouds poured water! / Mountains quaked before YHWH,[21] / one of Sinai, before YHWH, / the deity of Israel." Similar imagery abounds in reference to YHWH's military might. The psalmist in Ps 18 cries to YHWH from the temple for help (Ps 18:7), using storm

---

[18] "Rather, their purpose was at once to allude to the world of the sea myth, not only to that of the Babylonian Enuma Elish but also more generally to that of the common sea myth tradition, so as to make it visible to the reader's mind, but simultaneously to challenge and replace that world with a fresh vision of creation with YHWH, not Marduk, the god of their hated captors, enthroned in the cosmic temple" (Cho 2019, 78).

[19] This story is known from Ugarit, involving Baal and Yamm, from Old-Babylonia, involving Haddu and Temtum, from Neo-Babylonia, involving Marduk and Tiamat, and from a variety of myths from Anatolia. See Schwemer 2008b, 24–27; Greenstein 1982.

[20] See *KTU* 1.2.iv.32: *ym.lmt.b 'lm. yml*[*k*, "Yamm surely is dead! Baal rei[gns!(?)]" (Smith 1994, 319, 324). Note Smith's discussion (95–96) of the levels of kingship.

[21] My translation follows the LXX reading of *nozlû* as the niphal of *zll*, rather than MT's reading of qal *nzl*.

imagery to describe YHWH's arrival.[22] The skies bowed and thick darkness was under the deity's feet (v. 10). Their canopy was clouds dark with water (v. 12). Hailstones and coals of fire shot from the clouds (v. 13) as YHWH "thundered in the skies" (*yarʿēm bašāmayim*) and Elyon "uttered his voice" (*yittēn qōlô*) in verse 14. Psalm 29 famously employs a sevenfold description of YHWH's voice as lightning that shakes the wilderness and shatters trees.[23] Psalm 68:5 even applies to YHWH an epithet attributed to Baal in the Ugaritic literature: "Rider of the Clouds" (*rōḥēb bāʿărābôt*).[24]

YHWH's warrior status thus finds expression in a variety of ways that draw from and adapt features from the broader sociocultural matrix associated with divine war. The literary conventions associated with the storm-deity are among the most common means of reflecting that warrior nature, but battle can take place between deities, between YHWH and de-deified natural phenomena such as the sea or vague sea creatures like Leviathan, and between YHWH and human opponents. YHWH is also frequently called *YHWH ṣəbāʾôt*, "YHWH of Hosts," a reference to their command of military hosts.[25] While the securing of sovereignty was certainly one of the central purposes of employing warrior motifs, they also functioned in later texts as conceptual channels for YHWH's acts of creation and salvation.[26]

ACCESS TO STRATEGIC INFORMATION. Like other socially concerned deities, YHWH was understood to have full access to strategic information. Rhetoric regarding this access finds expression in many different ways in the Hebrew Bible. Isaiah 40:13, for instance, uses rhetorical questions to assert YHWH's incomparability regarding knowledge: "Who has ordered the *rûaḥ* of YHWH, and

---

[22] See Cross and Freedman 1953; Cross 1973, 158–62; Miller 1973, 121–23; Klingbeil 1999, 57–74; Green 2003, 269–71; Tsumura 2005, 149–51; Watson 2005, 74–83; Gray 2014.

[23] The majority of the scholarship on Ps 29 addresses its unity and poetic structures. See Craigie 1972; Freedman and Hyland 1973; Day 1979; Kloos 1986; Pardee 2005; Pardee and Pardee 2009; Barbiero 2016.

[24] In Ugaritic, *rkb ʿrpt* (*KTU* 1.2.iv.8, 29; 1.3.ii.40; iii.38 // iv.4; see Rahmouni 2008, 288–91). The resonance with Baal specifically is suggested by the Akkadian convention for the storm-deity to ride storms, not clouds (Rahmouni 2008, 290, n. 7). On the interchange of *bet* and *pe*, cf. Isa 5:30, where *ʿărîpîim* is used for "clouds." For more detail in this title in Ugaritic, see Wyatt 2007, 32–36.

[25] 260 occurrences, including 1 Sam 1:3, 11; 2 Kgs 23:5; Pss 46:7; 84:12; Deut 4:19; 17:3; Judg 5:20.

[26] While I am referring to battle with various forces, the relationship specifically between chaos and creation is not so clear. See Watson 2005, 19–25; Tsumura 2005. On the sea myth and its relationship to creation, see Cho 2019, 67–87. The convergence of divine battle, salvation, and creation occurs in Ps 74:12–17 (cf. Flynn 2014, 71–73).

what person being his counselor has instructed him?" Other passages assert YHWH's ability to monitor everyone's actions, activating the SOCIAL MONITORING domain (Ps 33:13–15): "From heaven YHWH looks down [*hibbîṭ*], / he sees all humanity [*rā'â 'et-kol-bənê hā'ādām*]. / From where he sits enthroned / he gazes upon all who dwell on earth [*hišgîḥa 'el kol-yōšəbê hā'āreṣ*]. / The one who fashions all their hearts / observes all their works [*mēbîn 'el-kol-ma'ăśêhem*]." Still other texts escalate this rhetoric, asserting YHWH's ability not only to observe actions, but to perceive the very thoughts and intentions of humanity (Ps 139:1–4): "O YHWH, you have searched me [*ḥăqartanî*] and you know me. / You know my sitting down and my getting up, / you discern my thoughts from afar [*bantâ lərê'î mērāḥôq*]. / You measure out my journey and my lying down, / and you are familiar with all my ways. / For before a word is on my tongue, / look, O YHWH, you know all of it [*yāda'tā kulāh*]."

One of the primary purposes of this access to strategic information was to benefit humanity by informing their decision-making. In the biblical literature, the verbs *drš*, "inquire, search, seek" (Gen 25:22; 1 Kgs 22:5–8; Ezek 20:1–3), and *š'l*, "ask" (Judg 18:5; 20:18; 1 Sam 22:13, 15; Isa 7:11–12) are used to refer to the accessing that information.[27] There were a variety of means available to inquire regarding YHWH's will, with some sanctioned by the authorities responsible for the biblical texts and some prohibited (although there was diachronic and synchronic variation on this). The previous chapter focused on some of the means of divination considered to be illicit by biblical authors and editors, but there were multiple cultic objects and agents that could be considered appropriate media for facilitating YHWH's full access to strategic information. In Num 27:21, for instance, Moses is instructed to have Aaron represent the concerns of the community before the high priest Eleazar, who would inquire (*š'l*) by means of the *'ûrîm*, "Urim," in the deity's presence (*lipnê YHWH*). Judges 20:27 suggests the ark of the covenant facilitated an inquiry (*š'l*) to YHWH. For Saul, it was YHWH's refusal to answer his inquiries through the Urim (1 Sam 28:6) or through dreams or prophets that compelled him to seek out the necromancer of En-dor.[28] This convention of inquiring of YHWH seems to have conceptually broadened in some texts to a more generic notion of "seeking" (*drš*) YHWH for purposes of communion or increased righteousness (Isa 55:6; 58:2;

---

[27] In many places, no method of inquiry is specified. For instance, in Judg 1:1–2, the author simply states that the Israelites asked (*wayyiš'ălû*) YHWH, and YHWH responded (*wayyō'mer YHWH*). The inquiry takes place after the death of Joshua, and they are asking who will function in Joshua's place, so the author may have needed to show the Israelites receiving divine guidance without acknowledging that they had no authorized means of doing so.

[28] Num 12:6 is an example of a connection between prophets and dreams.

Jer 29:13; Amos 5:4–6).²⁹ This may have roots in the cultic service that was commonly conducted in association with facilitating access to the deity's knowledge.

Prophets represent perhaps the most well-known medium for consulting the deity found across the biblical literature. Essentially professional diviners—although lay practitioners were likely not uncommon—prophets are known from across ancient Southwest Asia, and in many ways their portrayal in the biblical texts fits broader patterns, though there are important differences (cf. Sanders 2017). Jonathan Stökl (2012) identifies three broad categories of prophet: the ecstatic prophet, the technical diviner, and the writing prophet.³⁰ Ecstatic prophets and diviners are well represented in the cognate literature, though there is a great deal of overlap between the two in the Hebrew Bible. Stökl suggests the less stratified and diversified populations of Israel and Judah blurred the distinction between the roles, which contributed to a hybrid "messenger-type prophet," which is most clearly represented in the "writing prophets" attested first in the writings of Jeremiah and the Deuteronomistic literature (175–76).

The representation of prophets in the biblical texts is distinct in a variety of other ways (Sanders 2017).³¹ For instance, the prophets of the Bible represent only a single deity, rather than an entire pantheon. How much of this exclusivity is editorial in origin is unclear, but an occasional accusation against prophets who utilized illicit means or consulted other deities was that they dealt in some manner of false prophecy, which represents a degree of innovation on the genre (Huffmon 2012).³² Next, while prophets outside of Israel and Judah tended to operate in groups and directly in the service of the crown and/or temple, the biblical prophets are frequently portrayed as operating alone, and often independently of and even

---

²⁹ According to Lisbeth Fried (2013, 293), the infinitive construct *lidrôš*, "occurs 36 times in the Hebrew Bible and in all but three instances it is used to denote the act of seeking an oracle from a god, either directly or by means of a medium or prophet."

³⁰ Ecstatic prophets would be given access to information through ecstatic trances, while technical diviners studied texts in order to be able to divine information from the observation of material circumstances, such as the flight path of birds or the shape, color, and consistency of a sheep's liver.

³¹ On the terms for "prophet," see Stökl 2012, 155–200. Note, particularly, the following comment (167): "I have argued that *nabī* in Emar and Mari is related to some form of ancestor worship. If the word did not change its meaning in the process of borrowing, it would follow that the נביא was originally linked to some form of ancestor cult. A provisional, if very literal, translation of נביא is 'the called.'"

³² For instance, Jer 5:31 states, "the prophets prophesy falsely [*nibbʾû-baššeqer*]!" Ezek 12:24 asserts, "there will no longer be any false vision [*ḥăzôn šāwəʾ*] or flattering divination [*miqsam ḥālāq*] within the house of Israel." Huffmon (2012, 71–74) describes the prophets' fidelity to YHWH alone as a reflection of the vassal/king relationship.

4. YHWH in the Hebrew Bible

antagonistically towards the royal court.[33] The contrast with the broader pattern is punctuated in the story of Micaiah's prophecy regarding the death of Ahab (1 Kgs 22:8–28), which rhetorically mocks and derides the king's cadre of prophets as incompetent yes-men. The occasional antagonism towards specific kings (1 Kgs 21:17–22) and toward kingship more broadly (1 Sam 8:4–18) would have been rhetorically useful for criticizing past kings perceived to be impious or unjust, but more saliently for structuring values and power in the absence of kingship. A prophet who operates independently of the crown maintains access to the deity's strategic information even in exile or under direct foreign rule.

SOCIAL MONITORING AND PUNISHMENT. Perhaps the clearest illustration of how social monitoring informed the representation of YHWH in the Hebrew Bible is the Neo-Babylonian- or Achaemenid-period story of Achan from Josh 7.[34] In the story, Joshua's troops are routed in what was expected to be an easy victory at Ai (Josh 7:4–5). Joshua complains to YHWH, who informs him that they abandoned the troops in battle because someone stole from the spoils of Jericho. These were supposed to be *ḥerem*, or foreign spoils (or people) ritually devoted to destruction or to exclusively cultic use (Josh 7:11–12).[35] This term occurs also on the Mesha Stele (Monroe 2007; Del Monte 2005; Fleming 2021, 238–44). YHWH instructs Joshua to muster all Israel the next day so they can identify the guilty party and expunge the *ḥerem*, which is framed as a contaminant that infects the whole Israelite camp (cf. MacDonald 2003, 116–17). When Achan is identified, he confesses, "I sinned against YHWH, the deity of Israel" (Josh 7:20). Joshua then gathers at the Valley of Achor the recovered spoils, Achan, his family, and his

---

[33] See Albertz 2007, 361: "Such fundamental prophetic opposition during the ninth century against the ruling king is a new phenomenon in Israel's history. In the tenth century the prophets we hear about were ecstatic groups with no visible social function (1 Sam. 10.5–6, 10–12; 19.18–24), or court prophets like Nathan and Gad employed by the state, who predominantly functioned to stabilize the institution of monarchy (2 Sam. 7; 1 Kgs 1). Such prophets in the service of the kings are also mentioned later (1 Kgs 22). Only during the ninth century did individual prophets and prophetic groups with no ties to institutions emerge alongside these. Such prophets had largely detached themselves from ties of kinship and profession (1 Kgs 19.19–21) in order to earn their living as itinerant miraculous healers, exorcists, or oracle givers."

[34] On this dating, see Dozeman 2015, 350–61. Cf. Römer 2007, 87–88, which refers to the story of Achan as a "later interpolation" to the Deuteronomistic account of the conquest of Ai.

[35] On *ḥerem*, see Stern 1991; Crouch 2009, 174–89. Note Crouch (174–75) highlights that a national context is more likely for the development of these features of "holy war" than a tribal one. She also notes the "deuteronom(ist)ic" context for the majority of *ḥerem* narratives (177). On this last point, see MacDonald 2003, 108–22.

possessions, and they are all stoned and burned, which satiates YHWH's anger and enables the Israelites to take the city of Ai (Josh 8:1–29).

Achan here represents the quintessential free-rider, violating sociocultural mores in order to take advantage of resources facilitated by the broader cooperation of the social group. Achan's transgression in and of itself has no direct effect on the success of the social group, but if it goes unpunished, more free-riding is likely to follow, threatening the cohesion of the group. Because YHWH—who is fundamentally a prosocial agent—imposes and enforces the *ḥerem*, its violation results in YHWH's withdrawal of support from the siege of Ai, resulting in thirty-six deaths and Israel's defeat. Because Achan's sin is reflectively framed as a contaminant that must be rooted out from Israel, the punishment extends beyond the offender to all those within his household who stood to benefit, whether connected by kinship or servitude (cf. Berman 2014). This fictive account rhetorically elevates the stakes vis-à-vis free-riding for those hearers for whom the story was authoritative (it is referenced in a later warning in Josh 22:20).

The ritualization of this act of restraint by including it in the concept of *ḥerem* appropriates the powerful influences of divine scrutiny and punishment, as well as the CREDs (credibility enhancing displays) framework. The simple prohibition of taking the spoils of conquest on the grounds that leadership wants it, or that it advantages and disadvantages different groups and creates chaos, thereby undermining social cohesion and cooperation, would not go over incredibly well. Framing the prohibition as a ritual act, however, endows it with increased social salience and brings YHWH and their oversight into play. Enforcement with the death penalty could take place without the deity, but their ability to covertly monitor all members of the group changes the dynamic considerably. YHWH was the only one who knew that Achan had taken from the spoils, indicating that there is no hiding from the divine monitor (cf. Ps 139). The story additionally heightens the consequences of the violation of this putatively arbitrary ritual act by attributing to it the deaths of thirty-six Israelite troops and the melting of the hearts of the people. What is more, future military endeavors are threatened, not only by the deity's withdrawal of support, but also by the damage done to the reputation of Israel and its deity—this is not a victimless crime. The story of Achan presents one of the most unobstructed views in the Hebrew Bible of the conceptualization of YHWH as a prototypical socially concerned deity. It borrows the concept of *ḥerem* from an earlier period when it may have served to signal the equity and equal subordination of the different members of a loose federation to the deity that unified them, and leverages it as part of a terrifying warning regarding the deity's unseen monitoring.

DIVINE COUNCIL. Like the societies surrounding them, Israel and Judah structured their understanding of the pantheon's sociality and administration around the council.³⁶ The earliest iterations of this divine council appear to have been closely related to those of Ugarit, the coastal Syrian city that was destroyed around 1200 BCE, centuries before the establishment of an Israelite or Judahite national identity or literary tradition. Deuteronomy 32:8–9, for instance, preserves what may be the earliest biblical witness to the divine council, and in it the high deity (Elyon) divides and distributes the nations to their offspring (the *bene 'ĕlōhîm*, "children of deity," or "deities"; 4QDeutʲ) according to their number, with the nation of Israel assigned to YHWH, who would seem to be one of those offspring.³⁷ This not only distinguishes YHWH from Elyon, but also describes the divine council as composed of the high deity's offspring, which corresponds to the Ugaritic designations of the divine council as the *mpḫrt bn 'il*, "assembly of the children of El" (*KTU* 1.65.3), and *dr bn 'il*, "circle of the children of El" (*KTU* 1.40.25, 33–34). The table of nations in Gen 10 suggests there were understood to be seventy nations on earth, and this tradition appears in later literature in reference to seventy guardian angels over the nations of the earth (e.g., 1 En. 89.59; 90.22–25).³⁸ If this tradition of seventy nations was in circulation at the time of the composition of Deut 32:8–9, the number of nations would correspond with the number of the divine offspring, which would correspond with the Ugaritic literature's designation of the members of the divine council as the seventy offspring of Athirat, El's consort (*KTU* 1.4.vi.46; cf. Smith 2001, 41–43, 55–56).³⁹

Two major changes may be noted regarding the conceptualization of YHWH between the early iteration of the divine council in Deut 32 and the much later iteration in Ps 82. Perhaps the most significant difference is that YHWH appears to direct the council in the latter witness but is subordinate in the earlier. There has been a great deal of debate regarding the distinction of YHWH and El in Ps 82, but if El is identifiable in the psalm, they are utterly inoperative, and the exilic (or later) dating of the psalm renders unlikely the preservation of a firm distinction. There may be a relic of YHWH's subordination preserved in the

---

³⁶ As Robert Gordon (2007, 190) notes, "Old Testament references to this Divine Council … are too widely distributed among the individual books and across the canonical divisions for them to be regarded as simple 'vestigial' and immaterial to the presentation of God in the Hebrew scriptures. The Pentateuch, Former and Latter Prophets, Psalms, Job and Daniel all draw directly on the concept of the DC in their portrayal of the God of Israel."

³⁷ MT begins Deut 32:9 with *kî* ("because," "that," "but"), the interpretation of which has been a subject of some debate (Tsevat 1969, 132; Heiser 2006, 5–8), but it has largely facilitated identifying YHWH with Elyon and reading the passage to indicate YHWH reserved one of the allotments for themselves. The Septuagint, however, begins the verse with *kai egenēthē*, "and it happened that," which almost exclusively renders the narrative marker *wayəhî*.

³⁸ The number seventy was a conventionalized way to refer to a large number of something.

³⁹ Fleming (2021, 269) points out that a high deity distributing sovereignty over lands or peoples is "unknown from any ancient writing."

author's borrowing of a much older literary template, but YHWH is the only active deity in Ps 82 (McClellan 2018, 846).[40]

The other significant change in the conceptualization of YHWH's divine council is the inclusion of human witnesses and participants (Lenzi 2008, 50–64, 221–72). Human witnessing of divine council deliberations is known from texts from Mari, Deir 'Alla, and Mesopotamia, although in the latter instances, the witnessing is usually secretive (Nissinen 2002; Gordon 2007; Lenzi 2014). Several factors likely contributed to the adoption of this theme in the biblical texts, including a need to stock the council after the participation of other deities became problematic, a need to provide a context for human reporting on divine council proceedings, and perhaps a desire to structure power in favor of non-royal prophets. A detailed example of a prophet witnessing the divine council comes from 1 Kgs 22:15–23, in which the prophet Micaiah is goaded into contradicting the king's court prophets regarding the propriety of the king going to battle in Ramoth-gilead. Micaiah casts himself as witness to the divine council's deliberations in 1 Kgs 22:19: "I saw YHWH sitting upon his throne, and all the host of the heavens stood by him, on his right hand and on his left." He then goes on to describe YHWH asking which of the host of heaven in attendance would volunteer to seduce the king's prophets into leading the king into battle so he will be killed. Micaiah is punished for his insubordination, but his prophecy ultimately proves to be accurate. The sixth-century BCE prophet Jeremiah hints at his participation in the council itself when he rhetorically asks in Jer 23:18, "Who has stood in the council of YHWH [*běsôd YHWH*]?" More explicitly, Isa 6:8–10 has Isaiah volunteer to carry a message on behalf of YHWH's council (White 2014, 80–86). Prior to the request, a seraph purifies Isaiah with a coal from the altar of the temple (Isa 6:6–7), apparently to sanctify him so that he can be in the deity's presence and can participate in the council.

While these innovations show the creative work of the authors, editors, and authorities who influenced these traditions and the texts that transmitted them, the Hebrew Bible's representations of the divine council are clearly founded on broader Southwest Asian conventions and traditions adapted from patriarchal household and administrative institutions to structure and frame the conceptualization of divine sociality. YHWH's role fits this framing and this divine sociality in a way that demonstrates its rootedness in generic conceptualizations of deity.

INCOMPARABILITY. When directed at YHWH, the rhetoric of INCOMPARABILITY was generally brief, employing language closely parallel to that of surrounding

---

[40] Ellen White (2014, 33) suggests Ps 82 narrates YHWH's demotion not just of the other deities of the divine council, but also of its leader, the high deity El: "Thus while Yahweh is a character in this divine council type-scene he is not the head of it (El is) until possibly the end of the psalm when he takes over the position of the council."

societies: "Now I know that YHWH is greater than all the deities [*gādôl YHWH mikol-hā'ĕlōhîm*]" (Exod 18:11); "What deity [*mî-'ēl*] is there in heaven or on earth that could act according to your deeds and your might?" (Deut 3:24); "Because you, YHWH, are most high over all the earth. You are greatly exalted over all deities [*mə'ōd na'ălêtā 'al-kol-'ĕlōhîm*]" (Ps 97:9). This conceptual domain was not an assertion of philosophical monotheism (though it is frequently read as such),[41] but was a translatable feature of the generic concept of deity that was effectively and liberally employed by the authors and editors of the Hebrew Bible in reference to their preferred deity. While generic greatness or might was the most basic theme of the rhetoric of incomparability, YHWH's creative acts and military prowess were also frequently employed as a part of that rhetoric, as with praise for warrior and creator deities from other societies in ancient Southwest Asia.[42] Isaiah 37:16 is representative of this rhetoric: "YHWH of Hosts, Deity of Israel, who sits enthroned among the cherubim: You alone are the deity for all the kingdoms of the earth. You made the heavens and the earth."

HOLINESS. While the Hebrew Bible does use the lexeme *qādôš* in reference to deities other than YHWH, it reserves its most emphatic rhetoric regarding holiness for YHWH. *Qādôš* is frequently a title of YHWH, and particularly in Isaiah, where it occurs over two dozen times.[43] In several places, the concept of holiness is connected with the inspiration of awe and dread. For instance, Isa 29:23 asserts, "They will sanctify the Holy One of Jacob [*hiqdîšû 'et-qədôš ya'ăqōb*], and they will dread [*ya'ărîṣû*] the deity of Israel."[44] First Samuel 6:20 asks rhetorically, "Who is able to stand in the presence of YHWH, this holy deity?" Isaiah 6 elaborates on this when, after the seraphs chant in verse 3, "Holy, holy, holy [*qādôš qādôš qādôš*] is YHWH of hosts!," Isaiah cries out, "Woe is me! I am silenced! because I am a man of unclean lips, and I dwell in the midst of a people of unclean lips, yet my eyes have seen the king, YHWH of hosts!" One of the seraphs then takes a coal from the altar of the temple and touches Isaiah's lips with it, removing his sin and effectively rendering him "holy," thus able to withstand the presence of the deity.

The sense of holiness as overwhelming radiance is most frequently connected to the description of YHWH's appearance as like fire, although apart from

---

[41] For instance, Hewel Clifford (2010) argues that Deutero-Isaiah is adopting conventional rhetoric of incomparability, but is using it to assert divine exclusivity, since idol polemic elsewhere "encourages reading the exclusivity formulae with an absolute monotheism" (276). His argument relies on Rechenmacher (1997) but does not adequately engage discussions such as MacDonald's (2003, 82–85) regarding negating particles.

[42] Most explicit is "The Great Cairo Hymn of Praise to Amun-Re" (*COS* 1.25.i, iii).

[43] Isa 1:4; 5:19, 24; 10:17, 20; 12:6; 17:7; 29:19, 23; 30:11–12, 15; 31:1; 37:23; 40:25; 41:14, 16, 20; 43:3, 14–15; 45:11; 47:4; 48:17; 49:7; 54:5; 55:5; 60:9, 14.

[44] NRSV here renders, "they will stand in awe of the God of Israel."

Ezekiel, there appears to be a reticence—whether original or constructed—to elaborate on the appearance of the divine. Exodus 24:17 refers to the appearance of YHWH's "glory" (*kəbôd*) as a "devouring fire" (*'ēš 'ōkelet*). Isaiah 10:17 refers to Israel's "Holy One" (*qādôš*), as a flame. YHWH appears to Moses in Exod 3 in the midst of a fire (Exod 3:2). Even more explicitly, YHWH appears as a "pillar of fire" (*'ammûd 'ēš*), in leading the Israelites through the wilderness during the night (Exod 13:21). Rhetoric about holiness is also concentrated in P's Holiness Code, which emphasizes YHWH's holiness, but more saliently, the cultic and ritual requirements for Israel to become holy. Leviticus 19:2 states: "Speak to all the congregation of the children of Israel and say to them, "You will be holy [*qədōšîm tihyû*], because I—YHWH, your deity—am holy [*qādôš 'ănî*]" (cf. Lev 11:44–45; 20:7). As noted in the previous chapter, the sense of "holy" here seems to relate to purity and cleanliness, which likely influenced the conceptualization of YHWH as holy, making their purity and cleanliness a more salient aspect of their divine profile.

IMMORTALITY. Immortality was generally assumed of deities and was really only explicitly addressed in the context of rhetoric about humanity's status as non-divine (as in Ezek 28:9) or the revocation and demotion of undesirable deities (as in Ps 82). YHWH's immortality, a prototypical feature of generic deity, was most frequently framed in terms of their eternal nature,[45] as in Gen 21:33, which appositionally refers to YHWH as "Eternal El/Deity [*'ēl 'ôlām*]." Similarly, Exod 15:18 asserts "YHWH will reign forever and ever [*lə'ōlām wā'ed*]." In Deut 32:40, the Song of Moses has the deity swear an oath on their own life: "As I live forever [*ḥay 'ānōkî lə'ōlām*]." These descriptions of the deity's eternal existence were most rhetorically useful in referring to the eternity of YHWH's covenants and promises (Gen 17:19; Exod 31:16–17; 32:13), and to YHWH's sovereignty over the heavens, the earth, and the inhabitants of both, evinced by their pre-existence before the universe and before their antagonists. YHWH's role as creator takes center stage in much of this rhetoric. For example, Jer 10:11 mocks as mortal those deities that were not involved in the creation of the earth: "Thus will you say to them: 'The deities who did not create the skies or the earth will perish from the earth [*yē'badû mē'r'ā'*] and from under these skies.'" Similarly, Ps 136 represents a lengthy hymn of praise to YHWH for their various creative

---

[45] While I render "eternal" for *'ôlām*, the term's sense does not match the contemporary notion of philosophical eternity. Rather, it referred to perpetuity or a duration with no perceptible end. This is also not to say deities could not die or be killed, whether with or without permanent effect. On this, see Smith 2001, 104–31; Machinist 2011.

and salvific acts, punctuating each of the twenty-six verses with "For his mercy [ḥesed]⁴⁶ is eternal [lə 'ōlām]."

COMMUNICABLE AGENCY. As with other deities, YHWH's agency was conceptualized as communicable, and not uncommonly through material media. Within the Hebrew Bible, the Jerusalem temple and whatever cultic image may have been housed in the inner sanctum constituted the single most prominent means of presencing YHWH, but a number of cultic objects and other entities functioned to presence the deity's agency. The ark of the covenant and the messenger of YHWH are two examples that will be discussed in much greater detail below. One of the more explicit examples of a Yahwistic cult object facilitating YHWH's communicable agency is that of the bronze serpent created by Moses in Num 21:4–9. In verse 8, YHWH instructs Moses to produce a śārāp ("seraph") and set it on a pole to facilitate the healing of those Israelites suffering from the bites of "the fiery serpents" (hannəḥāšîm haśśərāpîm). In verse 9, Moses makes a bronze serpent (nəḥaš nəḥōšet), and those who look at it are healed. Attributing its construction to YHWH's command sidesteps the prohibitions on such practices, but it also suggests it is YHWH's agency that is ultimately responsible for the healing, even though it is channeled through an explicitly human-made cultic object (Gertz 2016).⁴⁷

The description in 2 Kgs 18:4 of the later destruction of this object by Hezekiah on the grounds that incense offerings were being made to it may suggest the editors could tolerate the object's conceptualization as a Yahwistic tool, but not as an object of worship. It is possible they understood the icon to mediate worship directed ultimately at YHWH, or they may have understood that worship to suggest its independent divine status. In other words, directing worship at the object centered its status as "is not YHWH,"⁴⁸ which was unacceptable for an ideology that sought a monopoly on accessing divine agency (cf. Eichler 2019). The authors of 2 Kgs 18:4 suggest someone (the subject is not perfectly clear) named the object Nehushtan, which may be an attempt to frame it as an independent agent. Whatever the case, COMMUNICABLE AGENCY was clearly a salient semantic domain.

I suggest the entities that presenced that agency could be profiled along a spectrum from deity to divine image, depending on how independently the hearer/reader understood the cultic object and the agency it presenced to be operating from the primary loci of the deity's self. The rhetorical compartmentalization of those loci from the vehicles of the deity's agency subordinated and

---

⁴⁶ "Mercy" is admittedly an imperfect gloss for ḥesed. For a helpful cognitive linguistic interrogation of the term, see Ziegert 2020.
⁴⁷ On the relationship of the sounds used in the story to broader sociocultural notions of the "magic" of words, see Hurowitz 2004.
⁴⁸ This is in reference to Jacobsen's "is" and "is not" dichotomy (see introduction).

separated the latter, likely contributing to concern with worship directed at it. The more independent it was understood to be from the locus of divine selfhood, the more of a threat it may have been perceived to be. The next chapter will discuss some rhetorical methods used by authors and editors used to exploit that compartmentalization while mitigating the potential threats.

ANTHROPOMORPHISM. Similar to the representation of other deities, YHWH is predominantly presented in the Hebrew Bible as thoroughly anthropomorphic (Stavrakopoulou 2021). However—and also similar to the representation of other deities—there was a concerted effort at times to mitigate or obscure that anthropomorphism. In the case of the other deities, this could be part of a campaign of denying their relevance, influence, and access, but in the case of YHWH, it was usually a corollary to efforts to rhetorically exalt the deity and safeguard control of access to them. This rhetorical tug-of-war seems to have been a product of the conflict of intuitive and reflective reasoning about deity. A host of reflective conceptualizations served the structuring of power and values on the part of cultic authorities, while more intuitive conceptualizations based more directly on familiar anthropomorphic frameworks facilitated the more efficient transmission and perseverance of deity concepts. Curating a divine profile that maintains the fundamental invisible and non-anthropomorphic nature of a deity across all domains and dimensions cuts against the intuitive grain and would require intentional, authoritative, and sustained reflective reasoning that would be difficult to achieve outside of the frameworks of powerful social institutions.

Even then, however, unless a person is consciously subordinating their deity concepts to those authoritative frameworks, they will frequently default to more intuitive conceptualizations. Experiments conducted by Justin Barrett and his colleagues in the 1990s and 2010s demonstrated that firmly held theological beliefs in all-present, all-powerful, nonanthropomorphic deities still gave way to thoroughly anthropomorphic conceptualizations when those theological frameworks were not the active focus of cognition (Barrett and Keil 1996; Barrett 1999, 2011). In the case of YHWH and the Hebrew Bible, the reflective conceptualizations of deity that served the authors' structuring of power opposed the gravitational pull of intuition, and so there was a need for constant curation.[49] Removing the deity from the narratives, however, created a disconnect from earlier narratives where the deity appears to interact directly with figures like Abraham and Moses. One tool for getting around this problem was the messenger of YHWH, whose literary utility will be discussed in greater detail in the next chapter.

---

[49] A convenient modern example of this conflict is the Christian concept of the Trinity, which is authoritatively maintained in the interest of specific rhetorical needs, but is difficult to reduce to cognitively efficient frameworks.

As with the representation of other deities in the cognate literature, YHWH's body was frequently portrayed as enormous in size and power (Wagner 2019; Cornelius 2017; cf. Reynolds 2002). Mark Smith (2001, 84) notes that Baal was described in Ugaritic literature as "large as his own mountain, Saphan." This is reflected in descriptions of the enormous size of the deity's temple/palace, but also their throne and footstool, which dwarf other deities, whose feet do not even reach the footstool. The 'Ain Dara temple, in Syria, reflects this enormous size by depicting in stone a series of one-meter-long footprints, representing the deity's stride toward the sanctuary (Lewis 2020, 341). A pair of them appear at the portico, with a single footprint representing a left foot immediately before the antechamber, and a single right foot several meters ahead before the main hall. While Isa 6:1 describes the train of YHWH's robe filling the whole Jerusalem temple (the enormous size of which is described in 1 Kgs 6), the rhetoric describing the exaggerated size of Baal's throne is amplified several times over in Isa 66:1's postexilic description of the heavens as YHWH's throne and the earth as their footstool. As with the representation of other deities in the cognate literature and material culture, the representation of the body and its parts was symbolically rich. The deity's body and its parts were not materially represented merely for the purpose of representing the deity's form; rather, over time, the intuitive impulse to conceptualize the deity as anthropomorphic was adorned with elaborations on the significance and symbolism of the various parts of the deity's body. These elaborations were quite flexible, since, like the deity itself, they were unavailable for verification or falsification.

CONCLUSION

Despite some of the distinctive characteristics of YHWH's background among national deities of ancient Southwest Asia, YHWH's conceptualizations were rooted in the same intuitive dynamics responsible for the conceptualization of generic deity in ancient Southwest Asia. The direct relationship with the broader ancient Southwest Asian conceptualizations is most evident in the cultic artifacts from preexilic Israel and Judah and in the oldest literary strata of the Hebrew Bible, but even the innovations of later periods represented incremental elaborations on conceptual frameworks descended from those earliest periods and arising within and in response to Israel and Judah's own cognitive ecologies. Israel and Judah's rhetorical goals and needs, their sociomaterial circumstances, the nature and complexity of their institutions, and the events of history drove changes that nuanced and adapted older and more generic concepts, while the emerging technology of text facilitated the cumulative and layered aggregation over time of these different approaches to deity, collapsing the disparities of time and space that had previously separated these ideas, thereby enriching and expanding the literary palette of those who would come after. It is with that dynamic in mind that we turn to the biblical presentation of YHWH's divine agents.

5.
YHWH's Divine Agents:
The Ark of the Covenant and the *Kābôd*

The discussion up to this point has been laying the groundwork for a more careful interrogation of YHWH's own presencing media in the Hebrew Bible. We have seen that the people of Iron Age Israel and Judah constructed their understandings of the nature and function of deity on the same cognitive foundations—those "fundamentals of ancient thought"—on which the peoples of the surrounding societies constructed their own understandings of the same. YHWH emerges in the earliest literary strata as a prototypical ancient Southwest Asian deity that possessed many of the characteristics and performed many of the functions that have been identified by cognitive scientists as critical to the transmission and perseverance of concepts of socially concerned deities. This includes the manifestation of the deity's presence through material media, which is demonstrated by the cultic media that have been discovered among the material remains of Iron Age Israel and Judah. The Hebrew Bible itself, however, also attests to the centrality of presencing media. Stelai and other media pepper the texts in ways that demonstrate their normativity, but even more centrally, the Hebrew Bible repeatedly and emphatically insists on the temple itself as the principal material medium for facilitating the deity's presence and the principal sign of that presence.

Having said that, beginning in the seventh century BCE and continuing for some time, significant changes were introduced regarding the way that presencing media was understood, particularly by the authors and editors responsible for the D, Dtr, and P literary strata, as well as those responsible for consolidating the various traditions into the corpora that became the Hebrew Bible. There were no doubt different motivations for these changes prior to the destruction of the Jerusalem temple,[1] but following that destruction, those motivations seem to have

---

[1] For instance, Max Weber (1952) posited the theory later taken up by Baruch Halpern (1991), Joseph Blenkinsopp (1995), and Susan Ackerman (2012) that one of the primary goals of D's earliest campaign of cult centralization was to undermine the power of kin-based communities and their commitment to cultic relationships with deceased kin.

been focused on making sense of the destruction of the temple, codifying authoritative knowledge, and formulating a more easily delineated and enforced identity for the followers of YHWH. There was some degree of abstraction introduced by these innovations and maintained by the institutions responsible for them, but there was no severing of the gravitational pull of the intuitive longing for the deity's material presence. As this and the next two chapters will demonstrate, the use of presencing media persevered throughout the Hebrew Bible, and is even *emphasized* in different ways in the literature of the Greco-Roman and later periods.² We can make sense of the innovations introduced in these later literary strata without needing to posit a unique and revolutionary rejection or abandonment of earlier frameworks (Sommer 2009, 58–79; Smith 2008, 131–85; Gnuse 1997; Clifford 2011). Rather, I would suggest we make more constructive sense of these innovations through the lens of social memory—they are part of the constant renegotiation that must take place between a community's shared past and the exigencies of its present.³

This chapter will examine two of the earlier and more prominent vehicles for divine agency in the Hebrew Bible, namely the ark of the covenant and the *kābôd*, or "glory," of YHWH. The interrogation begins with the ark of the covenant, the closest thing to a sanctioned Yahwistic cult image found in the Hebrew Bible.⁴ Some manner of discomfort with the early nature and function of the ark incentivized its renegotiation by later editors, but despite the conclusion of some scholarship, the relationship with its presencing functions was not so easily obscured. Following the discussion of the ark, I will move onto the *kābôd*, or "glory," of YHWH, which became a critical vehicle of divine presence in P and later in Ezekiel. Its nature and function were also renegotiated, but more clearly under Mesopotamian influence.

While the changes discussed in this chapter were primarily rooted in opposition to certain types and functions of cultic objects—opposition that arose from anxiety associated with social insularity and security—I will argue that the authors and editors did not reject presencing media outright, they simply introduced new ways of understanding and curating them. In short, the deity's self was more

---

² Sommer (2009, 126) notes that notions of divine fluidity and multiple embodiments, "recur in rabbinic literature, in various forms of Jewish mysticism, and in Christianity." As we will see in the Appendix, the Christian identification of Jesus with the deity of Israel is an elaboration on the same themes.

³ Alan Kirk (2005, 5) writes, "through recitation of its master narrative a group continually reconstitutes itself as a coherent community, and as it moves forward through its history it aligns its fresh experiences with this master narrative, as well as vice versa."

⁴ Timothy McNinch (2021) has suggested the ark narrative (1 Sam 4:1b–7:2) so directly parallels the representation of a cult image that the word *'ărôn* ("ark") may have been an interpolation meant to conceal explicit mention of just such an image.

firmly compartmentalized from the partible loci of their agency, which were altered in ways that initially mitigated their accessibility, their private reproduction, and their vulnerability. This allowed the media to adequately presence the deity's agency while the divine self was asserted to be located elsewhere, such as in the heavens or exclusively in the Jerusalem temple. These authors and editors trod a precarious line, however, in light of the risk that this compartmentalization could incentivize worship of the loci of agency (as we saw above with the bronze serpent, Nehushtan). Narratives could be produced to malign that worship, but authorities also developed certain characteristics for that media—such as locating them within authoritative texts—that also proved to be effective and durative.[5]

THE ARK OF THE COVENANT

According to the biblical texts, the ark of the covenant (*'ărôn habbərît*) was first and foremost a box.[6] The vast majority of the 202 uses of *'ărôn* in the Hebrew Bible refer to YHWH's cultic object, but the term is also used generically, as in Gen 50:26, in which Joseph's corpse was embalmed and placed in an *'ărôn*, and 2 Kgs 12:10–11, in which Jehoiada placed an *'ărôn* alongside the altar for the collection of money (cf. 2 Chr 24:8, 10–11). The more specialized use of the term in reference to YHWH's cult object derives from this generic sense, which is why the former almost always occurs in a construct phrase, such as the ark *of the testimony* (*'ărôn hā'ēdut*, Exod 25:22), the ark *of the covenant* (*'ărôn habbərît*, Josh 3:6), the ark *of YHWH* (*'ărôn YHWH*, Josh 3:13), or the ark *of (the) Deity* (*'ărôn [hā]'ĕlōhîm*, 1 Sam 3:3).

If YHWH's material presencing is rooted in the frameworks and conventions of the surrounding cultures, as I have argued, then the ark of the covenant ought to parallel, in form and function, presencing media from surrounding societies, and this is precisely what we find. Most simply, it was said to be stored, as with other cultic media, in the most holy space in the tent shrine and in the temple. David Aaron (2001, 172–75) has highlighted an interesting observation regarding the ark's function within the temple in a late segment of Exodus attributed to P.

---

[5] As we will see, there was an additional rhetorical campaign toward both the textualization of the vehicles of divine agency and the ritualization of the texts of the law.

[6] The cognates terms suggest closely related meanings. Issam Halayqa (2008, 61) glosses "chest" for Ugaritic *arn*, "chest," "box," and "coffin," for Phoenician *'rn*, "ossuary" and "coffin" for Punic *'rn*, and "sarcophagus" for Epigraphic Hebrew *'rn* (cf. del Olmo Lete and Sanmartín 2003, 1.104). The Septuagint primarily renders *kibōtos*, "box, chest, coffer," although the translator of the 2 Chronicles passages (2 Chr 24:8, 10–11) rendered *glōssokomon*, "box, money bag, coffin." The ark of the covenant was likely known in its earliest iterations as the ark of YHWH (*'ărôn YHWH*), the ark of El (*'ărôn 'ēl*), or the ark of deity (*'ărôn ĕlōhîm*).

In contrast to other passages where the testimony is put *"in* the ark" (*bā'ārôn*; Deut 10:2, 5; 1 Kgs 8:9), these passages command Moses to "give" (*ntn*) the testimony *"to* the ark" (*'el-hā'ārôn*). Similarly, in Num 17, Aaron's staff is described in verse 22 [ET v. 7] as being set "before YHWH" (*lipnê YHWH*), while in verse 25 [ET v. 10], it is set "before the testimony" (*lipnê hā'ēdût*), which is generally read as metonymy for the ark.[7] This closely parallels Southwest Asian conventions about treaties being placed *before* or *at the feet of* divine images for approval or enforcement (Noegel 2015, 228–29). It suggests the ark was functioning primarily as presencing media, but the language may have been just ambiguous enough to have been reinterpreted in harmony with developing understandings of the ark's function, helping it to evade excising editorial hands.

It is in the ark's nature and function as a shrine model, however, that we find the strongest and most numerous connections with the presencing media of surrounding societies.[8] The closed type of shrine model known from around ancient Southwest Asia matches the ark's nature as a container, and one such shrine model discovered at Megiddo and dated roughly to the ninth century depicts a windowed building flanked by volutes and winged entities reminiscent of sphynxes or perhaps cherubim (May 1935; see fig. 5.1). Herbert May (1936) described the shrine as a "miniature temple," and argued for understanding the ark of the covenant as the same (cf. Morgenstern 1942–1943). Wall reliefs commissioned by Tiglath-Pileser III in the late-eighth century BCE (fig. 5.2), and by Sennacherib in the early-seventh century (fig. 5.3), depict Neo-Assyrian forces carrying off cultic media, and each depicts a box containing a miniature divine image as one of the media. While anthropomorphic imagery is not attested in Iron Age Israel and Judah, it is not an enormous conceptual leap to link the tablets that contained some iteration of the law (depending on the source) with cultic stelai, particularly in light of the command to write the words of the law upon cultic stelai in Deut 27:1–10 and Josh 8:32, 34–35. The tablets of the law are also

---

[7] Metonymy is a figure of speech in which something is referred to by mentioning something closely related to it. To say someone is headed "to the altar," for instance, is usually metonymy for the act of getting married, even though there may not be any altar involved.

[8] Raanan Eichler (2021) rejects this comparison primarily on the grounds that the ark (1) is always described as made of wood and not of stone or clay, (2) is often described with features that are not found on shrine models, and (3) most closely parallels wooden chests, rather than miniature temples. This depends on the latest descriptions of the ark, however, which likely come from well after its disappearance. Eichler's assertion that it was a container and not a "miniature structure" seems a distinction without a difference, given shrine models were containers. The most detailed descriptions of the ark's construction and features also represent later elaborations on the ark's nature and function. Eichler also rejects the conceptualization of the tablets as stelai on the grounds that there is no hint anywhere that the ark's contents were thought to represent deity.

5. YHWH's Divine Agents: The Ark of the Covenant and the Kābôd

rhetorically cast in Exod 32 (P) as the authorized alternative to the golden calf—a sanctioned medium for divine presencing. Both entities function as cultic images in different ways. For instance, the golden calf and the stone tablets made use of materials traditionally associated with the divine. The divine production of the text of the tablets is emphasized in Exod 32:16, while Aaron asserts in verse 24 that the golden calf just "came out" of the fire, as if it were not the work of human production. Both were smashed. A critical distinction was Aaron's assertion that the calf actually presenced the locus of the deity's identity (Exod 32:4: "these are your deities, O Israel!"). This stands in contrast to the treatment of the tablets as a secondary divine agent.

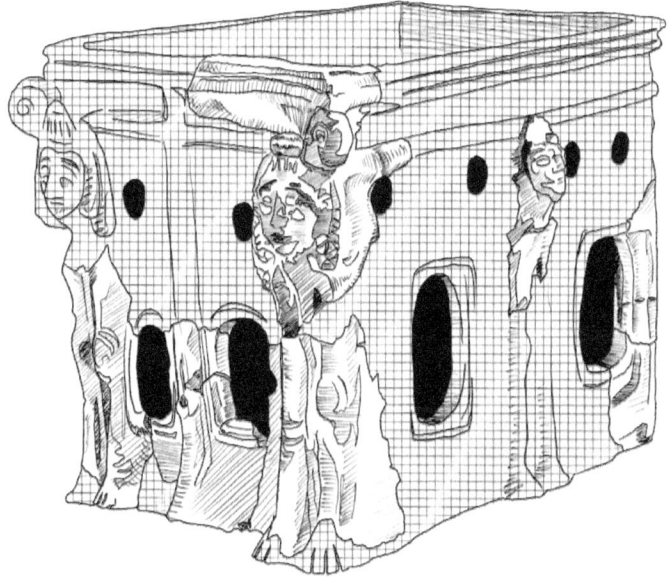

Figure 5.1. A reconstruction of a closed shrine model discovered at Megiddo. Source: May 1935, 13–17, plates 13 and 14. Drawing by the author.

Youn Ho Chung (2010, 82) argues that in narrating their intentional destruction by Moses' hand, Deuteronomy "attests to the fact that the tablets themselves are not holy: stone tablets are unlike the 'pillar.'" For Deuteronomy, however, presencing media is only "holy" if the deity's agency is intentionally inhabiting it. The root *šbr* occurs only four times in Deuteronomy, with two occurrences referring to Moses' destruction of the tablets (Deut 9:17; 10:2), and two referring to breaking unauthorized stelai (Deut 7:5; 12:3). Rather than indicating the tablets were unlike stelai, I would suggest the force of the narrative more directly compares them to stelai. Their destruction was not in reference to their function as cultic stelai, though. The covenant was already broken, and so the now-voided contract was to be destroyed before their eyes (Weinfeld 1991, 410). The new set of tablets were immediately placed within the ark (Deut 10:5), and three verses later (10:8), the text clarifies the presencing function of the ark by explaining that the tribe of Levi was to bear the ark of the covenant and (as a result) to stand "before YHWH" (*lipnê YHWH*) to minister to them.

Figure 5.2. Tiglath-Pileser III wall relief depicting a shrine model being carted off from a conquered city. Not depicted in this detail are anthropomorphic divine images depicting two seated female deities and one striding storm deity clutching lightning bolts. Source: British Museum 118931. Drawing by the author.

If figurines such as the small bronze bull discovered near Dothan and the miniature anthropomorphic statue that may be jutting its hand out from the enthroned box in the Tiglath-Pileser III relief discussed above are representative of the kind of media used in conjunction with shrine models, those media could have been miniature versions of full-scale divine images used in larger sites. The most explicit examples we have of full-scale divine images used in an Israelite/Judahite cultic site are the stelai that were located in the cella of the Arad temple. We have already seen that such stelai were ubiquitous across the regions inhabited by ancient Israel and Judah, and the biblical texts are replete with references to cultic stelai, so they are likely to have been broadly representative of the type of divine image employed in Israel and Judah. Tablets could very easily function as miniature stelai, and here the presencing function of cultic objects and of text converge (Watts 2016). The significance of this will be discussed in greater detail in chapter 7, but given the ubiquity of stelai in and around Israel and Judah, and the general paucity of anthropomorphic statuary, the ark may have been deployed at some point as a portable shrine model that housed one or more stelai that presenced the deity or the deity and their consort.

Figure 5.3. Sennacherib wall relief depicting cultic objects being carried off from a conquered city. Drawing by the author.

Scott Noegel (2015) has argued for Egypt's sacred bark as the primary conceptual seedbed for the ark. There were many variations on the theme, but a sacred bark was essentially a miniature boat that held either a coffin or a closed shrine model, and was transported with carrying poles. Unlike the clay models that have been discovered all over Iron Age Israel and Judah, but like the (late) description of the ark of the covenant (Exod 25:10–16), the Egyptian barks could be constructed of wood and covered in gold plating. They were frequently flanked by winged protective creatures reminiscent of cherubim, and could also be veiled with a curtain or canopy. As Noegel points out, the Hebrew term 'ărōn could also refer to a coffin (see Gen 50:1–14, 26).

In Num 10:35–36 and in 1 Sam 4–6, the ark seems to function exclusively as a war palladium that presences the deity (Römer 2019, Finkelstein and Römer

2020).⁹ Its role as a container for the law or as a throne or footstool is entirely absent, as is its association with cherubim.¹⁰ This suggests the passages may represent some of the earliest recoverable memories of the ark, before its nature and function were altered to serve the changing priorities and sensitivities of Judah's authorities. Numbers 10:35–36, known as the Song of the Ark (and also quoted in Ps 68:2), looks to be an archaic poem preserved within a pre-P seam that joins two larger P strands (Levine 1993, 311). As mentioned in the introduction, it seems to equate the activity of the ark with the activity of YHWH:¹¹

> When the ark set out [*binsōaʻ hāʼārōn*], Moses would say,
>   "Advance [*qûmâ*], O YHWH!
>   Your enemies shall scatter!
>   Those who hate you shall flee from your presence!"
> And when it rested [*ûbnuḥōh*], he would say,
>   "Bring back [*šûbâ*], O YHWH,
>   the ten thousand thousands of Israel!"¹²

First Samuel 4–6, which is widely understood as an early narrative embedded within a later Dtr layer, tells of the loss of the ark in battle with the Philistines at Ebenezer, its recovery in Beth-Shemesh, and its subsequent installation in Kiriath-

---

⁹ Sommer (2009, 93–94) and Natalie May (2015) both compare the ark and the tabernacle with Neo-Assyrian military practices related to the *qersu*, or portable shrine. In English, the word "palladium" has been used for centuries to refer to some manner of cultic object that offers protection within military contexts.

¹⁰ The closest the text comes to referring to any contents is the muddled statement in 1 Sam 6:19 that seventy (or 50,070) Beth-Shemites who "looked in the ark" (*rāʼû baʼărōn*) were struck down by YHWH (cf. Tsumura 2007, 226). If Exod 33:20 is in the background of this verse, then to look at the ark's contents is to look upon the face of the deity. In the LXX, however, 1 Sam 6:19a reads, "The children of Jeconiah were not happy with the men of Beth-Shemesh, because they saw the ark of the Lord. And he struck down 50,070 men." Miller and Roberts (2008, 77) believe the NAB's reconstruction is preferable: "The descendants of Jeconiah did not join in the celebration with the inhabitants of Beth-shemesh when they greeted the ark of the Lord, and seventy of them were struck down." Ted Lewis (2020, 874, n. 77) however, agrees with P. Kyle McCarter (1980, 131, 136–37) that the deaths were likely precipitated by the lack of Levites handling the ark, and with Levine (1993, 174) that their addition in verse 15 is a later interpolation.

¹¹ See also Ps 132:8, which similarly equates the activity of YHWH and the ark: "Ascend, O YHWH, to your resting place—you and the ark of your strength [*ʼattâ waʼărôn ʼuzzekā*]!"

¹² This translation is influenced by Levine 1993, 318.

Jearim.[13] According to 1 Sam 4, after it is retrieved from Shiloh to accompany the troops into battle, the ark fails to secure victory for the Israelites and is captured by the Philistines, who bring it back to their temple at Ashdod. After the ark's first night in the Philistine temple at Ashdod alongside their deity, Dagon, the latter's statue is knocked over.[14] After the second night, it is knocked over and its head and hands are severed. As the head and hands are important symbols of perception and action, this severing rhetorically renders the Philistine deity ignorant and impotent. The city is then stricken with a plague, so the ark is sent to Gath and then Ekron, where similar events take place (1 Sam 5:6–10). The Philistines have no choice but to return the ark to Israel, so they put it on a cart pulled by two cows, along with some offerings to appease the anger they have stoked, and set it loose. The text makes a point of highlighting that the cows set out directly for Beth-Shemesh and stopped upon arrival (1 Sam 6:12–14), as if guided by some agency (or perhaps driven like a chariot). At this point, in verse 15, the presencing function of the ark again comes to the fore. After the residents set up the ark next to or upon (*'el*) a "great stone" (*'eben gədôlâ*), they offer burnt offerings and sacrifices "to YHWH" (*la-YHWH*).

Sommer (2009, 101–7) argues that the Deuteronomic editors have adapted this narrative to argue *against* the perception that the ark presences the deity, but also to maintain a degree of tension between that perception and its rejection. The clearest expressions of the ark's presencing functions, for Sommer, are put into the mouths of individuals who don't know any better. For instance, the Israelite elders call for the ark before the battle, hoping that either YHWH or the ark (the third masculine singular verb is not clear) "will come into our midst and save us from the hand of our enemies" (1 Sam 4:3). This reflects, for Sommer, the erroneous notion associated with the "Zion-Sabaoth" tradition that Zion (Israel) was invincible as a result of YHWH's presence, facilitated by the ark. The hated Philistines realize the ark is present in 1 Sam 4:6 and equate the ark and the deity, lamenting in verse 7, "the Deity has come into the camp!"[15] Sommer (2009, 104–5) suggests as well that the name that the widow of Phinehas gives her child as she dies following delivery may reflect the understanding that the loss of the ark equals the loss of the divine presence/body. The name Ichabod (*'î-kābôd*)

---

[13] For a discussion of the likely core of the narrative, the archaeological data associated with the mentioned sites, and the social memory that may be indexed by it, see Finkelstein and Römer 2020.

[14] Note the text refers to the cultic image simply as *dāgôn*, "Dagon," reflecting—perhaps antagonistically—the identification of the image as the deity.

[15] The verb *bā'* is singular in verse 7, but verse 8 uses the word *'ĕlōhîm* in conjunction with a plural pronoun and a plural participle. Sommer (2009, 104) notes the Septuagint has the plural in verse 7, suggesting the plural reading in verse 7 may be older (cf. Miller and Roberts 2008, 45, n. 21).

means either "There is no *kābôd*" or "Where is the *kābôd*?" and seems to link the ark with the *kābôd*.

Sommer (2009, 106) suggests that, "If it ended at the close of chapter 4, the ark narrative might have been taken as a complete rejection of the notion that the ark is anything more than a box with several important texts inside it." 1 Samuel 5, however, goes on to narrate the story of the ark's defeat of Dagon, which, according to Sommer, shows that the ark does retain some manner of access to divine power. A tension is thus maintained between chapter 4's "complete rejection" of the ark's presencing function and the other chapters' presentation of a "mysteriously powerful" ark. For Sommer (2009, 107), "The Deuteronomistic editors front-loaded their critique without completely reworking the whole. The front-loaded critique provides the context in which to understand the miracles that follow."

Sommer seems to derive the "critique" that he identifies in chapter 4 entirely from the fact that the ark failed to facilitate the defeat of the Philistines. Nothing else in the chapter complicates the ark's presencing function, and every other character, Israelite or Philistine, expresses precisely the perspective that Sommer argues is being completely rejected. I would suggest that even by Sommer's own framework, this is an insufficient basis for his reading. A more likely explanation for the ark's failure is found in Sommer's (2009, 22) earlier discussion of Mesopotamian concepts of fluidity. There he explains, "it seems that, just as an *ilu* could enter an object, an *ilu* could also leave it. According to various historical texts, a god, when angry at a city, might abandon it, ascending from temple to heaven. The statues, however, were left behind—and now they consisted of nothing more than wood, stone, and metal. Further, the god could reenter the object." This is the abandonment motif, or the notion that an angry deity may abandon their presencing media in reaction to wickedness or disloyalty.

So that raises the question: do we have any indication in the texts that YHWH was angry? The answer is resoundingly in the affirmative.[16] To begin with, in contrast with other pre-battle narratives, such as Judg 20:27–28 or 2 Sam 5:19, there is no effort described to seek the will or disposition of the deity before engaging in battle.[17] The deployment of the ark, and perhaps even the battle itself, are unsanctioned. Even more explicitly, however, the comment in 1 Sam 4:4 that Hophni and Phinehas (Eli's sons) were with the ark in Shiloh connects the narrative with 1 Sam 2:12–17, 22–25, which interrupts the narrative in that

---

[16] According to Thomas Römer (2007, 116), attributing these losses to divine anger is in keeping with one of the overarching themes of Dtr: "In a way, the whole Deuteronomistic History maintains the assertion that the end of the monarchy, the destruction of Jerusalem and the loss of the land result from Yahweh's anger."

[17] Note that in Judg 20:27, the presence of the ark—before which a different Phinehas ministered—seems to have facilitated the inquiry.

5. YHWH's Divine Agents: The Ark of the Covenant and the Kābôd

chapter only to describe Hophni and Phinehas as corrupt priests *whom YHWH intended to kill*.[18] They ultimately meet their demise in 1 Sam 4:11, after the ark—which they appear to have accompanied—fails to precipitate a victory over the Philistines and is captured. YHWH's withdrawal of divine military aid, and thus the ark's failure, is attributed to the wickedness of the priests and to YHWH's intention to have them killed. A similar military loss in Josh 7:11–12 is attributed to sin among the Israelites that resulted in the withdrawal of YHWH's presence: "I will no longer be with you [*lō' 'ôsîp lihyôt 'immākem*] if you do not destroy the *ḥerem* from among you." Note Joshua communicates with YHWH "before the ark" (*lipnê 'ărôn*). In both Josh 7 and 1 Sam 4, the authors/editors appeal to the MORAL MONITORING and PUNISHMENT domains to blame the deity's refusal to protect their nation on wickedness within the nation. Returning to the ark narrative: after hearing of the loss of the ark, Eli also falls over dead. The ark thus fails while the corrupt priests and their enabling father remain alive, and it is only after their contaminating influence is removed from Israel's midst that YHWH's agency begins to return (incrementally?) to the ark, first toppling and then dismembering its Philistine counterpart.

The ark's continued presencing function is reinforced by passages elsewhere in D/Dtr where the phrase *lipnê YHWH*, "before YHWH," is employed to describe actions performed away from a temple, but in the presence of the ark. An example is 2 Sam 6:5, 14–16, in which David and all the house of Israel were, "dancing before YHWH [*lipnê YHWH*]," while they traveled with the ark towards Jerusalem. In a slight twist on that formula, Josh 7:6 describes Joshua tearing his clothes and falling down on his face, "before [*lipnê*] the ark of YHWH." (LXX here reads simply "before the Lord" [*enantion kyriou*].) Deuteronomy 10:8 describes the tribe of Levi as being set apart to "carry the ark of the covenant of YHWH, to stand before YHWH to minister to him, and to bless in his name, until this day." Anne Knafl (2014, 131) explains, "By carrying the ark, the Levites stand before Yhwh and there minister to him." Second Samuel 6:2 even states that the ark is, "called by the name [*niqrā' šēm*], the name of YHWH of hosts."

Like the fire out of which YHWH spoke to Israel in Deut 4, the ark does not necessarily reify the single or even primary locus of the deity's presence or body, but it does function as a channel for the deity's agency, thereby intuitively presencing the deity. Presence can be reified through a variety of separable loci of divine agency, not just through the deity's "body" (as Sommer's framework seems to require). The ark's theft does, however, seem to play into a broader rhetorical campaign of compartmentalization on the part of D/Dtr by employing

---

[18] Literally, "YHWH was delighted to kill them" [*ḥāpēṣ YHWH lahămîtām*]. Most scholars seem to accept the identification of these passages with the core of the account that was integrated into 1 Samuel. See, for instance, Miller and Roberts 2008, 27–32, 37–41; Levtow 2008, 135; Herring 2013, 68.

the abandonment motif to highlight the fact that the ark is most appropriately understood as a channel for divine agency and not as the very body of the deity. Much like the temple itself—which is miniaturized and mobilized in the ark[19]—the deity's agency can depart at will, and the righteousness not only of Israel, but also of its cultic specialists, is critical to the continued functioning of that channel. This abstracts the deity a bit and suggests something akin to a "secondary" status for presencing media could be reflectively employed by Judah's institutions to the degree they and their technologies could maintain and enforce the necessary "alternative realities" (see chapter 1). I suggest this rhetoric served in part to rationalize the destruction of the temple, in part to disincentivize private reproduction of cultic media, and in part to insulate the deity from the vulnerabilities of those media.

For Sommer, the tension he finds in the ark narrative serves to create an ambiguity meant to mitigate the potential for people to spread inappropriate deity concepts (presumably to prevent inappropriate worship practices from following after). This argument is part of Sommer's broader argument that these competing ideologies and their salience within the various biblical strata should not be reduced to reactions to historical circumstance, but should be recognized as the products of the universal wrestle with the "two religious impulses" of *fascinans* (the yearning for divine presence) and *tremendum* (the awe and terror of divine presence).[20] This point is developed in his discussion of P's dualistic approach to the deity's presence as mobilized in connection with the tabernacle while also inseparably linked to one single shrine (Sommer 2009, 90–99). For Sommer (2009, 96), scholars who understand the frameworks of these literary strata only in reference to historical events are reducing these complex religious phenomena to "nothing more than a historical reaction." The tension of these two impulses is not "confined to a particular period, place, or culture," and interpreters should "first of all at least consider the possibility that we can understand a religious text as manifesting religious intuitions that are essentially timeless" (97).

I am obviously sympathetic to the need to consider contributions from widespread cognitive frameworks to the production of the Hebrew Bible's concepts of deity, but my approach raises some concerns with Sommer's. *Fascinans* and *tremendum* are not innate "religious impulses," but rather everyday cognitive predispositions that happen to resonate with the ways socially concerned deities tend to be represented. I would argue that compartmentalizing those predispositions in order to serve the rhetoric of religious exceptionalism distorts them more than it clarifies them. Second, if using geopolitics to situate a particular conceptualization of divine presence reduces deity concepts to "nothing more than

---

[19] Knafl (2014, 131, n. 190) finds that the ark "represents a mobile divine presence, unbounded to the mandated cult site."
[20] Both frameworks developed by Rudolf Otto (1917).

a historical reaction," surely it is equally if not more reductive and distorting to treat such concepts as the exclusive products of pure and independent theological reflection detached from any historical circumstances. This is not to suggest that Sommer is engaged in that rhetoric, but I worry he approximates it in arguing so strenuously against identifying the historical circumstances most likely to generate the rhetoric we find in the biblical literature. This is always methodologically fraught, but no authoritative texts are composed independent of historical circumstances, and Sommer (2009, 101) seems to recognize as much in identifying P's rhetorical goal as mitigating the potential for people to view these cultic objects as "magical objects or as the earthly residence of the divine." Historical circumstance clearly plays a role not only in the salience of such perceptions of the ark or the tabernacle, but also in the desire on the part of the authorities to tamp them down.

This is all to say that the exile represents the most likely context for Dtr's deployment of the ark narrative. It makes use of the abandonment motif to assert the severability of the deity's agency from the ark and to account for the loss of the ark to the Philistines, but this does not indicate the outright rejection of any and all presencing facilities on the part of the ark. Such a dichotomous view of divine presencing is a presentistic scholarly imposition. The rhetorical exigency of denigrating the worship of idols could be satisfied without abandoning the entire premise upon which the ideology of the Jerusalem temple was based (namely that the structure in some sense presenced YHWH). Instead, the data support a more nuanced renegotiation of the deity's relationship to the temple and its cultic accoutrements that compartmentalized the loci of their agency and their body or primary locus of self. The ark remained a medium for, or extension of, YHWH's power and agency, even as it was decoupled or distanced from the main locus of the deity's self.

By the time these texts were written and in circulation, however, any ark or arks that may have occupied Israel or Judah's sacred precincts were long gone.[21] D/Dtr's distancing of the deity's self from the ark served several rhetorical functions vis-à-vis that absence. By presenting the absent ark as a uniquely situated medium for the deity's agency, the authors/editors of D/Dtr limited the

---

[21] David Rothstein (2021) argues that the absence of the ark during the period of the Chronicler was lamented, but did not prevent the presencing of the deity as a result of their promotion of Moses' tent (the *miškān*) as a second authorized piece of presencing media. As evidence of this, Rothstein points to the reference in 1 Chr 16:39 to the Zadokite priests ministering "before the dwelling-place of YHWH" (*lipnê miškān YHWH*) at Gibeon, as well as to the statement in 1 Chr 21:29 that David was afraid to inquire of YHWH at the *miškān* in Gibeon. These and other passages, according to Rothstein, suggest the Chronicler was positioning the *miškān* in Gibeon as an authorized facilitator of divine presence independent of the ark.

other available objects of potential worship. This mitigated the risk of other divine images replacing the ark. YHWH's abandonment of the ark was also a more favorable outcome than the deity's willful self-exile to the sacred precinct of whatever empire absconded with it. It allowed for the assertion that YHWH could remain with their people. The authoritative knowledge these rationalizations helped codify served their immediate functions, but also created new conceptual relationships that would have to be renegotiated as the corpus of Israel and Judah's authoritative texts began to take shape.[22]

The fronting of the ark's contents as the focal point of divine authority also played a role in this later rhetoric. Shrine models primarily functioned to house miniature divine images, with the former providing the appropriately set apart environment, and the latter constituting the primary facilitator of divine agency. Whatever the original contents of the ark, the tablets of the law become the centerpiece elsewhere in D/Dtr. The intersection of text and ark, and the eclipsing of the latter by the former, may be interpreted to suggest the replacement of one by the other—a passing of the torch as the primary medium of presencing the divine. The complexities of this transition will be addressed in much more detail in the next two chapters, but for now I turn my attention to that locus of divine presence and agency that seems so entangled with the ark itself, the divine "glory," or *kābôd*.

KĀBÔD

The word *kābôd* is thought to refer fundamentally to heaviness, and by metaphorical extension to wealth, reputation, and honor (Gen 31:1; 45:13; 1 Kgs 3:13).[23] While this conceptual matrix governs the term's usage across the various literary strata of the Hebrew Bible, there are a variety of domains that can be foregrounded, depending on the context (see Burton 2017). In this section, I examine different conceptualizations of the *kābôd YHWH*, as well as its rhetorical utility related to the divine presence, and particularly in later literary strata like P and Ezekiel, where its deployment is concentrated.

I suggest the representation of the *kābôd* can be productively plotted along a continuum of abstraction, though as with the ark, a dimension related to partibility

---

[22] For a fascinating discussion of how the ubiquity of abducted divine images may have undermined Neo-Assyria's traditional conceptualization of the relationship of cult statues to their deities, see Richardson 2012.

[23] See de Vries 2016, 51: "Both כָּבוֹד and יְקָר are expressed in splendor, greatness, might, brightness, etc. Texts that establish a relationship between the כָּבוֹד and the physical stature of a person are congruent with the meaning 'be weighty' of the root כבד. כָּבוֹד can also be connected with ornaments or clothing. Where that is so, there is a relationship both with someone's riches and with his external appearance."

from YHWH's own self seems to have developed in response to a growing need for that compartmentalization. On the most concrete side of that continuum, we find *kābôd* with a basic sense of "body" or some weighty constituent part of it, and it often appears in early poetic usage in parallel to references to human corporeality and to the loci of the self:[24]

> Genesis 49:6
> Into their council may my soul [*napšî*] never enter;
>   with their assembly may my *kābôd* never unite
>
> Isaiah 17:4:
> the *kābôd* of Jacob will shrink,
>   and the fatness of his flesh [*mišman bəśārô*] will dwindle
>
> Psalm 16:9
> my heart [*libbî*] rejoices,
>   and my *kābôd* shouts with joy.
> Indeed, my flesh [*bəśārî*] dwells securely.

The *kābôd* in this usage seems not only to have referred to corporeality, but also to have functioned as one of the loci of the self in the conceptualization of the human person. For this reason, scholars have frequently emphasized the association of the term with the notion of "presence."[25] Baruch Levine (2011, 216, n. 2), for instance, suggests "in more cases than not, we should eliminate the elements of greater abstraction, so understandably evoked by divine association, and emphasize rather the element of real presence."

Shawn Aster (2012, 264) similarly argues that the term refers to two related concepts in the Pentateuch: (1) "the perceptible Presence of YHWH," or (2) "signs and wonders which demonstrate His importance." He continues: "The phrase *kebod YHWH* refers simply to the 'person' or 'self' of YHWH, and is used in passages where YHWH appears and is perceived by humans." An example from P is Moses' encounter with YHWH in Exod 33. There Moses asks to see "your *kābôd*" (v. 18). YHWH responds that their *ṭôb*, "goodness" or "beauty," will pass by Moses, but as it does, YHWH states, "I will cover you with my hand until I have passed by." This seems to identify the *kābôd* with YHWH's *ṭôb*, and both with YHWH's own self. This identification occurs again in Exod 34:6, when YHWH carries out the actions described above. The text explains that "YHWH

---

[24] These examples are drawn from Sommer 2009, 60. Sommer additionally refers to Ps 7:6; Isa 10:3–4; 10:16; 22:18.

[25] David Aaron (2001, 53) prefers to avoid the term *presence* because of how theological loaded it is, but similarly concludes the term here "appears to be indicative of the physical being of the deity."

passed by [*ya'ăbōr YHWH*] before him." The *kābôd* thus refers to YHWH's very body, the primary locus of their self. These passages also mention YHWH's hand, back, and face, suggesting a fully anthropomorphic conceptualization of the deity. There is no particular visual phenomenon specifically associated with the divine body or self in this usage. The term refers to YHWH's body, self, or presence, but not to any particular visual aspect of it (though the danger of seeing the deity's face is emphasized).

On the most abstract side of the continuum (and less germane to this discussion) are to be placed those events, circumstances, objects, or behaviors that are understood as evidences or manifestations of *kābôd*, and with the more figurative sense of reputation, power, honor, or glory (cf. Burton 2017, 128–50). This usage occurs across the Hebrew Bible's literary layers, and while this evidence of power and honor can be *seen* in passages like Ps 96:3; Isa 35:2; 40:5, another reflection of this use of *kābôd* is found in those passages that call on people and even other deities to ascribe *kābôd* to YHWH (Josh 7:19; Ps 29:1–2), or to tell of their *kābôd* (Ps 19:2; 96:3). Acknowledging YHWH's *kābôd* is a means of manifesting and proliferating it (Aster 2012, 285–89). YHWH themselves can also be referred to as the manifestation of Israel's *kābôd* (Ps 106:20), of Jerusalem's *kābôd* (Zech 2:9 [ET 2:5]), and even as the *kābôd* of the psalmist (Ps 3:4).

In the middle of the continuum we should probably place those slightly abstract uses of *kābôd* that refer to the deity's presence, but less directly to the deity's own body. This usage is concentrated in P and functions in a few different ways. For instance, in response to misdeeds or complaints (e.g., Exod 16:7–10; Num 16:19; 17:7; 20:6), it serves to intimidate the Israelites in the wilderness and focus their attention on the deity and their power (Aster 2012, 275–78). It is also used as a signal of the sanctification of the tent of meeting (*'ōhel-mô'ēd*), as explained in Exod 29:43: "I will meet there with the children of Israel, and it will be sanctified [*wəqiddaštî*] by my *kābôd*." When this sanctification occurs, beginning in Exod 40:34, a cloud (*'ānān*) covered the tent of meeting, and the *kābôd YHWH* filled the "dwelling-place" (*miškān*). Here, according to Aster, the cloud is distinct from the *kābôd*, and is a means, as with the fire, of visually signaling the presence of the *kābôd*.

Fire and clouds are associated with deity elsewhere via the storm-deity profile and other frameworks, but the symbols seem to have dovetailed nicely with the rhetorical goals of the authors and editors deploying the *kābôd* for the purpose of signaling the divine presence while also obscuring its nature. Exodus 24:17, for instance, describes the appearance (*mar'ēh*) of the *kābôd YHWH* as "a devouring fire [*'ēš 'ōkelet*] on the top of the mountain in the sight of the children of Israel." As noted by Aster (2012, 268–70), Exod 19:18's description of the same events from Exod 24:17 has YHWH in the place of the *kābôd YHWH*, stating that "YHWH descended [*yārad*] upon it [Sinai] in fire [*bā'ēš*]." YHWH in this passage is not the fire, but descended *in* the fire. By analogy with this passage, Aster reads

Exod 24:17 to be distinguishing the *kābôd* from the fire. The "appearance" would thus refer to some separable visual phenomenon that cloaked the deity. This is similar to the notion that *melammu* is a covering for deity, rather than a visual phenomenon that is innate to the deity, though Aster (2012, 274) is adamant that parallels here to "Akk. *puluḥtu* and *melammu* are not consistent with the plain meaning of *kabod YHWH* in these passages."

While Aster treats the final form of these passages, they may reflect chronologically disparate concepts. Mettinger (1982, 85–87) notes the convergence of some features in Exod 24 that suggest P is appropriating an earlier pre-P tradition about a tent of meeting that simply facilitated dialogue between humans and the deity, who arrived cloaked in a cloud (de Vries 2016, 120–24). An example of this earlier tradition is preserved in Exod 33:7–9, where Moses enters the "tent of meeting" (*'ōhel mô'ēd*) and the cloud descends (*yrd*) and sits at the entrance to speak with Moses inside. Verse 11 explains, "And YHWH spoke to Moses face to face [*pānîm 'el-pānîm*]." There is no mention of *kābôd*. The cloud seems to obscure the deity themselves, who descends—perhaps from the heavens or from the summit of the holy mountain—to meet with Moses.[26] The difference between this narrative and those involving the *kābôd* go beyond just the addition of the *kābôd*. The verb *yrd*, for instance, describes YHWH's movement towards the place of meeting, but it never occurs in connection with the *kābôd*, which may or may not be incidental. The closest we get to that concept of descent is the use of *škn*, "to dwell, settle," to describe the action of the *kābôd* upon the summit of Sinai in Exod 24:16.[27] The traditions that lack the concept of the *kābôd*, and likely predate it, also lack reference to the dwelling-place (*miškān*), instead preferring *'ōhel mô'ēd*, "tent of meeting." The concept of the *miškān* and the description of the *kābôd* "settling" on the summit of Sinai were likely introduced in conjunction with each other.[28] It seems likely that the cloud—as a vehicle and attendant of the

---

[26] Note Exod 25:22: "And I will meet with you there [*wənô'adtî ləkā šām*]."

[27] Elsewhere, however, the cloud departs by ascending (*'lh*; Exod 40:35–36). This may suggest the dogmatic avoidance of the term *yrd* more than any systematic restructuring of the entire conceptualization of the function of the cloud and the divine presence. See de Vries 2016, 124 and note 18. In Exod 29:43–45, YHWH connects their own dwelling with that of the *kābôd*. In verse 43, YHWH puts the *kābôd* parallel to themselves, stating in reference to the tabernacle, "I will meet with the children of Israel there, and it will be sanctified by my *kābôd*." In verse 45, YHWH further states, "I will dwell among the children of Israel."

[28] The close relationship of the *miškān* and the *kābôd* is reflected in the materials used to accent and adorn the former. According to Exod 25–27, the interior of the *miškān* was adorned with gold, silver, and brass—materials most naturally and frequently compared to the radiance of deity—and covered with linen curtains of blue, purple, and scarlet, reflecting darkness and heavy clouds (de Vries 2016, 122–23; Kline 1980, 40). Even the cherubim intended to adorn the interior curtains of the *miškān* materialize the beings and

storm deity, the "rider of the clouds" (Ps 68:5)— predated the use of the *kābôd* as a literary vehicle for YHWH's presence and agency in the sanctuary,[29] but once the *kābôd* became the vehicle of choice, the cloud remained a convenient means of obscuring its precise nature.

The statement in Exod 40:34 that the *kābôd* "filled [*mālē'*] the *miškān*" further raises the question of the *kābôd*'s precise conceptualization. Aster (2012, 273–75) firmly maintains the distinction of the *kābôd* from any visual phenomena associated with it, but does not address the question of how the *kābôd* itself "fills" the *miškān*. It is not outside the realm of possibility that the *kābôd* was understood anthropomorphically, but it seems more likely the *kābôd* was understood as a substance capable of taking the shape of its container, such as the cloud, the fire, or even some manner of radiance. An additional question is whether this substance that fills the *miškān* is an extension or emanation from the divine body that is also located within the *miškān*, or a locus of divine agency that was partible from that body, which was itself located elsewhere.[30] It is, of course, not unlikely that there was no clear conceptualization of the *kābôd* undergirding these passages. They may be intentionally ambiguous precisely to muddy the waters regarding the *kābôd*'s partibility and form. If this is the case, the *kābôd* would function as literary prophylaxis for the deity's precise nature (cf. Hundley 2011, 32). The *kābôd* may have thus added an additional obfuscating layer to the presence of the deity, allowing the Priestly authors to preserve the notion of YHWH meeting with Moses in the tabernacle (Exod 25:22) while also obscuring the deity's form and providing an explanation for the dangers associated with seeing the deity. This seems to be the primary rhetorical thrust of P's renegotiation of the vehicles of divine agency: they manifest YHWH's presence, but they cannot be duplicated or destroyed, they obscure the deity's nature, and they are only accessible through the priestly class, of whom they are the exclusive purview. Even in its absence, the centrality of the temple—that fundamental material sign of divine presence— can still be maintained in the literary heritage that has been handed down to Judah

---

reflect their presence around the deity and the divine throne. These features of divine radiance are themselves obscured by coverings of goats' hair and tanned rams' skins. These skins can be connected to the practice of incubation, or sleeping within a cultic space to facilitate divine favors or visions in dreams. Animal skins and untasted sacrifices have been suggested to have been central features of the incubation ritual (Ackerman 1991).

[29] Thomas Wagner (2012, 117) states, "From the Pentateuch tradition came the idea of YHWH's covering with a cloud, which was transferred to the *kābôd*" ("Aus der Pentateuchtradition stammt die Vorstellung von der Umhüllung JHWHs von der Wolke, die auf den *kābôd* übertragen wird").

[30] Peter de Vries (2016, 56) describes the *kābôd* as a hypostasis in those places where "we see mention of a fire or an effulgence that has a degree of independence from the identity of YHWH himself."

while also providing a means of accounting for the deity's separability from it. In this regard, it is parallel to Dtr's renegotiation of the significance of the ark: both cultic objects presenced the deity, but always as a vehicle of its agency to which it was never inseparably bound.

Strengthening this understanding are those passages that promote even more explicitly abstract and partible conceptualizations of the *kābôd*. Deuteronomy's sole use of the term *kābôd*, in Deut 5:24, is the clearest example of this (Lewis 2020, 353–56): "our deity, YHWH, has shown us [*her'ānû*] his *kābôd* and his greatness [*gādlô*], and we heard his voice from the midst of the fire [*mitôk hā'ēš*]." The reference here is to YHWH's communication with Israel from the fire that engulfed Mount Horeb and was itself surrounded by dark clouds, described in Deut 4:11–12. The main rhetorical point there seems to be Deut 4:12's insistence that, "you heard the sound of the words [*qôl dəbārîm*], but you didn't see any form [*ûtmûnâ 'ênkem rō'îm*]—there was only a voice [*zûlātî qôl*]." According to verses 16–19, 23, 25, and 28, the goal is explicitly to undermine the compulsion to produce a divine image (*pesel*). For Sommer (2009, 63–64), this is a manifestation of Deuteronomy's rejection of the fluidity model. The fire, like the *šēm*, does not "refers to God's essence or to some deity that overlaps with God. Instead, it refers to *a token of divine attention*." Thus, the Israelites did not actually "see" YHWH's *kābôd*, but only came to abstractly understand it, similar to the statement in verse 24 that "we have seen that [*rā'înû kî*] deity can talk to humanity and it will survive." The usage of the root *r'h*, "to see," followed by *kî*, "that," and a subordinate clause, however, is a very different construction from the use of the root in the *hiphil* with the direct object marker *'et* connected to two direct objects that most commonly refer to visible phenomena.[31] Deuteronomy 4:36 also explains, parallel to 5:24, that YHWH caused Israel to see "his great fire [*'išô haggədôlâ*]," while they heard YHWH's words out of the midst of that fire.

This is not a rejection of the communicability of the deity's divine agency, but a renegotiation in line with the concerns described above related to the ark. The Dtr authors and editors seem to be more clearly compartmentalizing the deity's own self from their partible *kābôd* and the visible signs of its presence. Moses more explicitly asserts this compartmentalization in Deut 4:36, partly quoted just above: "From the heavens [*min-haššāmayim*] he caused you to hear his voice, in order to instruct you, while upon the earth, he showed you [*her'ăkā*]

---

[31] In Deut 5:4, Moses explains, "YHWH spoke with you face to face [*pānîm bəpānîm*] in the mount from the midst of the fire." The use of the preposition *b-* in the phrase *pānîm bəpānîm* is unique, however. The preposition *'el* occurs in every other occurrence of this phrase. The *beth* may be intended to qualify somewhat the sense in which they spoke "face to face" (Deut 34:10 says Moses is unique for having spoken with YHWH *pānîm 'el-pānîm*). While the reference may not be to visible faces, I suggest it indicates the fire reified the deity's presence.

his great fire, and you heard his words out of the midst of the fire [*mitôk hā'ēš*]." The repeated emphasis that this should disincentivize Israel from creating a divine image (vv. 16–19, 23, 25, 28) betrays the underlying motivation for the rhetorical compartmentalization. Both P and D emphasize a difficult to replicate manifestation of divine presence as a symbol of divine approbation of a cult location. P additionally restricts the vehicles of divine identity to the *kābôd*, limiting access to the appropriate authorities, and also obscures the deity's form, emphasizing the danger of exposure to it, perhaps to discourage the desire for unauthorized access to it or attempts to reproduce it.[32] This structures power in favor of the priestly classes. Their interests may have been further advanced (at least by the time of the Second Temple period) by the visual correspondence of two of the natural byproducts of the ongoing functioning of the temple cult (namely, fire and smoke), and the two main visual attendants of the *kābôd* (namely, fire and a cloud). Seeing a cloud of smoke hovering over the temple by day and that cloud of smoke and the temple structures illuminated at night by the fires of the altar may have suggested to the observer the constant presence of YHWH while the cult was operative.

Ezekiel's innovations on P's presentation of the *kābôd* relate to its anthropomorphism, visibility, and mobility.[33] While P is interested in prophylactically obscuring the divine form, Ezek 1:26–28a provide a frank description of the *kābôd*'s form that anthropomorphizes it while still emphasizing its radiance and transcendence:

> 26 And above the dome which was over their heads was the likeness of a throne that looked like sapphire; and higher above the likeness of the throne was a likeness that looked like a human. 27 And I saw what looked like sparkling amber, like what looked like fire, above what looked like its loins, enclosing it all around. And beneath what looked like its loins, I saw what looked like fire, and radiance was all around it. 28 Like a bow that was in the clouds on a rainy day, such was the appearance of the radiance all around. This was the appearance of the likeness of the glory of YHWH.

---

[32] Sommer concludes (2009, 76): "For P, God has only one body, and it is located either in heaven or on earth, but not in both places." Hundley (2011, 37) notes, "In the Priestly texts, Yhwh limits his point of contact with humanity to a single place and to an indescribable form, which may not be reproduced, and gives a single protocol for interaction, thereby eliminating all other places, modes of contact and means of representation."

[33] On this innovation as a reiteration of "Zion-Sabaoth" theology, see McCall 2014, 376–89. As Aster (2012, 311–15) notes, this is the only literary layer where parallels with the Mesopotamian concept of the *melammu* are evident, but the rhetorical purposes for its deployment differ from those of Mesopotamia.

In P, a cloud shrouds and obscures the divine form, while the author of Ezekiel appears to have an unobstructed view, apparently abandoning any concern for protecting authorized priestly viewers from the overwhelming radiance of the divine vision. There is one reference to the cloud in Ezek 1:4, but it employs imagery also found in Exod 9:24 regarding lightning continuously flashing forth. This does not obstruct Ezekiel's view, however, and may be repurposing the cloud to indicate the danger associated with the coming deity by associating it with violent weather instead of with overwhelming radiance (cf. McCall 2014, 380–81). The deity's appearance is still obscured, but the author of Ezekiel achieves this obscuring through literary hedging, or qualifying their descriptions as mere approximations. These descriptions employ the inseparable prefix *k-*, "like, as," six times, *mar'â*, "appearance of," nine times, and *dəmût*, "likeness of," four times. Robin McCall (2014, 381) concludes, "As the first prophetic book to be constructed as a work of literature, it is fitting that Ezekiel marries literary form and function this way."

Finally, for Ezekiel, the *kābôd* is not confined to the temple. As an exilic author seeking to rationalize the destruction of the temple and the continued commitment to YHWH and their cult, Ezekiel's account must make room for YHWH's continued activity beyond the bounds of the temple walls. It must also find a way to do this without entirely marginalizing the temple and its cult. This is primarily achieved through the mobilization and universalization of the *kābôd* and its throne.[34] The cherubim throne that located the deity within the tabernacle in pre-P tradition is preserved in Ezekiel, but altered and relocated above the primeval dome of Gen 1:6–7. Rather than two cherubim with wings touching over the ark, the author describes four *ḥayyôt*, "living things," each humanoid in form with four faces and four wings, in addition to other theriomorphic features (Ezek 1:5–12). The living things are described as traveling with the deity's *rûaḥ*, darting around like lightning (Ezek 1:12, 14). Ezekiel 1:15–21 also describe a wheel associated with each of the four living beings. These wheels all moved in unison with each living thing, since, according to Ezek 1:20, "the *rûaḥ* of the living thing [*haḥayyâ*] is in the wheels." The things' own locus of agency—their (shared?) *rûaḥ*—appear to animate the wheels. If Ezek 1:12's reference to the things moving around where the deity's *rûaḥ* went is to be understood analogously, the *rûaḥ* of YHWH may be animating each living thing. Ezekiel thus expands on the central stream of their received tradition (P) by incorporating and innovating older pre-P material regarding the conceptualization of YHWH's *kābôd*, the primary locus of divine identity, in order to meet the author's rhetorical demands. As with P, the rhetoric focuses on a unified divine presence.

---

[34] Ezekiel also envisions the rebuilding of a significantly larger temple in chapters 40–47.

As Sommer notes, P is concerned with "boundaries, their formation, and their maintenance," but I would argue against insisting this approach represents a rejection of "fluidity."[35] Sommer's (2009, 38) framework of the "fluidity of divine selfhood and multiplicity of divine embodiment" addresses a phenomenon that extends beyond and is separable from the locus of the deity's self or "body." Like human persons, divine personhood was multifaceted and situationally emergent, which allowed multiple different loci for their agency to be operative. While P is absolutely concerned with restricting access to the loci of identity, the deity's agency must still be free to operate in the world and among YHWH's people.[36] As with D, compartmentalization appears to be the key. For instance, the *kābôd* was not the only alternative to a cult statue. In describing humanity as created *bəṣelem 'ĕlōhîm*, "in the image of deity" (Gen 1:27), P also recasts humanity as an alternative divine image.[37] Similarly, Moses is rendered a deity (Exod 7:1), even radiating divinity after his mountain-top encounter with YHWH (Exod 34:29–35).[38] Even the tablets of the law, inscribed by the very hand of the deity themselves, were offered as an alternative to the golden calf, which (according to the text) was naively presented by Aaron as the deities that brought Israel up out of Egypt. As with D, the P source still reflects the communicability of divine agency, even if more clearly distinguished from the deity's own self.[39] Ezekiel employs some of the central features of divine identity from P, but incorporates other traditions while expanding on and innovating both, mobilizing the deity's self beyond the confines of the temple while still employing concepts of separable loci of agency and acknowledging the centrality of the temple within their sacred past.

---

[35] Hundley (2011, 30) has concerns of his own, arguing that Sommer's model would entrap YHWH in the tabernacle, "thereby circumscribing his potentiality and potency."

[36] Hundley (2011, 40) agrees that this is not a rejection of the fluidity model, but rather than address agency apart from a locus of self, he concludes, "in P the deity centralizes the point of contact between heaven and earth, limiting access to a single place so as to avoid divine fragmentation, divine overlap and competing means of and protocols for access."

[37] See Herring 2013, 209–18; cf. McDowell 2015, 207.

[38] As Herring (2013, 127) notes, "Exodus 32–34 was consciously included in the Priestly redaction of the book of Exodus and can, therefore, be read from a Priestly perspective." Herring develops this argument further on pages 128–37.

[39] Sommer (2009, 71–72) uses his characterization of P's understanding of the divine body as "fire" to account for its variations in size, but I would argue this imposes a far stricter reflective framework than is necessary. These variations are the result of rhetorical expediency, not of some systematic accounting of the deity's size and its variability.

CONCLUSION

The ark of the covenant and the *kābôd* served to presence the deity in a variety of ways throughout their occurrences in the biblical literature. They did not function as a means of rhetorically severing the deity's presence from material media, but rather as a means of renegotiating the precise nature of that presencing. For the ark, this involved compartmentalizing the vehicles of agency from those of the deity's self and subordinating the former to the latter, resulting in the "secondary divine agent" status described in Pongratz-Leisten's (2011) model. The ark was described employing a variety of conventions associated with the nature and function of presencing media from cognate societies, and it came to be viewed as a material medium which the deity could inhabit or could abandon. The *kābôd* was not subject to the volatilities of a human-made cultic object, and so it was a more rhetorically flexible vehicle of divine agency that came to be used to abstractly mark as well as obscure the deity's presence. In both cases, a salient rhetorical goal appears to be the creation of space between the deity's body and their people. The deity was still accessible through a variety of acts, such as prayer, but their material presence was compartmentalized, obscured, and often more abstract. The growing use and salience of text was one of the technological innovations that facilitated the maintenance and enforcement of such an abstract conceptualization of deity.

The ark and the *kābôd* were among the most visible and concrete presencing media from the Iron Age preserved by the texts of the Neo-Babylonian and Achaemenid periods. While their relationships to the agency and identity of YHWH were renegotiated in order to respond to pressing rhetorical needs regarding the deity's presence, for the exilic worshippers of YHWH, both pieces of media were also conspicuously absent. The temple was gone, and with it, the ark of the covenant and any pillar of fire or cloud of smoke that might have visibly manifested the deity's presence to previous generations. They existed only in written, spoken, and performed tradition. This reality imposed additional prosocial exigencies upon authorities and community leaders whose interests were tangled up with the insularity and survival of the Israelite/Judahite identity. In the absence of the temple and the divine presence and oversight it helped facilitate, other strategies for social cohesion and for conceptualizing the relationship of YHWH to their people would come to the fore, and particularly through the medium of text. It is to those strategies that I now turn.

6.
YHWH's Divine Agents: The Messenger and the Šēm

The compartmentalization of loci for divine self and divine agency in the texts of the late-seventh and sixth centuries BCE opened the door for a number of entities to take on presencing roles in the biblical literature. As that literature arrogated increased authority in certain circles, and in the absence of the temple and its trappings, cult seems to have given way to text as the primary backdrop against which those entities facilitated both the assertion of divine imminence and the sheltering of the deity's primary locus of self from the prying eyes and destructive hands of humanity. The most explicit vehicle for divine agency and the divine self in the narratives of the Hebrew Bible is the messenger of YHWH, and that vehicle will be interrogated in the chapter's first section. As a part of this interrogation, I discuss one biblical author/editor's use of YHWH's šēm, or "name," to rationalize the messenger's occasional identification with—even self-identification as—YHWH, the very deity of Israel.[1] This rationalization relates to a broader conceptual matrix found in Dtr and certain layers of D in which the šēm is the vehicle for presencing the deity in the temple. That matrix will be the subject of the chapter's final section.

THE MESSENGER OF YHWH

This section considers the use of the construct phrase "messenger of YHWH" (*mal'ak YHWH*) in the apparent conflation of the deity and their messenger in a handful of early biblical narratives: Gen 16:7–13; 21:17–19; 22:11–18; 31:11–13; Exod 3:2–6; Num 22:22–35; Judg 2:1–5; 6:11–23; 13:3–23. Camille Hélena von Heijne (2010, 1), in her discussion of the reception of the messenger of YHWH in early Jewish engagement with the book of Genesis, includes Gen 48:15–16 and Josh 5:13–15; 6:2 in her list of texts that merge the identity of the messenger with that of YHWH. I would suggest the situation is slightly distinct in theses verses,

---

[1] For a discussion of the significance of the divine name within Judaism from a cognitive perspective, see Levy 2014.

however. In the poetic blessing of Joseph in Gen 48, Jacob refers to "the messenger who redeemed me from all evil" in one colon, and to *'ĕlōhîm* in the parallel colon, which does not refer to the *mal'ak YHWH*. Similarly, in Josh 5:13–15, Joshua's interlocutor is not described as a messenger, but as "the commander of YHWH's host" (*śar-ṣəbā'-YHWH*). In Josh 6:2, YHWH is described as speaking to Joshua, but the continuity with 5:13–15 is not clear.[2] The situation in Zech 3 is unclear, in that the messenger of YHWH uses the formula, "thus says YHWH" (*kōh-'āmar YHWH*) in verse 7, which can be a messenger formula, but is also sometimes put into YHWH's own mouth. Zechariah 4:1 refers to a messenger, independent of the divine name, but the compositional relationship with chapter 3 is unclear. This may be a later narrative that incorporates some of the features of the conflated narratives while also maintaining the distinction of the messenger and YHWH.

The passages that conflate the identities of YHWH and the messenger refer specifically to a *mal'ak YHWH*, "messenger of YHWH," but in addition, they (1) alternatively refer to that messenger as YHWH or *'ĕlōhîm*, (2) describe them self-identifying as YHWH or *'ĕlōhîm*, and/or (3) attribute authority and power to them that was usually understood to be the sole prerogative of YHWH. Similar to the cult statues of surrounding societies, the messenger appears to be both identified as the deity and also distinguished from them. Sommer (2009, 40–44) treats these passages as one of the main prototypes of divine fluidity, but he combines these passages with others that do not incorporate the *mal'ak YHWH* formula, such as Hos 12:4–6 and Gen 32:24–30, producing a "messenger" theology that is broader than the phenomenon in question. His models of fragmentation and overlap result in the notion that "the selves of an angel and the God Yhwh could overlap or that a small-scale manifestation or fragment of Yhwh can be termed a *mal'akh*" (2009, 41). In other words, messengers may have existed as potential avatars with which YHWH may merge at any point, or alternatively, the term *mal'ak* may have served simply to designate any of the many different avatars of YHWH.

I would suggest that Sommer is on to something, but the story is a bit more complex than he describes, beginning from the specific and peculiar occurrence of the *mal'ak YHWH* formula. Exodus 3:2–6 is a representative example of this occurrence that can serve as a jumping-off point:

And the messenger of YHWH appeared [*wayyērā' mal'ak YHWH*] to him in a flame of fire in the midst of the bush. And he saw, and—look!—the bush was on fire, but it was not burning up. And Moses said, "I'm going to turn aside and take

---

[2] Though even if this continuity is secondary, it would have had to have been accepted following the spread of this form of the text. That identification is accounted for with my framework of communicable divine agency, though my interrogation here is limited to the messenger of YHWH. For another approach, see Chambers 2019.

a look at this incredible sight, why the bush is not burning." And YHWH saw [*wayyarə' YHWH*] that he turned aside to look, so the deity called out to him from the midst of the bush [*wayyiqrā' 'ēlāyw 'ĕlōhîm mittôk hassəneh*] and said, "Moses! Moses!" And he said, "I'm here." Then he said, "Don't come over here. Take your sandals off your feet, because the place where you are standing—it is holy ground." And he said, "I am the deity of your father [*'ānōkî 'ĕlōhê 'ābîkā*], the deity of Abraham, the deity of Isaac, and the deity of Jacob." And Moses hid his face, because he was afraid to look at the deity [*yārē' mēhabbîṭ 'el-hā'ĕlōhîm*].

Verse 2 describes the messenger appearing to Moses in the burning bush, but YHWH is the one observing Moses' actions in verse 4, a verse that also states that the *'ĕlōhîm* called out from the bush. This may exploit the semantic vagaries of the term *'ĕlōhîm*—a divine messenger could be referred to as a deity, or as Sommer (2009, 41) designates it, "a lower ranking divine being"—or it may have been understood to refer specifically to YHWH, in which case, the author has understood the identities of the messenger and of YHWH to have merged, and for some reason is highlighting that merger. In verse 6, the entity identifies themselves as the deity of Moses' ancestors. If we understand verse 2 to contextualize verses 3–6, as most do, then the messenger is appropriating the diving name, identifying themselves as YHWH. Here's the rub, though: the simple removal of the single occurrence of the Hebrew word *mal'āk* from verse 2 results in a perfectly consistent and clear narrative about the deity YHWH appearing to Moses in a burning bush (cf. Fischer 2007).

I will argue in following that that conflation of the identities of YHWH and their messenger is rooted in the textual interpolation of the word *mal'āk* in passages that initially narrated the deity's own direct interactions with humanity. As the deity's profile accreted more abstractions and more rhetoric associated with their transcendence and the dangers of looking upon the divine glory, and the deity was distanced from certain earthly acts, earlier passages were edited with the addition of the word *mal'āk* in order to obscure the deity's presence and replace it with that of the messenger (traditionally, "angel"). This resulted in some narratives in which the messenger self-identifies as the deity, or in which an individual refers to their interlocuter alternatively as the deity and as their messenger. These circumstances appear to have been acceptable to the communities in which the texts ultimately circulated, which has caused a great deal of debate among scholars. The theoretical framework of communicable divine agency I have developed in this book, however, accounts for all the idiosyncrasies of these narratives, including those of a late passage in Exod 23 that explicitly distinguishes the two entities, but also seems to appeal to communicable agency in an attempt to accommodate and account for their conflation.

ACCOUNTING FOR THE MESSENGER OF YHWH

Four general approaches to this phenomenon have gained some degree of currency among scholars (Heidt 1949, 69–101; van der Woude 1963–1964; Gieschen 1998, 53–57; von Heijne 2010, 114–20). The prevailing view, which has been called the "identity theory," holds that the messenger is a hypostasis, avatar, or some manner of extension or manifestation of YHWH's own self.[3] A second theory, the "representation theory," suggests the messenger is a separate and individualized entity who, as an authorized representative, may speak in the first person as their patron (López 2010; cf. Malone 2011). The third approach—for which I argue below—is the "interpolation theory," which holds that the word *mal'āk* is a textual interpolation (Irvin 1978; Meier 1999a). A final approach is closely related to the first two, and contends that the authors have intentionally blurred the distinction between the two entities to create a tension and ambiguity that signals the unknowability and mysteriousness of the divine form (Newsom 1992, 250). This theory has yet to be given a short-hand designation in the scholarly literature, but I will refer to it as the "ambiguity theory."

Among the most conspicuous indicators that the *mal'āk* is an interpolation is the fact that the messenger in the relevant passages acts in ways entirely inconsistent with the responsibilities of divine messengers within the broader Southwest Asian literary tradition. This was briefly addressed by Samuel Meier (1999b, 96–97) in his monograph, *The Messenger in the Ancient Semitic World*, and more forcefully by Dorothy Irvin (1978, 93–104) in her book, *Mytharion*. While Michael Hundley (2016, 7–12) highlights this inconsistency in arguing for the "idiosyncratic" representation of the messenger in the biblical texts, I would argue the messenger's activity is not so idiosyncratic—it matches the responsibilities of the deities themselves as represented elsewhere in ancient Southwest Asian literature. Even within the biblical context itself, the messenger seems to take on features and roles exclusively possessed in the relevant literature by full-fledged deities.

Note, for instance, that the fearful reactions to the messenger in several places reflect Exod 33:20's warning regarding the deadliness of seeing the deity's own face:

Exodus 3:2a, 6
And the messenger of YHWH appeared to him in a flame of fire in the midst of the bush.... And he said, "I am the deity of your father, the deity of

---

[3] Heidt 1949, 95–100; van der Woude 1963/1964, 6–13; Olyan 1993, 89–91; Friedman 1995, 13; Carrell 1997, 27–28; Gieschen 1998, 67–69; White 1999; Kugel 2003, 18–20; Tuschling 2007, 99–101; Eynikel 2007, 109–23; Sommer 2009, 40–44.

6. YHWH's Divine Agents: The Messenger and the Šem

Abraham, the deity of Isaac, and the deity of Jacob." And Moses hid his face because he was afraid to look at the deity [*hā-'ĕlōhîm*].

Judges 6:22
And Gideon saw that it was the messenger of YHWH, and Gideon said, "Help, Lord YHWH! For I have seen the messenger of YHWH face to face!"

Judges 13:21–22
And the messenger of YHWH did not again appear to Manoah and to his wife. Then Manoah realized that it was the messenger of YHWH, and Manoah said to his wife, "We will definitely die, because we have seen deity [*'ĕlōhîm rā'înû*]."

There is no such threat associated with communication with the deity's messenger anywhere in the Hebrew Bible. Indeed, it entirely undermines the function of a divine messenger for direct communication to be deadly.[4] From the biblical to the wider Southwest Asian contexts, the texts reflect the literary motifs associated with direct communication between humans and full-fledged deities. The removal alone of the word *mal'āk* resolves all the complications.

Another consideration that adds further support to the interpolation theory is the frequent interpolation of the messenger in the ancient versions.[5] A famous example is YHWH's confrontation with Moses in Exod 4:24, which in the Hebrew reads, "And when YHWH met him [*wayyipgəšēhû YHWH*], he sought to kill him." In the Septuagint, however, the passage differs slightly: "a messenger of the Lord met him [*syntēntēsen auto angelos kyriou*] and sought to kill him." The messenger was interpolated, either by the translator or by a scribe responsible for their source text, to obscure the deity's physical interaction with Moses, and likely also their attempted murder (Olyan 1993, 27–28).[6] In the story of God's

---

[4] Sommer (2009, 43) states, "The expression of God's presence known as the *mal'akh* is accessible precisely because it does not encompass God's entirety." This is a perfectly reasonable interpretation of the use of the divine messenger, but it betrays the interpolation, since the terror of seeing the deity is identical to what is expressed by those who see the messenger of YHWH, who is supposed to be "accessible." We cannot reason that in all instances the individuals simply mistakenly thought they were looking at the deity's entirety, since the omniscient narrator states in Judg 13:21 that Manoah, "realized [*yd'*] it was the messenger of YHWH [*mal'ak YHWH*]," and immediately afterwards in verse 22 has Manoah express fear of death for seeing *'ĕlōhîm*. For another take on this fear, see Chavel 2012.

[5] Sommer (2009, 43) understands these variations to "strengthen the impression that the boundary between angel and Yhwh was regarded in the texts underlying the translations as indistinct."

[6] A similar prophylactic alteration takes place with the biblical *śāṭān*, "satan," who

bedside chats with Balaam, the Samaritan Pentateuch adds *mal'āk* before *'ĕlōhîm* in Num 22:20. No such addition is made in verse 12, at the first nightly chat, but there the verb used to describe the deity's action is *'mr*, "to speak," while in v. 20 it is the more physical *bw'*, "to come." The theological concern seems to be with their explicit physical presence. SP Numbers 23:4 has the same addition of *mal'āk* where the verb is *mṣ'*, "to find," or "meet," and SP Num 23:5 has the *mal'ak YHWH* putting the deity's word in the mouth of Balaam. The *mal'āk* of Num 23:4 is also found at Qumran in 4QNum^b, and the spacing suggests it also appeared in that manuscript at Num 22:20 and 23:5.

This interpolative practice flourished in the Targumim, which also added other personified attributes of deity to mediate divine presence and activity. Targum Onqelos adds "messenger" at Exod 4:24 in agreement with LXX. Targumim Pseudo-Jonathan and Neophiti edit Jacob's encounter at Peniel in Gen 32:31 to read, "I have seen messengers of the Lord." Targum Pseudo-Jonathan also amends Eve's famous claim in Gen 4:1 to have conceived a man with YHWH, rendering, "I have got a man from the messenger of the Lord." Many of our scenes show textual instability in the versions, as well. In MT's version of the Hagar episode in Gen 16, the *mal'ak YHWH* appears in verses 7, 9, 10, and 11. The Septuagint adds an additional reference in verse 8, but the Vulgate lacks the references in verses 10 and 11. In the Vulgate's version of Exod 3:2, there is no messenger; only the Lord appears to Moses. In paraphrasing Exod 3, Josephus only mentions a "voice" calling Moses by name. In Gen 22, Josephus lacks all references to a messenger; there it is only the deity calling out to Abraham.

As with so many theories in biblical studies, James Barr (1960, 33) seems to be responsible for the most frequently quoted criticism of the interpolation theory: "The introduction of the mal'ak is too extremely spasmodic, and leaves too many fierce anthropomorphisms untouched, for its purpose to be understood in this way. The voice and presence of the mal'ak alternates in a number of stories so much with the voice and appearing of Yahweh that it is hardly possible to understand his place as a substitute for the latter." This concern hardly undermines the theory, however. First, the concern is not anthropomorphism, but the deity's immediate physical presence. Second, there is no reason to alter or add to every single verse in order to massage a text's interpretation when the hearer/reader needs little more than a contextualizing suggestion, particularly when it resolves or—if the ambiguity theory identifies the right rhetorical goals—muddies a theologically thorny reading. In Gen 32:24–32, Jacob's sparring partner is nowhere called a

---

functions as a sort of prosecutor. In 2 Sam 24:1, YHWH is described as influencing David to conduct a census of Israel and Judah. The much later version of this pericope preserved in 1 Chr 21:1 describes the *śāṭān* as the agent of influence. The insertion of the *śāṭān* here protects YHWH from the implications of engaging in what was considered inappropriate behavior.

messenger, and even though Jacob states in verse 31, "I have seen deity face to face" (rā'îtî 'ĕlōhîm pānîm 'el-pānîm), it has been read as a reference to a messenger for millennia. This is reflected in the received version of Hos 12:4–5, which makes reference to the tradition and refers to the entity first as an 'ĕlōhîm and then as a mal'āk (although the latter is likely itself an early interpolation).[7] Similarly, the Samaritan Pentateuch was selective in those passages that were emended, but it influenced the reading of nearby passages that it had left untouched. The comprehensive approaches of later Greek and rabbinic authors and editors are products of much more systematic and self-conscious literary conventions that cannot be so arbitrarily retrojected into the mid-first millennium BCE. The clearest and most definitive evidence that one need not change all the occurrences to influence interpretation is the fact that the vast majority of Jewish and Christian readers have interpreted the texts over the millennia precisely as those interpolations would have them read.

THE MESSENGER OF YHWH AS DIVINE AGENT

The interpolation theory best accounts for those passages in which the identity of the messenger overlaps or appears to be conflated with that of the deity. This does not fully explain the perpetuation and accommodation of these ostensibly conflated identities down through the ages, though. These passages grate against today's reflective conceptualizations of self, constructed as they are on binary Aristotelian notions of classification.[8] However, for ancient audiences, whose intuitive perspectives regarding the individual as both partible and permeable were far more salient, and who intuitively accepted the communicability of agency in their sociomaterial interactions with deity, the notion of a divine messenger somehow endowed with divine agency was no more the logical paradox than was the endowment of a cultic image with that agency.[9] One passage

---

[7] I would suggest that 'ĕlōhîm in verse 4 is intended to parallel 'ēl, "deity," in verse 5. This results in the phrase wāyyāśar 'ēl, "he contended with El," at the beginning of verse 5—a tidy etiology for the name yiśrā'ēl. Instead, the mal'āk is interpolated, 'ēl is reread as the preposition 'el, and the etiology vanishes. Note Sommer's (2009, 41) reading: "in Hosea 12 the being who wrestled with Jacob was not a mal'akh who also could be called an 'ĕlōhîm; rather, it was the God Yhwh, who can also be termed a mal'akh."

[8] Jonathan Jong (2015, 16) quips, "the ghost of Aristotle haunts us still."

[9] Anyone who has ever spoken to a deceased loved one via a gravestone is likely aware it only becomes a paradox when a reflective account is required. The act itself is quite intuitive. The presencing of deity in the societies around Iron Age Israel and Judah prototypically used inanimate objects, however, so the messenger is a bit idiosyncratic as a medium for divine agency (but this is likely just a product of its incidental creation via textual interpolation).

in the Hebrew Bible even appears to construct a conceptual framework for this endowment.

Following a series of commandments in Exod 23 regarding cultic expectations upon entry into the promised land, the deity explains in verses 20 and 21, "Look, I am sending a messenger [*'ānōkî šōlēaḥ mal'āk*] before you to guard you on the way and to bring you to the place I have established. Pay attention to him and listen to his voice. Do not rebel against him, because he won't pardon your transgressions [*lō' yiśśā' ləpiš'ăkem*], for my name is in him [*šəmî bəqirbô*]." The passage explicitly distinguishes the deity from their messenger, but it also seems to describe the latter as having the divine prerogative to not forgive sins, which in Josh 24:19 is attributed directly to YHWH in identical terms—*lō' yiśśā' ləpiš'ăkem*. The statement that "my name is in him" serves as an explanation for the messenger's exercising of the deity's prerogative (Johansson 2011).[10] The composer of this passage was aware of—if not responsible for—the conflated identities of YHWH and their messenger in the other passages discussed above, and they were likely providing a reflective rationalization for that conflation. Perhaps most directly in view is Judg 2:1, which narrates the story of YHWH's leading the Israelites out of Egypt and likely had the messenger interpolated.

We may leverage the theoretical framework of communicable agency to posit that the "name" operates in Exod 23 as a conceptual vehicle for YHWH's communicable agency. Thus, possession of the name not only allowed the messenger to be referred to as YHWH, but it endowed them with YHWH's power and authority. They were more or less a divine image that was already sentient and animated (though confined to the texts). According to this theory, with the interpolation of the *mal'āk*—or perhaps between the initial interpolation of the *mal'āk* and the composition of this passage in Exod 23—the conflated identities of YHWH and their messenger were rationalized using the notion of the "indwelling" of YHWH's name.[11] This concept is closely related to the so-called "Name Theology" of D and Dtr (discussed in the next section).

---

[10] Sommer (2009, 42) recognizes this as well: "by stating that His name is in the angel, Yhwh indicates that the angel carries something of Yhwh's own essence or self; it is not an entirely separate entity." Here Sommer seems to acknowledge that loci of the self that are distinct from the "body" are indeed communicable, but this acknowledgement does not influence the application of the broader fluidity model elsewhere.

[11] An alternative explanation is that the notion of the name indwelling the messenger in Exod 23 inspired the later interpolations, but this would make Exod 23:20–21 prior to texts like Judg 2:1 and raises more questions about the presence of the messenger in Exod 23 than it answers. If the messenger is an interpolation in the other passages, Exod 23 is most likely an elaboration on those interpolations. The literary progression would begin with YHWH themselves leading the Israelites (Exod 13:21; 33:14–17), then an interpolated messenger (Exod 14:19; Judg 2:1), and then the rationalized messenger (Exod 23:20–21).

The exclusively literary context of the origins of the composite "messenger of YHWH" merits further discussion. Because it operated within a literary medium under the control of authorities, the messenger could presence not just the deity's agency, but the deity's own self in a way that could not be privately reproduced and was not subject to the violence to which the temple and its accouterments could be. The agent's animate and anthropomorphic representation in that literary medium blurred the traditional boundaries that could be reified between the deity and its presencing media. The messenger was not a cultic object or a cultic installation whose theft or destruction the authorities found themselves having to rationalize, nor was the goal to discourage the followers of YHWH from worshipping an already accessible material object, at least initially (see below). Rather, the interpolation of the messenger initially answered a reflective concern for theological propriety and was subordinated and initially confined to the text. It would take on a life of its own within the community's broader discourse about divine presencing, but this marks a unique innovation born of text and its features, rather than of rationalizing and/or accommodating uncomfortable cultic practices. This may account for the literary survival of this specific medium for the presencing of the deity's own self.

The veneration of divine messengers may have become an unintended consequence of the survival and expansion of this text-based medium for divine presencing. As the Jewish literary imagination expanded in the Greco-Roman period, writers began to explore in greater detail the hierarchical structure of the heavens, producing complex social structures for the residents of the heavens, even developing names and mediatory responsibilities for a variety of different divine messengers (Reed 2020, 65–81). In some cases, divine attributes that appear to be personified in the biblical texts become identified with these messengers, such as "Anger" (Ps 78:49), "Wrath" (Isa 66:15), "Qeṣeph" (Num 17:11), and even "Shem" (Isa 30:27). Texts like Ps 78:49 may have influenced the reading of attributes like these as divine messengers: "He sent against them his burning anger [ḥărôn 'apô], wrath ['ebrâ], and indignation [zaʻam] and distress [ṣārâ]—a company of messengers of evil [malʼăkê rāʻîm]." In the later literature in which these figures appear explicitly as messengers, a common modification to the biblical iterations was the addition of the theophoric element -ʼēl, as in Qaṣpîʼēl from Sepher Ha-Razim 4:22 and 3 En. 1.3. Other names are carried through without alteration, such as ʻĀzāʼzēl, from Lev 16:8, 10, and 26, who appears as a messenger in several places in 1 Enoch and in the Apocalypse of Abraham (Olyan 1993, 109–11).

Scholars have alternatively dated the so-called "appendix" to the Covenant Code (of which Exod 23:20–21 are the opening verses) to a pre-D setting and a late-D setting. For the former, see Baden 2012, 119; Wright 2016. For the latter, see Blum 1990, 377.

The risk of worship appears to have been most acute in that literature which pondered the relationship of divine mediators and the possession of the divine name. Jarl Fossum (1985, 86) explains that the appeal to the divine name in Exod 23:20–21 "shows the individualization and personification of the Name of God in the figure of the Angel of the Lord.... this means that he has put his power into the angel and thus will be with his people through the agency of the angel."[12] The messenger Yahoel, from the *Apocalypse of Abraham*—whose name means "YHW is El"—is referred to by the deity as "the namesake of the mediation of my ineffable name" (Apoc. Ab. 10.3).[13] When Yahoel encounters Abraham, they explain, "I am a power in the midst of the Ineffable who put together his names in me" (10.8). This is what facilitates the performance of deeds normally restricted to the deity. While this messenger is not worshipped in the *Apocalypse of Abraham*, 1 En. 48 does refer to worship in discussion of the relationship of the divine name, the divine glory, and Dan 7's bar 'ĕnāš, "Son of Humanity." There the "Son of Humanity" is endowed before the creation of the earth with a special name: "And at that hour that Son of Humanity was named by the Name in the presence of the Lord of Spirits, the Before-Time; even before the creation of the sun and the moon, before the creation of the stars, he was named by the name in the presence of the Lord of Spirits" (1 En. 48.2–3).[14] And then two verses later: "all those who dwell upon the dry ground will fall down and worship before him, and they will bless, and praise, and celebrate with psalms the Name of the Lord of Spirits" (1 En. 48.5).[15] Charles Gieschen (2007, 240) states that the genuflecting masses "will use the name of the Lord of Spirits in worshiping the Son of Humanity because both possess the same divine Name."

Through this and related literature and cult, the divine council that had once been deposed was now being reconstituted by subordinate divine messengers and other mediating entities. Following this expansion, internal prohibitions against— and external accusations of—the worship of these entities began to proliferate, which has commonly been interpreted as evidence that people were worshipping

---

[12] Regarding the temple, Fossum (1985, 87) asserts, "YHWH certainly inhabits the earthly temple, but not in person; he is present through the agency of his Name." Biblical figures besides the messenger were also endowed with the power of the divine name. Moses, for instance, is said to be "vested with prophethood and the divine Name" in the Samaritan text, Memar Marqah (2.4; quoted in Orlov 2017, 30).

[13] This translation and the next are from Orlov 2017, 73.

[14] Following Gieschen 2007, 240, this translation is from Isaac 1983, 35, but restores the more literal rendering of "named by the name" that is relegated to the footnotes in the text.

[15] This translation is from Orlov 2017, 43–44.

them to one degree or another.[16] The mediation of divine messengers would provide an attractive alternative to the sanctioned cult for privately accessing divine presence and favor, particularly for the growing diaspora communities and those increasingly finding themselves outside the shrinking boundaries of "orthodoxy."

Internal prohibitions are particularly concentrated in rabbinic literature, such as *Mekhilta de-Rabbi Ishmael*'s commentary on Exod 20:20, which interprets the prohibition of fashioning images to include "the likeness of my servants who serve before me on high: not a likeness of messengers, not a likeness of ophanim, and not a likeness of cherubim" (Lauterbach 2004, 2.344; cf. Stuckenbruck 1995, 57–59). Most of the accusations about worship came from other groups, such as Clement of Alexandria's accusation in *Stromata* 6.5.41 that Jewish people were worshipping (*latreuō*) messengers. Origen of Alexandria reported in the third century CE that a Greek philosopher named Celsus accused Jewish people of worshipping messengers (Origen, *Cels.* 1.26). Already in the Christian Epistle to the Colossians (late first century CE), the author refers to "worship of messengers" (*thrēskeia tōn angelōn*; Col 2:18).[17] Beginning in the fifth century CE, petitions and incantations addressed to divine messengers appear on bowls and amulets. These practices drew from existing conventions directed at high deities, but it is not clear how early they began to be aimed at divine messengers.[18] What *is* clear is that the intuitive compulsion to access divine agency could not be entirely quashed by the machinations of authority. More effective was to redirect the impulse to an agent more directly under the control of cultic authority, which brings us back to the *šēm*.

ŠEM

While the narratives that involve the messenger of YHWH make the most thorough and explicit use of the *šēm* as a vehicle for divine identity and presence, its use as a sort of proxy for the deity is known from several passages in the Hebrew Bible (Lewis 2020, 279–92). One example is Ps 76:2–3:[19] "God is known in

---

[16] See, for instance, Ehrman 2014, 55: "Ancient authors insisted that angels not be worshiped precisely because angels were being worshiped." For broader discussions, see Stuckenbruck 1995; Gieschen 1998, 124; Olyan 1993; Tuschling 2007.

[17] On the influence of this passage on later Christian engagement with the veneration of divine messengers, see Cline 2011, 137–46.

[18] See Shaked, Ford, and Bhayro 2013. There is also discussion in Cline 2011, 137–65 and throughout de Bruyn 2017. For the reconstruction of an invocation of mediatory divine figures at Qumran, see Penney and Wise 1994.

[19] S. Dean McBride (1969, 67) employs the concept of "nominal realism," which he describes as a belief in "a concrete, ontological relationship ... between words and the

Judah, / in Israel, great is his name. / His abode was in Salem, / and his habitation in Zion" (Sommer 2009, 65). In Isa 30:27, the *šēm* seems to be treated as one of the partible components of the deity's agency: "The name of YHWH comes [*šēm-YHWH bā'*] from far off, his anger burning." The partibility of one's name, and particularly a divine name, is well known from ancient Southwest Asia. In the first chapter I discussed some of the ways the "name" could be conceptualized as a communicable locus of agency. In addition to reifying agency, it could refer to one's reputation or legacy, to their social presence, or to their authority. The materialization of the name through inscription created a durative invocation that rendered the intended reference or reification as permanent as was the medium of the inscription. While there was frequently a desire for someone to read or pronounce the name, it was not absolutely necessary for the materialization of the name to perpetuate one's agency. As Radner (2005, 130) notes, the continued existence of the name itself was most critical to the perpetuation of the existence of the named, and hidden texts were particularly effective, removed as they were from prying hands and eyes.

For humans, the most salient use of the partible "name" was in funerary and mortuary inscriptions, where it was inscribed on stelai, painted on plaster, or carved into wall inscriptions. The invocation of the name by readers of these inscriptions, whether descendants or passers-by, was often intended to facilitate the continued memory and existence of the deceased. The clearest example from the Hebrew Bible of this function of the name may be Absalom's lament, "I have no son to cause my name to be remembered" (2 Sam 18:18), which necessitated his erection of his own stele in the Valley of the King to facilitate his care and feeding throughout the afterlife. In her discussion of the power of the name, Radner (2005, 22) observes that in ancient Southwest Asia, the juxtaposition of name and image could serve to amplify the desired effect: "The 'written name' is closely related in its meaning and usage to the representative image, and is often used in conjunction with it to ensure the presence of the individual."[20]

Divine names had additional functions associated with their partibility. In one of the inscriptions from Kuntillet 'Ajrud, parallel cola bless "Baal on the day of war" and "The name of El on the day of war," suggesting the deity (whether YHWH or Baal) personifies or employs the name of El in battle. A related inscription is the Ugaritic *KTU* 1.16.6.54–57, in which King Kirta curses his son Yassubu, declaring:

---

things and actions which the words describe. A name is consubstantial with the thing named ... [or] a physical extension of the name bearer, an attribute which when uttered evokes the bearer's life, essence, and power" (as quoted in Sommer 2009, 26).

[20] "Der 'geschriebene Name' ist in seiner Bedeutung und Anwendung dem repräsentativen Bild eng verwandt und wird häufig im Verbund mit diesem verwendet, um die Präsenz des Individuums zu sichern."

yṯbr ḥrn ybn	May Horanu break, my son,
yṯbr ḥrn r'išk	May Horanu break your head,
'ṯtrt šm b'l qdqdk	'Athtartu-Name-of-Ba'lu your skull[21]

The same epithet is restored in a fragmentary portion of the Baal Cycle (*KTU* 1.2.1.7–8), and even makes an appearance in the fifth-century BCE Eshmunazor inscription (KAI 14.18).

These texts seem to objectify and weaponize the divine name. Theodore Lewis (2011) notes that several scholars understand 'Athtartu to be functioning in the role of "hypostatic" extension of Baal, but he finds additional interpretive clues in some rhetoric from ancient Egypt. In a relief from the fourteenth-century BCE Egyptian Thutmosis IV, the name of the pharaoh is represented with a fighting cartouche that goes into battle on behalf of the pharaoh. In a twelfth-century BCE inscription from Medinet Habu, Ramses III declares, "When they (the Sea Peoples) mention my name in their land, may it consume them, while I sit on the throne of Harakhte." These texts seem to suggest the weaponization of the name, which leads Lewis to the conclusion that 'Athtartu is not simply an extension of Baal's agency, but an independent agent incantationally wielding the name of Baal as a weapon. Lewis (2011, 227) concludes, "Certain specific words when correctly wielded by the right persons—an exorcist priest or a goddess such as 'Athtartu—were thought by the ancients to contain effectual power." He even points to several passages from the Hebrew Bible that could be read to weaponize the name of YHWH, such as 1 Sam 17:45, Isa 41:25, and Ps 118:10–11.[22]

Divine names could also function similarly to personal names in their memorialization and reification of agency. Cultic spaces are commonly referred to in the biblical literature as places where the deity's name was invoked, remembered, or placed. YHWH directs Moses to build an altar of earth in "every place where I cause my name to be remembered [*'azkîr 'et-šəmî*]," so that YHWH may come and bless him. D and Dtr make oblique reference to the Jerusalem temple as the place YHWH chose "to place his name" (*ləšakkēn šəmô*; Deut 12:11; 14:23; 16:2, 6, 11; 26:2).[23] This formula represents an expansion on the earlier "short centralization formula" found in Deut 12:14: "the place that YHWH will choose [*'ăšer-yibḥar YHWH*] among one of your tribes." There is a distinction between

---

[21] The translation is from Lewis 2011.
[22] These readings largely rely on reading the *bet* instrumentally in the construction *bəšēm*.
[23] Following Richter 2002, 2007, who argues (2002, 127–205) the Deuteronomistic usage adapted the Akkadian phrase *šuma šakānu*, "the place a name." (In Deut 12:21 and 14:24, the Hebrew is, "to place his name there" [*lāśûm šəmô šām*].) Cf., however, Morrow 2010. On the relationship of the passage in Exod 23 to the Deuteronomistic literature, see Ausloos 2008.

this usage and that of Ps 76 and other texts, however. Deuteronomy 4:36 and 5:24 rather explicitly locate the deity's self in the heavens, and not in their temple. There seems to be a renegotiation of the sense in which the *šēm* presences the deity. The recognition of this compartmentalization of the loci of divine agency and self, and attempts to make sense of it, have given rise to a concept conventionally called "Name Theology." This is a theory classically promulgated in 1947 by Gerhard von Rad (1947) that holds that D and Dtr significantly altered the conceptualization of divine presence by removing the divine self from the temple and locating it in the heavens, leaving only the deity's name to inhabit the temple as a hypostasis of sorts. This is thought to be reflected in the construction *ləškēn šəmô*, which is understood according to this theory to mean "to cause his name to dwell." This reading is supported by the later Dtr phrase *libnôt bayit ləšēm YHWH*, "to build a house for the name of YHWH" (2 Sam 7:13; 1 Kgs 5:17, 19 [ET 5:3, 5]; 8:16, 17).

A variety of positions regarding "Name Theology" have been developed since Von Rad's initial formulation (see Richter 2002, 26–36). Some have turned to comparative philology to gain better interpretive purchase on the constructions involved, pointing to the Amarna Letters and the broader Akkadian corpora as evidence that the intended sense was not "to cause his name to dwell," but "to put/place his name." This placement was most commonly achieved through the erection of stelai or inscriptions or the depositing of other media that could bear the royal or divine name.[24] These media were ubiquitous in ancient Southwest Asia. William Schniedewind (2009, 76) explains,

> Everywhere a king places his name, he claims exclusive ownership. Kings, in particular, put their names on monuments, stelae, and border inscriptions to claim exclusive ownership of things. It is not a coincidence that Semitic royal inscriptions often begin with the expression, 'I am X, son of Y, king of Z.' The king puts his name in a place and thereby claims ownership and exclusive dominion.

Now, Schniedewind (2009, 78) here did not have available Seth Sanders' (2010, 114; 2015, 72) argument that royal self-identification in inscriptions appears to have developed as a "ventriloquizing" presencing of the king, but he does suggest that Second Temple biblical texts that address this theme appear to reflect a "hypostatization of the Tetragrammaton."[25] Other scholars suggest the "put/place his name" reading supports the continuation of much earlier

---

[24] Tigay (2017) argues that there was likely an inscription of some kind bearing the divine name in the sanctuary.
[25] He elaborates: "Strikingly, the very symbol of God's presence in the temple, namely the ark of the covenant, was absent from the Second Temple; however, the divine name serves in its stead as the symbol of God's physical presence in the Jerusalem temple" (79).

conceptualizations of name and presence (e.g., de Vaux 1967), or have argued for the relevance of the Akkadian antecedent without denying that D and Dtr are overturning existing conceptualizations of that presencing (McBride 1969).[26] Still others have continued to defend both the "dwell" reading and Dtr's reformation of the divine presence (Mettinger 1982, 41–46, 56–59). Some see no reformation taking place, but just a nuancing of the same concept of divine presence found elsewhere (McConville 1979; Wilson 1995; Knafl 2014, 99–109, 184–87).

In addition to the many stelai that were in use around Israel and Judah that did have or could have had inscribed or painted divine names, votives and other offerings set within sacred precincts could also include the names of human persons seeking favor through the presence of their names before the deities. Anne Katrine de Hemmer Gudme (2003) interrogates second-century BCE Aramaic votive inscriptions from Mount Gerizim that include the petition, "Remembered be PN before DN." According to Gudme, the goal of including the personal name would be to catalyze the invocation of the names by visitors and passers-by, thereby ensuring the deity's remembrance of the individual. I would suggest this and other conventions that link one's name to their presence and interests flatly undermine the argument for the secularization of the name.

The most salient approach to "Name Theology" for this discussion is that of Sommer (2009, 65–66), who firmly sides with the reformative reading. He concludes that,

> According to the deuteronomic Name theology, then, the *shem* is not God, it is not a part of God, and it is not an extension of God. The *shem* is merely a name in the sense that Western thinkers regard names: a symbol, a verbal indicator that points toward something outside itself.… the deuteronomists used the term *shem* not to endorse or even modify its more common theological use but to deflate it.

---

[26] See also Hundley 2009, 542, citing Van Seters 2003, 871–72. I would agree with Hundley that Richter's argument regarding semantic content may not be off target, but that does not necessarily preclude presencing. Even the use of the formula in the Akkadian literature could have a presencing dimension. William Hallo (1962, 6), for instance, insists the inscription of one's name functioned "to proclaim one's ownership of, or presence in, the inscribed object or place" (quoted in Richter 2002, 131). A good critique of Hallo and Richter by William Morrow (2010) concludes, "common to all of these interpretations surveyed is the inference that Y$_{HWH}$ sets his name in the place he chooses in order to promote his divine presence and his claims to sovereignty" (381). Morrow posits that the "Assyrianism" of the specific form of the phrase is a product of "hybridity" or "colonial mimicry": "In the very act of mimicking the dominating culture's linguistic forms, there is an effort to make an ideological expression that serves the interests of the colonized, not the colonizer" (382).

Sommer (2009, 65) cites McBride's "nominal realism" framework as "one of the most thorough and sensitive discussions of this topic,"[27] but goes further than McBride in entirely denying any presencing function of the *šēm*. For Sommer (2009, 65), the *šēm* is completely secularized, which stands in stark contrast to its pre-D use, and thus supports his position regarding D and Dtr's rejection of the fluidity model: "As Deuteronomy 26.2 reminds us, it is the *shem* that is located there. Unlike Psalm 76, Deuteronomy 26 does not put God and the *shem* in the same place or allow them to overlap. In short, the author of Deuteronomy has put the *shem* where others thought God Himself to be."

Concern can be raised with the conclusions Sommer draws from the differences between earlier usage of the *šēm* and those of D and Dtr. As the discussion in previous chapters has demonstrated, loci of agency were not necessarily isometric with the self, and particularly for imagined unseen agents (like deities) whose partibility was bound only by the limits of imagination and the dynamics of counter-intuitiveness. For Sommer, the deity's body and self are the only vehicles of their presence, but just as the self could be parted from the body, other loci of agency could be parted from the body *and* the self.[28] The location of the deity's "self" in the heavens in no way indicates that a known vehicle of divine agency cannot be presencing that agency on earth. That is, after all, one of the primary functions of the partibility and communicability of divine agency. Deuteronomy also appeals in several places to the prototypical language of divine presencing in referring to the temple. Ian Wilson (1995, 152–59, 192–97), in his own critique of Name Theology, highlights multiple ways in which Deuteronomy actually strengthens the sense of the divine presence over and against the earlier narratives (see also Knafl 2014, 99–109, 184–87). For instance, *lipnê YHWH*, "before YHWH," is used frequently in Deuteronomy in reference to events occurring

---

[27] Sommer cites Richter's criticisms of the notion of "nominal realism," which is the framework McBride uses to develop his notion of divine presencing via the name (190, n. 101), and levels a lengthier critique at her work (based primarily on McBride's arguments) on pages 218–19, note 47.

[28] Sommer briefly considers the notion of the presencing of the name in relation to the Amarna Letters, which refer to the placement of the name of the Egyptian Pharaoh in Jerusalem. Sommer (2009, 66) asserts, "The phrase *šakan šumšu* (precisely cognate to the Hebrew לשכן את שמו) does not mean that Abdi-Ḫeba thought that Pharaoh was physically present in Jerusalem; rather, Abdi-Ḫeba acknowledges Pharaoh's claim over the city." This constitutes a bit of a straw man, though, as the partibility and presencing capabilities of deities were considerably more dynamic than those of human beings, and in the case of the Hebrew Bible, the *šēm* was being implanted within a literary tradition that already had an active tradition of divine presencing. Additionally, Abdi-Ḫeba's own presence may not have been understood to be reified by the name, but some sense of his agency or authority would have been there.

in the temple,[29] even where it was not used in previous iterations of the same narratives (cf. Hundley 2009, 537–40). As with the ark and the *kābôd*, the renegotiation between the community's past and the needs of its present was not a matter of a sharp and sudden severance, but of a gentle nuancing or reorienting.

The framework of divine agency formulated in this book is employed in one form or another from the beginning to end of the Hebrew Bible and beyond, undermining the primary contention of "Name Theology," namely that D and Dtr employed the concept of the name's installation in the temple precisely to deny the deity's presence therein. Rather, these authors maintained the presencing function of the temple while insulating the deity's "self" from the risks associated with traditional hosts for the vehicles of divine identity. The identification of the *šēm* as the salient locus of divine agency also likely served these authors' structuring of power and of authoritative knowledge, isolating the temple as the only appropriate host for this primarily textual vehicle of divine agency over which they had unique purview. That is, until the interpolation of the messenger.

Names were conceptualized as powerful agents in ancient Southwest Asia, and Iron Age Israel and Judah were active participants in the sociomaterial conventions associated with that conceptualization. Scholars sometimes appeal to the notion that inscriptions on stelai or other monuments served solely memorializing, commemoratory, or authoritative functions, but in a sociomaterial ecology where memory could perpetuate the afterlife of the deceased (for example, through invocation), and reify the presence of human or divine agency (for example, through ventriloquization), we cannot draw such firmly prescriptive lines. The sociomaterial functions of names in glyptic and literary texts were much more complex than is generally allowed by the traditional retrojection of twenty-first century CE reflective rationalizations. The significance of those functions to the changing means of presencing deity as well as to the development and authority of the biblical corpora will be discussed in greater detail in the next chapter.

CONCLUSION

The messenger of YHWH began with the appropriation of a figure from a lower tier of the conventional divine hierarchy for purposes of rhetorical prophylaxis. This was likely initiated by redactors who sought to obscure the deity's direct physical interactions with humanity, but it ultimately overlapped conceptually with expectations regarding divine agency and its communicability, giving rise to a new and dynamic literary framework for divine presencing. This was a textual solution to a textual problem that laid the conceptual groundwork for the elaboration of a new rhetorically flexible divine agent: the messenger of YHWH. I have

---

[29] See Deut 12:7, 12, 18; 14:23, 26; 15:20; 16:11, 16; 18:7; 26:5, 10, 13.

argued that the messenger of YHWH's reification of the divine presence was rationalized in Exod 23:20–21 via the indwelling of the *šēm*, a traditional vehicle for divine agency that would also be employed by D/Dtr to serve their own rhetorical ends regarding the divine presence. By virtue of possessing the divine name, the messenger may not only be referred to by YHWH's own name—thus the first-, second-, and third-person references in the interpolated passages to the messenger as YHWH—but they may also exercise YHWH's own power and authority. In this sense, both the identity theory and the representation theory approximate some of the rhetorical goals of the messenger's function, but are off target regarding the governing conceptual framework. The ambiguity theory also likely accounts at least in part for the rhetorical salience of the messenger, as an additional layer of ambiguity was no doubt helpful for those authorities who were concerned to keep the community from getting too firm a grasp on the nature of deity, or too comfortable with the deity's immanence. The utility of that ambiguity also likely contributed to the survival of the discordant texts that seemed to conflate the identity of the messenger with the identity of YHWH. There would have been no compelling need to resolve a tension that so well served the interests of those authorities.

7.
YHWH's Divine Agents: Texts

One final and perhaps unexpected means of materially encountering deity in ancient Israel and Judah that grew out of the rhetorical machinations of cultic authorities is that of text, and particularly the text of the law (Stavrakopoulou 2013; Watts 2016; 2017). The materiality of text has been acknowledged a number of times already in this book for methodological purposes, but I have not addressed the fact that that materiality facilitated important sociomaterial roles for texts in Israel and Judah (cf. Levy 2012, Mandell and Smoak 2016). Writing as a material technology had been in use for many generations by the time of the authors and editors of the D source, but the literary innovations and expansions that began with their project signal a new and expansive significance (Polaski 2007; Levtow 2012). While those innovations and expansions increased the social capacity for abstraction, imagination, and memory (Schaper 2007, 2019), this in no way suppressed the fundamentally material nature of the medium of writing, and in many ways expanded its flexibility and utility in that regard. Texts themselves could still function as cultic media, both as constituent elements of other media and as media in their own right. To demonstrate this continued function and its utility, this chapter will interrogate two broad categories of texts that performed presencing functions for unseen agency in general and for YHWH more specifically. The first section will look at amulets, inscriptions, and other texts often referred to as "magical" in the scholarship,[1] and the second will interrogate the text of the law of Moses (in its various iterations).

---

[1] *Magic* is a notoriously difficult category, but it falls under the rubric of unseen agency. Similar to the way we may describe the word *cult* as a pejorative label for "a religion I don't like," magic largely originates as a pejorative label for (according to my theoretical framework) "unseen agency I don't like." It has since been rationalized in a variety of ways in relation to the Hebrew Bible (Milgrom 1991, 42–43; Schmitt 2008; Cohn 2008, 21–24; Bohak 2008; Stökl 2012, 8). Further consideration of the term is outside the scope of this book, but would benefit greatly from interrogation through the methodological frameworks discussed here (see, for example, Czachesz 2013).

This is not remotely an exhaustive look at texts that were widely understood to transmit agency, however. There are many and varied ways in which texts performed such functions in the Hebrew Bible and in other related material remains. The ritual described in Num 5:11–31 is one such example. Part of the prescribed process includes writing out the priest's curse and then wiping the ink of the text off either with or into the water that had been prepared with dust from the floor of the sacred space. This seems to imbue the water with the words of the curse, which, while already materialized in their pronunciation, took on a more durative and manipulable state when written out. When mixed with water and drunk, the curse is interiorized, physically and conceptually, by the drinker. This passage clearly indicates the primarily artifactual function of the text, as well as the perception that, when properly produced in the appropriate circumstances and environments, cultic text can transmit the agency necessary to reify the events or states prescribed by the text.

The necessity of embeddedness within the appropriate environment should be emphasized here. Prior to the destruction of the Jerusalem temple, the temple and other cultic structures, including city gates and other significant locations, delineated sacred space and provided an environment dedicated to acts associated with the divine and its agency. That space could be controlled so that sociomaterial cues and ritualistic acts facilitated the desired encounter with divine agency, but in the absence of such sacred spaces, textual means of presencing the divine could rise to the challenge of enacting the appropriate cognitive ecology. This challenge could be overcome by embedding the engagement with the text within narrative, within ritual (such as recitation), within a closed-off space, or within some combination of the three. In this way, conventionalized means of reifying boundaries between mundane cognitive acts and the presencing media could provide that sense of separation and facilitate the desired cognitive effects.

AMULETS, INSCRIPTIONS, AND OTHER MAGICAL TEXTS

Among the earliest material witnesses to magical texts among worshippers of YHWH is the eighth-century BCE Khirbet el-Qôm inscription, discussed in chapter 1 (cf. Schmidt 2016, 144–62; cf. Cohn 2008). Like other presencing texts, the function of this inscription must be interrogated in connection with the sociomaterial ecology in which it was situated, which includes (1) its separation from everyday activities (Suriano 2018, 43–49), (2) its location within a darkened tomb, and (3) the funerary and mortuary rites associated with it. Alice Mandell and Jeremy Smoak (2017, 190) describe this and related inscriptions as "bound to the protection of the dead, and burial and funerary ritual enacted by the living kin. These inscriptions also communicated a warning to unseen malevolent forces, such as ghosts, demons, or potential intruders seeking to loot the tomb." Such inscriptions frequently occur with pictorial reliefs—the Khirbet el-Qôm inscription, for instance, surrounds an impression of a downward-facing hand—which suggests the overlap of the semiotic and performative functions of picture and text. Both were often combined in inscriptions like these to invoke the agency of the deities whose names the inscription materialized in order to (hopefully) ward off the influence of malevolent forces operating among the living or the dead.[2] Touching or tracing these words may have been just as salient a means of engagement as reading, and repetition of divine names may have been a way to amplify their power. Even many of those who could not read were likely able to recognize a small number of words, and particularly names, even if only from the pattern they visually formed and not from the characters themselves. A standardized way to write a divine name could be recognizable to literate and illiterate alike, in a sense functioning for both as a divine image in and of itself.[3]

The commonality of inscriptions like these was likely due to the ubiquitous perception of the pervasiveness of unseen agents and agency in the surrounding world, as well as the notion that those agents and agencies could be employed, controlled, or at least held at a distance through the recitation and/or inscription of their names.[4] Another medium for influencing this agency was inscribed amulets, which have been described as "the most pervasive of magical tools in antiquity" (Cohn 2008, 17; cf. Smoak 2010). Yehuda Cohn (2008, 19) has traced the apotropaic use of written amulets back to eighth-century BCE Egypt, at the latest, from where it soon spread out to Greek, Phoenician, Mesopotamian, and other societies.[5] Cohn (2008, 18) favorably cites John Gager's (1992, 220)

---

[2] In a discussion of the apotropaic use of the "evil eye," Sarah Bond (2015) highlights the combination on mosaics of text and a plurality of images in what she calls the "'kitchen sink' approach to protecting one's self."

[3] William Schniedewind (2003, 228) has argued that by the time of the second temple, "the name of God became a hypostasis of Yahweh himself." Writing the name could therefore reify the divine presence, and for some became taboo in most circumstances.

[4] Note John Gager's (1992, 12) comments prefacing his discussion of the use of curse tablets and binding spells: "The role of images and figures as mediators of power brings us finally to the names of deities and other spiritual entities on *defixiones*. In discussing these names, it is essential to keep in mind three fundamental characteristics of the 'spiritual universe' of ancient Mediterranean culture: first, the cosmos literally teemed, at every level and in every location, with supernatural beings; second, although ancient theoreticians sometimes tried to sort these beings into clear and distinct categories, most people were less certain about where to draw the lines between gods, *daimones*, planets, stars, angels, cherubim, and the like; and third, the spirit or soul of dead persons, especially of those who had died prematurely or by violence, roamed about in a restless and vengeful mood near their buried body."

[5] Psalm 91 pops up throughout the history of early Judaism and even early Christianity as a text with a clear apotropaic function. It is not unlikely it was inscribed on amulets or other

rhetorical flourish regarding the ubiquity of amulets: "given the conventional cognitive map of that world, it would have been foolish and unreasonable to behave otherwise." By the Late Antique period, some amuletic templates had become widespread across Jewish, Christian, and other Mediterranean societies.[6] For example, a fifth- or sixth-century CE amulet (see fig. 7.1) recently discovered in the Byzantine Jewish settlement of Arbel, in northern Israel, depicts a horse rider with a halo over their head thrusting a spear down at a female figure. A Greek inscription reads "The One God Who Conquers Evil." Between the rider and the female figure is a Greek variation on the Tetragrammaton that reads *IAŌTH*. Chance Bonar notes that, "All across the Galilee, Lebanon, and Syria, we've discovered amulets that depict the holy rider spearing a dragon or a woman. Jews, Christians, and pagans all commissioned and used this same amuletic template, sometimes labelling it as Solomon or Saint Sissinos" (Moss 2021).

Figure 7.1. Front and back of a fifth- or sixth-century CE amulet discovered at Arbel. Source: Tercatin 2021. Drawing by the author.

---

media and brandished as a means of warding off evil. See Nitzan 1994, 359–63; Cohn 2008, 94; Breed 2014, 298–303.

[6] James Watts (2017, 77) writes, "These traditions stimulated the belief that the Hebrew name of God is very powerful. Its use in prayer and incantations became popular across the Mediterranean world in Late Antiquity. Amulets reproduced IAΩ, the Greek equivalent of the Hebrew יהו YHWH, in combination with the names of Greek gods. Greek magical papyri utilized IAΩ more than any other divine name."

Stamp seals likely represent our earliest and most common examples of powerful inscriptions that could operate on a personal and a social level.[7] These were small carved seals intended to create impressions in clay or other materials to mark ownership or to "sign" a transaction or contract. Most stamp seals had primarily administrative or legal functions, but there were also personal seals that in many cases could be more accurately described as "seal amulets."[8] Frequently inscribed with the names or symbols of deities, and likely worn on rings or threaded on necklaces, seal amulets could have been understood as perpetual invocations of divine agency. The use of particularly precious, reflective, or transparent ores for some seals supports the conclusion that they may have been seen as appropriate media for conducting divine agency. These were likely used throughout life and were commonly included in grave goods, suggesting their power was thought to extend into the afterlife. In support of this conclusion, some scholars (Hallo 1985; Uehlinger 1993, 274; Vermeulen 2010, 9) have highlighted a reference to sealing in Song 8:6, in which the narrator compares herself to a seal amulet that can protect her lover from death: "Place me like a seal upon your heart, / like a seal upon your arm. / For as strong as death is love, / as resilient as Sheol is passion."

While anthropomorphic divine imagery is known from the seals of broader ancient Southwest Asia, in Israel and Judah, the preference was for symbols or symbolic animals (Ornan 1993, 63). For instance, the Egyptian *uraeus* cobra—an apotropaic symbol that became associated with the biblical seraphim and with divinity in general—commonly occurs in Hebrew iconic seals from the eighth century BCE (Vermeulen 2010, 56–57). The sun disk also appears on a number of seals from the end of the eighth century, including on multiple seals bearing the name of the Judahite king Hezekiah (Vermeulen 2010, 64–66). In the seventh century BCE, however, the appearance of Yahwistic theophoric elements on Hebrew seals began to correlate significantly with an *absence* of iconography on the same seal (Golub 2018; cf. Vermeulen 2010, 57–69). Despite the development of a more programmatic aniconographic tradition, there is still ample evidence for the power of seal inscriptions to presence divine agency. Keel and Uehlinger (1998, 24–26), for instance, highlight the use of a Greek omega (Ω) symbol on seals ranging from Mesopotamia to Judah. The symbol was associated in Old Babylonian iconography with miscarriage, and seals bearing the symbol were commonly included in the graves of children. The symbol may have represented

---

[7] Because of their commonality, Keel and Uehlinger (1998, 10) suggest, "they can virtually serve as the standard by which religious history is documented, particularly because they are more or less public artifacts and can thus serve as a sensitive seismograph to detect subtle shifts in religious history." See also Münger 2003.
[8] See Uehlinger 1993, 273–74; Vermeulen 2010. As Uehlinger notes, "seal-amulet" was coined by Hornung and Staehelin 1976.

the womb, and its inclusion in Iron Age IIC graves in Judah may reflect the conceptualization of the grave as a womb. Whatever the precise association, scholars believe it was included in order to grant protection to the miscarried child.

Another preexilic example of inscribed amulets from ancient Judah is that of the Ketef Hinnom silver scrolls (see fig. 7.2). The scrolls were briefly mentioned in chapter 1, but the relationship of the text inscribed on the scrolls to the blessing Aaron is instructed to give to the children of Israel in Num 6:23–27 was not discussed in much detail. That text is the earliest attestation of any version of a text that would ultimately constitute part of the later Torah. In

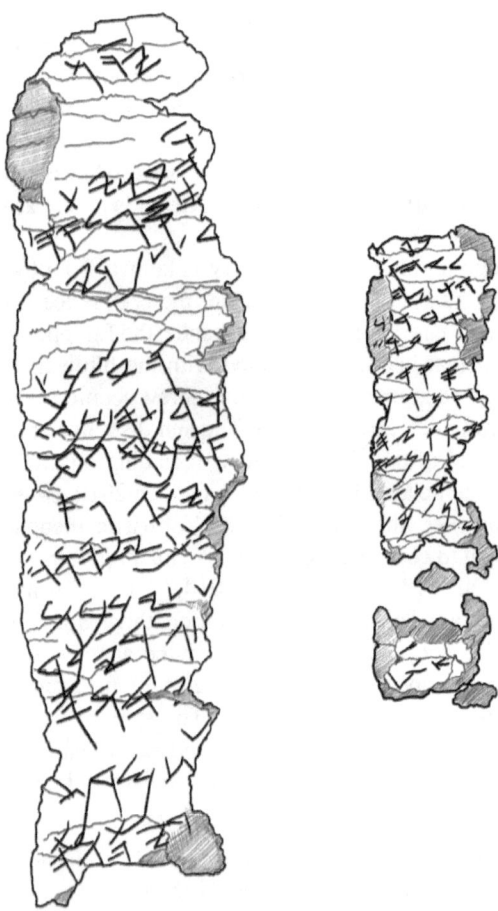

Figure 7.2. The Ketef Hinnom Silver Scrolls. Drawing by the author.

the version found in the book of Numbers, verse 27 explains, "So they will put my name upon [*wəśāmû 'et-šəmî 'al*] the children of Israel and I will bless them ['*ăbārăkēm*]." The notion that YHWH's name is "upon" the people of Israel is frequently understood to suggest the community's identification as the people of YHWH, but the silver scrolls demonstrate another sense in which that blessing could be realized, namely in bearing the materially present divine name.[9]

As was mentioned in chapter 1, the scrolls likely served apotropaic functions, perhaps both in life and death, but some additional observations may be made about their materiality. First, the scrolls were silver, which we have seen in previous chapters was one of a limited number of substances thought to either originate with the divine or be particularly conducive to transmitting divine agency. That would have made them more effective conduits for the divine agency that would have aided in warding off evil. Unlike the JPFs, however, they were explicitly associated with a specific deity, namely YHWH, whose name was inscribed at least seven times in the silver. This leads to a second observation: the use of the divine name was likely understood as a means of invoking that deity's specific agency, particularly via the possessor's vocal recitation of the blessing. Even when not speaking the blessing, however, the material inscription of the name in the silver could be understood as a means of perpetual invocation (Radner 2005; Tigay 2007). Third, the text on the scrolls appears to have been closely connected with the temple cult, which may indicate the small-scale and private appropriation and reallocation of ritual practices prototypically associated with the temple (see Smoak 2017). Finally, the scrolls were rolled up, meaning the text inscribed upon them, including the divine name, was not immediately accessible.[10] The text itself was closed off, separate, and yet, still materially present and available to remind the person (who likely wore them on a chain or string around their neck) of their presence and of the words of the blessing. Jeremy Smoak (2019, 445) comments, "It did not matter if the words on the amulets were visible to the eye. Their silver scripts touched the wearer's body and projected the words of the divine blessing into the wearer's mind. The brilliance of these metal objects was their ability to 'produce the presence' of Yahweh's blessings and protection throughout the day as the body 'awakened,' 'jarred,' and 'livened' their words."[11]

---

[9] Gabriel Levy (2012, 104–5) states, "these verses are clearly focused on a mantra-like reinscription of the divine name, and this is perhaps where they get their 'numinous power.'" Note that a Greek-Aramaic silver amulet discovered in Egypt and dating to the late Roman period (Kotansky, Naveh, and Shaked 1992, 11) begins the Aramaic section with "I bind this amulet from Jerusalem, in the name of YH."

[10] They were likely too small to easily read, as well. On this, see Smoak 2018.

[11] This is related to Radner's (2005, 130) observation, mentioned in chapter 6 (see above, p. 168), that hidden texts were particularly effective at perpetuating the existence of the named while protecting the written name from prying hands and eyes.

The Ketef Hinnom scrolls are likely to be plotted along the early stages of a trajectory of innovation toward the primary textual—which is not to say immaterial—presencing of deity, an innovation born of circumstance and rhetorical utility, more fully realized in the Achaemenid, Greco-Roman, and Late Antique periods.[12] It appropriated for certain texts some of the features of larger-scale divine images known from elsewhere in early Southwest Asia, including the use of precious metals and the incantational employment of the divine name. Several texts from the Hebrew Bible betray similar attempts at appropriation, but instead of being understood as a means of renegotiating the meaning of materialization, they are frequently misunderstood through the Reformation and Enlightenment lenses of scripturalization precisely as a means of *dematerialization*. This is not only a presentistic understanding of textualization, but it also ignores the constraints of cognition and of mnemohistory. The sociomaterially embedded memories of these media and practices are not so easily abandoned, particularly in light of their foundation upon universal principles of intuitive cognition. Where scholars have posited the rejection of this or that fundamental ideology, a renegotiation of their nature and function is a conclusion far more in line with what we know about how communities engage with their past. This is the case for Sommer's (2009, 58–79) discussion—addressed above—of the "rejection of the fluidity model," which, I have argued, was no rejection at all. The Ketef Hinnom silver scrolls overlap with and underline an even more significant example of renegotiated presencing media that is frequently overlooked in the scholarship, namely that of the Torah itself.

THE LAW

Portions of the texts now known collectively as the Torah or the "law of Moses" have likely existed in some form or another since the eighth century BCE, but the corpus does not seem to have achieved its status as Judah's preeminent charter myth and principal identity marker until the reforms of Ezra in the Achaemenid period at the earliest (Watts 2011; 2017; Collins 2017; cf. Honigman and Ben Zvi 2020). While P and D repeatedly assert the unilateral authority of the laws their texts consolidate, and command the people to give them priority, as Collins (2017, 26) notes, "official recognition of these laws is not clearly attested before the time of Ezra." That official recognition may have been achieved much quicker had the laws been composed with the intent of constituting the basis of a legal system, but that does not seem to have been their primary purpose.[13] Rather, as Collins (2017,

---

[12] For some fascinating Aramaic bowl spells from Late Antiquity that appeal to a wide variety of divine names and roles, see Shaked, Ford, and Bhayro 2013.

[13] As Collins (2017, 43) notes, the consolidation of the Pentateuch did not involve ironing out differences or creating a univocal text. "Rather, they created a composite document, in

41) explains, "In the exilic context, without king or temple, the Law provided a new identity for the remnant of Judah. 'Israel' was still a people bound by blood ties, and closely identified with the land. Most fundamentally, however, Israel was the people bound exclusively to the God Yahweh by covenant."[14] This covenant relationship provided an overarching framework of identity that could adapt the notion of kinship while also extending the boundaries beyond it,[15] but without the temple or the king, and embedded within a foreign nation, that relationship required a new and more robust set of ritual observances in order to generate the opportunities for costly signaling and the senses of social monitoring and punishment that could facilitate YHWH's performance of their prosocial functions. Things like sabbath observance and circumcision became particularly salient in this period, but this would not be enough without the deity's presence in the people's midst and some manner of material locus for that presence.[16]

The previous two chapters have discussed some of the ways preexisting modes of divine presencing were renegotiated in order to reflectively account for the loss of the temple and to insulate the deity's presencing media against unauthorized access, duplication, and harm. The heavy restriction of that media, and particularly its confinement to literary channels, limited the ability of the people to experience that presence, which represents a significant prosocial liability. Different authors responded to this liability in different ways, and one such way was to further exalt and expand the deity's purview and power, which we see taking place progressively in the literature (cf. Achenbach 2016). Jeremiah 3:16–17 prophesy of a time when the ark will be forgotten, and Jerusalem will be called "the throne of YHWH" (*kissē' YHWH*). The idea here is to render the absent cultic medium obsolete by framing the entire city as the throne that facilitated the deity's presence. Chapters 1 and 10 of Ezekiel engage in similar rhetoric, but rather than discounting the ark, they present a portable cherubim throne that allowed the deity to travel beyond the confines of a material temple. In Isa 66:1,

---

which their differing theologies, including the older Yahiwst and Elohist ones, stood in tension." This is precisely what we would expect from a document whose function was always intended to extend beyond the mere import of its words.

[14] MacDonald 2003 is an excellent discussion of the nature of this exclusive relationship.

[15] Sylvie Honigman and Ehud Ben-Zvi (2020, 375) note, "In the absence of alternative institutions having the required cultural, mnemonic, and social capital, the literati (and priests) took on the task of shaping a construction of an ethno-cultural group, which although from a certain perspective was a shadow of its glorious past instantiations, was nevertheless perceived in continuity with them, and, to a large extent, their necessary 'historical' continuation."

[16] James Watts (2008) has formulated a three-dimensional understanding of the function of scripture (semantic, performative, and iconic), and through that lens, this section would be focusing on the "iconic" function of the Torah as one of the more salient functions prior to the Achaemenid period.

the whole earth is the deity's footstool, and the earth is their throne. While this rhetoric allowed authors to rationalize the loss of the temple and also assert the presence of the deity, while also further exalting that deity, these were still literary abstractions not widely accessible—the liability remained and would become more acute as the deity's transcendence distanced them further.

Another means of renegotiating modes of divine presence involved the text of the law's conflation on the part of cultic authorities with more traditional presencing media. The Ketef Hinnom Scrolls show this conflation was more an adaptation of existing technology than a revolutionary breakthrough, but its accommodation and rationalization by institutional authorities would represent a starker departure. In chapter 5 I discussed the functional overlap between the ark and shrine models. The latter are known from glyptic depictions and from the material remains to have been able to house divine images of different types. As I mentioned there, it is no enormous leap to link the tablets of the law with cultic stelai. Though the ark's function as a container for the tablets of the law is a later innovation, that function conflates the text with a central piece of presencing media in a way that may have been intended to facilitate the transition of presencing functions *to* the text of the law, and likely via the material imposition of the divine name. Indeed, James Watts (2016, 21) has argued that the Pentateuch "was shaped to lay the basis for Torah scrolls to replace the ark of the covenant as the iconic focus of Israel's worship." There is no mention anywhere of the text inscribed on the tablets being read, so their primarily function seems to be artifactual rather than literary. The texts describe scrolls that were prepared from which the law could be read, but even those seem to have served a primary artifactual function in some places, and in ways that targeted traditional presencing media other than the ark for the imposition of the law.

In Deut 27:2–3, Moses gives the following instructions to the people of Israel, "you will erect [*hăqēmōtā*] for yourselves great stones [*'ăbānîm gədōlîm*] and plaster them with plaster. And you will write upon them all the words of this instruction [*hattôrâ hazzō't*]." Following the erection of these stelai (vv. 5–7), they are to build an altar, offer burnt offerings to YHWH, share a communal meal, and "rejoice before YHWH, your deity [*śāmaḥtā lipnê YHWH 'ĕlōhêkā*]." The stones here seem to function as presencing media, facilitating the deity's presence so that the sacrifice can be offered "before YHWH." The words of the law are not spoken or read here—it is only the materialization of the words that seem relevant to their function within the prescribed ritual acts. Stavrakopoulou (2013, 228) notes, "The narrator appears less concerned with the specifics of the 'message' of Torah than with the performance of writing and other rituals.... it is the material manifestation of Torah that is of central concern in this passage."

A related event is narrated in Josh 24:25–27. Joshua makes a covenant with the people of Israel, writing the words of the law on a scroll and erecting a large stone (*'eben gədôlâ*) under an oak near the sanctuary at Shechem. The stone in this episode is described as a witness (*'ēdâ*) against the people, in case they attempt to deceive their deity. While in this episode the law is written on a scroll and not the stele that is erected, the scroll is not read, but is immediately backgrounded to the stele and the ritual entering of the covenant. The stone does not seem to presence YHWH, but does act as an independent agent that "witnesses" the ritual and "testifies" against the people in the sense that it serves as a material reminder of the covenant and reifies a sense of monitoring, even though it is not identified with a specific unseen agency.

The law itself, and particularly the Decalogue, is identified with a specific named unseen agency, and it is that naming that may have provided the initial point of contact between the law and the presencing media that came before it (cf. Hogue 2019a). Seth Sanders (2008, 2010, 2012, 2015, 2019) has argued in several places that the use of first-person speech on monumental inscriptions not only served to assert ownership of property and authority over sociomaterially significant space, but to "ventriloquize" the author, or manifest the sense of their presence. The Mesha Stele (see fig. 7.3) is the earliest extant example of this phenomenon, as Sanders (2010, 114) explains:

> The stela of Mesha is the first known alphabetic inscription to address an audience in the first-person voice of the king. It presents a man who claims, in Moabite, to be the king of Moab. The shift in participants from earlier alphabetic royal inscriptions is decisive. The inscription now designates itself by the speaker, not the object, No longer "(this is) *the stela* which Mesha set up" but "*I am* Mesha, son of Kemoashyat, King of Moab, the Dibonite." The inscription presents royal power by making the king present in language, ventriloquizing Mesha as if he were standing in front of us.

This represents "an unrecognized landmark in West Semitic literature" for Sanders (2008, 99).

Another example that is more directly relevant to this chapter's discussion is that of the Katumuwa inscription, which was discussed in relation to personhood in the first chapter. Note the first-person address in the first line:

1   *'nk.ktmw. 'bd.pnmw.zy.qnt.ly.nṣb.b.*
2   *ḥyy…*

1   I am Katumuwa, servant of Panamuwa, who created this stele for myself during
2   my life…[17]

---

[17] I have followed Timothy Hogue and my own precedent in understanding the verb *qny* to be able to reflect creation in certain contexts (but see Thomas 2018). Hogue (2019b) bases his argument on the conventions of Luwian monumental inscriptions.

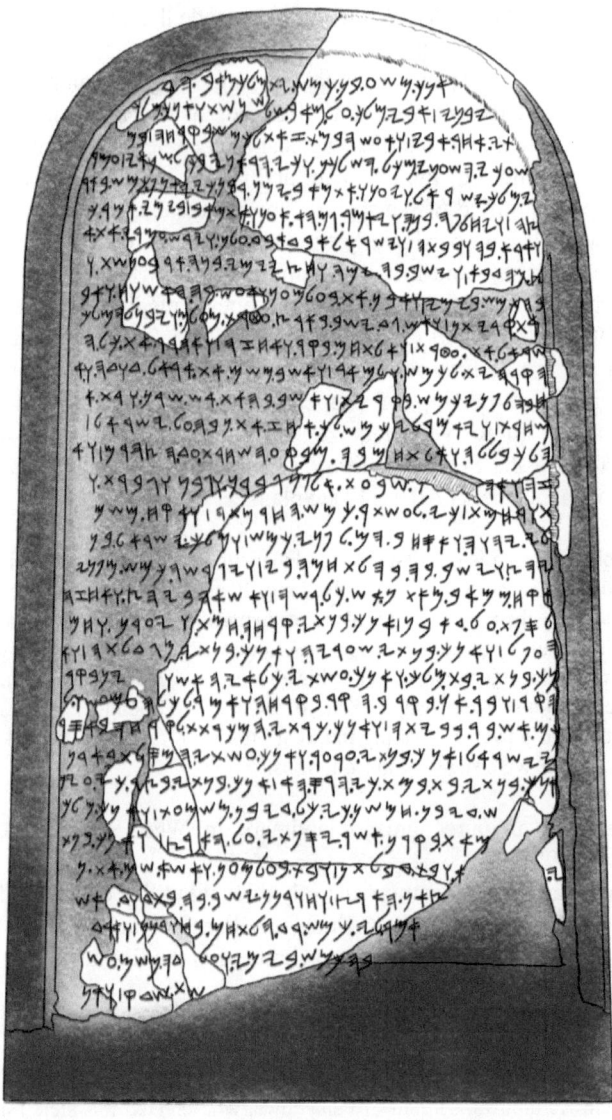

Figure 7.3. The Mesha Stele, discovered in 1868 in Jordan. The dark areas represent portions of the stele that had to be reconstructed after it was destroyed in 1869 by a Bedouin community reacting against pressure from Ottoman authorities to hand the stele over so it could be given to Germany. This specific reconstruction is based on Jackson and Dearman 1989 and Langois 2019. Drawing by the author.

The first-person speech here, according to Timothy Hogue (2019b, 200) helped facilitate "the materialization of Katumuwa's presence and agency so that he might interact with future users of the monument." Seth Sanders (2012, 35) also addresses mortuary inscriptions, insisting the shift to first-person address represents an innovation on the form: "The new inscriptions and monuments actually speak on behalf of the dead and make demands for themselves. They are designed to produce the presence of the dead and demand their feeding."[18]

The Decalogue also begins with first-person speech that identifies the speaker, namely YHWH: "I am YHWH, your deity [*'ānôkî YHWH 'ĕlōhêkā*], who brought you up from the land of Egypt, from the house of slavery." The theories of both Sanders and Hogue would suggest this is an adoption of an existing convention intended essentially to presence the speaker. Hogue (2019c) asserts,

> The result is an imagined encounter with the projected speaker implied by the pronoun 'I.' This process of deictic projection thus conjures a speaker—reembodying them in the imagination of the audience. The opening line of the Decalogue—'I am Yahweh'—is not a prosaic statement nor even a mere adaptation of royal monumental rhetoric. This statement actually produces the presence of Yahweh in the minds of the readers and hearers of the text. It is a theophany condensed into a formula.

As the opening statement of the Decalogue, these words would have been understood to have been the first inscribed by the deity's own finger (Exod 31:18) on the tablets of stone (cf. Doak 2014). The tablets would thus be a product of divine rather than human production and the deity's own first-person speech, in contrast to the golden calf (cf. Exod 32:15–16; Deut 9:8–21).[19] This touches multiple traditional bases for the production of presencing media. As miniature stelai bearing the divine name and the deity's own words, they are functionally parallel to the stelai mentioned above in Deut 27, and were no doubt also understood to be able to facilitate ritual acts "before YHWH." The later passages in which the law was to be written in some iteration or another upon (or in the presence of) stelai represent different variations on this shared theme: the law, whether written or spoken, has the power to presence the deity.[20] Even without stelai, the law could be conceptualized as presencing media. Note Neh 8:5–6 describe Ezra opening the book of the law from an elevated position (away from

---

[18] See also Radner 2005, 114–55.

[19] Moses goes on to shatter these tablets (Exod 32:19), but Exod 34:1 has YHWH command Moses to carve two new tablets, on which YHWH would again write the words of the law. According to Exod 34:28, however, Moses wrote on the tablets.

[20] See Watts 2016, 21: "the Pentateuch was shaped to lay the basis for Torah scrolls to replace the ark of the covenant as the iconic focus of Israel's worship." Cf. Schniedewind 2009, 78–79; Fried 2013.

the temple), then the people standing and—after Ezra blesses YHWH—replying "Amen! Amen!" and bowing down to worship YHWH. Describing this scene, Lisbeth Fried (2013, 294) comments, "the torah scroll has become a manifestation or an epiphany of the god Yhwh, and a medium through which God may be accessed."[21]

The recognition of these presencing capabilities is reflected in the later texts that deploy them in the democratization of access to the deity's agency through the integration of the law not with stelai—which were no longer acceptable—but with practices associated with inscribed amulets. Exodus 13:9, 16 and Deut 6:6–9; 11:18–21 (usually understood as Achaemenid period compositions) prescribe discussing, reciting, and meditating on specific passages from the law (since identified as Exod 13:1–10, 11–16; Deut 6:4–9; 11:13–21; cf. Cohn 2008, 33–48). The texts in Exodus and Deuteronomy would come to be understood to prescribe the materialization of the identified texts on small scrolls that were to be a sign upon the hands of the people, an emblem between their eyes, and were to be written on doorposts and gates.[22] Appropriating the mode of divine presencing found in the Ketef Hinnom scrolls, these passages of the law that repeated the divine name (and also included the deity's own first-person speech) were to be inscribed on small scrolls and enclosed within small containers that were worn on the body (*tafillîn*), but could also be placed, much like stelai, at the threshold of the home and perhaps the city (*mezûzôt*).[23] The words of the law here are more salient—as they were to be recited—but as with the stelai of Deut 27, it is their material presence that is most important (Schaper 2007, 14–16). While cultic leaders in earlier periods sought to restrict access to the deity's presence and the private production of presencing media, the law provided a new means of expanding that access without compromising their structuring of power. The integration of specific texts of the law with more traditional small-scale media allowed those leaders to subjugate that media to their own authority and refocus

---

[21] She also notes that in Ezra 7:10, the infinitive construct *lidrôš* is used in connection with the *tôrat YHWH*. As noted above in chapter 4, that infinitive construct is used overwhelmingly to refer to "seeking an oracle from a god, either directly or by means of a medium or prophet" (Fried 2013, 293).

[22] These practices are not clearly attested in the periods of these text's composition, and so it may not have been the intention of the authors and editors to institutionalize them (cf. Cohn 2008, 49–53). The gaps in the data are too numerous to reach firm conclusions.

[23] Note Gabriel Levy's (2012, 105) comments on the *tafillîn*: "One is literally binding the texts, and by extension the name of God, onto his arm. This aspect of being able to touch the text, by extension the name—is what makes writing so powerful. So it is the extensional feature of spoken and written language—the fact that it is materially present in the world, and then can interact with the higher mental functions of meaning and reference—that make is [sic] so compelling in practice."

the ritual attention of the people onto the leaders' own institutional purview, namely the law. The "doctrinal" mode of the associated ritual acts also helped to reinforce the preeminence of YHWH, the authority of those leaders, and the people's shared identity through a shared memory of the past.[24]

By the late-sixth century BCE, the temple had been rebuilt and temple sacrifices were ongoing, but cultic leaders had in the interim extended their influence over private ritual practices and were in no hurry to give it up.[25] The special function and treatment of texts bearing the divine name in later Jewish practices indicates the continued perception of their presencing capabilities. The reduced occurrence of Yahwistic theophoric elements in personal names in this period suggests an increased reverence for the name and a desire to avoid its pronunciation (Schniedewind 2009, 75). The intuitive perception that its pronunciation in some way presenced the deity may have contributed to discomfort with its pronunciation in profane contexts and the desire to avoid such pronunciation.

Other practices associated with texts and their transcription further attest to this sensitivity, though it is not incredibly consistent. For example, some twenty-eight or twenty-nine of the Dead Sea Scrolls manuscripts were written in the square Aramaic script, with the Tetragrammaton written in a paleo-Hebrew script. Scribes frequently left gaps in the transcription where the divine name was to appear, with senior scribes inserting the divine name in the paleo-Hebrew script at a later time. 11QPs^a demonstrates that this treatment was more than just stylistic. In that manuscript, twenty-eight words were erased from the transcription, but the Tetragrammaton was left untouched.[26] Cancellation dots appear over two occurrences the divine name, and none were erased. The goal of offsetting the divine name may have been to protect against accidental erasure,[27] but these scribal practices were not consistent, and the Tetragrammaton frequently occurs in the square script throughout the Qumran corpora. Similarly, while most LXX manuscripts substitute YHWH with the Greek word *kyrios*, "lord," in some Greek

---

[24] For some additional discussion about the effacement of the cult and the prioritization of the text (particularly in the Common Era), see Schmid 2012b.

[25] See Watts 2016, 33: "the priests' monopoly over temple rituals was strengthened by shifting the focus of veneration from the ark of the covenant to the Torah scroll. High priests in Jerusalem rode the rising prestige of both temple and Torah to unprecedented heights of religious and political influence. Only at the end of the Second Temple period did scribal and prophetic challenges to Aaronide priestly precedence gain significant influence in Rabbinic Judaism and early Christianity."

[26] In another eight manuscripts, the divine name was substituted with four dots, sometimes called the "Tetrapuncta." See Tov 2004, 238–45. Cf. Parry 1996.

[27] The Talmudic text Shev. 35a, which dates to the fifth century CE at the earliest, explains that while adjectives describing the deity may be erased, terms like *'ēl*, *'ĕlōhîm*, either term with second person singular or plural suffices, *'ehyeh 'ăšer 'ehyeh*, *šadday*, and other divine epithets may not be erased.

manuscripts from Qumran, such as 4Q120 and 4QpapLXX-Lev^b, the divine name appears as *iaō* (Shaw 2002; Rösel 2007; Lichtenberger 2018). In others, such as the Greek Minor Prophets Scroll from Naḥal Ḥever (8ḤevXII gr), the divine name is written in a paleo-Hebrew script. The lack of consistency shows that conventions for handling texts bearing the divine name were still developing.

Following the destruction of the Jerusalem temple in 70 CE, authorities once again had to wrestle with facilitating the deity's presence in the absence of the temple. The text of the law was already functioning within the society's memory as a species of presencing media, however, which allowed authorities to more clearly codify, standardize, and demarcate that function. Those texts that were understood to be written under divine inspiration "defile the hands," according to early rabbinic literature. Tosefta Yadayim 2:14, for instance, indicates that the Song of Songs defiles the hands as a result of being written under divine inspiration, while Ecclesiastes (or Qohelet) merely constitutes the wisdom of Solomon, and therefore does not defile the hands. The idea seems to be that the texts that defile the hands are endowed with some vestigial degree of divine agency. The initial reflective logic behind this notion of defiling the hands has been lost to the ages, but the intuitive aversion to touching presencing media in profane contexts (Baumgarten 2016)—by this period all contexts were profane—is not difficult to appreciate in light of this book's theoretical framework.[28] Martin Goodman (2007, 74–75) has even suggested ("very tentatively") that the notion of "defiling hands" may have arisen as a rationalization for treating scrolls of the law with a degree of reverence that paralleled to an embarrassingly close degree the pagan treatment of idols.[29] The consequences were reduced to matters of ritual impurity, however, no doubt at least in part because of the frequency of incidental contact with the scrolls, which would have been handled by some individuals on a daily basis. According to some rabbis, there were different degrees to which divine inspiration was understood to have attended different texts, depending, for instance, on whether they were inspired to be recited or inspired to be written.

As with other presencing media, there were also appropriate materials that had to be used and prescribed processes that had to be undertaken by appropriately authorized individuals. The Talmud prescribes the acceptable manner of the preparation and handling of the scrolls, as well as the types of animal skins that were appropriate for creating the parchment. By the end of the third century CE, m. Yad. 4:5 explained that biblical texts did not "defile the hands" unless they

---

[28] See, for instance, Lim 2010, who argues that the sacred contagion of the scriptures is best understood in parallel to the lethality of the unauthorized touching of the ark of the covenant.

[29] An example of the superlative degree of that reverence is the public execution (ordered by a Roman procurator) of a Roman soldier in the 50s CE who destroyed a copy of the law (Josephus, *J.W.* 2.229–231; *Ant.* 20.115).

were "written in the Assyrian script, on parchment, and in ink."[30] Codices, by then closely associated with Christian scripture (Nongbri 2018, 21–46), were an explicitly *inappropriate* textual vehicle for the law. By the sixteenth century, we find in the *Shulkhan Arukh* the requirement to state out loud before beginning to transcribe a scroll of the law, "I have the intent to write the holy name." This indicates for Marianne Schleicher (2010, 15) that "every Jew writing a scroll had to remind himself of its numinosity and thereby contribute to the maintenance of the status of the Torah as a holy artifact." The connections with the treatment of presencing media does not end there, according to Schleicher:

> Once written, inspected, accepted, and used for ritual purposes, the Torah had to be chanted aloud using a special melody (*bTalmud*, 'Megillah' 32a). These artifactual prescriptions for the preparation and transmission of the physical text provided and continue to provide tools within the Rabbinic tradition for projecting a status of holy *axis mundi* onto the Torah scroll…. In line with this conception, the Torah is even referred to as God's temple (*mikdashyah*) in medieval writings.

The widespread use of Torah arks, which use dates back to the second or third century CE, attests to the special status of the scrolls of the law (Watts 2017, 77–80).

Disposal of texts bearing the divine name required special care, as well. If the divine name cannot be erased, then it also cannot be simply thrown in the trash. The Talmudic text Shabb. 115a states that in the case of a fire, all parts of the Hebrew Bible are to be saved, as well as the *tefillin* (phylacteries) and the *mezuzot*. Other texts and fragments bearing the divine name (or eighty-five coherent letters from the law) were known as *shemot* ("names"), and they, too, were required to be reverently disposed of. The method of disposal that became normative was storage in a *genizah* ("storing"), which was a special storeroom in a synagogue or a designated area in a cemetery where worn-out scrolls of the law as well as other heretical or disgraced texts could be held. The use of a cemetery cues one to the texts' proximity to personhood (they were also sometimes buried with respected deceased persons), and in much the same way that decommissioned stelai are known to have been plastered into walls in Iron Age Israel and Judah, worn-out scrolls have been found plastered into the walls of synagogues (Schleicher 2010, 21). The law's bearing of divine agency is also suggested by its protection of the deceased through the afterlife. A medieval Jewish mystical text called Sefer haZohar points to the apotropaic capacities of the law (Sefer haZohar 1.185a): "When a man's body is laid in the grave, the Torah keeps guard over it; it goes in

---

[30] For a brief discussion of the reception of translations of the Hebrew Bible as holy writings, see Smelik 1999. See also the contributions in Law and Salvesen 2012.

front of his soul when it soars upwards, breaking through all barriers until the soul reaches its proper place; and it will stand by the man at the time when he is awakened at the resurrection of the dead, in order to defend him against any accusations."[31]

Unsurprisingly, this treatment of the scrolls of the law and of other biblical and parabiblical texts facilitated their conceptualization at the periphery of and beyond rabbinical orthodoxy as "magical" objects (Sabar 2009; cf. Bohak 2017). A fascinating tradition related to this conceptualization is that of the *golem*, an artificial clay or mud creature animated by the invocation of divine names (Idel 1990). The traditions regarding the activities of golems vary regarding their capacities, purposes, and comportment. Gershon Scholem's (2007, 735) entry in the Encyclopedia Judaica describes the golem in the following way:

> The golem is a creature, particularly a human being, made in an artificial way by the virtue of a magic art, through the use of holy names. The idea that it is possible to create living beings in this manner is widespread in the magic of many people. Especially well known are the idols and images to which the ancients claimed to have given the power of speech.

While there are indeed several ancient analogues to the notion of animated anthropomorphic statues (Idel 1990, 3–8)—some have already been discussed in this book—the tradition is largely inspired by the medieval mystical text, *Sefer Yeṣirah*, which explores the capacity for special combinations of letters and numbers to reify divine creative powers (Idel 1990, 9–26; Weiss 2018). More broadly, the tradition hearkens back to the initial creation of humanity in Gen 2:7 from the dust of the earth. The Talmudic tractate Sanh. 38b even refers to Adam as a "golem." Later Jewish sages would assert their access to similar life-giving power through their knowledge of the law. In Sanh. 65b, for instance, Rabbi Rava is said to create a *gbr'*, "man," which is sent to Rabbi Zeira, but is unable to speak and is commanded to *hdr l'pryk*, "return to your dust."

CONCLUSION

By the time of the exile, several campaigns associated with cult centralization and the restriction of access to the divine appear to have converged in a way that incentivized the prioritization of text as a medium for presencing the deity and their agency. The compartmentalization of presencing media from the primary loci of divine identity, the emphasis on the name as a vehicle for divine agency, the salience of the Torah in the absence of the temple, and the deemphasis of traditional divine images, all trained the focus of cultic elites on the texts. As a

---

[31] Quoted in Schleicher 2010, 25.

material bearer of the divine name, text was in every sense an appropriate medium for the presencing of deity, despite today's overwhelming focus on the abstract concepts indexed by a text over and against its materiality. The primary function of text in these periods was more artifactual than literary for the majority of the populations in which they exercised authority, and as time passed and their compositional origins faded into obscurity, they would be reinterpreted as divine in origin (cf. Parmenter 2009), further facilitating their conceptualization as media for presencing the divine.

One point of this chapter has been to throw into sharp relief the damage the presentistic dichotomy of book religion can do to the reconstruction of the perspectives of the authors, editors, and consumers of the Hebrew Bible. The prioritization of the law was not a rejection in any sense whatsoever of the material mediation of the divine presence.[32] Rather, it was the very deployment of it. It incorporated, in its earliest strata, the very same cultic media to presence the deity that existed in the earliest days of Israel and Judah's worship of YHWH, only altering the conventions as far as necessary to accommodate contemporary circumstances and sensitivities, and to restrict access to the desired authorities. When stelai, too, fell out of favor, other more personal media were incorporated to facilitate access to the Torah and to thus democratize and personalize the central and critical experience that was made available centuries before through corporate temple worship, namely communion with the divine presence.

---

[32] Stavrakopoulou (2013, 228) refers to "the pervasive imaging of Torah as a material entity, rather than solely as abstract 'teaching.'"

Conclusion

This book set out to answer a complex question: how is it that cultic images and certain divine representatives can appear to be simultaneously identified *with*, as well as distinguished *from*, the deities they index? Answering this question required a fundamental reevaluation of the concepts of deity and divine agency, which occasioned the development of a theoretical framework regarding both that departs in significant ways from consensus views within the study of the Hebrew Bible.[1] I have argued that conceptualizations of deity represented elaborations on the conceptualization of the partible and permeable human person, whose personhood and presence could be communicated—particularly after death—through socially constructed notions of loci of agency and through socially curated material media. This framework links the form and function of funerary and mortuary cults to those cults dedicated to deities, and it accounts for the intuitive perception that a deity's presence could inhabit and be manifested through such media. It also accounts for the practice of addressing those media—as well as thinking and communicating about them—as if they were the deity themselves. The fifth through seventh chapters of the book then deployed that framework to interrogate the Hebrew Bible's representation of YHWH's presencing media.

As noted in the introduction, this framework is surely wrong in many ways that other scholars will no doubt be able to expose and correct. This book represents a crude draft of a map, not actual territory. It is primarily an argument for the usefulness and the potential of this framework and a plea for its further development and refinement. In this conclusion I'd like to review the way the framework has contributed to my argument, as well as some of the ways it could be useful to Hebrew Bible and other scholarship moving forward. In the introduction, I briefly discussed cognitive linguistics and the cognitive science of religion, describing two important frameworks—dual process cognition and

---

[1] At the same time, this approach is also not entirely novel. As noted in the introduction, Pongratz-Leisten's (2011) essay on Mesopotamian concepts of deity and divinization had already productively applied Alfred Gell's (1998) concept of distributed agency as well as a cognitive framework for personhood to the question in an Assyriological context.

prototype theory—that would undergird the approach of the rest of the book. In addition to contributing to a better understanding of the role of intuitive cognition in the structuring of our knowledge regarding ourselves and the world around us, the frameworks also demonstrate the necessity of weighing the features of intuitive cognition against any reflective account of deity, divine images, and divine agency, whether emic or etic. No such account (my own included) operates in a social or rhetorical vacuum, and when we set out to draw hard boundary lines around the relevant concepts, we run the risk of distorting them, particularly because our approaches are so frequently influenced by concerns for structuring values and power—concerns to which none of us is by any means immune. There is often a lot at stake in both academic and devotional approaches, which is one of the reasons the hard and fast lines of dictionary semantics and contemporary philosophical frameworks have persevered for so long despite their distortions and their methodological shortcomings. If nothing else, bringing intuitive cognition to the surface of this discussion should equip and incentivize scholars to better identify and confront the frameworks that we presume, create, deploy, and defend to serve our own interests.[2]

The first chapter constructed a theoretical framework for deity based on the insights of the cognitive science of religion, and particularly the supernatural agency hypothesis. I argued that deity concepts (1) are sparked by humanity's hypersensitivity to unseen agency in the world around us, (2) further develop through reflective elaborations on intuitive reasoning about the agency of the partible and permeable person, (3) proliferate within large and complex societies as deities perform prosocial functions that increase social cohesion, and (4) are most effective as prosocial agents when they are backed by powerful social institutions and can be reified and presenced through some form of material media. Reconstructing deity concepts from their roots in agency detection and personhood is intended to sidestep many of the contemporary philosophical and academic frameworks regarding ontology, identity, and deity that have for so long complicated the academic study of deity in the Bible. To illustrate how this framework can help challenge such tendentiousness outside the study of the Hebrew Bible, I apply it in the appendix to a very brief interrogation of the study of early christology.[3]

---

[2] Paula Fredriksen (2006) published a wonderful article entitled "Mandatory Retirement: Ideas in the Study of Christian Origins Whose Time Has Come to Go," and one of the ideas she discussed that is still central to the study of the Hebrew Bible is "monotheism" (see also Fredriksen 2022). I would suggest we carefully interrogate this and other ideas and frameworks common to the historical-critical study of the Hebrew Bible—such as religion—that may need to be reapplied or that may offer little to no analytical value beyond that structuring of values and power.

[3] Multiple scholars working on the conceptualization of deity in the Christian scriptures have recognized a philosophical tendentiousness. Brittany Wilson (2021, 11) comments,

In my discussion about Israelite conceptualizations of the person, I pushed against the grain a bit (with the help of Richard Steiner) to argue the ancient Southwest Asian person was indeed partible and permeable, and that the biblical texts do indeed attest to body-agency partibility. This significantly closes the gap asserted by Sommer between deity and humanity (a gap that is one of degrees, not kind), but I would suggest it also indicates that our field would stand to benefit from the application of this model of personhood to the renewed interrogation of biblical anthropology that is currently underway (Carol Newsom [2021] is already pushing in that direction). Cognitive perspectives on personhood and the insights of prototype theory can advance our understanding of a variety of topics such as gender, disability, sexuality, class, trauma, ethnicity, emotion, mortality, nationality, and other topics salient to the study of the person within the societies of ancient Israel and Judah, as well as the broader world of ancient Southwest Asia. The development and proliferation of concepts like omniscience and omnipresence could be more productively interrogated considering CSR's insights regarding the cultural evolutionary selection for unseen agents with full access to strategic information and the ability to covertly monitor behavior. The study of concepts of purity/impurity and holiness, as well as associated rituals and laws, could benefit significantly from applying cognitive lenses regarding personhood and divine agency to the biblical concepts of contamination, which are a part of what some cognitive scientists have called our "hazard precaution system."[4] Insights regarding the prosocial functions of ritual as well as the different modes of ritual likewise could help biblical studies catch up with the advances that have been made in the broader field of religious studies (see Whitehouse 2021).

In chapters 3 and 4, I offered a careful interrogation of the conceptualizations of deity and of YHWH in the Hebrew Bible, applying theoretical frameworks from cognitive linguistics to the biblical texts in order to identify conceptual domains central to the representation of deity. I suggested that our reconstruction

---

for instance, "it is, in fact, our modern-day philosophical dispositions that largely lead us to assume that the God of the New Testament is an invisible, immaterial being." See also Michael Peppard's (2011, 11–14) interrogation of the role of Platonism in modern scholarly approaches to christology and divinity.

[4] According to Robert McCauley (2014, 144), this includes, "maturationally natural systems for avoiding environmental contaminants and for producing ordered environments. Both includes principles that cut across cultures, however particular cultures may tune the systems in question. Religious rituals routinely exploit these predilections in ways that have implications for their shapes and locations. They cue human preoccupations with environmental order and vertical symmetry." Some steps have already been taken in this direction with Risto Uro's (2013) study of corpse impurity and relic veneration in early Christianity. I am hopeful that Yitzhaq Feder's (2022) *Purity and Pollution in the Hebrew Bible* will further advance the discussion.

must begin from the language that is used in the Hebrew Bible to represent and describe deity, and that language treats the category as a generic one with many members who have several standardized characteristics and fill several standardized social roles that closely align with characteristics and roles identified by cognitive scientists of religion. The cognitive sciences can fill some gaps that currently exist in our understanding of the development of deity concepts and their interactions with social groups. This can shed light on the earliest history of YHWH and their divine profile (a popular topic that must wrestle with an unfortunate dearth of data; cf. Smith 2017, Fleming 2021). In the fourth chapter, I argued that YHWH's profile also closely fits those characteristics and roles of generic deity, and that writers began to elaborate and innovate on them as Israel's state and cult leaders responded to crisis and became incentivized to distinguish YHWH from other deities and to push for the increasingly exclusive worship of YHWH. This would lead to the marginalization of other deities and to their rhetorical relegation to the periphery of the category of deity as that category was narrowed around YHWH. This led not to monotheism, but to dismissive rhetoric that has been so misidentified by scholars bringing monotheistic lenses to the text. This book's framework, and particularly prototype theory, have a great deal to offer the study of the development of monotheism as well as its conceptualization in different historical and rhetorical contexts.

Chapters 5, 6, and 7 interrogated the Bible's representations of YHWH's divine agents, focusing on their nature as presencing media, their relationships to YHWH, and the renegotiation of those relationships in response to the changing needs and interests of state and cultic authorities. I argued that the ark of the covenant represents an early divine image that paralleled shrine models in both form and function, and that its status as presencing media would be renegotiated to compartmentalize it and distance it from YHWH's own self in order to protect YHWH from the perception of vulnerability and its easy accessibility through such media. Within this rhetorical context, the *kābôd* became a more salient means of obscuring the nature of YHWH's presence and of its relationship to YHWH's own self. In chapter 6 I addressed the messenger of YHWH, whose identity seems in several stories to be conflated with that of YHWH. I argued textual interpolation to distance YHWH from physical interaction with humanity was the cause of that initial conflation, but that it was ultimately reconciled with the broader tradition through the assertion in Exod 23 that the messenger possessed the divine name, a central vehicle for communicable divine agency. From there, the discussion moved on to the divine name as an important piece of presencing media that facilitated the further compartmentalization on the part of Deuteronomy and the Deuteronomists of YHWH's own self from that media. The textual materialization of the divine name provided a segue into chapter 7's discussion of text as presencing media, beginning with amulets and other magical texts, but ultimately focusing on the biblical texts themselves, and particularly the texts of the law, which would in later periods be incorporated into a variety of material media and associated authoritative knowledge that facilitated different modes of worship and access to deity in the absence of the temple. In short, material copies of the law became the central piece of presencing media within early Judaism. This allowed access to the divine presence to be democratized while simultaneously prohibiting the deployment of older and more traditional cultic media, resulting in a distinctive and effective new suite of means of costly signaling.

The findings from these chapters, and particularly chapter 7, have the most wide-ranging implications for the study of the Hebrew Bible in the ancient world down to today. The more direct implications were discussed in those chapters, but many other vehicles of divine agency from the Hebrew Bible, early Judaism, and early Christianity could be productively studied through this framework, including the deity's "spirit" (*rûaḥ*; *pneuma*), "wisdom" (*ḥŏkmâ*; *sophia*), "word" (*mêmra*; *logos*), "presence" (*šəkînâ*), and others. The framework could also benefit the study of the epiphanic traditions of Greece and Rome, which have already been the subject of significant scrutiny (e.g., Platt 2011). The theoretical model of text as presencing media could also be productively applied to the Dead Sea Scrolls, the Septuagint, the Targumim, other Rabbinic literature, and the engagement with the Tanakh since the Rabbinic period. Insight may also be gained from the framework's application to the study of the eucharist and the doctrine of transubstantiation, to the use of images in Catholic veneration, and to the iconic use of the Bible among Christians from late antiquity down to American Evangelicalism today (cf. Parmenter 2009).

This book's framework and its findings related to presencing media also have broader relevance to research within the cognitive science of religion today. While there has been a great deal of study regarding the origin and nature of the mental representation of deities, there has been very little study of the means and methods of presencing deity or the relationship of those means and methods to the presencing of the deceased. Cognitive scientists of religion could use the findings of this book as a jumping off point for research with living informants regarding presencing media that could significantly refine and advance both fields and inspire other future research related to concepts of partible and permeable personhood, of deity, and of the communicability of agency.

Appendix:
Divine Agency and Early Christology

The framework developed in this book, and particularly the treatment of the messenger of YHWH's endowment with the divine name, has direct relevance to ongoing debates about early christology, and it lends significant support to frameworks known as divine agency christology and angelomorphic christology. These debates more or less orbit around questions related to the trajectory and mechanism of Jesus's identification with the very deity of Israel. The perspective that appears to me to come closest to a consensus view among those scholars who assert that Jesus was clearly identified with Israel's deity by the time the canonical gospels were written is a model that is known as "divine identity christology." Richard Bauckham (2008) is responsible for what I see as the most commonly cited articulation of that model, which argues that first-century Jewish communities asserted a "'strict' monotheism" (2) that is most clearly attested in the centrality of those divine roles—such as creator of all things—that "distinguish God absolutely from all other reality" (9). This ontological dichotomy of one single creator over and against all creation means that Jesus is either included "in the unique identity of this one God" (4), or is a created being that therefore cannot possess any "real divinity" (2). Since Jesus is so frequently identified as in some sense being one with, or being identified with, the deity of Israel, the former conclusion is preferred. The rhetorical goal here seems largely to be to find the core of Nicene trinitarianism in the Christian scriptures in order to assert a shared identity with the earliest community of Christians. The weight of Bauckham's argument rest almost entirely on the clear and sharp conceptual boundaries he draws around identity, and between the dichotomies of monotheism/polytheism and creator/created.

My fundamental concern with Bauckham's model is the fact that these strict dichotomies simply cannot be shown to have been in circulation in the first century CE.[1] The two most problematic are his notion of "identity," which he

---

[1] Bauckham also argues for dichotomous conceptualizations of deity and of monotheism, which I do not consider here, but see McClellan 2017 for some discussion within a cognitive framework.

acknowledges is drawn from contemporary Christian theologizing,² and his ontological dichotomy of the creator over and against "all other reality," which is a philosophical principle that presupposes creation *ex nihilo*, a reflective innovation of the second century CE (May 1994; Young 1991; Hubler 1995; cf. Niehoff 2005; Frederiksen 2020). There is certainly emphatic rhetoric in first-century Jewish literature regarding YHWH's creation of "all things"—and this frequently included assertions that there is nothing created that was not created by YHWH—but this rhetoric is clearly aimed at asserting the deity's sovereignty over all things and not at articulating a philosophical model of creation out of nothing.³ That is a thoroughly counterintuitive and reflective framework that cannot simply be presumed to be present in the absence of any articulation of it. The catalyst for that subsequent articulation and transmission was the accommodation of the Christian gospel to philosophical frameworks by the apologists of the late-second century, and more specifically, their need to defend the resurrection from the dead against the criticisms of Greek philosophy and groups usually labeled "gnostic."

Without the imposition of these two dichotomies, the framework of Jesus's inclusion "within the unique identity of the one God of Israel" (Bauckham 2008, ix) has no evidentiary purchase to gain among the first-century CE material remains. "Divine identity christology" presupposes the salience of philosophical frameworks that did not then exist, and therefore cannot adequately inform our reconstruction of the earliest conceptualizations of Jesus's relationship with the deity of Israel. The relationship of YHWH to the messenger of YHWH, however,

---

² Citing Kevin J. Vanhoozer (1997), Bauckham states (2008, 6, n. 5), "Reference to God's identity is by analogy with human personal identity, understood not as a mere ontological subject without characteristics, but as including both character and personal story (the latter entailing relationships). These are the ways in which we commonly specify 'who someone is.'" He cites several other late-twentieth-century theologians who, as far as I can tell, all base their concepts of "identity" on contemporary philosophical and theological models. Note that while Bauckham asserts the centrality of "who" the deity is (relationships and story) over and against "what" the deity is (ontology), the concern for "character and personal story" seems aimed primarily at facilitating the identification of the deity as the creator of all things who is therefore distinct from "all other reality," which pivots back to the ontological dichotomy that is the key to the whole model.

³ Bockmuehl (2012) argues that the "meaning and substance of the doctrine, though not the terminology, is firmly rooted in scripture and pre-Christian Jewish literature, even if in formal terms it seems to be adopted by Jews only in the rabbinic period" (270). Bockmuehl may be going beyond the evidence he adduces if he is arguing the concept of creation out of nothing was in present but just not explicitly mentioned. His evidence seems to me to more securely demonstrate that the central conceptual building blocks of the doctrine were present in the literature of the first century, though their arrangement into that doctrine would not occur until the rhetorical exigencies of the second century compelled it.

directly parallels, in the earliest Christian literature, that of Jesus and the deity of Israel (Gieschen 1998).[4]

The two most salient parallels are their shared exercise of divine prerogatives and their shared possession of the divine name. As discussed above, the messenger of YHWH is said in Exod 23:21 to have the authority to not forgive Israel's sins, an allusion to Josh 24:19 and YHWH's prerogative to do the same (Johansson 2011). The story in Mark 2:1–12 of Jesus's healing of a paralyzed man and forgiving of his sins alludes to the same exclusive prerogative, which is put into the thoughts of the scholars, who incredulously wonder, "who can forgive sins except for the deity alone?" After discerning their thoughts, Jesus demonstrates that "the Son of Humanity [*ho huios tou anthrōpou*] has authority on earth to forgive sins" (v. 10) by healing the man's paralysis. There are many other ways that Jesus's exercise of divine prerogatives is demonstrated throughout the Christian scriptures, but this is the most closely related to the same assertion on the part of the messenger of YHWH. That the Christian scriptures are far more extensive, varied, and emphatic about that assertion should come as no surprise. The goal of Exod 23:21 (as described in chapter 6) seem simply to be to provide a rationalization for conflated identities arising from a set of textual interpolations. The rhetorical goal in the Christian scriptures appears to be not just to assert Jesus's possession of YHWH's divine agency, but also to link Jesus with the rich and complex messianic tradition that had been developing over the previous centuries and included elaboraton and innovation on the significance of messenger's possession of the divine name.

This possession of the divine name as a vehicle for divine agency is central to both the messenger of YHWH as well as to the christological frameworks of the Christian scriptures (Gieschen 2003). Regarding the story above from Mark 2, the title "Son of Humanity" is linked with the messianic endowment with the divine name via 1 Enoch, which describes this "Son of Humanity" possessing the "hidden name" (1 En. 69.14) and being "named in the presence of the Lord of Spirits, the Before-Time" (1 En. 48.2).[5] A more explicitly Christian articulation of Jesus's endowment with the divine name is found in the christological hymn of Phil 2:9: "Therefore the Deity has highly exalted him [*auton hyperypsōsen*] and has given him the name that is above every name [*to onoma to hyper pan onoma*], so that at the name of Jesus every knee may bend—in heaven and on earth and

---

[4] While I am only addressing the divine name in this appendix, the Christian scriptures assert Jesus's possession and deployment of a number of the communicable vehicles for divine agency, such as the deity's spirit, glory, power, and so on (cf. Sommer 2009, 135–37; Wilson 2021, 121–45). The consolidation of these vehicles within the figure of Jesus no doubt amplified the power and salience of Jesus's claim to divine sonship and authority.

[5] These translations are from Nickelsburg and VanderKam 2012.

under the earth—and every tongue may confess that Jesus Christ is Lord [*kyrios*], to the glory of the Deity, the Father" (cf. Holloway 2017, 114–29). The assertion that Jesus is "Lord" can also be understood to reflect Jesus's possession of the divine name, in light of the fact that *kyrios* ("Lord") by this time period was overwhelmingly the preferred substitute for the Tetragrammaton in Greek Jewish literature.[6] We may also point to the book of Revelation, which in the nineteenth chapter describes Jesus as "having a name written that no one knows except he himself" (Rev 19:12).[7]

The gospels add an additional rhetorical layer by repeatedly putting the Greek verbal phrase *egō eimi*, "I am," into Jesus's mouth (e.g., Matt 24:5; Mark 14:62; Luke 22:70; John 4:26; 8:58). While this verbal phrase is not incredibly unusual, the contexts of its usage in the gospels is understood by many to allude in two specific ways to the divine name and to the deity's self-identification in the Greek translation of the Hebrew Bible. One of these allusions appears to be to the Greek translation of Exod 3:14, which renders the Hebrew Bible's folk etiology for the Tetragrammaton, *'ehyeh 'ăšer 'ehyeh* ("I will be what I will be"), with the Greek *egō eimi ho ōn* ("I am the one who is"). *Egō eimi* is also the rendering for the Hebrew *'anî hû*, "I am he," which appears most prominently in Isaiah (Isa 43:10; 48:12; 52:6) and in Deuteronomy (Deut 32:39) as the deity's emphatic self-identification (Williams 2000). These allusions are most pervasive in the gospel of John, where *egō eimi* occurs twenty-four times, all either in Jesus's own statements or in the narrator's quoting of Jesus. Bauckham (2008, 40) is most emphatic about the weight of this usage: "The series of sayings thus comprehensively identifies Jesus with the God of Israel who sums up his identity in the declaration 'I am he.'"

Viewed through the framework developed within this book, the Christian scriptures are not including Jesus within the "unique identity" of the deity of Israel, they are literally asserting his endowment with the divine name, enabling

---

[6] Note Bauckham (2008, 37) describes the climax of this hymn as "when Jesus is exalted to the position of divine sovereignty over all things and given the divine name itself, which names the unique divine identity." He then highlights parallels between the hymn and YHWH's self-revelation in Isa 45:22–23, concluding, "The Philippians passage is, therefore, no unconsidered echo of an Old Testament text, but a claim that it is in the exaltation of Jesus, his identification as YHWH in YHWH's universal sovereignty, that the unique deity of the God of Israel comes to be acknowledged as such by all creation" (38).

[7] The text does not specify where the name was written, but the statement follows immediately after a reference to "many diadems" [*diadēmata polla*] on his head, and so suggests the name was written on the diadems, similar to the inscription of the divine name on the high priest's turban (Exod 28:36–37) and the writing of the deity's name on those who are victorious [*ho nikōn*] and are made a pillar in the deity's temple in Rev 3:13 (cf. Isa 56:5).

him—as with the messenger of YHWH—to exercise divine power and to be both identified with and distinguished from that deity. The Christian scriptures nowhere go remotely as far as having Jesus declare "I am the deity of your father," as we read in the received version of Exod 3:6, but that declaration originally resulted from a textual interpolation, not from an original composition. The Christian authors are much more circumspect, satisfied to present a messianic figure who was more clearly compartmentalized from the deity, but enjoyed an ambiguous relationship with them that facilitated access to the necessary power and authority through the deity's agency, communicated via the name. All this is not necessarily to identify Jesus as an "angel"—though early Christians frequently saw Jesus in the manifestations of the messenger of YHWH (Hannah 1999)—but to say the conceptual template that facilitated the messenger of YHWH's unique and ambiguous relationship with YHWH was the most intuitive and proximate way to represent Jesus's relationship to divinity. Authors further fleshed out the content of those representations in a variety of ways (on Mark's gospel as adoptionist, for instance, see Peppard 2011), but undergirding it all was the intuitive concept of divine agency communicated via the divine name.[8]

---

[8] Michael Bird (2014b, 35–38) works to distance Jesus from the messenger framework in order to reject an angelomorphic christology, but none of the arguments are relevant to the case made above, which is not necessarily that Jesus was first an "angel" and then later graduated to being worshipped, but that Jesus's conceptualization built on the same foundation laid by that of the messenger of YHWH.

Bibliography

Aaron, David H. 2001. *Biblical Ambiguities: Metaphor, Semantics and Divine Imagery.* Leiden: Brill.
Abusch, Tzvi. 1998. "Ghost and God: Some Observations on a Babylonian Understanding of Human Nature." Pages 363–83 in *Self, Soul and Body in Religious Experience.* Edited by Albert I. Baumgarten, Jan Assmann, and Guy G. Stroumsa. Leiden: Brill.
———. 1999. "Etemmu אטים." *DDD*, 309–12.
Achenbach, Reinhard. 2016. "The Empty Throne and the Empty Sanctuary: From Aniconism to the Invisibility of God in Second Temple Theology." Pages 35–53 in *Ritual Innovation in the Hebrew Bible and Early Judaism.* Edited by Nathan MacDonald. Berlin: de Gruyter.
Ackerman, Susan. 1991. "The Deception of Isaac, Jacob's Dream at Bethel, and Incubation on Animal Skin." Pages 92–120 in *Priesthood and Cult in Ancient Israel.* Edited by Gary A. Anderson and Saul M. Olyan. Sheffield: Sheffield Academic.
———. 2012. "Cult Centralization, the Erosion of Kin-Based Communities, and the Implications for Women's Religious Practices." Pages 19–40 in *Social Theory and the Study of Israelite Religion. Essays in Retrospect and Prospect.* Edited by Saul M. Olyan. Atlanta, GA: Society of Biblical Literature.
Aharoni, Yohanan. 1968. "Arad: Its Inscriptions and Temple." *BA* 31.1: 2–32.
Aḥituv, Shmuel, Esther Eshel, and Ze'ev Meshel. 2012. "The Inscriptions." Pages 73–142 in *Kuntillet 'Ajrud (Ḥorvat Teman): An Iron Age II Religious Site on the Judah-Sinai Border.* Edited by Ze'ev Meshel. Jerusalem: Israel Exploration Society.
Albertz, Rainer. 1994. *A History of Israel Religion in the Old Testament Period. Volume I: From the Beginnings to the End of the Monarchy.* Translated by John Bowden. Louisville, KY: Westminster/John Knox.
———. 2003. *Israel in Exile: The History and Literature of the Sixth Century B.C.E.* Translated by David Green. Atlanta: Society of Biblical Literature.
———. 2007. "Social History of Ancient Israel." Pages 347–67 in *Understanding the History of Ancient Israel.* Edited by H. G. M. Williamson. Oxford: Oxford University Press.
———. 2008. "Family Religion in Ancient Israel and its Surroundings." Pages 89–112 in *Household and Family Religion in Antiquity.* Edited by John Bodel and Saul M. Olyan. Malden, MA: Blackwell.

———. 2012. "Personal Names and Family Religion." Pages 245–386 in *Family and Household Religion in Ancient Israel and the Levant*. Edited by Rainer Albertz and Rüdiger Schmitt. Winona Lake, IN: Eisenbrauns.

Allen, James P. 2014. *Middle Egyptian: An introduction to the Language and Culture of Hieroglyphs. Third Edition*. Cambridge: Cambridge University Press.

Allen, Spencer L. 2015. *The Splintered Divine: A Study of Ištar, Baal, and Yahweh Divine Names and Divine Multiplicity in the Ancient Near East*. Berlin: de Gruyter.

Anderson, Marc. 2019. "Predictive Coding in Agency Detection." *RBB* 9.1: 65–84.

Anderson, Marc, Thies Pfeiffer, Sabastian Müller, and Uffe Schjødt. 2019. "Agency Detection in Predictive Minds: A Virtual Reality Study." *RBB* 9.1: 52–64.

Anthonioz, Stéphanie. 2014. "Astarte in the Bible and her Relation to Asherah." Pages 125–39 in *Transformation of a Goddess: Ishtar – Astarte – Aphrodite*. Edited by David T. Sugimoto. Fribourg: Academic Press; Göttingen: Vandenhoeck & Ruprecht.

Appuhamilage, Udeni M. H. 2017. "A Fluid Ambiguity: Individual, Dividual and Personhood." *APJA* 18.1: 1–17.

Arav, Reuma, Sagi Filin, Uzi Avner, and Dani Nadel. 2016. "Three-Dimensional Documentation of *masseboth* Sites in the 'Uvda Valley Area, Southern Negev, Israel." *DAACH* 3: 9–21.

Asher-Greve, Julia M. 1997. "The Essential Body: Mesopotamian Conceptions of the Gendered Body." *G&H* 9.3: 432–61.

Assmann, Jan. 1998. "A Dialogue between Self and Soul: Papyrus Berlin 3024." Pages 384–403 in *Self, Soul and Body in Religious Experience*. Edited by Albert I. Baumgarten, Jan Assmann, and Guy G. Stroumsa. Leiden: Brill.

———. 2005. *Death and Salvation in Ancient Egypt*. Translated by David Lorton. Ithaca, NY: Cornell University Press.

———. 2010. "Memory, Narration, Identity: Exodus as a Political Myth." Pages 3–18 in *Literary Constructions of Identity in the Ancient World*. Edited by Hanna Liss and Manfred Oeming. Winona Lake, IN: Eisenbrauns.

———. 2012. "Konstellative Anthropologie: Zum Bild des Menschen im alten Ägypten." Pages 35–55 in *Der ganze Mensch: Zur Anthropologie der Antike und ihere europäischen Nachgeschichte*. Edited by Bernd Janowski. Berlin: Akademie Verlag.

Aster, Shawn Zelig. 2012. *The Unbeatable Light: Melammu and Its Biblical Parallels*. Münster: Ugarit-Verlag.

———. 2015. "Ezekiel's Adaptation of Mesopotamian *Melammu*." *WO* 45: 10–21.

———. 2017. *Reflections of Empire in Isaiah 1–39: Responses to Assyrian Ideology*. Atlanta, GA: SBL Press.

Astuti, Rita, and Paul L. Harris. 2008. "Understanding Mortality and the Life of the Ancestors in Rural Madagascar." *CogSci* 32.4: 713–40.

Atkinson, Quentin D., and Pierrick Bourrat. 2011. "Beliefs about God, the Afterlife and Morality Support the Role of Supernatural Policing in Human Cooperation." *EHB* 32.1: 41–49.

Atran, Scott. 2012. "Psychological Origins and Cultural Evolution of Religion." Pages 209–38 in *Grounding Social Sciences in Cognitive Sciences*. Edited by Ron Sun. Cambridge, MA: The MIT Press

Aufrecht, Walter E. 1997. "Urbanization and the Northwest Semitic Inscriptions of the Late Bronze and Early Iron Ages." Pages 116–29 in *Urbanism in Antiquity: From Mesopotamia to Crete*. Edited by Walter E. Aufrecht, Neil A. Mirau, and Steven W. Gauley. Sheffield: Sheffield Academic.

Ausloos, Hans. 2008. "The 'Angel of YHWH' in Exod. xxiii 20–33 and Judg. ii 1–5. A Clue to the 'Deuteronom(ist)ic' Puzzle?" *VT* 58.1: 1–12.

Avalos, Hector. 1995. *Illness and Health Care in the Ancient Near East: The Role of the Temple in Greece, Mesopotamia, and Israel*. Chico, CA: Scholars Press.

Avner, Uzi. 2002. "Studies in the Material and Spiritual Culture of the Negev and Sinai Populations, during the Sixth–Third Millennia B.C." PhD diss. Hebrew University.

———. 2018. "Protohistoric Developments of Religion and Cult in the Negev Desert." *TA* 45.1: 23–62.

Avner, Uzi, and Liora Kolska Horwitz. 2017. "Animal Sacrifices and Offerings from Cult and Mortuary Sites in the Negev and Sinai, Sixth–Third Millennia BC." *ARAM* 29.1–2: 35–70.

Baden, Joel S. 2012. *The Composition of the Pentateuch: Renewing the Documentary Hypothesis*. New Haven, CT: Yale University Press.

Bahrani, Zainab. 2003. *The Graven Image: Representation in Babylonia and Assyria* (Philadelphia: University of Pennsylvania Press.

Barbiero, Gianni. 2016. "The Two Structures of Psalm 29." *VT* 66.3: 378–92.

Barkay, Gabriel. 1992. "The Priestly Benediction on Silver Plaques from Ketef Hinnom in Jerusalem." *TA* 19.2: 139–92.

Barr, James. 1960. "Theophany and Anthropomorphism in the Old Testament." Pages 31–38 in *Congress Volume Oxford 1959*. Edited by G. W. Anderson, P. A. H. de Boer, G. R. Castellino, Henri Cazelles, E. Hammbershaimb, H. G. May, and W. Zimmerli. Leiden: Brill.

Barrett, Justin L. 1999. "Theological Correctness: Cognitive Constraint and the Study of Religion." *MTSR* 11: 325–39.

———. 2000. "Exploring the Natural Foundations of Religion." *TCS* 4.1: 29–34.

———. 2011. *Cognitive Science, Religion, and Theology: From Human Minds to Divine Minds*. West Conshohocken, PA: Templeton Press.

Barrett, Justin L., and Frank C. Keil. 1996. "Conceptualizing a Nonnatural Entity: Anthropomorphism in God Concepts." *CogPsych* 31: 219–47.

Barton, Carlin A., and Daniel Boyarin. 2016. *Imagine No Religion: How Modern Abstractions Hide Ancient Realities*. New York: Fordham University Press.

Bateson, Melissa, Daniel Nettle, and Gilbert Roberts. 2006. "Cues of Being Watched Enhance Cooperation in a Real-World Setting." *BL* 2: 412–14.

Bateson, Melissa, Luke Callow, Jessica R. Holmes, Maximilian L. Redmond Roche, and Daniel Nettle. 2013. "Do Images of 'Watching Eyes' Induce Behaviour That Is More Pro-Social or More Normative? A Field Experiment on Littering." *PLoSONE* 8.12: 1–9.

Bauckham, Richard. 2008. *Jesus and the God of Israel:* God Crucified *and Other Studies on the New Testament's Christology of Divine Identity*. Grand Rapids: Eerdmans.

Bauks, Michaela. 2016. "'Soul-Concepts' in Ancient Near Eastern Mythical Texts and Their Implications for the Primeval History." *VT* 66: 181–93.

Baumgarten, Albert I. 1981. *The* Phoenician History *of Philo of Byblos: A Commentary.* Leiden: Brill.

———. 2016. "Sacred Scriptures Defile the Hands." *JJS* 67.1: 46–67.

Beal, Richard H. 2002. "Dividing A God." Pages 197–208 in *Magic and Ritual in the Ancient World.* Edited by Paul Mirecki and Marvin Meyer. Leiden: Brill.

Beck, Pirhiya. 1994. "The Cult Stands from Taanach: Aspects of the Iconographic Tradition of Early Iron Age Cult Objects in Palestine." Pages 352–81 in *From Nomadism to Monarchy: Archaeological and Historical Aspects of Early Israel.* Edited by Israel Finkelstein and Nadav Na'aman. Washington: Biblical Archaeology Society.

———. 2012. "The Drawings and Decorative Designs." Pages 143–203 in *Kuntillet 'Ajrud (Ḥorvat Teman): An Iron Age II Religious Site on the Judah-Sinai Border.* Edited by Ze'ev Meshel. Jerusalem: Israel Exploration Society.

Becking, Bob, and Dirk Human, eds. 2009. *Exile and Suffering: A Selection of Papers Rad at the Fiftieth Anniversary Meeting of the Old Testament Society of South Africa. OT-WSA/OTSSA, Pretoria August 2007.* Leiden: Brill.

Beckman, Gary. 2010. "Temple Building among the Hittites." Pages 71–89 in *From the Foundations to the Crenellations: Essays on Temple Building in the Ancient Near East and Hebrew Bible.* Edited by Mark J. Boda and Jamie Novotny. Münster, Ugarit-Verlag.

Beckman, John C. 2013. "Pluralis Majestatis: Biblical Hebrew." *EHLL* 3.145–46.

Beerden, Kim. 2013. *World Full of Signs: Ancient Greek Divination in Context.* Leiden: Brill.

Ben-Ami, Doron. 2006. "Early Iron Age Cult Places—New Evidence from Tel Hazor." *TA* 33.2: 121–33.

Ben-Dov, Jonathan. 2016. "The Resurrection of the Divine Assembly in the Divine Title El in the Dead Sea Scrolls." Pages 9–31 in *Submerged Literature in Ancient Greek Culture: The Comparative Perspective.* Edited by Andrea Ercolani and Manuela Giordano. Berlin: de Gruyter.

Ben-Tor, Amnon, and Y. Portugali. 1987. *Tell Qiri, A Village in the Jezreel Valley: A Report of The Archaelogical Excavations 1975–1977.* Jerusalem: The Institute of Archaeology, The Hebrew University of Jerusalem.

Benzel, Kim. 2015 "'What Goes in Is What Comes Out'—But What Was Already There? Divine Materials and Materiality in Ancient Mesopotamia." Pages 89–118 in *The Materiality of Divine Agency.* Edited by Beate Pongratz-Leisten and Karen Sonik. Berlin: de Gruyter.

Berendt, Erich A., and Keiko Tanita. 2011. "The 'Heart' of Things: A Conceptual Metaphoric Analysis of *Heart* and Related Body Parts in Thai, Japanese and English." *ICS* 20.1: 65–78.

Bering, Jesse M. 2002. "Intuitive Conceptions of Dead Agents' Minds: The Natural Foundations of Afterlife Beliefs as Phenomenological Boundary." *JCC* 2.4: 263–308.

———. 2006. "The Folk Psychology of Souls." *BBS* 29: 453–98.

Bering, Jesse M., and David F. Bjorklund. 2004. "The Natural Emergence of Reasoning about the Afterlife as a Developmental Regularity." *DevPsych* 40: 217–33.

Bering, Jesse M., Katrina McLeod, and Todd K. Shackelford. 2005. "Reasoning about Dead Agents Reveals Possible Adaptive Trends." *HN* 16.4: 360–81.

Berlejung, Angelika. 1998. *Die Theologie der Bilder: Herstellung und Einweihung von Kultbildern in Mesopotamien und die alttestamentliche Bilderpolemik*. Fribourg: Silberamuletten von Ketef Hinnom." Pages 37–62 in *Mensch und König: Studien zur Anthropologie des Alten Testaments. Rüdiger Lux zum 60. Geburtstag*. Edited by Angelika Berlejung and Raik Heckl. Freiburg: Herder.

Berman, Joshua. 2014. "The Making of the Sin of Achan (Joshua 7)." *BibInt* 22.2: 115–31.

Bertolotti, Tommaso, and Lorenzo Magnani. 2010. "The Role of Agency Detection in the Invention of Supernatural Beings: An Abductive Approach." Pages 239–62 in *Model-Based Reasoning in Science and Technology: Abduction, Logic, and Computational Discovery*. Edited by Lorenzo Magnani, Walter Carnielli, and Claudio Pizzi. Berlin: Springer-Verlag.

Beyer, Klaus, and Alasdair Livingstone. 1987. "Die neuesten aramäischen Inschriften aus Taima." *ZDMG* 137.2: 288–90.

Bird, Michael F. 2014a. "The Story of Jesus as the Story of God." Pages 11–21 in *How God Became Jesus: The Real Origins of Belief in Jesus' Divine Nature*. Edited by Michael F. Bird. Grand Rapids, MI: Zondervan.

———. 2014b. "Of Gods, Angels, and Men." Pages 22–40 in *How God Became Jesus: The Real Origins of Belief in Jesus' Divine Nature*. Edited by Michael F. Bird. Grand Rapids, MI: Zondervan.

Black, Jeremy, and Anthony Green. 1992. *An Illustrated Dictionary of Gods, Demons and Symbols of Ancient Mesopotamia*. London: British Museum Press.

Blair, Judit M. 2009. *De-Demonising the Old Testament: An Investigation of Azazel, Lilith, Deber, Qeteb, and Reshef in the Hebrew Bible*. Tübingen: Mohr Siebeck.

Blenkinsopp, Joseph. 1995. "Deuteronomy and the Politics of Post-Mortem Existence." *VT* 45.1: 1–16.

Bloch-Smith, Elizabeth M. 1992a. *Judahite Burial Practices and Beliefs about the Dead*. Sheffield: Sheffield Academic.

———. 1992b. "The Cult of the Dead in Judah: Interpreting the Material Remains." *JBL* 111.2: 213–24.

———. 2006. "Will the Real *Massebot* Please Stand Up: Cases of Real and Mistakenly Identified Standing Stones in Ancient Israel." Pages 64–79 in *Text, Artifact, and Image: Revealing Ancient Israelite Religion*. Edited by Gary Beckman and Theodore J. Lewis. Providence, RI: Brown Judaic Studies.

———. 2007. "*Maṣṣēbôt* in the Israelite Cult: An Argument for Rendering Implicit Cultic Criteria Explicit." Pages 28–39 in *Temple and Worship in Biblical Israel*. Edited by John Day. London: T&T Clark.

———. 2009. "From Womb to Tomb: The Israelite Family in Death as in Life." Pages 122–31 in in *The Family in Life and in Death. The Family in Ancient Israel: Sociological and Archaeological Perspectives*. Edited by Patricia Dutcher-Walls. New York: T&T Clark.

———. 2015. "Massebot Standing for Yhwh: The Fall of a Yhwistic Cult Symbol." Pages 106–10 in *Worship, Women, and War: Essays in Honor of Susan Niditch*. Edited by

John J. Collins, T. M. Lemos, and Saul M. Olyan. Providence, RI: Brown Judaic Studies.
Block, Daniel I. 2000. *The Gods of the Nations: Studies in Ancient Near Eastern Theology. Second Edition*. Grand Rapids, MI: Baker Academic.
Blum, Erhard. 1990. *Studien zur Komposition des Pentateuch*. Berlin: de Gruyter.
———. 2009. "Hosea 12 und die Pentateuchüberlieferungen." Pages 291–321 in *Die Erzväter in der biblischen Tradition: Festschrift für Matthias Köckert*. Edited by Anselm C. Hagedorn und Henrik Pfeiffer. Berlin: de Gruyter.
Bockmuehl, Markus. 2012. "*Creatio ex nihilo* in Palestinian Judaism and Early Christianity." *Scottish Journal of Theology* 65: 253–70.
Boden, Peggy Jean. 1998. "The Mesopotamian Washing of the Mouth (*mīs pî*) Ritual." PhD diss. Johns Hopkins University.
Bohak, Gideon. 2008. *Ancient Jewish Magic: A History*. Cambridge: Cambridge University Press.
———. 2017. "Dangerous Books: The Hekhalot Texts as Physical Objects." *Henoch* 39.2: 306–24.
Bokovoy, David. 2008. "שמעו והעידו בבית יעקב: Invoking the Council as Witnesses in Amos 3:13." *JBL* 127.1: 37–51.
Bond, Sarah Emily. 2015. "The (Evil) Eyes Have It: Welcoming and Warning Ancient Visitors." *History From Below*. 21 July. http://sarahemilybond.com/2015/07/21/the-evil-eyes-have-it-welcoming-and-warning-ancient-visitors/.
Borg, Barbara E. 1997. "The Dead as a Guest at Table? Continuity and Change in the Egyptian Cult of the Dead." Pages 26–32 in *Portraits and Masks: Burial Customs in Roman Egypt*. Edited by Morris L. Bierbrier. London: British Museum Press.
Bourrat, Pierrick, Quentin Atkinson, and Robin I. M. Dunbar. 2011. "Supernatural Punishment and Individual Social Compliance across Cultures." *RBB* 1.2: 119–34.
Boyer, Pascal. 2001. *Religion Explained: The Evolutionary Origins of Religious Thought*. New York: Basic Books.
———. 2003. "Are Ghost Concepts 'Intuitive,' 'Endemic' and 'Innate'?" *JCC* 3.3: 233–43.
———. 2012. "Cognitive Predispositions and Cultural Transmission." Pages 288–319 in *Memory in Mind and Culture*. Edited by Pascal Boyer and J. V. Wertsch. Cambridge: Cambridge University Press.
Boyer, Pascal, and H. Clark Barrett. 2016. "Intuitive Ontologies and Domain Specificity." Pages 161–79 in *Foundations*. Vol. 1 of *The Handbook of Evolutionary Psychology*. Edited by David M. Buss. 2nd ed. Hoboken, NJ: Wiley & Sons.
Breed, Brennan. 2014. "Reception of the Psalms: The Example of Psalm 91." Pages 297–311 in *The Oxford Handbook of the Psalms*. Edited by William P. Brown. Oxford: Oxford University Press.
Bridge, Edward J. 2013. "The Metaphoric Use of Slave Terms in the Hebrew Bible." *BBR* 23.1: 13–28.
Broyles, Craig C. 1989. *The Conflict of Faith and Experience in the Psalms: A Form-Critical and Theological Study*. Sheffield: JSOT Press.
Bubic, Andreja, D. Yves von Cramon, and Ricarda I. Schubotz. 2010. "Prediction, Cognition and the Brain." *FHN* 4.25: 1–15.

Burnett, Joel S. 2001. *A Reassessment of Biblical Elohim*. Atlanta, GA: Society of Biblical Literature.
———. 2006. "Forty-Two Songs for Elohim: An Ancient Near Eastern Organizing Principle in the Shaping of the Elohistic Psalter." *JSOT* 31.1: 81–101.
Burns, John Barclay. 1990. "Why Did the Besieging Army Withdraw? (II Reg 3,27)." *ZAW* 102.2: 187–94.
Burton, Marilyn E. 2017. *The Semantics of Glory: A Cognitive, Corpus-based Approach to Hebrew Word Meaning*. Leiden: Brill.
Busby, Cecilia. 1997. "Permeable and Partible Persons: A Comparative Analysis of Gender and Body in South India and Melanesia." *JRAI* 3.2: 261–78.
Bynum, Caroline Walker. 2015. "The Animation and Agency of Holy Food: Bread and Wine as Material Divine in the European Middle Ages." Pages 70–85 in *The Materiality of Divine Agency*. Edited by Beate Pongratz-Leisten and Karen Sonik. Berlin: de Gruyter.
Byrne, Máire. 2011. *The Names of God in Judaism, Christianity, and Islam*. London: Continuum.
Byrne, Ryan. 2004. "Lie Back and Think of Judah: The Reproductive Politics of Pillar Figurines." *NEA* 67.3: 137–51.
Cai, Wei, Xiangqin Huang, Song Wu, and Yu Kou. 2015. "Dishonest Behavior Is Not Affected by an Image of Watching Eyes." *EHB* 36.2: 110–16.
Carmi, Israel, and Dror Segal. 2012. "^{14}C Dates from Kuntillet 'Ajrud." Pages 61–64 in *Kuntillet 'Ajrud (Ḥorvat Teman): An Iron Age II Religious Site on the Judah-Sinai Border*. Edited by Ze'ev Meshel. Jerusalem: Israel Exploration Society.
Carr, David M. 2005. *Writing on the Tablet of the Hebrew: Origins of Scripture and Literature*. Oxford: Oxford University Press, 2005.
Carrell, Peter R. 1997. *Jesus and the Angels: Angelology and the Christology of the Apocalypse of John*. Cambridge: Cambridge University Press.
Chambers, Nathan. 2019. "Reading Joshua with Augustine and Sommer: Two Frameworks for Interpreting Theophany Narratives." *JSOT* 43.3: 273–83.
Chavel, Simeon. 2012. "The Face of God and the Etiquette of Eye-Contact: Visitation, Pilgrimage, and Prophetic Vision in Ancient Israelite and Early Jewish Imagination." *JSQ* 19.1: 1–55.
Cho, Paul K.-K. 2019. *Myth, History, and Metaphor in the Hebrew Bible*. Cambridge: Cambridge University Press.
Christensen, Dorthe Refslund, and Kjetil Sandvik. 2014. "Death Ends a Life, Not a Relationship: Objects as Media on Children's Graves." Pages 251–71 in *Mediating and Remediating Death*. Edited by Dorthe Refslund Christensen and Kjetil Sandvik. Surrey: Ashgate.
Chudek, Maciej, Rita Anne McNamara, Susan Birch, Paul Bloom, and Joseph Henrich. 2018. "Do Minds Switch Bodies? Dualist Interpretations across Ages and Societies." *RBB* 8.4: 354–68.
Chung, Youn Ho. 2010. *The Sin of the Calf: The Rise of the Bible's Negative Attitude Toward the Golden Calf*. New York: T&T Clark.
Claassens, L. Juliana, and Irmtraud Fischer. 2021. *Prophecy and Gender in the Hebrew Bible*. Atlanta, GA: SBL Press.

Clark, Andy, et al. 2013. "Whatever Next? Predictive Brains, Situated Agents, and the Future of Cognitive Science." *BBS* 36: 181–253.

Clifford, Hywel. 2010. "Deutero-Isaiah and Monotheism." Pages 267–89 in *Prophecy and Prophets in Ancient Israel*. Edited by John Day. New York: T&T Clark.

Cline, Rangar. 2011. *Ancient Angels: Conceptualizing Angeloi in the Roman Empire*. Leiden: Brill.

Clines, Dave J. A. 2021a. "Alleged Basic Meanings of the Hebrew Verb *qdš* 'Be Holy': An Exercise in Comparative Hebrew Lexicography." *VT* (Advance Article):1–21.

———. 2021b. "Alleged Female Language about the Deity in the Hebrew Bible." *JBL* 140.2: 229–49.

Cohen, Emma. 2013. *The Mind Possessed: The Cognition of Spirit Possession in an Afro-Brazilian Religious Tradition*. Oxford: Oxford University Press.

Cohen, Emma, and Justin L. Barrett. 2008. "When Minds Migrate: Conceptualizing Spirit Possession." *JCC* 8.1: 23–48.

———. 2011. "In Search of 'Folk Anthropology': The Cognitive Anthropology of the Person." Pages 104–22 in *In Search of Self: Interdisciplinary Perspectives on Personhood*. Edited by J. Wentzel van Huyssteen and Erik P. Wiebe. Grand Rapics, MI: Eerdmans.

Cohn, Yehuda B. 2008. *Tangled Up in Text: Tefillin and the Ancient World*. Providence, RI: Brown Judaic Studies.

Collard, David. 2013. "When Ancestors Become Gods: The Transformation of Cypriote Ritual and Religion in the Late Bronze Age." Pages 109–29 in *Ritual Failure: Archaeological Perspectives*. Edited by Vasiliki G. Koutrafouri and Jeff Sanders. Leiden: Sidestone Press.

Collins, John J. 2017. *The Invention of Judaism: Torah and Jewish Identity from Deuteronomy to Paul*. Oakland, CA: University of California Press.

Conklin, Beth A. 1995. "'Thus Are Our Bodies, Thus Was Our Custom': Mortuary Cannibalism in an Amazonian Society." *AE* 22.1: 75–101.

Cook, Stephen L. 2007. "Funerary Practices and Afterlife Expectations in Ancient Israel." *RC* 1.6 (2007): 660–83.

———. 2009. "Death, Kinship, and Community: Afterlife and the חסד Ideal in Israel." Pages 106–21 in *The Family in Life and in Death. The Family in Ancient Israel: Sociological and Archaeological Perspectives*. Edited by Patricia Dutcher-Walls. New York: T&T Clark.

Cornelius, Izak. 2017. "The Study of the Old Testament and the Material Imagery of the Ancient Near East, with a Focus on the Body Parts of the Deity." Pages 195–227 in *Congress Volume Stellenbosch 2016*. Edited by Louis C. Jonker, Gideon R. Kotzé, and Christl M. Maier. Leiden: Brill.

Cornell, Collin, ed. 2020. *Divine Doppelgängers: YHWH's Ancient Look-Alikes*. University Park, PA: Eisenbrauns.

Cox, Benjamin D., and Susan Ackerman. 2012. "Micah's Teraphim." *JHS* 12.11: 1–37. doi: 10.5508/jhs.2012.v12.a11.

Cradic, Melissa S. 2017. "Embodiments of Death: The Funerary Sequence and Commemoration in the Bronze Age Levant." *BASOR* 377: 219–48.

Craffert, Pieter F. 2015. "When is an Out-of-Body Experience (Not) an Out-of-Body Experience? Reflections about Out-of-Body Phenomena in Neuroscientific Research." *JCC* 15.1–2: 13–31.
Craigie, Peter C. 1972. "Psalm XXIX in the Hebrew Poetic Tradition." *VT* 22.2: 143–51.
Crespi, Bernard. 2021. "The Kin Selection of Religion." Pages 135–52 in *The Oxford Handbook of Evolutionary Psychology and Religion*. Edited by James R. Liddle and Todd K. Shackelford. Oxford: Oxford University Press.
Croft, William, and D. Alan Cruse. 2004. *Cognitive Linguistics*. Cambridge: Cambridge University Press.
Cross, Frank Moore. 1973. *Canaanite Myth and Hebrew Epic: Essays in the History of the Religion of Israel*. Cambridge, MA: Harvard University Press.
Cross, Frank M., and David Noel Freedman. 1953. "A Royal Song of Thanksgiving: II Samuel 22=Psalm 18." *JBL* 72.1: 15–34.
Crouch, C. L. *War and Ethics in the Ancient Near East: Military Violence in Light of Cosmology and History*. Berlin: de Gruyter, 2009.
Czachesz, István. 2013. "A Cognitive Perspective on Magic in the New Testament. Pages 164–79 in *Mind, Morality and Magic: Cognitive Science Approaches to Biblical Studies*. Edited by István Czachesz and Risto Uro. Durham: Acumen.
Darby, Erin. 2014. *Interpreting Judean Pillar Figurines: Gender and Empire in Judean Apotropaic Ritual*. Tübingen: Mohr Siebeck.
Davis, Richard H. 1997. *Lives of Indian Images*. Princeton: Princeton University Press.
Day, John. 1979. "Echoes of Baal's Seven Thunders and Lightnings in Psalm XXIX and Habakkuk III 9 and the Identity of the Seraphim in Isaiah VI." *VT* 29.2: 143–51.
———. 1985. *God's Conflict with the Dragon and the Sea: Echoes of a Canaanite Myth in the Old Testament*. Cambridge: Cambridge University Press.
De Bruyn, Theodore. 2017. *Making Amulets Christian: Artefacts, Scribes, and Contexts*. Oxford: Oxford University Press.
De Neys, Wim. 2014. "Conflict Detection, Dual Processes, and Logical Intuitions: Some Clarifications." *T&R* 20: 167–87.
De Roche, Michael. 1983. "Yahweh's *Rîb* against Israel: A Reassessment of the So-Called 'Prophetic Lawsuit' in the Preexilic Prophets." *JBL* 102.4: 563–74.
De Vaux, Roland. 1967. "Le lieu que Yahvé a choisi pour y établir son nom." Pages 219–28 in *Das ferne und nahe Wort, Festschrift Leonhard Rost zur Vollendung seines 70. Lebensjahres am 30. November 1966 gewidmet*. Edited by Fritz Mass. Berlin: Alfred Töpelmann.
De Vries, Pieter. 2016. *The Kābôd of Yhwh in the Old Testament: With Particular Reference to the Book of Ezekiel*. Leiden: Brill.
De Waal, Frans B. M. 2008. "Putting the Altruism Back in Altruism: The Evolution of Empathy." *ARP* 59: 279–300.
Dean, Lewis G., Gill L. Vale, Kevin N. Leland, Emma Flynn, and Rachel L. Kendal. 2014. "Human Cumulative Culture: A Comparative Perspective." *BiolRev* 89.2:284–301.
Dearman, Andrew, ed. 1989. *Studies in the Mesha Inscription and Moab*. Atlanta, GA: Scholars Press.

———. 2020. "Who Is Like You among the Gods? Some Observations on Configuring YHWH in the Old Testament." Pages 77–87 in *Divine Doppelgängers: YHWH's Ancient Look-Alikes*. Edited by Collin Cornell. University Park, PA: Eisenbrauns.

Del Monte, Giuseppe F. 2005. "The Hittite Ḥerem." Pages 21–46 in *Memoriae Igor M. Diakonoff. Babel und Bibel 2*. Edited by Leonid E. Kogan, Natalia Koslova, Sergey Loesov, and Serguei Tishchenko. Winona Lake, IN: Eisenbrauns.

Del Olmo Lete, Gregorio, and Joaquín Sanmartín. 2003. *A Dictionary of the Ugaritic Language in the Alphabetic Tradition*. Translated by Wilfred G. E. Watson. 2 vols. Leiden: Brill.

DeLapp, Nevada Levi. 2018. *Theophanic "Type-Scenes" in the Pentateuch: Visions of YHWH*. London: Bloomsbury.

Dick, Michael B. 1999. "Prophetic Parodies of Making the Cult Image." Pages 16–45 in *Born in Heaven Made on Earth: The Making of the Cult Image in the Ancient Near East*. Edited by Michael B. Dick. Winona Lake, IN: Eisenbrauns.

Dion, Paul E. 1991. "YHWH as Storm-god and Sun-god: The Double Legacy of Egypt and Canaan as Reflected in Psalm 104." *ZAW* 103.1: 43–71.

Dirven, René, and Marjolijn Verspoor. 2004. *Cognitive Explorations of Language and Linguistics. Second Revised Edition*. Amsterdam: John Benjamins Publishing Company.

Doak, Brian R. 2014. "Written with the Finger of God: Divine and Human Writing in Exodus." Pages 81–110 in *Children of the Calling: Essays in Honor of Stanley M. Burgess and Ruth V. Burgess*. Edited by Eric Nelson Newberg and Lois E. Olena. Eugene, OR: Wipf & Stock.

———. 2015. *Phoenician Aniconism in Its Mediterranean and Ancient Near Eastern Contexts*. Atlanta, GA: SBL Press.

Dobbs-Allsopp, F. W., J. J. M. Roberts, C. L. Seow, and R. E. Whitaker, eds. 2005. *Hebrew Inscriptions: Texts from the Biblical Period of the Monarchy with Concordance*. New Haven, CT: Yale University Press.

Douglas, Mary. 1999. *Implicit Meanings: Selected Essays in Anthropology*. 2nd ed. London: Routledge.

Dozeman, Thomas B. 2006. "The Commission of Moses and the Book of Genesis." Pages 107–29 in *A Farewell to the Yahwist? The Composition of the Pentateuch in Recent European Interpretation*. Edited by Thomas B. Dozeman and Konrad Schmid. SymS 34. Atlanta, GA: Society of Biblical Literature.

———. 2015. *Joshua 1–12: A New Translation with Introduction and Commentary*, AB. New Haven, CT: Yale University Press, 2015.

Dozeman, Thomas B., and Konrad Schmid, eds. 2006. *A Farewell to the Yahwist? The Composition of the Pentateuch in Recent European Interpretation*. SymS 34. Atlanta, GA: Society of Biblical Literature.

Draycott, Catherine M., and Maria Stamatopoulou, eds. 2016. *Dining and Death: Interdisciplinary Perspectives on the 'Funerary Banquet' in Ancient Art, Burial and Belief*. Leuven: Peeters.

Duncan, William N., and Kevin R. Schwarz. 2014. "Partible, Permeable, and Relational Bodies in a Maya Mass Grave." Pages 149–70 in *Commingled and Disarticulated*

Human Remains: Working Toward Improved Theory, Method, and Data. Edited by Anna J. Osterholtz, Kathryn M. Baustian, and Debra L. Martin. New York: Springer.
Durand, Jean-Marie. 1998. "Réalités Amorrites et traditions bibliques." *RAAO* 92.1: 3–39.
Edelman, Diana Vikander. 1991. *King Saul in the Historiography of Judah*. Sheffield: JSOT Press.
———, ed. 2014. *Deuteronomy–Kings as Emerging Authoritative Books: A Conversation*. Atlanta, GA: Society of Biblical Literature.
———. 2017. "Adjusting Social Memory in the Hebrew Bible: The *Teraphim*." Pages 115–42 in *Congress Volume Stellenbosch 2016*. Edited by Louis C. Jonker, Gideon R. Kotzé, and Cristl M. Maier. Leiden: Brill.
Ehrman, Bart. 2014. *How Jesus Became God: The Exaltation of a Jewish Preacher from Galilee*. New York: HarperOne.
Eichler, Raanan. 2019. "The Priestly Asherah." *VT* 69.1:33–45.
Elkaisy-Friemuth, Maha, and John M. Dillon, eds. 2009. *The Afterlife of the Platonic Soul: Reflections of Platonic Psychology in the Monotheistic Religions*. Leiden: Brill.
Ember, Aaron. 1905. "The Pluralis Intensivus in Hebrew." *AJSLL* 21.4: 195–231.
Emelianov, Vladimir V. 2010. "On the Early History of *melammu*." Pages 1109–19 in *Language in the Ancient Near East: Proceedings of the 53rd Rencontre Assyriologique Internationale. Vol. 1, Part 1*. Edited by Leonid E. Kogan, Natalia Koslova, Sergey Loesov, and Serguei Tishchenko. Winona Lake, IN: Eisenbrauns.
Emerton, J. A. 1982. "Leviathan and *ltn*: The Vocalization of the Ugaritic Word for the Dragon." *VT* 32: 327–31.
———. 1999. "'Yahweh and His Asherah': The Goddess or Her Symbol?" *VT* 49.3: 315–37.
Emmerson, Grace I. 1984. *Hosea: An Israelite Prophet in Judean Perspective*. Sheffield: JSOT Press.
Evans, Jonathan St. B. T., and Keith E. Stanovich. 2013. "Dual-Process Theories of Higher Cognition: Advancing the Debate." *PPS* 8.3: 223–41.
Eynikel, Erik. 2007. "The Angel in Samson's Birth Narrative: Judg 13." Pages 109–23 in *Yearbook 2007. Angels: The Concept of Celestial Beings – Origins, Development and Reception*. Edited by Friedrich V. Reiterer, Tobias Nicklas, and Karin Schöpflin. Berlin: de Gruyter.
Fabry, Heinz-Josef. 1995. "לב lēḇ." *TDOT* 7:401–34.
———. 2004. "רוּחַ rûaḥ." *TDOT* 13:372–402.
Fauconnier, Gilles, and Mark Turner. 2002. *The Way We Think: Conceptual Blending and the Mind's Hidden Complexities*. New York: Basic Books.
Faust, Avraham. 2019. "The World of P: The Material Realm of Priestly Writings." *VT* 69.2: 173–218.
Feder, Yitzhaq. 2014. "The Semantics of Purity in the Ancient Near East: Lexical Meaning as a Projection of Embodied Experience." *JANER* 14: 87–113.
———. 2019. "Death, Afterlife and Corpse Pollution: The Meaning of the Expression *ṭāmēʾ la-nepeš*." *VT* 69.3: 408–34.
———. 2022. *Purity and Pollution in the Hebrew Bible: From Embodied Experience to Moral Metaphor*. Cambridge: Cambridge University Press.

Feldman, Marian H. 2014. *Communities of Style: Portable Luxury Arts, Identity, and Collective Memory in the Iron Age Levant.* Chicago: University of Chicago.
Fensham, F. Charles. 1962. "Widow, Orphan, and the Poor in Ancient Near Eastern and Wisdom Literature." *JNES* 21.2: 129–39.
Finkelstein, Israel. 2013. *The Forgotten Kingdom: The Archaeology and History of Northern Israel.* Atlanta, GA: Society of Biblical Literature.
———. 2017. "Major Saviors, Minor Judges: The Historical Background of the Northern Accounts in the Book of Judges." *JSOT* 41.4: 431–49.
———. 2020. "Jeroboam II's Temples." *ZAW* 132.2: 250–65.
Finkelstein, Israel, and Eli Piasetzky. 2008. "The Date of Kuntillet 'Ajrud: The ^{14}C Perspective." *TA* 35: 175–85.
Finkelstein, Israel, and Thomas Römer. 2014. "Comments on the Historical Background of the Jacob Narrative in Genesis." *ZAW* 126.3: 317–38.
———. 2020. "The Historical and Archaeological Background behind the Old Israelite Ark Narrative." *Biblica* 101.2: 161–85.
Fischer, Alexander A. 2007. "Moses and the Exodus-Angel." Pages 79–93 in *Yearbook 2007. Angels: The Concept of Celestial Beings – Origins, Development and Reception.* Edited by Friedrich V. Reiterer, Tobias Nicklas, and Karin Schöpflin. Berlin: de Gruyter.
Fitzgerald, Timothy. 2015. "Critical Religion and Critical Research on Religion: Religion and Politics as Modern Fictions." *CRR* 3.3: 303–19.
Fleming, Daniel E. 1989. "The Divine Council as Type Scene in the Hebrew Bible." PhD diss. Southern Baptist Theological Seminary.
———. 1992. *The Installation of Baal's High Priestess at Emar: A Window on Ancient Syrian Religion.* Atlanta, GA: Scholars Press.
———. 2000. *Time at Emar: The Cultic Calendar and the Rituals from the Diviner's Archive.* Winona Lake, IN: Eisenbrauns.
———. 2021. *Yahweh before Israel: Glimpses of History in a Divine Name.* Cambridge: Cambridge University Press.
Flynn, Shawn W. 2014. *YHWH Is King: The Development of Divine Kingship in Ancient Israel.* Leiden: Brill.
Forschey, Harold O. 1975. "The Construct Chain *naḥᵃlat YHWH/ᵉlōhîm*." *BASOR* 220: 51–53.
Forstmann, Matthias, and Pascal Burgmer. "Adults are Intuitive Mind-Body Dualists." 2015. *JEPG* 144.1: 222–35.
Fossum, Jarl E. 1985. *The Name of God and the Angel of the Lord: Samaritan and Jewish Concepts of Intermediation and the Origin of Gnosticism.* Tübingen: Mohr Siebeck.
Fowler, Chris. 2004. *The Archaeology of Personhood: An Anthropological Approach.* New York: Routledge.
Frandsen, Paul John. 2007. "The Menstrual 'Taboo' in Ancient Egypt." *JNES* 66.2: 81–106.
Fredriksen, Paula. 2020. "How High Can Early Christology Be?" Pages 293–319 in *Monotheism and Christology in Greco-Roman Antiquity.* Edited by Matthew V. Novenson. Leiden: Brill.

———. 2022. "Philo, Herod, Paul, and the Many Gods of Ancient Jewish 'Monotheism.'" *HTR* 115.1: 23–45.
Freedman, David Noel, and C. Franke Hyland. 1973. "Psalm 29: A Structural Analysis." *HTR* 66: 237–56.
Frey-Anthes, Henrike. 2008. "Concepts of 'Demons' in Ancient Israel." *WO* 38: 43–48.
Friedman, Richard Elliott. 1995. *The Hidden Face of God.* San Francisco: HarperCollins.
Friedman Richard Elliott, and Shawna Dolansky Overton. 1999. "Death and Afterlife: The Biblical Silence." Pages 35–59 in *Judaism in Late Antiquity 4. Death, Life-After-Death, Resurrection in the World-to-Come in the Judaisms of Antiquity.* Edited by Alan J. Avery-Peck and Jacob Neusner. Leiden: Brill.
Gager, John G. 1992. *Curse Tablets and Binding Spells from the Ancient World.* Oxford: Oxford University Press.
Gahlin, Lucia. 2007. "Private Religion." Pages 325–39 in *The Egyptian World.* Edited by Toby Wilkinson. New York: Routledge.
Galbraith, Deane. 2019. "The Origin of Archangels: Ideological Mystification of Nobility." Pages 209–240 in *Class Struggle in the New Testament.* Edited by Robert J. Myles. Lanham, MD: Lexington Books.
Galen, Luke W. 2016. "Big Gods: Extended Prosociality or Group Binding?" *BBS* 39: 29–30.
Gamble, Clive. 2007. *Origins and Revolutions: Human Identity in Earliest Prehistory.* Cambridge: Cambridge University Press.
Gardiner, Alan. 1957. *Egyptian Grammar. Third Edition.* Oxford: Griffith Institute.
Garfinkel, Yosef. 2018. "The Standing Stones." Pages 55–70 in *Khirbet Qeiyafa Vol. 4. Excavation Report 2007–2013: Art, Cult, and Epigraphy.* Edited by Yosef Garfinkel, Saar Ganor, and Michael G. Hasel. Jerusalem: Israel Exploration Society.
———. 2020. "Face of Yahweh?" *BAR* 46.4: 30–33.
Garfinkel, Yosef, and Madeleine Mumcuoglu. 2013. "Triglyphs and Recessed Doorframes on a Building Model from Khirbet Qeiyafa: New Light on Two Technical Terms in the Biblical Descriptions of Solomon's Palace and Temple." *IEJ* 63.2: 135–63.
———. 2015. "A Shrine Model from Tel Rekhesh." *SBA-IAS* 33: 77–87.
———. 2018. "An Elaborate Clay Portable Shrine." Pages 83–126 in *Khirbet Qeiyafa Vol. 4. Excavation Report 2007–2013: Art, Cult, and Epigraphy.* Edited by Yosef Garfinkel, Saar Ganor, and Michael G. Hasel. Jerusalem: Israel Exploration Society.
Garfinkel, Yosef, Saar Ganor, and Michael G. Hasel. 2018. *In the Footsteps of King David: Revelations from an Ancient Biblical City.* New York: Thames & Hudson.
Garr, W. Randall. 2003. *In His Own Image and Likeness: Humanity, Divinity, and Monotheism.* Leiden: Brill.
Geeraerts, Dirk. 2006. "Prototype Theory: Prospects and Problems of Prototype Theory." Pages 141–65 in *Cognitive Linguistics: Basic Readings.* Edited by Dirk Geeraerts. Berlin: de Gruyter.
Gell, Alfred. 1998. *Art and Agency: An Anthropological Theory.* Oxford: Oxford University Press.
Gertz, Jan Christian. 2016. "Hezekiah, Moses, and the Nehushtan: A Case Study for a Correlation between the History of Religion in the Monarchic Period and the History

of the Formation of the Hebrew Bible." Pages 745–60 in *The Formation of the Pentateuch: Bridging the Academic Cultures of Europe, Israel, and North America*. Edited by Jan Christian Gertz, Bernard M. Levinson, Dalit Rom-Shiloni, and Konrad Schmid. Tübingen: Mohr Siebeck.

Gertz, Jan Christian, Konrad Schmid, and Markus Witte, eds. 2002. *Abschied vom Jahwisten: Die Komposition des Hezateuch in der jüngsten Diskussion*. Berlin: de Gruyter.

Gervais, Will M., and Joseph Henrich. 2010. "The Zeus Problem: Why Representational Content Biases Cannot Explain Faith in Gods." *JCC* 10.3–4: 383–89.

Gieschen, Charles A. 1998. *Angelomorphic Christology: Antecedents and Early Evidence*. Leiden: Brill.

———. 2007. "The Name of the Son of Man in the Parables of Enoch." Pages 238–49 in *Enoch and the Messiah Son of Man: Revisiting the Book of Parables*. Edited by Gabriele Boccaccini. Grand Rapids, MI: Eerdmans.

Gilmour, Garth. 2009. "An Iron Age II Pictorial Inscription from Jerusalem Illustrating Yahweh and Asherah." *PEQ* 141.2: 87–103.

Gnuse, Robert Karl. 1997. *No Other Gods: Emergent Monotheism in Israel*. Sheffield: Sheffield Academic Press.

Golub, Mitka R. 2018. "Aniconism and Theophoric Names in Inscribed Seals from Judah, Israel and Neighbouring Kingdoms." *TA* 45.1: 157–69.

Gonzalez, A. 1963. "Le Psaume LXXXII." *VT* 13.3: 293–309.

Goodman, Martin. 2007. *Judaism in the Roman World. Collected Essays*. Leiden: Brill.

Gordon, Andrew A. 1996. "The K3 as an Animating Force." *JARCE* 33: 31–35.

Gordon, Robert P. 2007. "Standing in the Council: When Prophets Encounter God." Pages 190–204 in *The God of Israel*. Edited by Robert P. Gordon. Cambridge: Cambridge University Press.

Graesser, Carl F. 1972. "Standing Stones in Ancient Palestine." *BA* 35.2: 33–63.

Gray, Alison Ruth. 2014. *Psalm 18 in Words and Pictures: A Reading Through Metaphor*. Leiden: Brill.

Green, Alberto R. W. 2003. *The Storm-God in the Ancient Near East*. Winona Lake, IN: Eisenbrauns.

Greene, Nathaniel E. 2017. "Creation, Destruction, and a Psalmist's Plea: Rethinking the Poetic Structure of Psalm 74." *JBL* 136.1: 85–101.

Greenstein, Edward L. 1982. "The Snaring of Sea in the Baal Epic." *MAARAV* 3.2: 195–216.

Gudme, Anne Katrine de Hemmer. 2003. *Before the God in This Place for Good Remembrance: A Comparative Analysis of the Aramaic Votive Inscriptions from Mount Gerizim*. Berlin: de Gruyter.

Guillaume, Philippe. 2009. *Land and Calendar: The Priestly Document from Genesis 1 to Joshua 18*. New York: T&T Clark.

Gunkel, Hermann, and Joachim Begrich. 1998. *Introduction to Psalms: The Genres of the Religious Lyric of Israel*. Translated by James D. Nogalski. Macon, GA: Mercer University Press.

Guthrie, Stewart. 1993. *Faces in the Clouds: A New Theory of Religion*. Oxford: Oxford University Press.

Hachlili, Rachel. 2001. *The Menorah, the Ancient Seven-Armed Candelabrum: Origin, Form and Function*. Leiden: Brill.
Hadley, Judith M. 1987. "The Khirbet el-Qom Inscription." *VT* 37.1: 50–62.
———. 2000. *The Cult of Asherah in Ancient Israel and Judah: Evidence for a Hebrew Goddess*. Cambridge: Cambridge University Press.
Haidle, Miriam Noël. 2019. "The Origin of Cumulative Culture: Not a Single-Trait Event But Multifactorial Processes." Pages 128–48 in *Squeezing Minds From Stones: Cognitive Archaeology and the Evolution of the Human Mind*. Edited by Karenleigh A. Overmann and Frederick L. Coolidge. Oxford: Oxford University Press.
Halayqa, Issam H. K. 2008. *A Comparative Lexicon of Ugaritic and Canaanite*. Münster: Ugarit-Verlag.
Hallam, Elizabeth, and Jenny Hockey. 2001. *Death, Memory and Material Culture*. Oxford: Berg.
Hallo, William W. 1962. "The Royal Inscriptions of Ur: A Typology." *HUCA* 33: 1–43.
———. 1985. "As the Seal Upon Thy Heart." *BRev* 1.1: 20–27.
Hamori, Esther J. 2008. *"When Gods Were Men": The Embodied God in Biblical and Near Eastern Literature*. Berlin: de Gruyter.
———. 2015. *Women's Divination in Biblical Literature: Prophecy, Necromancy, and Other Arts of Knowledge*. New Haven, CT: Yale University Press.
Hampe, Beate, ed. 2005. *From Perception to Meaning: Image Schemas in Cognitive Linguistics*. Berlin: de Gruyter.
Handy, Lowell K. 1994. *Among the Host of Heaven: The Syro-Palestinian Pantheon as Bureaucracy*. Winona Lake, IN: Eisenbrauns.
Hannah, Darrell D. 1999. *Michael and Christ: Michael Traditions and Angel Christology in Early Christianity*. Tübingen: Mohr Siebeck.
———. 2007. "Guardian Angels and Angelic National Patrons in Second Temple Judaism and Early Christianity." Pages 413–36 in *Yearbook 2007. Angels: The Concept of Celestial Beings; Origins, Development and Reception*. Edited by Friedrich V. Reiterer, Tobias Nicklas, and Karin Schöpflin. Berlin: de Gruyter.
Haran, Menahem. 1993. "'Incense Altars'—Are They?" Pages 237–47 in *Biblical Archaeology Today, 1990: Proceedings of the Second International Congress on Biblical Archaeology, Jerusalem, June–July 1990*. Edited by Avraham Biran, J. Aviram, and Alan Paris-Shadur. Jerusalem: Israel Exploration Society/The Israel Academy of Sciences and Humanities.
Hausmann, Lucerne J. 2003. "צלח *ṣālāḥ*." *TDOT* 12:382–84.
Hayman, Peter. 1990. "Monotheism—A Misused Word in Jewish Studies?" *JJS* 42.1: 1–15.
Hays, Christopher B. 2015. *A Covenant with Death: Death in the Iron Age II and Its Rhetorical Uses in Proto-Isaiah*. Grand Rapids, MI: Eerdmans.
———. 2020. "Enlil, Isaiah, and the Origins of the *'ĕlîlîm*: A Reassessment." *ZAW* 132.2: 224–35.
Hays, Christopher B., and Joel M. LeMon. 2009. "The Dead and Their Images: An Egyptian Etymology for Hebrew *'ôb*." *JAEI* 1.4: 1–4.
Heidt, William George. 1949. *Angelology of the Old Testament: A Study in Biblical Theology*. Washington, DC: Catholic University of America Press.

Heiser, Michael S. 2006. "Are Yahweh and El Distinct Deities in Deut. 32:8–9 and Psalms 82?" *Hiphil* 3: 1–9.
———. 2008a. "Monotheism, Polytheism, Monolatry, or Henotheism? Toward an Assessment of Divine Plurality in the Hebrew Bible." *BBR* 18.1: 9–15.
———. 2008b. "Does Deuteronomy 32.17 Assume or Deny the Reality of Other Gods?" *BT* 59.3: 137–45.
———. 2015. *The Unseen Realm: Recovering the Supernatural Worldview of the Bible.* Bellingham, WA: Lexham Press.
Hemer, Susan. 2013. *Tracing the Melanesian Person: Emotions and Relationships in Lihir.* Adelaide: University of Adelaide Press.
Hendel, Ronald S. 2015. "The Exodus as Cultural Memory: Egyptian Bondage and the Song of the Sea." Pages 65–77 in *Israel's Exodus in Transdisciplinary Perspective: Text, Archaeology, Culture, and Geoscience.* Edited by Thomas E. Levy, Thomas Schneider, and William H. C. Propp. Switzerland: Springer.
Henrich, Joseph. 2009. "The Evolution of Costly Displays, Cooperation and Religion: Credibility Enhancing Displays and Their Implications for Cultural Evolution." *EHB* 30.4: 244–60.
Henrich, Joseph, Steven J. Heine, and Ara Norenzayan. 2010. "The Weirdest People in the World?" *BBS* 33.2–3: 61–135.
Herring, Stephen L. 2013. *Divine Substitution: Humanity as the Manifestation of Deity in the Hebrew Bible and the Ancient Near East.* Göttingen: Vandenhoeck & Ruprecht.
Herrmann, Christian. 1994–2006. *Ägyptische Amulette aus Palästina/Israel.* 3 vols. Fribourg: Universitätsverlag; Göttingen: Vandenhoeck & Ruprecht.
Herrmann, Virginia Rimmer, and J. David Schloen, eds. 2014. *In Remembrance of Me: Feasting with the Dead in the Ancient Middle East.* Chicago: University of Chicago Press.
Herzog, Ze'ev. 2002. "The Fortress Mound at Tel Arad: An Interim Report." *TA* 29.1: 3–109.
———. 2010. "Perspectives on Southern Israel's Cult Centralization: Arad and Beer-scheba." Pages 169–99 in *One God – One Cult – One Nation: Archaeological and Biblical Perspectives.* Edited by Reinhard G. Kratz and Hermann Spieckermann. Berlin: de Gruyter.
Hess, Richard. "Asherah or Asherata?" *Orientalia* 65.3 (1996): 209–19.
Hess, Sabine C. 2009. *Person and Place: Ideas, Ideals and the Practice of Sociality on Vanua Lava, Vanuatu.* New York: Berghan Books.
Hestrin, Ruth. 1987. "The Cult Stand from Taʿanach and Its Religious Background." Pages 61–77 in *Studia Phoenicia V: Phoenicia and the East Mediterranean in the First Millennium B.C.* Edited by E. Lipiński. Leuven: Peeters, 1987.
Hitchcock, Louise A. 2011. "Cult Corners in the Aegean and the Levant." Pages 321–45 in *Household Archaeology in Ancient Israel and Beyond.* Edited by Assaf Yasur-Landau, Jennie R. Ebeling, and Laura B. Mazow. Leiden: Brill.
Hobson, Nicholas M., and Michael Inzlicht. 2016. "Recognizing Religion's Dark Side: Religious Ritual Increases Antisociality and Hinders Self-Control." *BBS* 39: 30–31.
Hodder, Ian. 2006. *The Leopard's Tale: Revealing the Mysteries of Çatalhöyük.* New York: Thames & Hudson.

Hodge, K. Mitch. 2008. "Descartes' Mistake: How Afterlife Beliefs Challenge the Assumption that Humans Are Intuitive Cartesian Substance Dualists." *JCC* 8: 387–415.
Hogue, Timothy. 2019a. "The Monumentality of the Sinaitic Decalogue: Reading Exodus 20 in Light of Northwest Semitic Monument-Making Practices." *JBL* 138.1 (2019): 79–99.
———. 2019b. "*Abracadabra*, or 'I Create as I Speak': A Reanalysis of the First Verb in the Katumuwa Inscription in Light of Northwest Semitic and Hieroglyphic Luwian Parallels." *BASOR* 381: 193–202.
———. 2019c. "Image, Text, and Ritual: The Decalogue and the Three Reembodiments of God." Paper presented at the Annual Meeting of the Society of Biblical Literature. San Diego, CA.
Hohwy, Jakob. 2013. *The Predictive Mind*. Oxford: Oxford University Press.
Holloway, Paul A. 2017. *Philippians: A Commentary*. Hermeneia. Minneapolis: Fortress.
Holt, John Clifford. 2009. *Spirits of the Place: Buddhism and Lao Religious Culture*. Honolulu: University of Hawai'i Press.
Honigman, Sylvie, and Ehud Ben Zvi. 2020. "The Spread of the Ideological Concept of a (Jerusalem-Centred) *Tōrâ*-Centred Israel beyond Yehud: Observations and Implications." *HeBAI* 9.4: 370–97.
Hornung, Erik, and Elisabeth Staehelin. 1976. *Skarabäen und andere Siegelamulette aus Basler Sammlungen*. Mainz: Philipp von Zabern.
Hubler, James N. 1995. "Creatio ex Nihilo: Matter, Creation, and the Body in Classical and Christian Philosophy through Aquinas." PhD diss. University of Pennsylvania.
Huffmon, Herbert B. 2012. "The Exclusivity of Divine Communication in Ancient Israel: False Prophecy in the Hebrew Bible and the Ancient Near East." Pages 67–81 in *Mediating between Heaven and Earth: Communication with the Divine in the Ancient Near East*. Edited by C. L. Crouch, Jonathan Stökl, and Anna Elise Zernecke. London: T&T Clark.
Hundley, Michael B. 2009. "To Be or Not to Be: A Reexamination of Name Language in Deuteronomy and the Deuteronomistic History." *VT* 59.4: 533–55.
———. 2011. *Keeping Heaven on Earth: Safeguarding the Divine Presence in the Priestly Tabernacle*. Tübingen: Mohr Siebeck.
———. 2013. *Gods in Dwellings: Temples and Divine Presence in the Ancient Near East*. Atlanta, GA: Society of Biblical Literature.
———. 2016. "Of God and Angels: Divine Messengers in Genesis and Exodus in their Ancient Near Eastern Contexts." *JTS* 67.1: 1–22.
Hurowitz, Victor Avigdor. 2003. "The Mesopotamian God Image, from Womb to Tomb." *JAOS* 123.1: 147–57.
———. 2004. "Healing and Hissing Snakes—Listening to Numbers 21:4–9." *Scriptura* 87: 278–87.
———. 2006. "What Goes in Is What Comes Out: Materials for Creating Cult Statues." Pages 3–23 in *Text, Artifact, and Image: Revealing Ancient Israelite Religion*. Edited by Gary Beckman and Theodore J. Lewis. Providence, RI: Brown Judaic Studies.
Hutter, Manfred. 1999. "Lilith לילית." *DDD*, 520–21.

———. 2007. "Demons and Benevolent Spirits in the Ancient Near East: A Phenomenological Overview." Pages 21–34 in *Yearbook 2007. Angels: The Concept of Celestial Beings; Origins, Development and Reception*. Edited by Friedrich V. Reiterer, Tobias Nicklas, and Karin Schöpflin. Berlin: de Gruyter.

Idel, Moshe. 1990. *Golem: Jewish Magical and Mystical Traditions on the Artificial Anthropoid*. New York: State University of New York Press.

Irvin, Dorothy. 1978. *Mytharion: The Comparison of Tales from the Old Testament and the Ancient Near East*. Kevelaer: Butzon & Bercker.

Isaac, E. 1983. "1 Enoch." Pages 5–89 in *The Old Testament Pseudepigrapha*. Edited by James H. Charlesworth. Vol. 1. Garden City, NY: Doubleday, 1983.

Jackson, Kent P., and J. Andrew Dearman. 1989. "The Text of the Mesha Inscription." Pages 93–95 in *Studies in the Mesha Inscription and Moab*. Edited by Andrew Dearman. Atlanta, GA: Scholars Press.

Jacobsen, Thorkild. 1987. "The Graven Image." Pages 15–32 in *Ancient Israelite Religion: Essays in Honor of Frank Moore Cross*. Edited by Patrick D. Miller, Jr., Paul D. Hanson, and S. Dean McBride. Philadelphia: Fortress.

Janak, Jiri. 2011. "A Question of Size. A Remark on Early Attestations of the Ba Hieroglyph." *SAK* 40: 143–53.

Janowski, Bernd. 1999a. "Azazel עזאזל." *DDD*, 128–31.

———. 1999b. "Satyrs שעירים." *DDD*, 732–33.

Järnefelt, Elisa, Caitlin F. Canfield, and Deborah Kelemen. 2015. "The Divided Mind of a Disbeliever: Intuitive Beliefs about Nature as Purposefully Created Among Different Groups of Non-Religious Adults." *Cognition* 140.1: 72–88.

Järnefelt, Elisa, Liqi Zhu, Caitlin F. Canfield, Marian Chen, and Deborah Kelemen. 2019. "Reasoning about Nature's Agency and Design in the Cultural Context of China." *Religion* 9.2: 156–78.

Joffe, Laura. 2001. "The Elohistic Psalter: What, How and Why?" *SJOT* 15.1: 142–69.

Johansson, Daniel. 2011. "'Who Can Forgive Sins but God Alone?': Human and Angelic Agents, and Divine Forgiveness in Early Judaism." *JSNT* 33.4: 351–74.

Johnson, Carl Nils. 1990. "If You Had My Brain, Where Would I Be? Children's Understanding of the Brain and Identity." *ChildDev* 61.4: 962–72.

———. 2016. *God Is Watching You: How the Fear of God Makes Us Human*. Oxford: Oxford University Press, 2016.

Jong, Jonathan. 2015. "On (Not) Defining (Non)Religion." *SRC* 2.3: 15–24.

Kang, Sa-Moon. 1989. *Divine War in the Old Testament and in the Ancient Near East*. Berlin: de Gruyter.

Katz, Hava. 2016. *Portable Shrine Models. Ancient Architectural Clay Models from the Levant*. BARIS 2791. London: British Archaeological Reports Ltd.

Kay, Aaron C., Steven Shepherd, Craig W. Blatz, Sook Ning Chua, and Adam D. Galinsky. 2010. "For God (or) Country: The Hydraulic Relation between Government Instability and Belief in Religious Sources of Control." *JPSP* 99.5: 725–39.

Kee, Min Suc. 2007. "The Heavenly Council and Its Type-Scene." *JSOT* 31: 259–73.

Keel, Othmar. 1997. *The Symbolism of the Biblical World: Ancient Near Eastern Iconography and the Book of Psalms*. Translated by Timothy J. Hallett. Winona Lake, IN: Eisenbrauns.

Keel, Othmar, and Christoph Uehlinger. 1998. *Gods, Goddesses, and Images of God in Ancient Israel*. Translated by Thomas H. Trapp. Edinburgh: T&T Clark.

Kelemen, Deborah, and Evelyn Rosset. 2009. "The Human Function Compunction: Teleological Explanation in Adults." *Cognition* 111.1: 138–43.

Kelemen, Deborah, Joshua Rottman, and Rebecca Seston. "Professional Physical Scientists Display Tenacious Teleological Tendencies: Purpose-Based Reasoning as a Cognitive Default." *JEPG* 142.4 (2013): 1074–83.

Kim, Eun Young, and Hyun-joo Song. 2015. "Six-Month-Olds Actively Predict Others' Goal-Directed Actions." *CD* 33: 1–13.

King, Peter. 2012. "Body and Soul." Pages 505–24 in *The Oxford Handbook of Medieval Philosophy*. Edited by John Marenbon. Oxford: Oxford University Press.

Kinzler, Katherine D., and Elizabeth S. Spelke. 2007. "Core Systems in Human Cognition." *PBR* 164: 257–64.

Kiperwasser, Reuven. 2013. "Matters of the Heart: The Metamorphosis of the Monolithic in the Bible to the Fragmented in Rabbinic Thought." Pages 43–59 in *Judaism and Emotion: Texts, Performance, Experience*. Edited by Sarah Ross, Gabriel Levy, and Soham Al-Suadi. New York: Lang.

Kirk, Alan. 2005. "Social and Cultural Memory." Pages 1–24 in *Memory, Tradition, and Text: Uses of the Past in Early Christianity*. Edited by Alan Kirk and Tom Thatcher. Atlanta, GA: Society of Biblical Literature.

Kisilevitz, Shua. 2015. "The Iron IIA Judahite Temple at Tel Moẓa." *TA* 42: 147–64.

Kisilevitz, Shua, Ido Koch, Oded Lipschits, and David S. Vanderhooft. 2020. "Facing the Facts About the 'Face of God': A Critical response to Yosef Garfinkel." *BAR* 46.5: 38–45.

Kjærsgaard, Anne, and Eric Venbrux. 2016. "Still in the Picture: Photographs at Graves and Social Time." Pages 85–110 in *Materialities of Passing: Explorations in Transformation, Transition and Transience*. Edited by Peter Bjerresgaard, Anders Emil Rasmussen, and Tim Flohr Sørensen. Abingdon: Routledge.

Kletter, Raz. 1996. *The Judean Pillar-Figurines and the Archaeology of Asherah*. Oxford: Tempvs Reparatvm.

Kloos, Carola. 1986. *Yhwh's Combat with the Sea: A Canaanite Tradition in the Religion of Ancient Israel*. Leiden: Brill.

Knafl, Anne K. 2014. *Forming God: Divine Anthropomorphism in the Pentateuch*. Winona Lake, IN: Eisenbrauns.

Knauf, Ernst Axel. 2010. "History in Judges." Pages 140–49 in *The Texts*. Vol. 2 of *Israel in Transition: From Late Bronze II to Iron IIa (c. 1250–850 B.C.E.)*. Edited by Lester L. Grabbe. New York: T&T Clark.

Knauf, Ernst Axel, and Philippe Guillaume. 2016. *A History of Biblical Israel: The Fate of the Tribes and Kingdoms from Merenptah to Bar Kochba*. Sheffield: Equinox.

Knauft, Bruce. 1999. *From Primitive to Postcolonial in Melanesia and Anthropology*. Michigan: University of Michigan Press.

Kotansky, Roy, Joseph Naveh, and Shaul Shaked. 1992. "A Greek-Aramaic Silver Amulet from Egypt in the Ashmolean Museum." *Muséon* 105.1–2: 5–25.

Köckert, Matthias. 2007. "Divine Messengers and Mysterious Men in the Patriarchal Narratives of the Book of Genesis." Pages 51–78 in *Yearbook 2007. Angels: The*

Concept of Celestial Beings; Origins, Development and Reception. Edited by Friedrich V. Reiterer, Tobias Nicklas, and Karin Schöpflin. Berlin: de Gruyter.

———. 2010. "YHWH in the Northern and Southern Kingdom." Pages 357–94 in *One God—One Cult—One Nation: Archaeological and Biblical Perspectives.* Edited by Reinhard G. Kratz and Hermann Spieckermann. Berlin: de Gruyter.

Kövecses, Zoltán. 2020. *Extended Conceptual Metaphor Theory.* Cambridge: Cambridge University Press.

Kugel, James. 2003. *The God of Old: Inside the Lost World of the Bible.* New York: The Free Press.

Labuschagne, C. J. 1966. *The Incomparability of Yahweh in the Old Testament.* Leiden: Brill.

Lakoff, George. 1987a. *Women, Fire, and Dangerous Things: What Categories Reveal about the Mind.* Chicago: University of Chicago.

———. 1987b. "Image Metaphors." *MSA* 2.3: 219–22.

Lakoff, George, and Mark Johnson. 1999. *Philosophy in the Flesh: The Embodied Mind and Its Challenges to Western Thought.* New York: Basic Books.

Lambek, Michael, and Andrew Strathern, eds. 1998. *Bodies and Persons: Comparative Perspectives from Africa and Melanesia.* Cambridge: Cambridge University Press.

Langacker, Ronald. 1987. *Theoretical Prerequisites.* Vol. 1 of *Foundations of Cognitive Grammar.* Stanford, California: Stanford University Press.

———. 2002. "Theory, Method, and Description in Cognitive Grammar: A Case Study." Pages 13–40 in *Cognitive Linguistics Today.* Edited by Barbara Lewandowska-Tomaszczyk and Kamila Turewicz. Frankfurt am Main: Peter Lang, 2002.

LaRocca-Pitts, Elizabeth C. 2001. *'Of Wood and Stone': The Significance of Israelite Cultic Items in the Bible and Its Early Interpreters.* Winona Lake, IN: Eisenbrauns.

Lauterbach, Jacob Z. 2004. *Mekhilta de-Rabbi Ishmael.* 2nd ed. 2 vols. Philadelphia, PA: Jewish Publication Society.

Law, Timothy Michael, and Alison Salvesen, eds. 2012. *Greek Scripture and the Rabbis.* Leuven: Peeters.

Lenzi, Alan. 2008. *Secrecy and the Gods: Secret Knowledge in Ancient Mesopotamia and Biblical Israel.* SAAS 19. Helsinki: The Neo-Assyrian Text Corpus Project.

———. 2014. "Revisting Biblical Prophecy, Revealed Knowledge Pertaining to Ritual, and Secrecy in Light of Ancient Mesopotamian Prophetic Texts." Pages 65–86 in *Divination, Politics, and Ancient Near Eastern Empires.* Edited by Alan Lenzi and Jonathan Stökl. Atlanta, GA: Society of Biblical Literature.

Leprohon, Ronald J. 2013. *The Great Name: Ancient Egyptian Royal Titulary.* Atlanta, GA: Society of Biblical Literature.

Levin, Yigal. 2015. "How Did Rabshakeh Know the Language of Judah?" Pages 323–37 in *Marbeh Ḥokmah: Studies in the Bible and the Ancient Near East in Loving Memory of Victor Avigdor Hurowitz.* Edited by S. Yona, E. L. Greenstein, M. I. Gruber, P. Machinist, and S. M. Paul. Winona Lake, IN: Eisenbrauns.

Levine, Baruch. 1974. *In the Presence of the Lord: A Study of Cult and Some Cultic Terms in Ancient Israel.* Leiden: Brill.

———. 1993. *Numbers 1–20: A New Translation with Introduction and Commentary.* AB. New York: Doubleday.

———. 2011. *Religion*. Vol. 1 in *In Pursuit of Meaning: Collected Studies of Baruch A. Levine*. Edited by Andrew D. Gross. Winona Lake, IN: Eisenbrauns.

Levinson, Bernard M., and Jeffrey Stackert. 2012. "Between the Covenant Code and Esarhaddon's Succession Treaty." *JAJ* 3: 123–40.

Levinson, Hanne Løland. 2022. "Still Invisible after All These Years? Female God-Language in the Hebrew Bible: A Response to David J. A. Clines." *JBL* 141.2: 199–217.

Levtow, Nathaniel B. 2008. *Images of Others: Iconic Politics in Ancient Israel*. Winona Lake, IN: Eisenbrauns.

———. 2012. "Text Destruction and Iconoclasm in the Hebrew Bible and the Ancient Near East." Pages 311–62 in *Iconoclasm and Text Destruction in the Ancient Near East and Beyond*. Edited by Natalie Neomi May. Chicago: The Oriental Institute of the University of Chicago.

Levy, Gabriel. 2012. *Judaic Technologies of the Word: A Cognitive Analysis of Jewish Cultural Formation*. London: Routledge.

———. 2014. "'I Was El Shaddai, but Now I'm Yahweh': God Names and the Informational Dynamics of Biblical Texts." Pages 98–119 in *Mind, Morality and Magic: Cognitive Science Approaches in Biblical Studies*. Edited by István Czachesz and Risto Uro. Durham: Acumen.

Lewis, Theodore J. 2002. "How Far Can Texts Take Us? Evaluating Textual Sources for Reconstructing Ancient Israelite Beliefs about the Dead." Pages 169–217 in *Sacred Time, Sacred Place: Archaeology and the Religion of Israel*. Edited by Barry M. Gittlen. Winona Lake, IN: Eisenbrauns.

———. 2011. "'Athtartu's Incantations and the Use of Divine Names as Weapons." *JNES* 70.2: 207–27.

———. 2014. "Feasts for the Dead and Ancestor Veneration in Levantine Traditions." Pages 69–74 in *In Remembrance of Me: Feasting with the Dead in the Ancient Middle East*. Edited by Virginia Rimmer Herrmann and J. David Schloen. Chicago: University of Chicago Press.

———. 2020. *The Origin and Character of God: Ancient Israelite Religion through the Lens of Divinity*. Oxford: Oxford University Press.

Liberman, Zoe, Katherine D. Kinzler, and Amanda L. Woodward. 2018. "The Early Social Significance of Shared Ritual Actions." *Cognition* 171.1: 42–51.

Lichtenberger, Hermann. 2018. "The Divine Name in the Dead Sea Scrolls and in New Testament Writings." Pages 140–55 in *The Religious Worldviews Reflected in the Dead Sea Scrolls: Proceedings of the Fourteenth International Symposium of the Orion Center for the Study of the Dead Sea Scrolls and Associated Literature, 28–30 May, 2013*. Edited by Ruth A. Clements, Menahem Kister, and Michael Segal. Leiden: Brill.

Lim, Timothy H. 2010. "The Defilement of the Hands as a Principle Determining the Holiness of Scriptures." *JTS* 61.2: 501–15.

Long, A. A. 2015. *Greek Models of Mind and Self*. Cambridge, MA: Harvard University Press.

López, René A. 2010. "Identifying the 'Angel of the Lord' in the Book of Judges: A Model for Reconsidering the Referent in Other Old Testament Loci." *BBR* 20.1: 1–18.

Luo, Yuyan, and Renée Baillargeon. 2005. "Can a Self-Propelled Box Have a Goal? Psychological Reasoning in Five-Month-Old Infants." *PS* 16.8: 601–08.
Lys, Daniel. 1959. *Nèphèsh: Histoire de l'âme dans la revelation d'Israël au sein des religions proche-orientales*. Paris: Presses Universitaires de France.
MacDonald, Nathan. 2003. *Deuteronomy and the Meaning of Monotheism*. Tübingen: Mohr Siebeck.
———. 2013. "The Spirit of Yhwh: An Overlooked Conceptualization of Divine Presence in the Persian Period." Pages 95–120 in *Divine Presence and Absence in Exilic and Post-Exilic Judaism*. Edited by Nathan MacDonald and Izaak J. de Hulster. Tübingen: Mohr Siebeck.
MacDougal, Renata. 2014. "Remembrance and the Dead in Second Millennium BC Mesopotamia." PhD diss. University of Leicester.
Machinist, Peter. 2011. "How Gods Die, Biblically and Otherwise: A Problem of Cosmic Restructuring." Pages 189–240 in *Reconsidering the Concept of Revolutionary Monotheism*. Edited by Beate-Pongratz Leisten. Winona Lake, IN: Eisenbrauns.
Mageo, Jeanette Marie, and Alan Howard, eds. 1996. *Spirits in Culture, History, and Mind*. New York: Routledge.
Maher, E. F., and J. S. Lev-Tov. 2001. "Food in Late Bronze Age Funerary Offerings: Faunal Evidence from Tomb 1 at Tell Dothan." *PEQ* 133: 91–110.
Maiden, Brett E. 2020. *Cognitive Science and Ancient Israelite Religion: New Perspectives on Texts, Artifacts, and Culture*. Cambridge: Cambridge University Press.
Maij, David L. R., Hein T. van Shie, and Michiel van Elk. 2019. "The Boundary Conditions of the Hypersensitive Agency Detection Device: An Empirical Investigation of Agency Detection in Threatening Situations." *RBB* 9.1: 23–51.
Malone, Andrew S. 2011. "Distinguishing the Angel of the Lord." *BBR* 21.3: 297–314.
Mandell, Alice, and Jeremy Smoak. 2016. "Reconsidering the Function of Tomb Inscriptions in Iron Age Judah: Khirbet Beit Lei as a Test Case." *JANER* 16.2: 192–245.
———. 2017. "Reading and Writing in the Dark at Khirbet el-Qom: The Literacies of Ancient Subterranean Judah." *NEA* 80.3: 188–95.
Mandler, Jean M. 1992. "How to Build a Baby: II. Conceptual Primitives." *PsychRev* 99.4: 587–604.
Mandler, Jean M., and Cristóbal Pagán Cánovas. 2014. "On Defining Image Schemas." *LangCog* 6.4: 510–32.
Mandolfo, Carleen. 2014. "Language of Lament in the Psalms." Pages 114–30 in *The Oxford Handbook of the Psalms*. Edited by William P. Brown. Oxford: Oxford University Press.
Margalit, Baruch. 1989. "Some Observations on the Inscription and Drawing from Khirbet el-Qôm." *VT* 39.3: 371–78.
Martin, Luther H. 2013. "Past Minds: Evolution, Cognition, and Biblical Studies." Pages 15–22 in *Mind, Morality and Magic: Cognitive Science Approaches to Biblical Studies*. Edited by István Czachesz and Risto Uro. Durham: Acumen.
May, Gerhard. 1994. *Creatio Ex Nihilo: The Doctrine of 'Creation Out of Nothing' in Early Christian Thought*. Translated by A. S. Worrall. London: T&T Clark.

May, Natalie Naomi. 2015. "Portable Sanctuaries and Their Evolution: The Biblical Tabernacle ('*ōhel mô'ēd*/*miškān*) and the Akkadian *qersu*." *Marbeh Ḥokmah: Studies in the Bible and the Ancient Near East in Loving Memory of Victor Avigdor Hurowitz*. Edited by S. Yona, E. L. Greenstein, M. I. Gruber, P. Machinist, and S. M. Paul. Winona Lake, IN: Eisenbrauns.

Mazar, Amihai. 2015. "Religious Practices and Cult Objects during the Iron Age IIA at Tel Reḥov and Their Implications Regarding Religion in Northern Israel." *HeBAI* 4.1: 25–55.

Mazar, Amihai, and Nava Panitz-Cohen. 2008. "To What God? Altars and a House Shine from Tel Reḥov Puzzle Archaeologists." *BAR* 34.4: 40–76.

McBride, Samuel Dean. 1969. "The Deuteronomic Name Theology." PhD diss. Harvard University.

McCall, Robin C. 2014. "The Body and Being of God in Ezekiel." *RE* 111.4: 376–89.

McCarter, P. Kyle. 1980. *1 Samuel*, AB. Garden City, NY: Doubleday.

McCauley, Robert N. 2011. *Why Religion Is Natural and Science Is Not*. Oxford: Oxford University Press.

———. 2014. "Putting Religious Ritual in its Place: On Some Ways Humans' Cognitive Predilections Influence the Locations and Shapes of Religious Rituals." Pages 144–64 in *Locating the Sacred: Theoretical Approaches to the Emplacement of Religion*. Edited by Claudia Moser and Cecelia Feldman. Oxford: Oxbow Books.

McCauley, Robert N., and E. Thomas Lawson. 2002. *Bringing Ritual to Mind: Psychological Foundations of Cultural Forms*. Cambridge: Cambridge University Press.

McClellan, Daniel. 2013. "'You Will Be Like the Gods': The Conceptualization of Deity in the Hebrew Bible in Cognitive Perspective." MA thesis, Trinity Western University.

———. 2017. "Cognitive Perspectives on Early Christology." *BibInt* 25.3–4: 647–62.

———. 2018. "The Gods-Complaint: Psalms 82 as a Psalm of Complaint." *JBL* 137.4: 833–51.

McConville, J. Gordon. 1979. "God's 'Name' and God's 'Glory.'" *TynBul* 30: 149–63.

McDowell, Catherine L. 2015. *The Image of God in the Garden of Eden: The Creation of Humankind in Genesis 2:5–3:24 in Light of* mīs pî pīt pî *and* wpt-r *Rituals of Mesopotamia and Ancient Egypt*. Winona Lake, IN: Eisenbrauns.

McKay, Ryan, and Harvey Whitehouse. 2016. "Religion Promotes a Love for Thy Neighbor: But How Big is the Neighbourhood?" *BBS* 39: 35–36.

McNamara, Rita Anne, Rebekah Senanayake, Aiyana K. Willard, and Joseph Henrich. 2021. "God's Mind on Morality." *EHS* 3:1–19.

McNinch, Timothy. 2021. "The Ark in 1 Samuel as Aniconic Overlay." Paper presented at the Annual Meeting of the Society of Biblical Literature. San Antonio, TX.

Meier, Samuel A. 1999a. "Angel of Yahweh מלאך יהוה." *DDD*, 53–59.

———. 1999b. *The Messenger in the Ancient Semitic World*. Atlanta: Scholar's Press.

Meltzoff, Andrew N. 2011. "Social Cognition and the Origins of Imitation, Empathy, and Theory of Mind." Pages 49–75 in *The Wiley-Blackwell Handbook of Childhood Cognitive Development. Second Edition*. Edited by Usha Goswami. Malden, MA: Wiley-Blackwell.

Meshel, Ze'ev, ed. 2012. *Kuntillet 'Ajrud (Ḥorvat Teman): An Iron Age II Religious Site on the Judah-Sinai Border.* Jerusalem: Israel Exploration Society.

Meskell, Lynn M. 2002. *Private Life in New Kingdom Egypt.* Princeton: Princeton University Press.

Meskell, Lynn M., and Rosemary A. Joyce. 2003. *Embodied Lives: Figuring Ancient Maya and Egyptian Experience.* London: Routledge.

Mesoudi, Alex. 2011. *Cultural Evolution: How Darwinian Theory can Explain Human Culture and Synthesize the Social Sciences.* Chicago: University of Chicago Press.

Mettinger, Tryggve N. D. 1982. *The Dethronement of Sabaoth: Studies in the Shem and Kabod Theologies.* Translated by F. H. Cryer. Lund: CWK Gleerup.

———. 1995. *No Graven Image? Israelite Iconism in Its Ancient Near Eastern Context.* Stockholm: Almqvist & Wiksell International, 1995.

Meyer, Sias. 2010. "Dating the Priestly Text in the Pre-exilic Period: Some Remarks about Anachronistic Slips and Other Obstacles." *VEE* 31.1: 1–6.

Meyers, Carol L. 2003. *The Tabernacle Menorah: A Synthetic Study of a Symbol from the Biblical Cult.* Piscataway, NJ: Gorgias Press, 2003.

Meyers, Eric M. 1970. "Secondary Burials in Palestine." *BA* 33.1: 1–29.

Middlemas, Jill. 2007. *The Templeless Age.* Louisville, KY: Westminster John Knox.

———. 2014. *The Divine Image: Prophetic Aniconic Rhetoric and Its Contribution to the Aniconism Debate.* FAT 74. Tübingen: Mohr Siebeck.

Mikkelsen, Henrik Hvenegaard. 2016. "Chaosmology: Shamanism and Personhood among the Bugkalot." *HJET* 6.1: 189–205.

Milgrom, Jacob. 1991. *Leviticus 1–16.* AB 3.1. New York: Doubleday.

———. 1999. "The Antiquity of the Priestly Source: A Reply to Joseph Blenkinsopp." *ZAW* 111.1: 10–22.

Miller, Jared L. 2004. *Studies in the Origins, Development and Interpretation of the Kizzuwatna Rituals.* Weisbaden: Harrassowitz Verlag.

Miller, Patrick D., Jr. 1973. *The Divine Warrior in Early Israel.* Cambridge, MA: Harvard University Press.

———. 1987. "Cosmology and World Order in the Old Testament: The Divine Council as Cosmic-Political Symbol." *HBT* 9.2: 53–78.

Miller, Patrick D., Jr., and J. J. M. Roberts. 2008. *The Hand of the Lord: A Reassessment of the "Ark Narrative" of 1 Samuel.* Baltimore: Johns Hopkins University Press, 1977. Repr. Atlanta, GA: Society of Biblical Literature.

Miller, Robert D. 2021. *Yahweh: Origin of a Desert God.* Göttingen: Vandenhoeck & Ruprecht.

Mithen, Steven. 1998. "The Supernatural Beings of Prehistory and the External Storage of Religious Ideas." Pages 97–106 in *Cognition and Material Culture: The Archaeology of Symbolic Storage.* Edited by Colin Renfrew and Chris Scarre. Cambridge: McDonald Institute for Archaeological Research.

Moberly, R. W. L. 2004. "How Appropriate Is 'Monotheism' as a Category for Biblical Interpretation." Pages 216–34 in *Early Jewish and Christian Monotheism.* Edited by Loren T. Stuckenbruck and Wendy E. S. North. London: T&T Clark.

Monroe, Lauren A. S. 2007. "Israelite, Moabite and Sabaean War-*ḥērem* Traditions and the Forging of National Identity: Reconsidering the Sabaean Text RES 3945 in Light of Biblical and Moabite Evidence." *VT* 57: 318–41.
Morgan, Jonathan. 2014. "Religion and Dual-Process Cognition: A Continuum of Styles or Distinct Types?" *RBB* 6.2: 1–18.
Morgan, David. 2018. *Images at Work: The Material Culture of Enchantment*. Oxford: Oxford University Press.
Morgenstern, Julian. 1939. "The Mythological Background of Psalm 82." *HUCA* 14.1: 29–126.
———. 1942–1943. "The Ark, the Ephod, and the 'Tent of Meeting.'" HUCA 17: 153–266.
Moriguchi, Yusuke, and Ikuko Shinohara. 2012. "My Neighbor: Children's Perception of Agency in Interaction with an Imaginary Agent." *PLoSONE* 7: 1–6.
Morrow, William. 2010. "'To Set the Name' in the Deuteronomic Centralization Formula: A Case of Cultural Hybridity." *JSS* 55.2: 365–83.
Mosko, Mark. 1992. "Motherless Sons: 'Divine Kings' and 'Partible Persons' in Melanesia and Polynesia." *Man* 27.4: 697–717.
———. 2010. "Partible Penitents: Dividual Personhood and Christian Practice in Melanesia and the West." *JRAI* 16.2: 215–40.
Moss, Candida. 2021. "New Discovery Highlights How Jews and Christians Were Once Naughty with Magic." *The Daily Beast*, June 13, 2021. http://thedailybeast.com/new-discovery-highlights-how-jews-and-christians-were-once-naughty-with-magic.
Muentener, Paul, and Laura Schulz. 2014. "Toddlers Infer Unobserved Causes for Spontaneous Events." *FiP* 5: 1–9.
Mullen, E. Theodore, Jr. 1980. *The Divine Council in Canaanite and Early Hebrew Literature*. Chico, CA: Scholars Press.
Müller, Reinhard. 2008. *Jahwe als Wettergott: Studien zur althebräischen Kultlyrik anhand ausgewählter Psalmen*. Berlin: de Gruyter.
Münger, Stefan. 2003. "Egyptian Stamp-Seal Amulets and Their Implications for the Chronology of the Early Iron Age." *TA* 30.1: 66–82.
Mylonopoulos, Joannis ed. 2010. *Divine Images and Human Imaginations in Ancient Greece and Rome*. Leiden: Brill.
Nakhai, Beth Alpert. 2015. "Where to Worship? Religion in Iron II Israel and Judah." Pages 90–101 in *Defining the Sacred: Approaches to the Archaeology of Religion in the Near East*. Edited by Nicola Laneri. Oxford: Oxbow Books.
Nasuti, Harry P. 1999. *Defining the Sacred Songs: Genre, Tradition and the Post-Critical Interpretation of the Psalms*. Sheffield: Sheffield Academic.
Neubert, Frank. 2016. *Die diskursive Konstitution von Religion*. Heidelberg: Springer VS.
Newsom, Carol A. 1992. "Angels." *ABD* 1.248–55.
———. 2010. "Pairing Research Questions and Theories of Genre: A Case Study of the Hodayot." *DSD* 17.3: 241–59.
———. 2020. "In Search of Cultural Models for Divine Spirit and Human Bodies." *VT* 70.1: 104–23.
Nichols, Ryan, Edward Slingerland, Kristoffer Laigaard Nielbo, Peter Kirby, and Carson Logan. 2020. "Supernatural Agents and Prosociality in Historical China: Micro-

Modeling the Cultural Evolution of Gods and Morality in Textual Corpora." *RBB* 11.1: 46–64.

Nickelsburg, George W. E., and James C. VanderKam. 2012. *1 Enoch: The Hermeneia Translation*. Minneapolis: Fortress.

Niditch, Susan. 2015. *The Responsive Self Personal Religion in Biblical Literature of the Neo-Babylonian and Persian Periods*. New Haven, CT: Yale University Press.

Niehoff, Maren R. 2005. "*Creatio ex Nihilo* Theology in *Genesis Rabbah* in Light of Christian Exegesis." *HTR* 99.1: 37–64.

Niehr, Herbert. 1997. "In Search of YHWH's Cult Statue in the First Temple." Pages 73–95 in *The Image and the Book: Iconic Cults, Aniconism, and the Rise of Book Religion in Israel and the Ancient Near East*. Edited by Karel van der Toorn. Leuven: Peeters.

———. 2014. "The Katumuwa Stele in the Context of Royal Mortuary Cult at Sam'al." Pages 57–60 in *In Remembrance of Me: Feasting with the Dead in the Ancient Middle East*. Edited by Virginia Rimmer Herrmann and J. David Schloen. Chicago: University of Chicago Press.

Nielsen, Kirsten. 1978. *Yahweh as Prosecutor and Judge: An Investigation of the Prophetic Lawsuit (Rîb Pattern)*. Sheffield: Sheffield Academic.

Nissinen, Martti. 2002. "Prophets and the Divine Council." Pages 4–19 in *Kein Land für sich allein: Studien zum Kulturkontact in Kanaan, Israel/Palästina und Ebirnâri für Manfred Weippert zum 65. Geburtstag*. Edited by U. Hübner and E. A. Knauf. Fribourg: Universitätsverlag; Göttingen: Vandenhoeck & Ruprecht.

———. 2004. "What Is Prophecy? An Ancient Near Eastern Perspective." Pages 17–37 in *Inspired Speech: Prophecy in the Ancient Near East. Essays in Honor of Herbert B. Huffmon*. Edited by John Kaltner and Louis Stulman. London: T&T Clark.

Nitzan, Bilhah. 1994. *Qumran Prayer and Religious Poetry*. Leiden: Brill.

Noegel, Scott B. 2015. "The Egyptian Origin of the Ark of the Covenant." Pages 223–42 in *Israel's Exodus in Transdisciplinary Perspective: Text, Archaeology, Culture, and Geoscience*. Edited by Thomas E. Levy, Thomas Schneider, and William H. C. Propp. Switzerland: Springer.

Nongbri, Brent. 2008. "Dislodging 'Embedded' Religion: A Brief Note on a Scholarly Trope." *Numen* 55.4: 440–60.

———. 2013. *Before Religion. A History of a Modern Concept*. New Haven, CT: Yale University Press.

———. 2018. *God's Library: The Archaeology of the Earliest Christian Manuscripts*. New Haven, CT: Yale University Press, 2018.

Norenzayan, Ara. 2013. *Big Gods: How Religion Transformed Cooperation and Conflict*. Princeton: Princeton University Press.

Norenzayan, Ara, Azim F. Shariff, Will M. Gervais, Aiyana K. Willard, Rita A. McNamara, Edward Slingerland, and Joseph Henrich. 2016. "The Cultural Evolution of Prosocial Religions." *BBS* 39: 1–65.

Nyord, Rune. 2009. *Breathing Flesh: Conceptions of the Body in the Ancient Egyptian Coffin Texts*. Copenhagen: Carsten Niebuhr Institute of Near Eastern Studies.

Oda, Ryo, Yuta Kato, and Kai Hiraishi. 2015. "The Watching-Eye Effect on Prosocial Lying." *EP* 13.3: 1–5.

Olyan, Saul M. 1993. *A Thousand Thousands Served Him: Exegesis and the Naming of Angels in Ancient Judaism*. Tübingen: Mohr Siebeck.

———. 2012. "Is Isaiah 40–55 Really Monotheistic?" *JANER* 12: 190–201.

———. 2018. "The Territoriality of YHWH in Biblical Texts." Pages 45–52 in *Strength to Strength: Essays in Appreciation of Shaye J. D. Cohen*. Edited by Michael L. Satlow. Providence, RI: Brown Judaic Studies.

Oppenheim, A. L. 1943. "Akkadian *pul(u)ḫ(t)u* and *melammu*." *JAOS* 63.1: 31–34.

———. 1977. *Ancient Mesopotamia: Portrait of a Dead Civilization*. Edited by Erica Reiner. Chicago: University of Chicago Press.

Orlov, Andrei A. 2017. *Yahoel and Metatron: Aural Apocalypticism and the Origins of Early Jewish Mysticism*. Tübingen: Mohr Siebeck.

Ornan, Tallay. 1993. "The Mesopotamian Influence on West Semitic Inscribed Seals: A Preference for the Depiction of Mortals." Pages 52–73 in *Studies in the Iconography of Northwest Semitic Inscribed Seals*. Edited by Benjamin Sass and Christoph Uehlinger. Göttingen: Vandenhoeck & Ruprecht.

———. 2004. "Idols and Symbols: Divine Representation in First Millennium Mesopotamian Art and Its Bearing on the Second Commandment." *TA* 31: 90–121.

———. 2005. *The Triumph of the Symbol: Pictorial Representations of Deities in Mesopotamia and the Biblical Image Ban*. Fribourg: Academic Press; Göttingen: Vandenhoeck & Ruprecht.

———. 2011. "'Let Baʻal Be Enthroned': The Date, Identification, and Function of a Bronze Statue from Hazor." *JNES* 70.2:253–80.

Otto, Rudolph. 1917. *Das Heilige: Über das Irrationale in der Idee des Göttlichen und sein Verhältnis zum Rationalen*. Breslau: Trewendt und Granier.

Pantoja, Jennifer Metten. 2017. *The Metaphor of the Divine as Planter of the People: Stinking Grapes or Pleasant Planting?* Leiden: Brill.

Pardee, Dennis. 2005. "On Psalm 29: Structure and Meaning." Pages 153–81 in *The Book of Psalms: Composition and Reception*. Edited by Peter W. Flint and Patrick D. Miller, Jr. Leiden: Brill.

———. 2009. "A New Aramaic Inscription from Zincirli." *BASOR* 356: 51–71.

Pardee, Dennis, and Nancy Pardee. 2009. "Gods of Glory Ought to Thunder: The Canaanite Matrix of Psalm 29." Pages 115–25 in *Psalm 29 through Time and Tradition*. Edited by Lowell K. Handy. Cambridge: James Clarke & Co.

Parker, Simon B. 1995. "The Beginning of the Reign of God—Psalm 82 as Myth and Liturgy." *RB* 102.4: 532–59.

———. 2006. "Divine Intercession in Judah?" *VT* 56.1:76–91.

Parmenter, Dorina Miller. 2009. "The Bible as Icon: Myths of the Divine Origins of Scripture." Pages 298–309 in *Jewish and Christian Scripture as Artifact and Canon*. Edited by Craig A. Evans and H. Daniel Zacharias. London: T&T Clark.

Parry, Donald W. 1996. "4QSam^a and the Tetragrammaton." Pages 106–25 in *Current Research and Technological Developments on the Dead Sea Scrolls*. Edited by Stephen D. Ricks and Donald W. Parry. Leiden: Brill.

Penney, Douglas L., and Michael O. Wise. 1994. "By the Power of Beelzebub: An Aramaic Incantation Formula from Qumran (4Q560)." *JBL* 113.4: 627–50.

Peppard, Michael. 2011. *The Son of God in the Roman World: Divine Sonship in its Social and Political Context.* Oxford: Oxford University Press.
Pereira, Vera, Luís Faísca, and Rodrigo de Sá-Saraiva. 2012. "Immortality of the Soul as an Intuitive Idea: Towards a Psychological Explanation of the Origins of Afterlife Beliefs." *JCC* 12.1–2: 101–27.
Pfattheicher, Stefan, Simon Schindler, and Laila Nockur. 2018. "On the Impact of Honesty-Humility and a Cue of Being Watched on Cheating Behavior." *JEP* 71: 159–74.
Philpot, Joshua M. 2013. "Exodus 34:29–35 and Moses' Shining Face." *BBR* 23.1: 1–11.
Pioske, Daniel D. 2018. *Memory in a Time of Prose: Studies in Epistemology, Hebrew Scribalism, and the Biblical Past.* Oxford: Oxford University Press.
Pitard, Wayne T. 2002. "Tombs and Offerings: Archaeological Data and Comparative Methodology in the Study of Death in Israel." Pages 145–68 in *Sacred Time, Sacred Place: Archaeology and the Religion of Israel.* Edited by Barry M. Gittlen. Winona Lake, IN: Eisenbrauns.
Pitts-Taylor, Victoria. 2016. *The Brain's Body: Neuroscience and Corporeal Politics.* Durham, NC: Duke University Press.
Platt, Verity. 2011. *Facing the Gods: Epiphany and Representation in Graeco-Roman Art, Literature and Religion.* Cambridge: Cambridge University Press.
Polaski, Donald C. 2007. "What Mean These Stones? Inscriptions, Textuality and Power in Persia and Yehud." Pages 37–48 in *Approaching Yehud: New Approaches to the Study of the Persian Period.* Edited by Jon L. Berquist. Atlanta, GA: Society of Biblical Literature.
Pongratz-Leisten, Beate. 2011. "Divine Agency and Astralization of the Gods in Ancient Mesopotamia." Pages 137–87 in *Reconsidering the Concept of Revolutionary Monotheism.* Edited by Beate Pongratz-Leisten. Winona Lake, IN: Eisenbrauns.
Pongratz-Leisten, Beate, and Karen Sonik. 2015. "Between Cognition and Culture: Theorizing the Materiality of Divine Agency in Cross-Cultural Perspective." Pages 3–69 in *The Materiality of Divine Agency.* Edited by Beate Pongratz-Leisten and Karen Sonik. Berlin: de Gruyter.
Pope, Marvin H. 1955. *El in the Ugaritic Texts.* Leiden: Brill.
Porter, Barbara N. 2009. *What Is a God? Anthropomorphic and Non-Anthropomorphic Aspects of Deity in Ancient Mesopotamia.* Edited by Barbara N. Porter. Winona Lake, IN: Eisenbrauns.
Preston, Jesse Lee, and Ryan S. Ritter. 2013. "Different Effects of Religion and God on Prosociality with the Ingroup and Outgroup." *PSPB* 39: 1471–83.
Preston, Jesse Lee, Ryan S. Ritter, and J. Ivan Hernandez. 2010. "Principles of Religious Prosociality: A Review and Reformulation." *SPPC* 4.8: 574–90.
Propp, William H. C. 1996. "The Priestly Source Recovered Intact?" *VT* 46.4: 458–78.
Purves, Dal, Amita Shimpi, and R. Beau Lotto. 1999. "An Empirical Explanation of the Cornsweet Effect." *JN* 19.19:8542–551.
Purzycki, Benjamin Grant. 2013. "The Minds of Gods: A Comparative Study of Supernatural Agency." *Cognition* 129: 163–79.
Purzycki, Benjamin Grant, Daniel N. Finkel, John Shaver, Nathan Wales, Adam Cohen, and Richard Sosis. 2012. "What Does God Know? Supernatural Agents' Access to Socially Strategic and Non-Strategic Information." *CogSci* 36.5: 846–69.

Purzycki, Benjamin Grant, Omar Sultan Haque, and Richard Sosis. 2014. "Extending Evolutionary Accounts of Religion beyond the Mind: Religions as Adaptive Systems." Pages 74–91 in *Evolution, Religion, and Cognitive Science: Critical and Constructive Essays*. Edited by Fraser Watts and Léon P. Turner. Oxford: Oxford University Press.

Purzycki, Benjamin Grant, and Aiyana K. Willard. 2016. "MCI Theory: A Critical Discussion." *RBB* 6.3: 207–48.

Pyysiäinen, Ilkka. 2009. *Supernatural Agents: Why We Believe in Souls, Gods, and Buddhas*. Oxford: Oxford University Press.

———. 2014. "God Is Great—But Not Necessary? On Ara Norenzayan, *Big Gods* (2013)." *Religion* 44.4: 638–44.

Quirke, Stephen. 2015. *Exploring Religion in Ancient Egypt*. Malden, MA: Wiley-Blackwell.

Radner, Karen. 2005. *Die Macht des Namens: Altorientalische Strategien zur Selbsterhaltung*. Wiesbaden: Harrassowitz Verlag.

Rahlfs, Alfred, and Robert Hanhart. 2006. *Septuaginta. Editio altera*. Stuttgart: Deutsche Bibelgesellschaft.

Rahmouni, Aicha. 2008. *Divine Epithets in the Ugaritic Alphabetic Texts*. Translated by J. N. Ford. Leiden: Brill.

Ramachandran, Vilayanur S. 2011. *The Tell-Tale Brain: A Neuroscientist's Quest for What Makes Us Human*. New York: Norton.

Rasmussen, Susan J. 1995. *Spirit Possession and Personhood among the Kel Ewey Tuareg*. Cambridge: Cambridge University Press.

Ready, Jonathan L. 2012. "Zeus, Ancient Near Eastern Notions of Divine Incomparability, and Similes in the Homeric Epics." *ClassAnt* 31.1: 56–91.

Rechenmacher, Hans. 1997. *"Ausser mir gibt es keinen Gott!": Eine Sprach- und Literaturwissenschaft-liche Studie zur Ausschliesslichkeitsformel*. St. Ottilien: EOS Verlag.

Rendsburg, Gary A. *Linguistic Evidence for the Northern Origin of Selected Psalms*. Atlanta, GA: Scholars Press, 1990.

———. 2013. "Foreigner Speech: Biblical Hebrew." *EHLL* 1.903–04.

Rendtorff, Rolf. 1976. *Das überlieferungsgeschichtliche Problem des Pentateuch*. Berlin: de Gruyter.

———. 1977. "The 'Yahwist' as Theologian? The Dilemma of Pentateuchal Criticism." *JSOT* 3: 2–10.

Renehan, R. 1980. "On the Greek Origins of the Concepts Incorporeality and Immateriality." *GRBS* 21.2: 105–38.

Reynolds, Fances S. 2002. "Describing the Body of a God." Pages 215–27 in *Mining the Archives: Festschrift for Christopher Walker on the Occasion of His Sixtieth Birthday, 4 October 2002*. Edited by Cornelia Wunsch. Dresden: Islet.

Richardson, Seth. 2012. "The Hypercoherent Icon: Knowledge, Rationalization, and Disenchantment at Nineveh." Pages 231–58 in *Iconoclasm and Text Destruction in the Ancient Near East and Beyond*. Edited by Natalie Neomi May. Chicago: The Oriental Institute of the University of Chicago.

Richerson Peter, Ryan Baldini, Adrian V. Bell, Kathryn Demps, Karl Frost, Vicken Hillis, Sarah Matthew, Emily K. Newton, Nicole Naar, Lesley Newson, Cody Ross, Paul E.

Smaldino, Timothy M. Waring, and Matthew Zefferman. 2016. "Cultural Group Selection Plays an Essential Role in Explaining Human Cooperation: A Sketch of the Evidence." *BBS* 39: 1–68.

Richert, Rebekah A., and Paul L. Harris. 2008. "Dualism Revisited: Body vs. Mind vs. Soul." *JCC* 8.1: 99–115.

Richter, Sandra L. 2002. *The Deuteronomistic History and the Name Theology:* lᵉšakkēn šᵉmô šām *in the Bible and the Ancient Near East.* Berlin: de Gruyter.

———. 2007. "The Place of the Name in Deuteronomy." *VT* 57: 342–66.

Ringgren, Helmer. 1974. "אלהים *ᵉlōhîm.*" *TDOT* 1:267–84.

Rizzolatti, Giacomo, and Laila Craighero. 2004. "The Mirror-Neuron System." *ARN* 27: 169–92.

Roazzi, Maira, Melanie Nyhof, and Carl Johnson. 2013. "Mind, Soul and Spirit: Conceptions of Immaterial Identity in Different Cultures." *IJPsychRel* 23: 75–86.

Roes, Frans L., and Michel Raymond. 2003. "Belief in Moralizing Gods." *EHB* 24.2: 126–35.

Rogers, Robert William. 1912. *Cuneiform Parallels to the Old Testament.* New York: Eaton & Mains.

Rosch, Eleanor. 1973. "On the Internal Structure of Perceptual and Semantic Categories." Pages 111–44 in *CD and the Acquisition of Language.* Edited by T. E. Moore. New York: Academic Press.

———. 1975. "Cognitive Representations of Semantic Categories." *JEPG* 104.3: 192–233.

Roth, Ann Macy. 1992. "The *Psš-kf* and the 'Opening of the Mouth' Ceremony: A Ritual of Birth and Rebirth." *JEA* 78.1: 113–47.

Rothstein, David. 2021. "The Tent of Meeting and the Missing Ark: The Chronicler's View." *VT* 1–12.

Routledge, Bruce. 1997. "Learning to Love the King: Urbanism and the State in Iron Age Moab." Pages 130–44 in *Urbanism in Antiquity: From Mesopotamia to Crete.* Edited by Walter E. Aufrecht, Neil A. Mirau, and Steven W. Gauley. Sheffield: Sheffield Academic Press.

Römer, Thomas C. 2006. "The Elusive Yahwist: A Short History of Research." Pages 9–27 in *A Farewell to the Yahwist? The Composition of the Pentateuch in Recent European Interpretation.* Edited by Thomas B. Dozeman and Konrad Schmid. SymS 34. Atlanta, GA: Society of Biblical Literature.

———. 2007. *The So-Called Deuteronomistic History: A Sociological, Historical and Literary Introduction.* London: T&T Clark.

———. 2019. "L'arche de Yhwh: de la guerre à l'alliance." *ETR* 94.1:95–108.

Rösel, Martin. 2007. "The Reading and Translation of the Divine Name in the Masoretic Tradition and the Greek Pentateuch." *JSOT* 31.4: 411–28.

Sabar, Shalom. 2009. "Torah and Magic: The Torah Scroll and Its Appurtenances as Magical Objects in Traditional Jewish Culture." *EJJS* 3.1: 135–70.

Saeed, John I. 2003. *Semantics. Second Edition.* Malden, Massachusetts: Blackwell.

Saler, Benson. 2000. *Conceptualizing Religion: Immanent Anthropologists, Transcendent Natives, and Unbounded Categories.* New York: Berghahn Books.

Sanders, Paul. 1996. *The Provenance of Deuteronomy 32.* Leiden: Brill.

Sanders, Seth. 2008. "Writing and Early Iron Age Israel: Before National Scripts, Beyond Nations and States." Pages 97–112 in *Literate Culture and Tenth-Century Canaan: The Tel Zayit Abecedary in Context*. Edited by Ron E. Tappy and P. Kyle McCarter, Jr. Winona Lake, IN: Eisenbrauns.

———. 2010. *The Invention of Hebrew*. Urbana, IL: University of Illinois.

———. 2012. "Naming the Dead: Funerary Writing and Historical Change in the Iron Age Levant." *MAARAV* 19.1–2: 11–36.

———. 2015. "When the Personal Becomes Political: An Onomastic Perspective on the Rise of Yahwism." *HeBAI* 4.1: 78–105.

———. 2017. "Why Prophecy Became a Biblical Genre. First Isaiah as an Instance of Ancient Near Eastern Text-Building." *HeBAI* 1.6:26–52.

———. 2019. "Words, Things, and Death: The Rise of Iron Age Literary Monuments." Pages 327–49 in *Language and Religion*. Edited by Robert Yelle, Courtney Handman, and Christopher Lehrich. Berlin: de Gruyter.

Sanderson, Stephen K., and Wesley W. Roberts. 2008. "The Evolutionary Forms of the Religious Life: A Cross-Cultural, Quantitative Analysis." *AA* 110.4: 454–66.

Savran, George W. 2005. *Encountering the Divine: Theophany in Biblical Narrative*. London: T&T Clark.

Scanlon, Lauren A., Andrew Lobb, Jamshid J. Tehrani, and Jeremy R. Kendal. 2019. "Unknotting the Interactive Effects of Learning Processes on Cultural Evolutionary Dynamics." *EHS* 1:1–13. doi:10.1017/ehs.2019.17.

Schaper, Joachim. 2007. "The Living Word Engraved in Stone: The Interrelationship of the Oral and the Written and the Culture of Memory in the Books of Deuteronomy and Joshua." Pages 9–23 in *Memory in the Bible and Antiquity: The Fifth Durham-Tübingen Research Symposium (Durham, September 2004)*. Edited by Stephen C. Barton, Loren T. Stuckenbruck, and Benjamin G. Wold. Tübingen: Mohr Siebeck.

———. 2019. *Media and Monotheism: Presence, Representation, and Abstraction in Ancient Judah*. Tübingen: Mohr Siebeck.

Scheyhing, Nicola. 2018. "Fossilising the Holy. Aniconic Standing Stones of the Near East." Pages 95–112 in *Sacred Space: Contributions to the Archaeology of Belief*. Edited by Louis Daniel Nebelsick, Joanna Wawrzeniuk, and Katarzyna Zeman-Wiśniewska. Warsaw: University of Warsaw.

Schleicher, Marianne. 2010. "Accounts of a Dying Scroll: On Jewish Handling of Sacred Texts in Need of Restoration or Disposal." Pages 11–29 in *The Death of Sacred Texts: Ritual Disposal and Renovation of Texts in World Religions*. Edited by Kristina Myrvold. London: Routledge.

Schmid, Konrad. 2010. *Genesis and the Moses Story: Israel's Dual Origins in the Hebrew Bible*. Winona Lake, IN: Eisenbrauns.

———. 2012a. "Genesis and Exodus as Two Formerly Independent Traditions of Origins for Ancient Israel." *Biblica* 93.2: 187–208.

———. 2012b. "The Canon and the Cult: The Emergence of Book Religion in Ancient Israel and the Gradual Sublimation of the Temple Cult." *JBL* 131.2: 289–305.

———. "The Biblical Writings in the Late Eighth Century BCE." 2018. Pages 489–501 in *Archaeology and History of Eighth-Century Judah*. Edited by Zev I. Farber and Jacob L. Wright. ANEM 23. Atlanta, GA: SBL Press.

Schmidt, Brian B. 2016. *The Materiality of Power: Explorations in the Social History of Early Israelite Magic.* Tübingen: Mohr Siebeck.

Schmitt, Rüdiger. 2008. "The Problem of Magic and Monotheism in the Book of Leviticus." *JHS* 8.11: 2–12.

———. 2009. "'And Jacob Set Up a Pillar at Her Grave …': Material Memorials and Landmarks in the Old Testament." Pages 389–403 in *The Land of Israel in Bible, History, and Theology: Studies in Honour of Ed Noort.* Edited by J. T. A. G. M. Ruiten and Cor Vos. Leiden: Brill.

———. 2012. "Care for the Dead in the Context of the Household and Family." Pages 429–73 in *Family and Household Religion in Ancient Israel and the Levant.* Edited by Rainer Albertz and Rüdiger Schmitt. Winona Lake, IN: Eisenbrauns.

Schniedewind, William M. 2003. "The Evolution of Name Theology." Pages 228–39 in *The Chronicler as Theologian: Essays in Honor of Ralph W. Klein.* Edited by M. Patrick Graham, Steven L. McKenzie, and Gary N. Knoppers. London: T&T Clark.

———. 2004. *How the Bible Became a Book: The Textualization of Ancient Israel.* Cambridge: Cambridge University Press, 2004.

———. 2009. "Calling God Names: An Inner-Biblical Approach to the Tetragrammaton." Pages 74–86 in *Scriptural Exegesis: The Shapes of Culture and the Religious Imagination. Essays in Honour of Michael Fishbane.* Edited by Deborah A. Green and Laura S. Lieber. Oxford: Oxford University Press.

Scholem, Gershon. 2007. "Golem." *EncJud* 7:735–37.

Schroer, Silvia. 1983. "Zur Deutung der Hand unter der Grabinschrift von Chirbet el Qôm." *UF* 15: 191–99.

Schroer, Silvia, and Thomas Staubli. 2001. *Body Symbolism in the Bible.* Translated by Linda M. Maloney. Collegeville, MN: The Liturgical Press.

Schwemer, Daniel. 2008a. "The Storm-Gods of the Ancient Near East: Summary, Synthesis, Recent Studies. Part I." *JANER* 7.2: 121–68.

———. 2008b. "The Storm-Gods of the Ancient Near East: Summary, Synthesis, Recent Studies. Part II." *JANER* 8.1: 1–44.

Schjødt, Uffe. 2019. "Predictive Coding in the Study of Religion: A Believer's Testimony." Pages 364–79 in *Evolution, Cognition, and the History of Religion: A New Synthesis. Festschrift in Honour of Armin W. Geertz.* Edited by Anders Klostergaard Petersen, Ingvild Sælid Gilhus, Luther H. Martin, Jeppe Sinding Jensen, and Jesper Sørensen. Leiden: Brill.

Scurlock, JoAnn. 2002. "Soul Emplacements in Ancient Mesopotamian Funerary Rituals." Pages 1–6 in *Magic and Divination in the Ancient World.* Edited by Leda Ciraolo and Jonathan Siedel. Leiden: Brill.

Selz, Gebhard J. 2008. "The Divine Prototypes." Pages 13–31 in *Religion and Power: Divine Kingship in the Ancient World and Beyond.* Edited by Nicole Brisch. Chicago: The Oriental Institute of the University of Chicago.

Seow, C. L., and Robert K. Ritner. 2003. *Prophets and Prophecy in the Ancient Near East.* Atlanta, GA: Society of Biblical Literature.

Shaked, Shaul, James Nathan Ford, and Siam Bhayro. 2013. *Aramaic Bowl Spells: Jewish Babylonian Aramaic Bowls. Volume One.* Leiden: Brill.

Sharifian, Farzad, René Dirven, Ning Yu, and Susanne Niemeier, eds. 2008. *Culture, Body, and Language: Conceptualizations of Internal Body Organs across Cultures and Languages*. Berlin: de Gruyter.
Shaw, Frank Edward. 2002. "The Earliest Non-Mystical Use of Jewish Ιαω." PhD diss. University of Cincinnati.
Shennan, Stephen. 2004. "An Evolutionary Perspective on Agency in Archaeology." Pages 19–32 in *Agency Uncovered: Archaeological Perspectives on Social Agency, Power, and Being Human*. Edited by Andrew Gardner. London: UCL Press.
Shults, LeRon. 2010. "Spiritual Engtanglement: Transforming religious symbols at Çatalhöyük." Pages 73–98 in *Religion in the Emergence of Civilization: Çatalhöyük as a Case Study*. Edited by Ian Hodder. Cambridge: Cambridge University Press.
Shults, F. LeRon, and Wesley J. Wildman. 2018. "Simulating Religious Entanglement and Social Investment in the Neolithic." Pages 33–63 in *Religion, History and Place in the Origin of Settled Life*. Edited by Ian Hodder. Boulder, CO: University Press of Colorado.
Silver, Morris. 1995. "Prophets and Markets Revisited." Pages 179–98 in *Social Justice in the Ancient World*. Edited by K. D. Irani and Morris Silver. Westport, CT: Greenwood.
Singletary, Jennifer Elizabeth. 2021. "Incomparable or Prototypical" Yahweh among the Gods in the Hebrew Bible." Pages 401–15 in *With the Loyal You Show Yourself Loyal: Essays on Relationships in the Hebrew Bible in Honor of Saul M. Olyan*. Edited by T. M. Lemos, Jordan D. Rosenblum, Karen B. Stern, and Debra Scoggins Ballentine. Atlanta, GA: SBL Press.
Slingerland, Edward, Joseph Henrich, and Ara Norenzayan. 2010. "The Evolution of Prosocial Religions." Pages 335–48 in *Cultural Evolution: Society, Technology, Language, and Religion*. Edited by Peter J. Richerson and Morten H. Christiansen. Cambridge, MA: MIT Press.
Slingerland, Edward, and Maciej Chudek. 2011. "The Prevalence of Mind-Body Dualism in Early China." *CogSci* 35: 997–1007.
Smelik, Willem F. 1999. "The Rabbinic Reception of Early Bible Translations as Holy Writings and Oral Torah." *JAB* 1: 249–72.
Smith, Jonathan Z. 1990. *Drudgery Divine: On Comparison of Early Christianities and the Religions of Late Antiquity*. Chicago: The University of Chicago Press.
Smith, Mark S. 1990. *The Early History of God: Yahweh and the Other Deities in Ancient Israel*. San Francisco: HarperCollins Publishers.
———. 1994. *Introduction with Text, Translation and Commentary of KTU 1.1–1.2*. Vol. 1. *The Ugaritic Baal Cycle:* Leiden: Brill.
———. 1998. "The Heart and Innards in Israelite Emotional Expressions: Notes from Anthropology and Psychobiology." *JBL* 117.3: 427–36.
———. 2001. *The Origins of Biblical Monotheism: Israel's Polytheistic background and the Ugaritic Texts*. Oxford: Oxford University Press.
———. 2002. *The Early History of God: Yahweh and the Other Deities in Ancient Israel*. Second Edition. Grand Rapids, MI: Eerdmans; Dearborn, MI: Dove Booksellers.
———. 2004a. *The Memoirs of God: History, Memory, and the Experience of the Divine in Ancient Israel*. Minneapolis, MN: Fortress.

———. 2004b. "The Polemic of Biblical Monotheism: Outsider Context and Insider Referentiality in Second Isaiah." Pages 208–22 in *Religious Polemics in Context: Papers Presented to the Second International Conference of the Leiden Institute for the Study of Religions (LISOR) Held at Leiden, 27–28 April 2000*. Edited by T. L. Hettema and A. van der Kooij. Assen, The Netherlands: Van Gorcum.

———. 2008. *God in Translation: Deities in Cross-Cultural Discourse in the Biblical World*. Tübingen: Mohr Siebeck.

———. 2017. "Yhwh's Original Character: Questions about an Unknown God." Pages 23–43 in *The Origins of Yahwism*. Edited by Jürgen van Oorschot and Markus Witte. Berlin: de Gruyter.

Smith, Mark S., and Wayne T. Pitard. 2009. *Introduction with Text, Translation and Commentary of KTU/CAT 1.3–1.4*. Vol. 2 of *The Ugaritic Baal Cycle*. Leiden: Brill.

Smoak, Jeremy. 2010. "Amuletic Inscriptions and the Background of YHWH as Guardian and Protector in Psalm 12." *VT* 60.3: 421–32.

———. 2016. *The Priestly Blessing in Inscription and Scripture: The Early History of Numbers 6:24–26*. Oxford: Oxford University Press.

———. 2017. "From Temple to Text: Text as Ritual Space and the Composition of Numbers 6:24–26." *JHS* 17.2: 1–26.

———. 2018. "Words Unseen: The Power of Hidden Writing." *BAR* 44.1:53–59.

———. 2019. "Wearing Divine Words: In Life and Death." *MR* 15.4: 433–55.

Sommer, Benjamin D. 2009. *The Bodies of God and the World of Ancient Israel*. Cambridge: Cambridge University Press.

Sonik, Karen. 2015. "Divine (Re-)Presentation: Authoritative Images and a Pictorial Stream of Tradition in Mesopotamia." Pages 142–93 in *The Materiality of Divine Agency*. Edited by Beate Pongratz-Leisten and Karen Sonik. Berlin: de Gruyter.

Sosis, Richard, Howard C. Kress, and James S. Boster. 2007. "Scars for War: Evaluating Alternative Signaling Explanations for Cross-Cultural Variance in Ritual Costs." *EHB* 28.4: 234–47.

Speiser, E. A., trans. 1969. *Epic of Gilgamesh*. ANET, 72–99.

Stagnaro, Michael N., and David G. Rand. 2021. "The Coevolution of Religious Belief and Intuitive Cognitive Style via Individual-Level Selection." Pages 153–73 in *The Oxford Handbook of Evolutionary Psychology and Religion*. Edited by James R. Liddle and Todd K. Shackelford. Oxford: Oxford University Press.

Stahl, Michael J. 2021. *The "God of Israel" in History and Tradition*. Leiden: Brill.

Stark, Thom. 2011. *The Human Faces of God: What Scripture Reveals When It Gets God Wrong (and Why Inerrancy Tries to Hide It)*. Eugene, OR: Wipf & Stock.

Stavrakopoulou, Francesca. 2010. *The Land of Our Fathers: The Roles of Ancestor Veneration in Biblical Land Claims*. New York: T&T Clark.

———. 2013. "Materialist Reading: Materialism, Materiality, and Biblical Cults of Writing." Pages 223–42 in *Biblical Interpretation and Method: Essays in Honour of John Barton*. Edited by Katharine J. Dell and Paul M. Joyce. Oxford: Oxford University Press.

———. 2016. "Religion at Home: The Materiality of Practice." Pages 347–65 in *The Wiley Blackwell Companion to Ancient Israel*. Edited by Susan Niditch. West Sussex: John Wiley & Sons.

———. 2021. *God: An Anatomy*. London: Picador.
Stein, Peter. 2019. "Gottesname und Genitivattribut?" *ZAW* 131.1: 1–27.
Steiner, Richard C. 2015. *Disembodied Souls: The Nefesh in Israel and Kindred Spirits in the Ancient Near East, with an Appendix on the Katumuwa Inscription*. Atlanta, GA: SBL Press.
Steinert, Ulrike. 2012. *Aspekte des Menschseins im Alten Mesopotamien: Eine Studie zu Person und Identität im 2. Und 1. Jt. V. Chr*. Leiden: Brill.
Stern, Philip D. 1991. *The Biblical Ḥerem: A Window on Israel's Religious Experience*. Atlanta, GA: Scholars Press.
Stol, Marten. 1999. "Psychosomatic Suffering in Ancient Mesopotamia." Pages 57–68 in *Mesopotamian Magic: Textual, Historical, and Interpretative Perspectives*. Edited by Tzvi Abusch and Karel van der Toorn. Groningen: STYX Publications.
Stowers, Stanley. 2021. "What Is the Relation of God to the Ghost That Saul Did Not See?" 385–99 in *With the Loyal You Show Yourself Loyal: Essays on Relationships in the Hebrew Bible in Honor of Saul M. Olyan*. Edited by T. M. Lemos, Jordan D. Rosenblum, Karen B. Stern, and Debra Scoggins Ballentine. Atlanta, GA: SBL Press.
Stökl, Jonathan. 2012. *Prophecy in the Ancient Near East: A Philological and Sociological Comparison*. Leiden: Brill.
Stökl, Jonathan, and Corrine L. Carvalho, eds. 2013. *Prophets Male and Female: Gender and. Prophecy in the Hebrew Bible, the Eastern Mediterranean, and the Ancient Near East*. Atlanta, GA: Society of Biblical Literature.
Strathern, Marilyn. 1988. *The Gender of the Gift: Problems with Women and Problems with Society in Melanesia* . Berkeley: University of California Press.
Stroumsa, Guy G. 2010. *A New Science: The Discovery of Religion in the Age of Reason*. Cambridge, MA: Harvard University Press.
———. 2021. *The Idea of Semitic Monotheism: The Rise and Fall of a Scholarly Myth*. Oxford: Oxford University Press.
Struble, Eudora J., and Virginia Rimmer Herrmann. 2009. "An Eternal Feast at Sam'al: The New Iron Age Mortuary Stele from Zincirli in Context." *BASOR* 356: 15–49.
Stuckenbruck, Loren T. 1995. *Angel Veneration and Christology*. Tübingen: Mohr Siebeck.
Suriano, Matthew J. 2014. "Breaking Bread with the Dead: Katumuwa's Stele, Hosea 9:4, and the Early History of the Soul." *JAOS* 134.3: 385–405.
———. 2018. *A History of Death in the Hebrew Bible*. Oxford: Oxford University Press.
Taggar-Cohen, Ada. 2013. "Concept of the Divine in Hittite Culture and the Hebrew Bible: Expression of the Divine." *JISMOR* 9: 29–50.
Tate, Marvin. 1990. *Psalms 51–100, Volume 2, Word Biblical Commentary*. Dallas: Word Books.
Tattersall, Ian. 2009. "Language and the Origin of Symbolic Thought." Pages 109–16 in *Cognitive Archaeology and Human Evolution*. Edited by Sophie A. de Beaune, Frederick L. Coolidge, and Thomas Wynn. Cambridge: Cambridge University Press.
Taylor, John. 2002. *Cognitive Grammar*. Oxford: Oxford University Press.
———. 2003. *Linguistic Categorization. Third Edition*. Oxford: Oxford University Press.
Taylor, John H. 2001. *Death and the Afterlife in Ancient Egypt*. Chicago: University of Chicago Press.

Teinz, Katharina. 2012. "How to Become an Ancestor—Some Thoughts." Pages 235–44 in *(Re-) Constructing Funerary Rituals in the Ancient Near East*. Edited by Peter Pfälzner, Herbert Niehr, Ernst Pernucka, and Anne Wissing. Weisbaden: Harrassowitz.

Tercatin, Rossella. 2021. "Jewish Amulet against 'Evil Eye' Offers Insight into Talmudic Israel Life." *The Jerusalem Post*, May 26, 2021, http://jpost.com/archaeology/amulet-against-evil-eye-offers-look-at-jewish-life-in-talmudic-israel-669202.

Thomas, Ryan. 2016. "The Identity of the Standing Figures on Pithos A from Kuntillet 'Ajrud: A Reassessment." *JANER* 16: 121–91.

———. 2017. "The Meaning of *asherah* in Hebrew Inscriptions." *Semitica* 59: 157–218.

———. 2018. "אלקנהארץ: Creator, Begetter, or Owner of the Earth." *UF* 48: 451–521.

Tigay, Jeffrey H. 2007. "The Priestly Reminder Stones and Ancient Near Eastern Votive Practices." Pages 339–55 in *Shai le-Sara Japhet: Studies in the Bible, Its Exegesis and Its Language*. Edited by Moshé Bar-Asher, Dalit Rom-Shiloni, Emanuel Tov, and Nilil Wazana. Jerusalem: The Bialik Institute, 2007 [Hebrew].

———. 2017. "'To Place His Name There': Deuteronomy's Concept of God Placing His Name in the Temple." Pages 17–26 in *"Now It Happened in Those Days": Studies in Biblical Assyrian, and Other Ancient Near Eastern Historiography Presented to Mordechai Cogan on His 75th Birthday. Volume 1*. Edited by Amitai Baruchi-Unna, Tova Forti, Shmuel Aḥituv, Israel Aph'al, and Jeffrey H. Tigay. Winona Lake, IN: Eisenbrauns.

Tilford, Nicole L. 2017. *Sensing World, Sensing Wisdom: The Cognitive Foundations of Biblical Metaphors*. Atlanta, GA: SBL Press.

Tov, Emanuel. 2004. *Scribal Practices and Approaches Reflected in the Texts Found in the Judean Desert*. Leiden: Brill.

———. 2012. *The Textual Criticism of the Hebrew Bible*. 3rd ed. Rev. and exp. Minneapolis, MN: Fortress.

Tropper, Josef. 2017. "The Divine Name *Yahwa*." Pages 1–21 in *The Origins of Yahwism*. Edited by Jürgen van Oorschot and Markus Witte. Berlin: de Gruyter.

Tsevat, Matitiahu. 1969. "God and the Gods in Assembly: An Interpretation of Psalm 82." *HUCA* 40: 123–37.

Tsoraki, Christina. 2018. "The Ritualization of Daily Practice." Pages 238–62 in *Religion, History and Place in the Origin of Settled Life*. Edited by Ian Hodder. Boulder, CO: University Press of Colorado.

Tsumura, David Toshio. 2005. *Creation and Destruction: A Reappraisal of the Chaoskampf Theory in the Old Testament*. Winona Lake, IN: Eisenbrauns.

———. 2015. "The Creation Motif in Psalm 74:12–14? A Reappraisal of the Theory of the Dragon Myth." *JBL* 134.3: 547–55.

Tuschling, R. M. M. 2007. *Angels and Orthodoxy: A Study in their Development in Syria and Palestine from the Qumran Texts to Ephrem the Syrian*. Tübingen: Mohr Siebeck.

Tuzin, Donald. 2001. *Social Complexity in the Making: A Case Study among the Arapesh of New Guinea*. New York: Routledge.

Uehlinger, Christoph. 1993. "Northwest Semitic Inscribed Seals, Iconography and Syro-Palestinian Religions of Iron Age II: Some Afterthoughts and Conclusions." Pages

257–88 in *Studies in the Iconography of Northwest Semitic Inscribed Seals*. Edited by Benjamin Sass and Christoph Uehlinger. Göttingen: Vandenhoeck & Ruprecht.

———. 1997. "Anthropomorphic Cult Statuary in Iron Age Palestine and the Search for Yahweh's Cult Image." Pages 97–155 in *The Image and the Book: Iconic Cults, Aniconism, and the Rise of Book Religion in Israel and the Ancient Near East*. Edited by Karel van der Toorn. Leuven: Peeters.

Unzueta, Miguel M., and Brian S. Lowery. 2008. "Defining Racism Safely: The Role of Self-Image Maintenance on White Americans' Conceptions of Racism." *JESP* 44.6: 1491–97.

Uro, Risto. 2013. "From Corpse Impurity to Relic Veneration: New Light from Cognitive and Psychological Studies." Pages 180–96 in *Mind, Morality and Magic: Cognitive Science Approaches in Biblical Studies*. Edited by István Czachesz and Risto Uro. London: Routledge.

Van der Toorn, Karel. 1990. "The Nature of the Biblical Teraphim in the Light of the Cuneiform Evidence." *CBQ* 52.2: 203–22.

———. 1996. *Family Religion in Babylonia, Syria and Israel: Continuity and Change in the Forms of Religious Life*. Leiden: Brill.

———. 1999a. "God (I) אלהים." *DDD*, 352–65.

———. 1999b. "Nahor." *DDD*, 610.

———. 2007. *Scribal Culture and the Making of the Hebrew Bible*. Cambridge, MA: Harvard University Press.

Van der Woude, A. S. 1963/1964. "De Mal'ak Jahweh: Een Godsbode." *NTT* 18: 1–13.

Van Elk, Michiel, and André Aleman. 2017. "Brain Mechanisms in Religion and Spirituality: An Integrative Predictive Processing Framework." *NBR* 73: 359–78.

Van Koppen, Frans, and Karel van der Toorn. 1999b. "Holy One קדוש." *DDD*, 415–18.

Van Seters, John. 2003. "Review of *The Deuteronomistic History and the Name Theology*." *JAOS* 1233.4: 871–72.

Van Wolde, Ellen, ed. 2003. *Job 28: Cognition in Context*. Leiden: Brill.

———. 2005. "Cognitive Linguistics and Its Application to Genesis 28:10–22." Pages 125–48 in *One Text, A Thousand Methods: Studies in Memory of Sjef van Tilborg*. Edited by Patrick Chatelion Counet and Ulrich Berges. Leiden: Brill.

———. 2007. "Cognitive Linguistics and the Hebrew Bible. Illustrated with a Study of Job 28 and Job 38." Pages 247–77 in *The Professorship of Semitic Languages at Uppsala University 400 Years. Jubilee Volume from a Symposium Held at the University Hall, 21–23 September 2005*. Edited by Bo Isaksson, Mats Eskhult, and Gail Ramseay. Uppsala: Uppsala University.

———. 2009a. *Reframing Biblical Studies: When Language and Text Meet Culture, Cognition, and Context*. Winona Lake, IN: Eisenbrauns.

———. 2009b. "Why the Verb ברא Does Not Mean 'to Create' in Genesis 1.1–2.4a." *JSOT* 34.1: 3–23.

———. 2013. "Cognitive Linguistics: A Cognitive Linguistic Study of the Concept of Defilement in Ezekiel 22:1–16." Pages 257–71 in *Biblical Interpretation and Method: Essays in Honour of John Barton*. Edited by Katharine J. Dell and Paul M. Joyce. Oxford: Oxford University Press.

Vanhoozer, Kevin J. 1997. "Does the Trinity Belong in a Theology of Religions? On Angling in the Rubicon and the 'Identity' of God." Pages 41–71 in *The Trinity in a Pluralistic Age*. Edited by Kevin J. Vanhoozer. Grand Rapids, MI: Eerdmans.

Verderame, Lorenzo. 2017. "Demons at Work in Ancient Mesopotamia." Pages 61–78 in *Demons and Illness from Antiquity to the Early-Modern Period*. Edited by Siam Bhayro and Catherine Rider. Leiden: Brill.

Vermeulen, Floris Nicolas. 2010. "Egyptian Religious Symbols in Judah and Israel from 900 B.C.E. to 587 B.C.E.: A Study of Seal Iconography." PhD diss. University of South Africa.

Violi, Patrizia. 2000. "Prototypicality, Typicality, and Context." Pages 103–22 in *Meaning and Cognition: A Multidisciplinary Approach*. Edited by Liliana Albertazzi. Amsterdam: Benjamins.

Von Heijne, Camille Hélena. 2010. *The Messenger of the Lord in Early Jewish Interpretations of Genesis*. Berlin: de Gruyter.

Von Rad, Gerhard. 1947. *Deuteronomium-Studien*. Göttingen: Vandenhoeck & Ruprecht.

Von Stuckrad, Kocku. 2013. "Discursive Study of Religion: Approaches, Definitions, Implications." *MTSR* 25.1: 5–25.

Vriezen, Karel J. H. 2001. "Archaeological Traces of Cult in Ancient Israel." Pages 45–80 in *Only One God? Monotheism in Ancient Israel and the Veneration of the Goddess Asherah*. Edited by Bob Becking, Meindert Dijkstra, Marjo C. A. Korpel, and Karel J. H. Vriezen. London: Sheffield Academic.

Wagner, Andreas. 2019. *God's Body: The Anthropomorphic God in the Old Testament*. Translated by Marion Salzmann. London: T&T Clark.

Wagner, Thomas. 2012. *Gottes Herrlichkeit: Bedeutung und Verwendung des Begriffs kābôd im Alten Testament*. Brill: Leiden.

Walker, Christopher, and Michael B. Dick. 1999. "The Induction of the Cult Image in Ancient Mesopotamia: The Mesopotamian *mīs pî* Ritual." Pages 55–121 in *Born in Heaven Made on Earth: The Making of the Cult Image in the Ancient Near East*. Edited by Michael B. Dick. Winona Lake, IN: Eisenbrauns.

———. 2001. *The Induction of the Cult Image in Ancient Mesopotamia: The Mesopotamian Mīs Pî Ritual*. Finland: Neo-Assyrian Text Corpus Project.

Walter, Tony. 2017. "How the Dead Survive: Ancestors, immortality, memory." Pages 19–39 in *Postmortal Society: Towards a Sociology of Immortality*. Edited by Michael Hviid Jacobsen. New York: Routledge.

Wardlaw, Terrance. 2008. *Conceptualizing Words for "God" within the Pentateuch: A Cognitive-Semantic Investigation in Literary Context*. London: T&T Clark.

Watson, Rebecca S. 2005. *Chaos Uncreated: A Reassessment of the Theme of "Chaos" in the Hebrew Bible*. Berlin: de Gruyter.

Watts, James W. 2008. "The Three Dimensions of Scriptures." *Postscripts* 2.2–3: 135–59.

———. 2011. "Using Ezra's Time as a Methodological Pivot for Understanding the Rhetoric and Functions of the Pentateuch." Pages 489–506 in *The Pentateuch: International Perspectives on Current Research*. Edited by Thomas B. Dozeman, Konrad Schmid, and Baruch J. Schwartz. Tübingen: Mohr Siebeck.

———. 2016. "From Ark of the Covenant to Torah Scroll: Ritualizing Israel's Iconic Texts." Pages 21–34 in *Ritual Innovation in the Hebrew Bible and Early Judaism*. Edited by Nathan MacDonald. Berlin: de Gruyter.

———. 2017. *Understanding the Pentateuch as a Scripture*. Malden, MA: Wiley-Blackwell.

Weinfeld, Moshe. 1972. *Deuteronomy and the Deuteronomic School*. Oxford: Clarendon.

———. 1991. *Deuteronomy 1–11. A New Translation with Introduction and Commentary*. The Anchor Bible. New York: Doubleday.

Weisman, Kara, Carol S. Dweck, and Ellen M. Markman. 2017. "Rethinking People's Conceptions of Mental Life." *PNAS* 114.43: 11,374–79.

Weiss, Tzahi. 2018. *'Sefer Yeṣirah' and Its Contexts: Other Jewish Voices*. Philadelphia: University of Pennsylvania Press.

Wellman, Henry M. 2014. *Making Minds: How Theory of Mind Develops*. Oxford: Oxford University Press.

Westenholz, Joan Goodnick. 2012. "*Damnatio Memoriae*: The Old Akkadian Evidence for Destruction of Name and Destruction of Person." Pages 89–104 in *Iconoclasm and Text Destruction in the Ancient Near East and Beyond*. Edited by Natalie Neomi May. Chicago: The Oriental Institute of the University of Chicago.

White, Claire. 2015. "Establishing Personal Identity in Reincarnation: Minds and Bodies Reconsidered." *JCC* 15.3–4: 402–29.

———. 2016. "The Cognitive Foundations of Reincarnation." *MTSR* 28.3: 264–86.

———. 2021. *An introduction to the Cognitive Science of Religion: Connecting Evolution, Brain, Cognition, and Culture*. London: Routledge.

White, Ellen. 2014. *Yahweh's Council: Its Structure and Membership*. Tübingen: Mohr Siebeck.

White, Stephen L. 1999. "Angel of the Lord: Messenger or Euphemism?" *TynBul* 50.2: 299–305.

Whitehead, Amy. 2013. *Religious Statues and Personhood: Testing the Role of Materiality*. London: Bloomsbury.

Whitehouse, Harvey. 1992. "Memorable Religions: Transmission, Codification and Change in Divergent Melanesian Contexts." *Man* (N.S.) 27.4: 777–97.

———. 2021. *The Ritual Animal: Imitation and Cohesion in the Evolution of Social Complexity*. Oxford: Oxford University Press.

Whitehouse, Harvey, and Ian Hodder. 2010. "Modes of Religiosity at Çatalhöyük." Pages 122–45 in *Religion in the Emergence of Civilization: Çatalhöyük as a Case Study*. Edited by Ian Hodder. Cambridge: Cambridge University Press.

Wightman, Gregory J. 2015. *The Origins of Religion in the Paleolithic*. Lanham: Rowman & Littlefield.

Wilson, David Sloan. *Darwin's Cathedral: Evolution, Religion and the Nature of Society*. Chicago: University of Chicago Press, 2002.

Wilson, Ian. 1995. *Out of the Midst of Fire: Divine Presence in Deuteronomy*. Atlanta, GA: Scholars Press.

Wilson, Ian D. 2018. "History and the Hebrew Bible: Culture, Narrative, and Memory." *BRPBI* 3.2: 1–69.

Wilson, Margaret. 2002. "Six Views of Embodied Cognition." *PsychBullRev* 9.4: 625–36.

Winter, Irene J. 1992. "'Idols of the King': Royal Images as Recipients of Ritual Action in Ancient Mesopotamia." *JRS* 6.1: 13–42.

———. 2008. "Touched by the Gods: Visual Evidence for the Divine Status of Rulers in the Ancient Near East." Pages 75–101 in *Religion and Power: Divine Kingship in the Ancient World and Beyond*. Edited by Nicole Brisch. Chicago: The Oriental Institute of the University of Chicago.

Wittgenstein, Ludwig. 1958. *Philosophical Investigations*. Translated by G. E. M. Anscombe. Oxford: Basil Blackwell.

Wood, Connor, and John H. Shaver. 2018. "Religion, Evolution, and the Basis of Institutions: The Institutional Cognition Model of Religion." *ESIC* 2.2: 1–20.

Wright, David P. 2009. *Inventing God's Law: How the Covenant Code of the Bible Used and Revised the Laws of Hammurabi*. Oxford: Oxford University Press.

———. 2016. "The Covenant Code Appendix (Exodus 23:20–33), Neo-Assyrian Sources, and Implications for Pentateuchal Study." Pages 47–85 in *The Formation of the Pentateuch: Bridging the Academic Cultures of Europe, Israel, and North America*. Edited by Jan Christian Gertz, Bernard M. Levinson, Dalit Rom-Shiloni, and Konrad Schmid. Tübingen: Mohr Siebeck.

Wright, Jacob L. 2014. *David, King of Israel, and Kaleb in Biblical Memory*. Cambridge: Cambridge University Press.

Wunn, Ina, and Davina Grojnowski. 2016. *Ancestors, Territoriality, and Gods: A Natural History of Religion*. Berlin: Springer.

Wyatt, Nicolas. 2002. *Religious Texts from Ugarit. Second Edition*. Sheffield: Sheffield Academic Press.

———. 2007. *Word of Tree and Whisper of Stone, And Other Papers on Ugaritian Thought*. Piscataway, NJ: Gorgias.

———. 2012. "After Death Has Us Parted: Encounters between the Living and the Dead in the Ancient Semitic World." Pages 257–91 in *The Perfumes of Seven Tamarisks: Studies in Honour of Wilfred G. E. Watson*. Edited by Gregorio del Olmo Lete, Jordi Vidal, and Nicolas Wyatt. Münster: Ugarit-Verlag.

Young, Frances. 1991. "'Creatio Ex Nihilo': A Context for the Emergence of the Christian Doctrine of Creation." *SJT* 44:139–51.

Young, Stephen L. 2019. "'Let's Take the Text Seriously': The Protectionist Doxa of Mainstream New Testament Studies." *MTSR* 32.4–5: 328–63.

Yu, Ning. 2009. *The Chinese HEART in a Cognitive Perspective: Culture, Body, and Language*. Berlin: de Gruyter.

Žabkar, Louis V. 1968. *A Study of the Ba Concept in Ancient Egyptian Texts*. Chicago: University of Chicago Press.

Zevit, Ziony. 1984. "The Khirbet el-Qôm Inscription Mentioning a Goddess." *BASOR* 255: 39–47.

———. 2001. *The Religions of Ancient Israel: A Synthesis of Parallactic Approaches*. London: Continuum, 2001.

Zgoll, Annette. 2012. "Der oikomorphe Mensch: Wesen im Menschen und das Wesen des Menschen in sumerisch-akkadischer Perspektive." Pages 83–105 in *Der ganze Mensch: Zur Anthropologie der Antike und ihere europäischen Nachgeschichte*. Edited by Bernd Janowski. Berlin: Akademie Verlag.

Ziegert, Carsten. 2020. "What is חֶסֶד? A Frame-Semantic Approach." *JSOT* 44.4: 711–32.
Ziffer, Irit. 2020. "Moon, Rain, Womb, Mercy: The Imagery of the Shrine Model from Tell el-Fa'ah North—Biblical Tirzah. For Othmar Keel." Pages 133–56 in *Archaeology and Ancient Israelite Religion*. Edited by Avraham Faust. Basel: MDPI.
Zilberg, Peter. 2018. "A Simple Clay Portable Shrine." Pages 73–81 in *Khirbet Qeiyafa Vol. 4. Excavation Report 2007–2013: Art, Cult, and Epigraphy*. Edited by Yosef Garfinkel, Saar Ganor, and Michael G. Hasel. Jerusalem: Israel Exploration Society.
Zimmermann, Frank. 1962. "*'El* and *Adonai*." *VT* 12.2: 190–95.
Zukerman, Alexander. 2012. "A Re-Analysis of the Iron Age IIA Cult Place at Lachish." *ANER* 49: 24–60.

Ancient Sources Index

Hebrew Bible/Old Testament
Genesis

Reference	Page(s)
1	118
1:1	81
1:1–2:4	8
1:2	119
1:6–7	153
1:21	119
1:27	154
2	100
2:7	192
3:5	104
3:22	95
3:22–24	105
4:1	162
6:2	83, 84
6:2	82, 85, 98
6:3	95
6:4	82, 84, 85, 98
10	125
12:1–3	87
14:19–22	85
16	162
16:7	162
16:8	162
16:9	162
16:10	162
16:11	162
16:7–13	157
16:13	111
17:1–14	87
17:7	83
17:19	128
18:1–15	111
18:5	35
18:25	90
19:24–25	115
20:13	81
21:17–19	157
21:33	128
22	162
22:11–18	157
22:15–18	87
23	159
25:22	121
28:18	61
28:22	44, 60
31	109
31:1	146
31:11–13	157
31:29	110
31:30	83, 86
31:42	110
31:45	61
31:53	81, 86, 109
32:23–33	111
32:24–30	158
32:24–32	162
32:31	111, 162, 163
33:20	114, 160
35:2	83, 86
35:4	83, 86, 96
35:7	81
35:14	61

35:14–15	44, 60	20:20	167
35:20	44	20:23	96
45:13	146	21:2–6	83
46:3	114	22:7–8	83, 84
48	158	22:8–9	81
48:15–16	157	22:17	90
49:6	147	22:27	85, 115
50:1–14	139	23	164, 169, 198
50:26	135, 139	23:20	2, 164
		23:20–21	19, 164–66, 174
Exodus		23:21	203
3	128, 162	23:31	164
3:2a	160	24	149
3:2	2, 128, 159, 162	24:10	93
3:2–4	106	24:10–11	61
3:2–6	157, 158–59	24:16	149
3:3–6	159	24:17	128, 148–49
3:6	2, 87, 159, 160–61, 205	25–27	149
3:14	204	25:10–16	139
4:10	87	25:22	135, 149, 150
4:16	83	27:20	43
4:24	161, 162	28:36–37	204
6:3	85	29:43	148, 149
7:1	83, 154	29:43–45	149
9:24	153	29:45	149
13:1–10	188	31:16–17	128
13:9	188	32	137
13:11–16	188	32–34	154
13:16	188	32:4	106, 137
13:21	128, 164	32:8	2
14:19	164	32:13	128
15:1–12	116–17	32:15–16	187
15:3	117	32:16	137
15:11	119	32:19	187
15:18	128	32:24	137
16:7–10	148	32:31	83
18:11	101, 127	33	147
19:4	35	33:7–9	149
19:5–6	116	33:11	111, 149
19:18	148	33:14–17	164
20:1–23:19	87	33:18	147
20:2	187	33:20	94, 111, 112, 140
20:3	80, 82	34:1	187

34:6	147	17:22	138
34:14	80, 82	17:25	138
34:17	96	20:6	148
34:23	112	21:4–9	106, 129
34:28	187	21:8	129
34:29–35	94, 154	21:9	129
40:34	148, 150	22:12	162
40:35–36	149	22:20	162
		22:22–35	157
Leviticus		23:4	162
11:44–45	128	23:5	162
12:4	93	23:23	90
12:6	93	27:18–21	89
14	64	27:21	42, 89, 121
16:7–8	89		
16:8	102, 165	Deuteronomy	
16:10	102, 165	3:24	87, 127
16:16	112	4	143
16:26	102, 165	4:11–12	151
17:11	36	4:12	106, 151
17–26	8	4:16–19	151–52
19:2	128	4:19	87–88, 120
19:21	41	4:23	151–52
19:26	90	4:24	151–52
19:31	41	4:25	151–52
20:6	41, 90	4:28	61, 151–52
20:7	128	4:36	112, 151, 170
20:26	93	5:4	151
20:27	41, 90	5:7	80
26:1	61	5:24	151, 170
		6:4–5	7
Numbers		6:4–9	188
5	64	6:6–9	188
5:11–31	89, 176	6:14	85
6:23–27	180	7:5	137
6:24–26	39	7:6	93
6:27	181	7:9	114
10:35–36	2, 139, 140	7:21	114
12:6	121	9:8–21	187
16:19	148	9:17	137
17	136	10:2	136, 137
17:7	148	10:5	136, 138
17:11	165	10:8	138, 143

10:12	87	27:2–3	184
10:17	81, 101, 114	27:5–7	184
10:20	87	28:36	61
11:13–21	188	28:64	61, 101
11:18–21	188	29:3	35
12–13	7	29:12	83
12:3	137	29:17	61, 85
12:5–7	106	31:16	80
12:7	173	32	125
12:11	169	32:4	61
12:12	173	32:8–9	87–88, 93, 99, 125
12:14	169	32:9	125
12:18	173	32:12	80
12:21	169	32:15	61
12:31	106	32:16–17	101
13:6–11	87	32:18	61
14:2	93, 116	32:21	80, 82, 101
14:23	169, 173	32:37	61
14:24	169	32:39	204
14:26	173	32:40	128
15:20	173	33:8–10	89
16:2	169	33:26	114
16:6	169	34:10	111, 151
16:11	169, 173		
16:16	112, 173	Joshua	
17:3	120	3:6	135
17:14–20	87	3:13	135
18:7	173	5:13–15	157, 158
18:9–24	90	5:14	87
18:11	41, 42	6:2	157, 158
18:13	90	7	123, 143
21–25	7	7:4–5	123
22:15	82	7:6	143
26	172	7:9	148
26:2	169, 172	7:11–12	123, 143
26:5	173	7:19	148
26:10	173	7:20	123
26:13	170	8:1–29	124
26:14	39	8:32	136
26:17	83	8:34–35	136
26:18	116	22:20	124
27	187, 188	22:22	81, 101
27:1–10	19, 136	24:19	81, 164, 203

24:20	80	4	141–43
24:25–27	184	4–6	139, 140
		4:1b–7:2	134
Judges		4:3	141
1:1–2	121	4:4	142
2:1	164	4:7	141
2:1–2	87	4:8	141
2:1–5	157	4:11	143
5:4–5	119	4:18	90
5:20	120	5	142
6:11–23	157	5:2–4	106
6:22	161	5:6–10	141
6:25–26	106	6:12–14	141
11:24	86, 88	6:15	141
13:3–23	157	6:19a	140
13:21	161	6:19	140
13:21–22	102, 161	6:20	127
13:22	161	7:16–17	90
17	89	8:4–18	123
17–18	109	8:5	90
17:1–4	110	9:12–13	63
17:1–5	106	10:5–6	123
17:6	110	10:10–12	123
17:3	110	10:9	35
17:5	89, 96	10:20–22	89
18	89, 110	14:15	82
18:1–6	106	14:41	89
18:5	121	17:45	169
18:24	83, 89	19:13	110
19:5	35	19:18–24	123
19:8	35	22:3	61
19:22	35	22:13	121
20:18	121	22:15	121
20:27	121, 142	23:9–10	89
20:27–28	142	26:19	88, 115–16
		28	89
1 Samuel		28:3	41
1:3	120	28:3–25	42, 90
1:11	120	28:6	42, 121
2:2	61	28:7–9	41
2:12–17	142	28:8	42
2:22–25	142	28:9	41
3:3	135	28:13	42

2 Samuel		22	123
2:1	89	22:5–8	121
5:19	142	22:8–28	123
6:2	143	22:15–23	126
6:5	143	22:19	126
6:14–16	143		
7	123	2 Kings	
7:2	2	1	86
7:13	170	1:2	86, 89
7:23	81	1:2–3	81
8:3	37	1:3	86, 104
14:27	37	1:6	81, 86
18:18	37, 44	1:16	81, 86
22:32	61	3	89
24:1	162	3:18–19	88
		3:27	88, 115, 117
1 Kings		5:15–17	88
1	123	5:17	116
3:9	35	10:26–27	106
3:13	146	12:10–11	135
5:3	170	13:6	69
5:5	170	13:20–21	41
5:17	170	17:9–12	106
5:19	170	17:10	69
6	131	17:16	69
8:9	136	17:18	90
8:16	170	18:4	70, 106, 129
8:17	170	18:33	85
11:33	81, 82	19:10	88
12:27–29	106	19:12	88
17:22	35	19:36	89
18:18	168	21:7	106
18:19	69	23:4	70
18:23–24	106	23:5	120
18:24	106	23:6	106
18:27	81	23:13	106
18:26	115	23:24	41
18:39	115		
19:19–21	123	Isaiah	
20:23	86	1:4	127
20:28	86	1:12	112
20:35	83	1:17	98
21:17–22	123	2:4	90

5:19	127	37:23	127
5:24	127	38:14	36
5:30	120	40:5	148
6	127	40:13	120
6:1	131	40:25	127
6:3	127	41:14	127
6:6–7	126	41:16	127
6:8–10	126	41:20	127
7:11–12	121	41:23	104
8:19	41, 42	41:25	169
9:5	83	42:17	101
10:3–4	147	43:3	127
10:10	101	43:10	101, 204
10:16	147	43:14–15	127
10:17	127, 128	44:8	61
10:20	127	44:9	101
11:4	90	44:9–20	101
12:6	127	44:15	83
13:19	114	44:17	80
13:21–22	102	45:11	127
14:9	41	45:22–23	204
17:4	147	47:4	127
17:7	127	47:8	92, 101
17:10	61	47:10	92, 101
18:11–12	41	48:12	204
19:3	41	48:17	127
19:19–20	44	49:7	127
22:18	147	52:6	204
26:4	61	54:5	87, 127
26:14	41	55:5	127
26:19	35	55:6	121
27:1	102, 118	56:4–5	37, 43–44
29:4	41	56:5	204
29:19	127	58:2	121
29:23	127	60:9	127
30:11–12	127	60:14	127
30:15	127	63:1–6	117
30:27	165, 168	65:3–5	39
31:1	127	66:1	131, 183–84
31:3	80, 95, 105	66:15	165
34:14	102		
35:2	148	Jeremiah	
37:16	127	3:16–17	183

5:19	80	Habakkuk	
5:31	122	1:11	80
10:11	128		
21:1–7	89	Zephaniah	
23:18	126	2:15	92, 101
29:13	122		
50:39	102	Zechariah	
		2:9	148
Ezekiel		3	158
1	183	3:7	158
1:4	153	4:1	158
1:5–12	153	10:2	89
1:12	153	14:5	93–94
1:14	153		
1:15–21	153	Malachi	
1:20	153	2:11	80
1:26–28a	152		
6:8–14	87	Psalms	
7:8	90	3:4	148
8:5	83	4:8	35
10	183	7:6	147
12:24	122	8:6	100
21:26	89	11:1	36
24:17	41	13:3	35
28:2	82	16:9	147
28:9	82, 128	18	119
40–47	153	18:7	119
		18:10	120
		18:12	120
Hosea		18:13	120
2:1–20	87	18:14	120
3:4	44, 106	19:2	148
8:4–6	102	22:15	35
8:6	80, 82	27:3	35
12	163	29	120
12:4	163	29:1	83
12:4–5	163	29:1–2	148
12:5	163	33:13–15	121
12:4–6	158	34:19	35
		38:9	35
Amos		42:12	36
3:13	91	45:7–8	83
5:4–6	122	46:7	120

64:7	35	106:20	148
68:2	140	106:28	41
68:5	120, 150	115:2–7	102
74–76	96	118:10–11	169
74:10	97	124:7	36
74:12–14	118	132:8	140
74:12–17	120	135:4	116
74:14	102	136	128–29
74:15–17	118	136:2	81, 101
74:22	96	137:4	116
76	170, 172	139	124
76:2–3	167–68	139:1–4	121
78:49	165	143:3	38
79–82	96		
80:5	97	Job	
81:10	80	1:6	82, 98
82	85, 96–100, 116, 125, 126, 128	2:1	82, 98
		3:8	102
82:2	97	19:26	36, 95
82:2–4	97	38:7	82, 98
82:5	98	40:25	102
82:6	83, 98, 105		
82:6–7	94, 98	Proverbs	
83:19	99	4:23	35
84:8	81	9:18	41
84:12	120	14:30	35
88:6	38	25:3	35
88:11	41		
89:7	83	Song of Songs	
89:7–8	94	8:6	179
90:13	97		
91	177	Ecclesiastes	
95:3	101	9:5	41
96:3	148	12:7	36
96:4	101		
96:5	85, 101	Lamentations	
97:9	101, 127	3:6	38
103:1	36		
103:2	36	Daniel	
103:22	36	10:13–21	88
104:1	36	11:39	80
104:26	102		
104:35	36		

Ezra		Colossians	
7:10	188	2:18	167
Nehemiah		James	
8:5–6	187–88	2:21–22	15
		2:24	14
1 Chronicles			
16:25	101	Revelation	
16:26	101	3:13	204
16:39	145	19:12	204
18:3	37		
21:1	162	**Deuterocanonical Books**	
21:29	143	Tobit	
		4:17	39
2 Chronicles			
24:8	135	**Dead Sea Scrolls**	
24:10–11	135	4Q120	190
		4Q403	
		1.i:1–29	88
New Testament			
Matthew		4QNum[b]	
24:5	204	20–22.xv:14	162
		23–26.xvi:14–15	162
Mark			
2	203	4QpapLXX-Lev[b]	190
2:1–12	203		
2:10	203	8ḤevXII gr	190
14:62	204		
Luke		11QPs[a]	189
22:70	204		
		Greco-Roman Jewish Sources	
John		1 Enoch	
4:26	204	20	88
8:58	204	48	166
		48.2	203
Romans		48.2–3	166
3:28	14	48.5	166
4:2–3	15	69.14	203
		89.55–90.19	88
Philippians		89.59	125
2:9	203–04	90.22–25	125

Ancient Sources Index

3 Enoch
  1.3   165

Apocalypse of Abraham
  10.3   166
  10.6   166

Josephus, *Antiquities of the Jews*
  1.1.2.34   36
  20.115   190

Josephus, *Jewish War*
  2.229–31   190

Jubilees
  10.22–23   88

Philo, *Who Is the Heir?*
  55   36

Philo of Byblos, *Phoenician History*
  810.28   61

Sirach
  17:17   88

Testament of Naphtali
  8–10   88

Christian Sources
Clement of Alexandria, *Stromata*
  6.5.41   167

Origen, *Contra Celsus*
  1.26   167

Rabbinic Sources
Megillah
  32a   191

Mekhilta de-Rabbi Ishmael
  20:20   167

Mishnah Yadayim
  4:5   190–91

Sanhedrin
  38b   192
  65b   192

Sepher Ha-Razim
  4:22   165

Sefer haZohar
  1.185a   191–92

Shabbat
  115a   191

Shevuot
  35a   189

Shulkhan Arukh, Yoreh Deah
  274   191

Targum Neophiti Genesis
  32:31   162

Targum Onqelos Exodus
  4:24   162

Targum Pseudo-Jonathan Genesis
  4:1   162
  32:31   162

Tosefta Yadayim
  2:14   190

Samaritan Sources
Memar Marqah
  2.4   166

Samaritan Pentateuch Numbers
  22:20   162
  22:12   162
  23:4   162

23:5	162	1.5.i.1–3	118
		1.5.i.2	118
Northwest Semitic Sources		1.16.i.11	92
Amarna Tablets		1.16.i.21–22	92
47:11	81–82	1.16.ii.49	92
		1.16.vi.54–57	168–69
ANET		1.17.i.3	92
534–35	86	1.17.i.8	92
		1.17.i.10–11	92
COS		1.17.i.13	92
1.25.i	91, 127	1.17.i.22	92
1.25.iii	91, 127	1.17.i.26–27	53
		1.40.25	125
Katumuwa Inscription		1.40.33–34	125
1–2	185, 187	1.65.3	125
Khirbet el-Qôm		Kuntillet 'Ajrud	
1–6	39	3.1	71
		3.6	70
KAI		3.9	70
4.4	86	4.1.1	70
4.7	86		
14.18	169	Mesha Inscription	
14.19	86	5–6	90
214.17	34		
222 B.5–6	86	Silwan	
		1	40
KTU			
1.2.i.7–8	169	**Sumerian and Akkadian Sources**	
1.2.i.20–21	92	Atrahasis	
1.2.i.38	92	1.2.215	
1.2.iv.8	120	1.2.217	36
1.2.iv.10–30	117		
1.2.iv.32	119	Enuma Elish	
1.3.ii.40	120	1.138	92
1.3.iii.32	102	2.24	92
1.3.iii.38	120		
1.3.iii.40	118	Epic of Gilgamesh	
1.3.iii.41–42	118	10.3.3–5	105
1.3.iv.4	120		
1.3.v.32–33	91		
1.4.v.18–19	93		
1.4.vi.46	125		

Modern Authors Index

Aaron, David H.	135–36	Barrett, H. Clark	24
Abusch, Tzvi	31, 36	Barrett, James	12, 22, 28–29, 49, 130
Achenbach, Reinhard	183		
Ackerman, Susan	110, 133, 150	Barton, Carlin A.	xiii
Aharoni, Yohanan	44, 93	Bateson, Melissa	48
Aḥituv, Shmuel	69–70, 72	Bauckham, Richard	201–04
Albertz, Rainer	7, 39, 42–43, 106, 123	Bauks, Michaela	31, 34
		Baumgarten, Albert I.	61, 190
Aleman, André	13	Beal, Richard H.	56
Allen, James	30	Beck, Pirhiya	67, 70
Allen, Spencer L.	4	Becking, Bob	7
Anderson, Marc	13	Beckman, Gary	56
Anthonioz, Stéphanei	69	Beckman, John C.	81
Appuhamiliage, Udeni	28	Beerden, Kim	90
Arav, Reuma	52	Begrich, Joachim	97
Ahser-Greve, Julia	31	Ben-Ami, Doron	57, 61–62
Assmann, Jan	9, 30	Ben-Dov, Jonathan	76
Aster, Shawn Zelig	92, 147–50, 152	Ben-Tor, Amnon	63
Astuti, Rita	24	Ben-Zvi, Ehud	182–83
Atkinson, Quentin D.	48	Benzel, Kim	54
Atran, Scott	25	Berendt, Erich A.	xi
Aufrecht, Walter E.	46	Bering, Jesse M.	24, 28, 29
Ausloos, Hans	169	Berlejung, Angelika	39, 53
Avalos, Hector	63	Berman, Joshua	124
Avner, Uzi	52	Bertolotti, Tommaso	23–24, 46
Baden, Joel S.	8, 165	Beyer, Klaus	32
Bahrani, Zainab	3	Bhayro, Siam	167, 181–82
Baillargeon, Renée	23	Bird, Michael F.	2, 205
Barbiero, Gianni	120	Bjorklund, David F.	24
Barkay, Gabriel	39	Black, Jeremy	31
Barr, James	162	Blair, Judit	102

Blenkinsopp, Joseph	133	Clifford, Hywel	127, 134
Bloch-Smith, Elizabeth M.	37–39, 41, 43–44, 58, 60, 63	Cline, Rangar	167
		Clines, David J. A.	x, 92
Block, Daniel	87	Cohen, Emma	24, 28
Blum, Erhard	7, 165	Cohn, Yehuda	175–78, 188
Bockmuehl, Markus	202	Collard, David	46
Boden, Peggy Jean	53	Collins, John J.	182
Bohak, Gideon	175, 192	Conklin, Beth A.	28
Bokovoy, David	91	Cook, Stephen L.	37
Bond, Sarah Emily	177	Cornelius, Izak	131
Borg, Barbara E.	34	Cornell, Collin	75
Boster, James S.	48	Cox, Benjamin	110
Bourrat, Pierrick	48	Cradic, Melissa S.	28, 37
Box, George E. P.	1	Craffert, Pieter F.	28
Boyarin, Daniel	xiii	Craighero, Laila	23
Boyer, Pascal	12, 22, 24, 29, 42	Craigie, Peter C.	120
Breed, Brennan	178	Crespi, Bernard	46
Bridge, Edward J.	87	Croft, William	14
Broyles, Craig C.	97	Cross, Frank M.	120
Bubic, Andreja D.	13	Crouch, C. L.	123
Burgmer, Pascal	24	Cruse, D. Alan	14
Burnett, Joel S.	80–82, 85, 99	Czachesz, István	175
Burns, John Barclay	89	Darby, Erin	60, 63–64, 68–69
Burton, Marilyn E.	146–48	Davis, Richard H.	2
Busby, Cecilia	28	Day, John	118, 120
Bynum, Caroline Walker	2	De Bruyn, Theodore	167
Byrne, Máire	81	De Neys, Wim	11
Byrne, Ryan	63	De Roche, Michael	90
Cai, Wei	48	De Vaux, Roland	171
Carmi, Israel	70	De Vries, Pieter	146, 149–50
Canfield, Caitlin F.	11, 23	De Waal, Frans B. M.	46
Cánovas, Christóbal Pagán	15	Dean, Lewis G.	25
Carr, David M.	7	Dearman, Andrew	76, 90, 186
Carrell, Peter R.	160	Del Monte, Giuseppe F.	123
Carvalho, Corrine L.	90	Del Olmo Lete, Gregorio	93, 135
Chambers, Nathan	158	DeLapp, Nevada Levi	111
Chavel, Simeon	161	Dick, Michael B.	53–55, 85, 102
Cho, Paul K.-K.	118–20	Dillon, John M.	26
Christensen, Dorthe Refslund	29	Dion, Paul E.	117
Chudek, Maciej	26, 29	Dirven, René	15
Chung, Youn Ho	137	Doak, Brian R.	67, 69, 187
Claassens, L. Juliana	42	Dobbs-Allsopp, F. W.	39
Clark, Andy	13	Douglas, Mary	43

Dozeman, Thomas B.	8, 87, 123	Galen, Luke W.	49
Draycott, Catherine M.	32	Gamble, Clive	24
Dunbar, Robin I. M.	48	Ganor, Saar	60–63, 65, 67
Duncan, William N.	28	Gardiner, Alan	30
Durand, Jean-Marie	60	Garfinkel, Yosef	60–63, 65–68
Dweck, Carol S.	24	Garr, W. Randall	105
Edelman, Diana Vikander	7, 110	Geeraerts, Dirk	16
Ehrman, Bart	167	Gell, Alfred	3, 195
Eichler, Raanan	129, 136	Gertz, Jan Christian	8, 129
Elkaisy-Friemuth, Maha	26	Gervais, Will M.	23
Ember, Aaron	81	Gieschen, Charles A.	160, 166–67, 203
Emelianov, Vladimir V.	92		
Emerton, J. A.	72, 118	Gilmour, Garth	58
Emmerson, Grace	7	Gnuse, Robert Karl	134
Eshel, Esther	69–70, 72	Golub, Mitka R.	179
Evans, Jonathan St. B. T.	11	Gonzalez, A.	97
Eynikel, Erik	160	Goodman, Martin	190
Faísca, Luís	28	Gordon, Andrew A.	30
Fabry, Heinz-Josef	34–35	Gordon, Robert P.	125–26
Fauconnier, Gilles	29	Graesser, Carl F.	52, 60
Faust, Avraham	8, 64	Gray, Alison Ruth	120
Feder, Yitzhaq	35–37, 40	Green, Alberto R. W.	117–20
Feldman, Marian H.	34	Green, Anthony	31
Fensham, F. Charles	98	Greene, Nathaniel E.	118
Finkelstein, Israel	65, 70, 139–41	Greenstein, Edward L.	119
Fischer, Irmtraud	42	Grojnowski, Davina	18
Fitzgerald, Timothy	xii	Gudme, Anne Katrine de Hemmer 171	
Fleming, Daniel E.	60, 91, 103, 110, 123, 125, 198		
		Guillaume, Philippe	8
Flynn, Shawn W.	117, 120	Gunkel, Hermann	97
Ford, James Nathan	167, 181–82	Guthrie, Stewart	22
Forschey, Harold O.	99	Hachlili, Rachel	43
Forstmann, Matthias	24	Hadley, Judith M.	39, 67
Fossum, Jarl E.	166	Haidle, Miriam Noël	25
Fowler, Chris	26	Halayqa, Issam H. K.	135
Frandsen, Paul John	30	Hallam, Elizabeth	29
Fredriksen, Paula	196	Hallo, William W.	171, 179
Freedman, David Noel	120	Hamori, Esther J.	42, 90, 111
Frey-Anthes, Henrike	102	Hampe, Beate	15
Friedman, Richard Elliott	38, 160	Handy, Lowell K.	83, 87, 102
Gager, John G.	177	Hanhart, Robert	xiii
Gahlin, Lucia	30	Hannah, Darrell D.	88, 205
Galbraith, Deane	41	Haque, Omar Sultan	25, 48

Haran, Menahem	43	Hutter, Manfred	102–03
Harris, Paul L.	24, 28	Hyland, C. Franke	120
Hasel, Michael G.	60–63, 65, 67	Idel, Moshe	192
Hausmann, Lucerne	35	Inzlicht, Michael	49
Hayman, Peter	76	Irvin, Dorothy	160
Hays, Christopher B.	30–31, 41–42, 101	Isaac, E.	166
		Jackson, Kent P.	90, 186
Heidt, William George	160	Jacobsen, Thorkild	3, 129
Heine, Steven J.	10	Janak, Jiri	30
Heiser, Michael S.	81, 92, 95, 125	Järnefelt, Elisa	11, 23
Hemer, Susan	27	Joffe, Laura	99
Hendel, Ronald S.	117	Johansson, Daniel	164, 203
Henrich, Joseph	23	Johnson, Carl Nils	xi, 24
Hernandez, J. Ivan	49	Johnson, Mark	xi
Herring, Steven L.	3, 60, 100, 143, 154	Jong, Jonathan	163
		Joyce, Rosemary A.	30
Herrmann, Christian	39	Kang, Sa-Moon	88
Herrmann, Virginia Rimmer	32–33	Kato, Yuta	48
Herzog, Ze'ev	43–44, 58	Katz, Hava	65
Hess, Richard	72	Kay, Aaron C.	46
Hess, Sabine C.	28	Kee, Min Suc	91
Hestrin, Ruth	67, 70	Keel, Othmar	30, 57–58, 67, 69–70, 179
Hiraishi, Kai	48		
Hitchcock, Louise A.	63	Keil, Frank C.	25, 130
Hobson, Nicholas M.	49	Kelemen, Deborah	11, 23
Hockey, Jenny	29	Kim, Eun Young	23
Hodder, Ian	47–48	King, Peter	26
Hodge, K. Mitch	24	Kinzler, Katherine D.	24, 47
Hogue, Timothy	185, 187	Kiperwasser, Reuven	35
Hohwy, Jakob	13	Kirk, Alan	134
Holloway, Paul A.	204	Kisilevitz, Shua	61–62
Holt, John Clifford	29	Kjærsgaard, Anne	29
Honigman, Sylvie	182–83	Kletter, Raz	60, 63
Hornung, Erik	179	Kloos, Carola	120
Horwitz, Liora Kolska	52	Knafl, Anne K.	27, 143–44, 171–72
Howard, Alan	28–29	Knauf, Ernst Axel	7–8
Hubler, James N.	202	Knauft, Bruce	28
Huffmon, Herbert B.	90, 122	Köckert, Matthias	44, 102
Human, Dirk	7	Kotansky, Roy	181
Hundley, Michael B.	57, 150, 152, 154, 160, 171, 173	Kövecses, Zoltán	15
		Kress, Howard C.	48
Hurowitz, Victor Avigdor	21, 53–54, 129	Kugel, James	160
		Labuschagne, C. J.	91–92

Modern Authors Index

Lakoff, George xi, 13, 15–16, 78
Lambek, Michael 28
Langacker, Ronald 77–78
LaRocca-Pitts, Elizabeth C. 44
Lauterbach, Jacob Z. 167
Law, Timothy Michael 191
Lawson, E. Thomas 47
LeMon, Joel M. 41
Lenzi, Alan 91, 126
Leprohon, Ronald J. 30
Levin, Yigal 88
Levine, Baruch 57, 140, 147
Levinson, Bernard M. 87
Levinson, Hanne Løland x
Lev-Tov, J. S. 32
Levtow, Nathaniel B. 102, 143, 175
Levy, Gabriel 10, 157, 175, 181, 188
Lewis, Theodore J. 4, 32, 38, 58, 70, 83, 131, 140, 151, 167, 169
Liberman, Zoe 47
Lichtenberger, Hermann 190
Lim, Timothy H. 190
Livingstone, Alasdair 32
Long, A. A. 26
López, René 160
Lowery, Brian S. 17
Luo, Yuyan 23
Lys, Daniel 36
MacDonald, Nathan 35, 87, 91, 101, 106, 116, 123, 183
MacDougal, Renata 31–32
Machinist, Peter 95–96, 128
Mageo, Jeanette Marie 28–29
Magnani, Lorenzo 23–24, 46
Maher, E. F. 32
Maiden, Brett 1, 9
Maij, David L. R. 22
Malone, Andrew S. 160
Mandell, Alice 39, 175–76
Mandler, Jean M. 15–16
Mandolfo, Carleen 97
Margalit, Baruch 39

Markman, Ellen M. 24
Martin, Luther H. 9–10
May, Gerhard 202
Mazar, Amihai 63–65, 69
McBride, Samuel Dean 167, 171–72
McCall, Robin C. 152–53
McCarter, P. Kyle 140
McCauley, Robert N. 47, 64, 197
McClellan, Daniel O. 83, 96, 98, 126, 201
McConville, J. Gordon 171
McDowell, Catherine L. 53–55, 100, 154
McCkay, Ryan 49
McLeod, Katrina 29
McNamara, Rita Anne 47
McNinch, Timothy 134
Meier, Samuel A. 160
Meltzoff, Andrew N. 23
Meshel, Ze'ev 69, 72
Meskell, Lynn M. 30
Mesoudi, Alex 45
Mettinger, Tryggve N. D. 39, 58, 60–61, 149, 171
Meyer, Sias 8
Meyers, Carol L. 43
Meyers, Eric M. 37
Middlemas, Jill 70, 92, 101, 111, 114
Mikkelson, Henrik Henegaard 29
Milgrom, Jacob 8, 175
Miller, Jared L. 56
Miller, Patrick D., Jr. 88, 91, 120, 140–41, 143
Miller, Robert D., II 6
Mithen, Steven 25
Moberly, R. W. L. 92
Monroe, Lauren A. S. 123
Morgan, Jonathan 11
Morgan, David 3
Morgenstern, Julian 99, 136
Moriguchi, Yusuke 23

Morrow, William	169, 171	Penney, Douglas L.	167
Mosko, Mark	27–28	Peppard, Michael	197, 205
Moss, Candida	178	Pereira, Vera	28
Muentener, Paul	23	Pfattheicher, Stefan	48
Mullen, E. Theodore, Jr.	83	Philpot, Joshua M.	94
Müller, Reinhard	117	Pioske, Daniel D.	6–7
Mumcuoglu, Madeleine	65–66, 68	Pitard, Wayne T.	38, 93, 117–18
Münger, Stefan	179	Pitts-Taylor, Victoria	xi
Mylonopoulos, Joannis	2	Platt, Verity	2, 199
Nakhai, Beth Alpert	65	Polaski, Donald C.	175
Nasuti, Harry P.	97	Pongratz-Leisten, Beate	3, 45, 54–55, 155, 195
Naveh, Joseph	181		
Neubert, Frank	xiii	Pope, Marvin H.	80
Newsom, Carol A.	34–35, 160, 197	Porter, Barbara N.	21
Nichols, Ryan	49	Portugali, Y.	63
Nickelsburg, George W. E.	203	Preston, Jesse Lee	49
Niditch, Susan	97, 109	Propp, William H. C.	8
Niehoff, Maren R.	202	Purzycki, Benjamin Grant	21, 22, 25, 42, 48
Niehr, Herbert	34, 56–57		
Nielsen, Kirsten	90	Pyysiäinen, Ilkka	25, 27, 36, 49
Nissinen, Martti	90, 126	Quirke, Stephen	30
Nitzan, Bilhah	178	Radner, Karen	38, 168, 181, 187
Nockur, Laila	48	Rahlfs, Alfred	xiii
Noegel, Scott B.	136, 139	Rahmouni, Aicha	92, 120
Nongbri, Brent	xii, 191	Ramachandran, Vilayanur	12
Norenzayan, Ara	10, 46–47, 49	Rand, David G.	46
Nyhof, Melanie	24	Raymond, Michel	46
Nyord, Rune	15	Rasmussen, Susan J.	29
Oda, Ryo	48	Ready, Jonathan L.	91–92
Olyan, Saul M.	88, 92, 160–61, 165, 167	Rechenmacher, Hans	127
		Rendsburg, Gary A.	7, 86
Oppenheim, A. L.	3, 92	Rendtorff, Rolf	8
Orlov, Andrei A.	166	Renehan, R.	95
Ornan, Tallay	58, 112–13, 179	Reynolds, Frances S.	131
Otto, Rudolph	144	Richardson, Seth	146
Overton, Shawna Dolansky	38	Richerson, Peter	46
Panitz-Cohen, Nava	65	Richert, Rebekah A.	28
Pantoja, Jennifer Metten	117	Richter, Sandra L.	169–72
Pardee, Dennis	32, 120	Ringgren, Helmer	80
Pardee, Nancy	120	Ritner, Robert K.	90
Parker, Simon B.	40, 96	Ritter, Ryan S.	49
Parmenter, Dorina Miller	193, 199	Rizzolatti, Giacomo	23
Parry, Donald W.	189	Roazzi, Maira	24

Roberts, Gilbert	48
Roberts, J. J. M.	39, 140–41, 143
Roberts, Wesley W.	46
Roes, Frans L.	46
Rogers, Robert William	91
Rosch, Eleanor	16
Rothstein, David	145
Routledge, Bruce	46
Römer, Thomas C.	7–8, 123, 139, 141–42
Rösel, Martin	190
Rosset, Evelyn	23
Rottman, Joshua	11, 23
Sabar, Shalom	192
Saeed, John I.	15
Saler, Benson	xii
Salvesen, Alison	191
Sanders, Paul	99
Sanders, Seth	6, 34, 43, 46, 80, 97, 110–11, 122, 170, 185, 187
Sanderson, Stephen K.	46
Sandvik, Kjetil	29
Sanmartín, Joaquín	93, 135
Sá-Saraiva, Rodrigo	28
Savran, George W.	111
Scanlon, Lauren A.	45
Schaper, Joachim	3–4, 114, 175, 188
Scheyhing, Nicola	60
Schindler, Simon	48
Schjødt, Uffe	13
Schleicher, Marianne	191–92
Schloen, J. David	32
Schmid, Konrad	7–8, 87, 129, 189
Schmidt, Brian B.	39–40, 42, 176
Schmitt, Rüdiger	37–39, 44, 90, 175
Schniedewind, William M.	7, 170, 177, 187, 189
Scholem, Gershon	192
Schroer, Silvia	34–35, 40
Schubotz, Ricarda I.	13
Schulz, Laura	23
Schwarz, Kevin R.	28
Schwemer, Daniel	117, 119
Scurlock, JoAnn	31, 36
Segal, Dror	70
Selz, Gebhard	9
Seston, Rebecca	11, 23
Seow, C. L.	39, 90
Shaked, Shaul	167, 181–82
Shackelford, Todd K.	29
Sharifian, Farzad	26
Shaver, John H.	25
Shaw, Frank Edward	190
Shennan, Stephen	45
Shinohara, Ikuko	23
Shults, F. LeRon	48
Silver, Morris	98
Singletary, Jennifer Elizabeth	1, 4, 91
Slingerland, Edward	26
Smelik, Willem F.	191
Smith, Jonathan Z.	104
Smith, Mark S.	4, 21, 27, 35, 51, 55, 61, 76, 83, 85–89, 92–93, 95–96, 102, 104, 117–19, 125, 128, 131, 134, 198
Smoak, Jeremy	39, 175–77, 181
Sommer, Benjamin D.	4, 11, 26–27, 57, 60–61, 69, 72, 134, 140–45, 147, 151–52, 154, 158–61, 163–64, 168, 171–72, 182, 197, 203
Song, Hyun-joo	23
Sonik, Karen	3, 55
Sosis, Richard	25, 48
Speiser, E. A.	105
Spelke, Elizabeth S.	24
Stackert, Jeffrey	87
Staehelin, Elisabeth	179
Stagnaro, Michael N.	46
Stahl, Michael J.	7
Stamatopoulou, Maria	32
Stanovich, Keith E.	11
Stark, Thom	89
Staubli, Thomas	34–35

Stavrakopoulou, Francesca 37–38, 44, 63, 112, 130, 175, 184, 193
Stein, Peter 72
Steiner, Richard C. 30–32, 35–36, 197
Steinert, Ulrike 31
Stern, Philip D. 123
Stol, Marten 31
Stowers, Stanley 1, 3–4, 21
Stökl, Jonathan 90, 122, 175
Strathern, Andrew 28
Strathern, Marilyn 27
Stroumsa, Guy G. 1
Struble, Eudora J. 32–33
Stuckenbruck, Loren T. 167
Suriano, Matthew J. 34, 37–40, 176
Taggar-Cohen, Ada 56
Tanita, Keiko xi
Tate, Marvin 97
Tattersall, Ian 25
Taylor, John 16, 77–78
Taylor, John H. 30
Teinz, Katharina 37
Tercatin, Rossella 178
Thomas, Ryan 58, 69, 72, 185
Tigay, Jeffrey H. 170, 181
Tilford, Nicole L. 16, 35
Tov, Emanuel 8, 189
Tropper, Josef 72
Tsevat, Matitiahu 125
Tsoraki, Christina 47
Tsumura, David Toshio 118, 120, 140
Turner, Mark 29
Tuschling, R. M. M. 160, 167
Tuzin, Donald 46
Uehlinger, Christoph 57–58, 67, 69–70, 179
Unzueta, Miguel M. 17
Uro, Risto 197
Van der Toorn, Karel 7, 38, 43, 93, 109–111
Van der Woude, A. S 160

Van Elk, Michiel 13, 22
Van Koppen, Frans 93
Van Seters, John 171
Van Shie, Hein T. 22
Van Wolde, Ellen 9
VanderKam, James C. 203
Vanhoozer, Kevin J. 202
Venbrux, Eric 29
Verderame, Lorenzo 31
Vermeulen, Floris Nicolas 179
Verspoor, Marjolijn 15
Violi, Patrizia 17
Von Cramon, Yves 13
Von Heijne, Camille Hélena 157, 160
Von Rad, Gerhard 170
Von Stuckrad, Kocku xiii
Vriezen, Karel J. H. 93
Wagner, Andreas 4, 131
Wagner, Thomas 150
Walker, Christopher 53–55
Walter, Tony 29, 53
Wardlaw, Terrance 76, 80, 82–83, 114
Watson, Rebecca S. 118, 120
Watts, James W. 139, 175, 178, 182–84, 187, 189, 191
Weinfeld, Moshe 7, 138
Weisman, Kara 24
Weiss, Tzahi 192
Wellman, Henry M. 24
Westenholz, Joan Goodnick 38
Whitaker, R. E. 39
White, Claire 11, 28
White, Ellen 91, 126
White, Stephen L. 160
Whitehead, Amy 2
Whitehouse, Harvey 11, 47–49, 197
Wightman, Gregory J. 23
Wildman, Wesley J. 48
Willard, Aiyana K. 21
Wilson, David Sloan xi

Wilson, Ian 171–72
Wilson, Ian D. 6
Wilson, Brittany E. 1, 27, 196, 203
Wilson, Margaret xi
Winter, Irene J. 54, 83
Wise, Michael O. 167
Witte, Markus 129
Wittgenstein, Ludwig 17
Wood, Connor 25
Woodward, Amanda L. 47
Wright, David P. 42, 81, 165
Wright, Jacob L. 7
Wunn, Ina 18
Wyatt, Nicolas 32, 118, 120
Young, Fances 202
Young, Stephen L. 12
Žabkar, Louis V. 30
Zevit, Ziony 39, 44, 62–63, 65, 72
Zgoll, Annette 30
Ziegert, Carsten 129
Ziffer, Irit 69
Zilberg, Peter 66
Zimmermann, Frank 80
Zukerman, Alexander 60, 63

Subject Index

Aaron, 121, 135–37, 147, 154, 180, 189
abandonment motif, 142, 144–46, 155
abdominocentric, 26
Abdi-Ḫeba, 172
Abraham, 2, 15, 86–87, 109–10, 130, 159, 161–62, 165–66
Achaemenid period, 7, 72, 87, 96, 98, 123, 155, 182–83, 188
Adam, 8, 88, 192
adoptionism, 205
afterlife, 30, 32, 34, 168, 173, 179, 191
agency
  communicability of, 19–20, 35, 46, 56, 64, 72, 94, 96, 102, 106, 129–30, 151, 154, 158–59, 163–64, 168, 172–73, 198–99, 203
  divine, 41, 50, 51–73, 76, 79, 90, 96, 107, 129, 134–35, 143–44, 146, 150–51, 154–55, 157–59, 163, 167, 170, 172–74, 176, 179, 181, 190–92, 195–99, 201, 203, 205
  locus of, 26, 28, 30, 32, 34, 36, 44, 146, 150, 153, 168, 173
  unseen, 22, 25, 29, 45–47, 50–51, 58, 67, 84, 95, 99, 109, 111–13, 172, 175, 177, 185, 196–97

'Ain Dara, 131
altar, 43–44, 60, 63, 65, 93, 115, 126–27, 135–36, 152, 169, 184
Amarna Letters, 81, 170, 172
ambiguity theory, 160, 162, 174. *See also* identity theory, interpolation theory, *and* representation theory
amulet, 19, 39, 41, 69, 167, 175–79, 181, 188, 198
Anatolia, 18, 51, 119
ancestor, 41, 43–44, 52, 79, 87, 95, 101, 122, 159
angel, 88, 98–100, 102, 125, 158–59, 164, 166–67, 177, 201, 205. *See also* messenger *and mal'āk*
angelomorphic, 201, 205
aniconism, 58, 92
anthropomorphism, 12, 96, 111, 113, 130, 152, 162
Arad, 43–44, 58–60, 93, 139
Aramaic, 32, 56–57, 61, 171, 181–82, 189
ark of the covenant, 2, 18–19, 67, 73, 121, 129, 133–46
Asherah, 39–40, 63, 69–70, 104
Ashdod, 141
asherahs, 106
Assyria, 7, 60, 64, 87–88, 101, 103, 112, 136, 140, 171
Assyriology, 5, 21, 195
'Athtartu, 168–59

Azazel, 102
ba, 30–31, 36
Baal, 72, 86, 91–93, 101, 104, 106, 113, 115, 117–20, 131, 168–69
Baal-zebub, 104
Babylon, xi–xii, 7, 8, 53, 72, 81, 87, 91, 96, 98, 101, 103, 112, 114, 118, 119, 123, 155, 179
Babylonian exile, xii, 80–81, 83, 92, 99, 116, 118, 123, 125, 145, 153, 155, 183, 192. *See also* preexilic period *and* postexilic period
base (conceptual), 77–79, 84, 99, 109, 111–13
Beth-Shemesh, 60, 140–41
betyl, 60–61
birth, 10, 53, 55, 63, 79, 93, 102
body, xi, 1, 4–5, 13, 16, 19, 24–31, 34–37, 41, 45, 63, 65, 78, 95, 111, 131, 141, 143–50, 152, 154–55, 164, 172, 177, 181, 187–88, 191, 197
brain, xi, 5, 13, 26
burial, 28, 32, 37–39, 41, 43, 52, 176
calf, 2, 65, 67, 137, 154, 187
cardiocentric, 26
cephalocentric, 26
Chemosh, 86, 89–90, 104, 115
Christian(ity), xiii, 1, 2, 14, 26, 55, 134, 163, 167, 177–78, 189, 191, 196–97, 199, 201–05
christology, 12, 196–97, 201–05
Church
  of Jesus Christ of Latter-day Saints, 115
  Roman Catholic, 2, 115
clay, 31, 58, 61–69, 73, 100, 112, 136, 139, 179, 192. *See also* terracotta
Clement of Alexandria, 167
cloud, 148–53, 155,

cognition, xi, xiii, 10–14, 16, 22–24, 26, 34, 45, 50, 130, 182, 195–96
  intuitive, 5, 11–12, 15–16, 18–19, 21–26, 29–30, 32, 38, 45–46, 51, 56–58, 62, 75–77, 84, 95, 104, 111, 113, 115, 117, 130–31, 134, 143, 163, 167, 172, 182, 189–90, 195–96, 202, 205
  locus of, 24
  reflective, 11, 12, 22, 24–27, 29–30, 38, 45, 51, 53–54, 56, 58, 72, 90, 104, 112–13, 124, 130, 144, 154, 163–65, 173, 183, 190, 196, 202
cognitive linguistics, 9, 13–15, 18, 26, 75, 107, 121, 195, 197
cognitive science of religion, 1, 9, 11–12, 18, 23, 64, 107, 195–96, 199
cognitive sciences, ix, 3–4, 9–11, 24, 198
commemoration, 39, 43, 58, 60, 173
communicable agency. *See* agency, communicability of
concretized abstract plural, 82
contamination, 30, 39, 64, 123–24, 143, 197
costly signaling, 18, 22, 47, 183, 199
counterintuitiveness, 21, 25, 29, 95, 117, 202
credibility enhancing displays, 18, 47, 124
cult, 3, 8, 38–39, 43, 56–57, 72, 106, 112, 114, 129, 133, 152–53, 157, 166–67, 175, 181, 189, 192
  authority/leader/specialist, 49, 90, 93, 98, 112, 130, 144, 167, 175, 184, 198
  center, 7
  centralization, 133, 192

image/object/statue, 1, 2, 3, 19, 53–54, 58, 72, 86, 100, 106, 112, 129, 134–35, 137, 139–41, 144–45, 151, 154–55, 158, 163, 165, 195
installation/place/room, 56–57, 60–61, 62–63, 69, 144
stand, 57–58, 64, 67–70, 73
temple, 8, 43, 152, 181
D. *See* Deuteronomy
Dagon, 119, 141–42
David, 2, 37, 110, 115, 143, 145, 162
dead, 29, 31–32, 34, 36–39, 41–45, 83, 89, 119, 143, 176–77, 187, 192
Dead Sea Scrolls, 8, 189, 199
deadly, 94, 112–13, 160–61
debir, 59
Deborah. *See* Song of Deborah
demons, 81, 99, 101–02, 176
Deuteronomy, 7–8, 81, 87, 112, 137, 143, 146, 151, 164, 172–73, 169–73, 188, 198
Deuteronomistic source, 7, 86, 116, 133, 122–23, 140, 142–46, 151, 157, 164, 169–74, 198
DH. *See* Documentary Hypothesis
divination, 42, 89–90, 121–22
divine
 council, 83, 91, 93–94, 96–99, 124–26, 166
 image, 1, 3, 11, 19, 53, 55, 61, 73, 89, 96, 100, 110, 114, 129, 136, 138–39, 146, 151–52, 154, 164, 177, 179, 182, 184, 192, 196, 198
 name, 19–20, 56, 72, 157–58, 166–71, 174, 177–78, 181–84, 187–93, 198, 201, 203–05
 presence. *See* presence, divine
Documentary Hypothesis, 8
domain (conceptual), 13, 76–79, 84–91, 94, 96–100, 104, 109, 114–15, 121, 127, 129–30, 143, 146, 197
Dtr. *See* Deuteronomistic source
E. *See* Elohist source
Edom,
Egypt, 2, 18, 30–32, 34, 36, 38–39, 41, 51, 53, 55, 57, 65, 72, 95, 105, 117, 119, 139, 154, 164, 169, 172, 177, 179, 181, 187
Ekron, 104
El
 as a common noun, 60, 80–83, 95, 96, 97, 101, 114–15, 127–28, 163, 189
 as a divine name, 44, 61, 83, 85, 92, 97, 113–14, 125–26, 128, 135, 163, 165–66, 168
Elyon, 83, 85, 88, 97–99, 120, 125
Eli, 143. *See also* Hophni *and* Phinehas
Elijah, 35, 86, 101, 106, 115
'ĕlîlîm, 101
Elisha, 41, 89
'ĕlôha, 80–83, 101, 115
'ĕlōhîm, 42, 44, 60, 80–83, 85, 96–99, 101–02, 104–06, 110, 115, 125, 127, 135, 141, 154, 158–59, 161–63, 189
Elohist source, 8
En-dor, necromancer of, 42, 104, 121
Enlil, 101
eṭemmu, 31–32, 36, 41
Eusebius of Caesarea, 61
exodus (tradition), 7, 8, 87
figurine(s), 32, 58, 60–69, 73, 110, 113, 138
fire, 106, 115, 120, 127–28, 137, 143, 148–52, 154–55, 158, 160, 191
fluidity model, 4, 26–27, 134, 142, 151, 154, 158, 164, 172, 182
fragmentation, 4, 27, 154, 158. *See also* overlap

funerary, 32, 34, 38, 55, 168, 176, 195. *See also* mortuary
ghost, 29, 31, 41, 46, 102, 163, 176
Gibeon, 145
Gideon, 161
grave, 27, 36–37, 39–40, 179–80, 191
gravestone, 29, 32, 163
Greco-Roman period, 8, 88, 100, 102, 134, 165, 182
Greece, 2, 4, 88, 199
Greek, 26, 55, 60–61, 163, 167, 177–79, 181, 189–90, 202, 204
H. *See* Holiness Code
Hadad, 34
Hagar, 162
Harakhte, 169
Hazor, 60–62, 93
heart, xi, 5, 24, 26–27, 30–31, 34–35, 53, 121, 124, 147, 179. *See also lēb*
Hebron, 7
Hittites, 32, 56
holiness, 64, 92–94, 116, 127–28, 197
Holiness Code, 8, 128
Hophni, 142–43
hypostasis, 4, 150, 160, 170, 177
identity theory, 160, 174. *See also* ambiguity theory, interpolation theory, *and* representation theory
immaterial(ity), 1, 95, 125, 182, 197. *See also* material(ity)
immortality, 94–95, 98, 100, 105, 128–29
impurity, 64, 190, 197. *See also* purity
incense, 43, 65, 112, 129
indwelling, 164, 174
interpolation theory, 19, 85, 159–65, 173, 198, 203, 205. *See also* ambiguity theory, identity theory, *and* representation theory
Isaac, 2, 87, 110, 159, 161, 166

J. *See* Yahwist source
Jacob, 2, 44, 60, 83, 86–88, 110, 127, 129, 147, 158–63
Jerusalem, xi, 7, 59, 65, 88, 142–43, 148, 172, 181, 183, 189
 temple, 19, 44, 106, 129, 131, 133, 135, 145, 150, 152–55, 157, 165–66, 169, 170, 172–73, 176–77, 181, 183–84, 188–90, 192, 199
Jesus Christ, 20, 134, 201–05
Josephus, 36, 162, 190
Joshua, 121, 123, 143, 158, 184
Josiah, 7
Judean Pillar Figurines, 60, 63–64, 70, 73, 110, 181
kābôd, 18, 19, 111, 133–34, 141–42, 146–55, 173, 198
Katumuwa Stele, 32–34, 43, 185–87
Ketef Hinnom inscriptions, 19, 39, 180–82, 184, 188
Khirbet el-Qôm inscription, 39–40, 70, 176–77
Khirbet Qeiyafa, 60–61, 65–66
kinship, 28, 42–43, 46, 49, 77–78, 86, 110–11, 123–24, 183
Kirta, 168–69
kispu, 32
Kuntillet 'Ajrud inscriptions, 58, 70–71, 168
law, 136, 140, 182–93, 197
 of Moses, 87, 175, 182
 scrolls of the, 190–92
 tablets of the, 126, 146, 154
 text of the, 135, 175, 184, 188, 190, 199
 works of the, 15
lēb, 34–35. *See also* heart
Leviathan, 102, 118–20
Lilith, 102
LXX, 119, 140, 143, 162, 189–90. *See also* Septuagint

magic, 32, 54, 64, 129, 145, 175–78, 192, 198
mal'āk, 85, 102, 157–65. *See also* angel *and* messenger
Manoah, 102, 161
Marduk, 119
Masoretic Text, 8, 85, 112, 119, 125, 162
maṣṣēbâ. 32, 37, 44–45, 52, 60. *See also* stele
material(ity), xi, 1–3, 5–6, 9–10, 18–19, 22, 25–34, 37, 39, 44–62, 65, 72–73, 79–80, 92, 95–96, 102–07, 113–14, 122, 125, 129, 131, 133–37, 149–50, 153, 155, 163, 165, 168, 173, 175–90, 193, 195–98, 202. *See also* immaterial(ity)
matrix (conceptual), 32, 72, 77–79, 104, 118, 120, 146, 157
Megiddo, 63, 65, 136–37
metal, 53, 54, 58, 73, 110, 113, 142, 181–82
Mesha Stele, 6, 90, 123, 185–86
Mesopotamia, 2–4, 9, 18, 30–32, 34, 36, 38–39, 51, 53, 55, 60, 91, 112, 126, 134, 142, 152, 177, 179, 195
messenger, 2, 19, 85–86, 102, 122, 157–67, 173–74, 198, 203, 205. *See also* angel *and* mal'āk
of evil, 165
of YHWH, 2, 19, 20, 70, 89, 102, 129–30, 157–67, 173–74, 198, 201–203, 205
of the Lord, 161–62
Micah, 110
Micaiah, 123, 126
Milcom, 104
mind, x–xi, xiii, 9–16, 22–24, 29, 31, 53, 84, 119, 181, 187
miškān, 145, 148–50. *See also* tent
model shrine, 19, 58, 64–69, 73, 136–39, 146, 184, 198

Mormonism, ix. *See also* Church, of Jesus Christ of Latter-day Saints
mortuary, 28, 30–31, 34, 38, 52, 55, 168, 176, 187, 195. *See also* funerary
Moses, 2, 83, 87, 94, 121, 128–30, 136–37, 140, 145, 147, 149–51, 154, 158–59, 161–62, 166, 169, 175, 182, 184, 187
Nahar. *See* Yamm
Nahor, 86, 109–10
name, divine. *See* divine name
Name Theology, 164, 170–73
necromancy, 42, 90. *See also* Endor, necromancer of
Nehushtan. *See* serpent, bronze
nepeš, 32, 34–37, 147. *See also* soul
offering table, 43, 61–63, 65
ontology, 1, 3–4, 26, 56, 83–84, 102, 167, 196, 201–02
opening of the mouth, 53–55. *See also* washing of the mouth
Origen of Alexandria, 167
overlap, 4, 158, 163, 172. *See also* fragmentation
P. *See* Priestly source
Panamuwa, 34, 185
partible, 4, 5, 19, 22, 24, 27–29, 34, 37, 45, 56, 95, 135, 146, 150–51, 163, 168, 172, 195–99
patronage, 34, 85–90, 99–105, 111, 115–16, 160
patron deity, ix, 85–91, 97, 99–106, 111, 115–16
permeable, 4, 5, 19, 22, 27, 34–35, 163, 195–99
personhood, 4, 16, 21, 25–45, 57, 63, 113, 154, 185, 191, 195–199
pharaoh, 83, 117, 169, 172
Philistines, 42, 140–45
Philo of Alexandria, 36
Philo of Byblos, 61

Phinehas, 141–43
Platonism, 1, 197
plural of majesty, 81–82
post-P, 8
postexilic period, 44, 94, 102, 116, 131. *See also* Babylonian exile *and* preexilic period
pre-P, 140, 149, 153
preexilic period, 41, 64, 88, 112, 131, 180. *See also* Babylonian exile *and* postexilic period
presence, x–xi, 2, 13, 22–23, 27, 29, 32, 51, 62–63, 111, 140–41, 147, 168, 171, 173, 187
　divine, 35, 54, 57, 73, 112, 127, 133–34, 141, 143–55, 159, 161–67, 170–74, 177, 181, 183–85, 188, 190, 193, 195, 198–99
　locus of, 5, 26, 38, 137
presencing, x–xi, 3, 18–19, 22, 26–27, 32, 38, 44–45, 50–53, 58, 60, 63, 65, 72–73, 106, 129, 133–46, 155, 157, 165, 170–73, 175–76, 179, 182–84, 187–89, 192–93, 196, 199
　media, 5, 18–22, 29, 50–51, 57–58, 73, 106, 110–12, 114, 129, 134–46, 151, 155, 165, 176, 182–85, 187–88, 190–93, 195, 198–99
Priestly Blessing, 39
Priestly source, 4, 8, 116, 118, 128, 133–34, 144–54, 182
prototype, 17, 86, 100, 103–04, 158
　effects, 83, 103, 109
　theory, xi, 9, 16, 17, 76, 196–98
purity, 8, 64, 92–94, 116, 128, 197. *See also* impurity
Rachel, 44, 110
Rabshakeh, 88
Ramses III, 169

representation theory, 160, 174. *See also* ambiguity theory, identity theory, *and* interpolation theory
Rider of the Clouds, 120, 150
Rome, 2, 115, 199
sacrifice, 39, 43, 56, 60–63, 81, 89, 101, 106, 115, 141, 150, 184, 189
Samaritan Pentateuch, 162–63, 166
Saphan, 131
Saul, 7, 35, 42, 63, 89, 104, 111, 115, 121
Seir, 119
selfhood
　locus of, 27, 35–36, 73, 95, 130, 145, 148, 154, 157
šem, 19, 44, 143, 151, 157, 167–74
shrine model, 19, 58, 64–69, 73, 136–39, 146, 184, 198
Sinai, 119, 148–49
Second Temple period, 152, 170, 177, 189
Sennacherib, 19, 88–89, 136, 139
Septuagint, 8, 85, 97, 125, 135, 141, 161, 162, 199. *See also* LXX
serpent, 104, 118
　bronze, 129, 135
shaddays, 81, 101
Shechem, 7, 60, 184
Shem, 8, 165
social memory, 9, 134, 141
Son of Humanity, 166, 203
Song of Deborah, 117, 119
soul, 1, 5, 24, 31–36, 147, 177, 192
spirit, 5, 16, 24, 28–37, 41, 46, 95, 166, 177, 199, 203
standing stone. 19, 38, 44, 57. *See also* stele
stele, 6, 19, 32–34, 37–38, 43–44, 46, 52, 57–63, 70, 73, 83, 90, 106, 123, 133, 136–39, 168, 170–71, 173, 184–88, 191, 193

strategic information, 18, 22, 31, 41–42, 47–48, 50, 89–90, 95, 102, 104–05, 120–23, 197
Targumim, 162, 199
Taylor Swift, x–xi
Tel Dan, 60, 65
Tel Moẓa, 61–62
Tel Qiri, 60, 63
Tel Reḥov, 60, 63–65, 69
temple, 8, 43–44, 54, 56–61, 63, 65, 67, 92–93, 112, 119, 131, 136, 139, 141–44, 191, 193, 204. *See also* Jerusalem, temple
tent, 2, 135. See also *miškān*
of meeting, 145, 148–49
teraphim, 89, 109–10
terracotta, 57–58, 67, 69, 73. *See also* clay
theological correctness, 51, 130
Thutmosis IV, 169
Tiamat, 119
Timnah, 60
Tiglath-Pileser III, 136, 138–39
Tirzah, 60, 65
Torah, 8, 19, 180, 182–84, 187–89, 191–93
Ugarit(ic), 60, 91–93, 102, 117–20, 125, 131, 135, 168
Vulgate, 162
washing of the mouth, 53
Wê-ila, 32
Yahoel, 166
Yahwist source, 8
Yamm, 117, 119
Yassubu, 168–69
Zinçirli, 32
Zion, 141, 168
Zion-Sabaoth, 141, 152

www.ingramcontent.com/pod-product-compliance
Lightning Source LLC
Chambersburg PA
CBHW021348300426
44114CB00012B/1126